CRITICAL
THINKING
THERAPY

PRAISE FOR
CRITICAL THINKING THERAPY FOR HAPPINESS AND SELF-ACTUALIZATION:

"I have often wished there was a 'magic wand' that I could wave over the world to help people transition from being mere believers in all forms of nonsense to become effective critical thinkers. Linda Elder's clear and instructive book is as close to the magic wand as we're likely to get, a gift for which we can be grateful. Leading readers along the path to develop the profound skills of increasing the quality of our thinking and our mental health, Elder illuminates how to integrate these skills into managing the challenges of living we all inevitably face. Don't just read this valuable book—study it and discover the many rewards of knowing how to better use your mind's potential."

> — Michael D. Yapko, Ph.D., Psychologist, author of *Depression is Contagious* and *Breaking the Patterns of Depression*

"A tour-de-force application of critical thinking to psychotherapy! The human change processes are fraught with mysteries and unpredictability, but the tools in this book ensure those uncertainties are minimized. It presents a strong and important foundation for psychotherapists interested in helping people outside the failed medical and disease model of human distress. A must read!"

> — Chuck Ruby, Ph.D., psychologist and author of *Smoke and Mirrors: How You Are Being Fooled About Mental Illness—An Insider's Warning to Consumers*; Executive Director, International Society for Ethical Psychology and Psychiatry

"Who doesn't want to live a happier life in work, parenting, friendships, finances and all of its dimensions? In *Critical Thinking Therapy*, Linda Elder blends her extensive theoretical knowledge and teaching experiences to guide readers on new ways to achieve these goals—using explicit tools for better thinking. Her sane advice and easy exercises, if taken seriously, should help pave the way towards better mental well-being and greater self-fulfillment."

> — Elizabeth Loftus, Ph.D., Distinguished Professor of Psychological Science, University of California, Irvine, named by APA as one of the 100 most eminent psychologists of the 20th century

"Shout out to anyone interested in self-enquiry, reflection, learning, contemplating, inspiration and growth—whether you are in the healing professions or not!!! *Critical Thinking Therapy* by Linda Elder is one of those books that can be enjoyed by reading it cover to cover, or through focusing on one section at a time in any order, as one's inclination leads one to do. This book is written with immense skill and clarity, is beautifully set out, including many activities and exercises that encourage self-awareness and knowledge, with delightful photos and images—this book could be considered by many as a Self-Help Workshop, Nourishment for the Intellect, and in parts—a Spa for the Mind! Incorporating many elements of the pioneering and groundbreaking approach of Rational Emotive Behavior Therapy, yet primarily focused on presenting Critical Thinking's unique and particular aspects, elements and emphases, this book can indeed be a significant and powerful contribution to people who choose to create more meaningful and satisfying lives."

— Dr. Debbie Joffe Ellis, Psychologist and Coauthor with Albert Ellis of *Rational Emotive Behavior Therapy*

"This book takes you on a journey towards your mental well-being. The sound critical thinking theoretical framework and the corresponding tools woven throughout the book render the interactions between your mind and the book a wonderful journey. The experience is full of aha moments as the tools help you explore how your thoughts influence your feelings, how to break down your thoughts into their parts, assess these parts, and unpack the conscious and unconscious barriers that shape your thoughts. The tools help you make conscious moves towards improvement in your thinking and subsequently a more grounded state of mind. It is a journey; you will need to revisit the book and interact with the concepts and tools as often as needed to internalize and embody them. My experience working with the Paul-Elder's Critical Thinking theory and tools has been a transformative one toward my empowerment and mental well-being."

— Nadine Ezzeddine, MS, MN, Instructor, Dalhousie School of Nursing

"*Critical Thinking Therapy* is a seminal, much-needed guide for those seeking a path to better mental health—to greater happiness and self-actualization, and to therapists assisting them on that quest. Its central idea, that one's emotional well-being is determined by the quality of one's reasoning is like a beacon of light illuminating the way to successfully pursuing and achieving happiness and self-fulfillment. Filled with specific exercises for systematically improving one's thinking, *Critical Thinking Therapy* is a masterful exposition of how to take command of one's thoughts, emotions, and behavior. For those in therapy and, indeed, for all of us seeking to be better humans and contribute to a saner, happier, more just way to face and overcome the challenges each of us faces in today's world, *Critical Thinking Therapy* is a singular addition to the broader corpus of works on critical thinking that Dr. Elder, Richard Paul, and others have produced over the past forty-plus years. It couldn't have come at a more crucial time."

— Dr. Ken Stringer, retired US intelligence officer

"Linda Elder's *Critical Thinking Therapy* is a major contribution both to expanding the scope of critical thinking studies and to applying the concepts and tools of critical thinking to advancing people's self-actualization and thus their potential for happiness. She lays out both the irrational ways people standardly undermine their own self-actualization as well as straightforward, rational methods people can use to achieve greater mental health.

Elder's is the first (and only) book to apply robust, fairminded, explicit critical thinking to advancing greater mental health. The systematicity of the Paul-Elder Approach allows her to apply each of the vital dimensions of critical thinking— the elements of reasoning, the critical thinking standards, the critical thinking traits of mind, and the barriers that undermine our thinking—to our thoughts, desires, emotions, and actions. It is a down-to-earth book, reasonable throughout, a book that provides readers with sets of specific guidelines, as well as questions and activities they can use to analyze and evaluate the ways they interpret and respond to the world they live in. If worked through diligently, Elder's book offers a path to greater self-understanding and self-fulfillment."

— Dr. Gerald Nosich, Author, *Learning to Think Things Through: A Guide to Critical Thinking Across the Curriculum and Critical Writing: A Guide to Writing a Paper Using the Concepts and Processes of Critical Thinking*

"First, as a student of the Foundation for Critical Thinking, I have been fascinated by the highest level of intellectual standards incorporated into this book. It is comprehensive, clear and surprisingly easy to read, given the depth of its content. The critical thinking knowledge and tools people need to cultivate their mental health can be found in this book. Its universal breadth and deep concepts will aid any serious-minded person striving to find significant meaning in life. Insofar as a person actively seeks self-actualization, this book offers the best guidance. It is timeless and transformative—'a True Classic'."

— Behnam Jafari, *Investment Advisor*

"Critical Thinking Therapy" is a "masterwork" that brings the Paul-Elder framework for fairminded critical thinking and rational therapy models together in a profoundly helpful book. Thank you, Dr. Elder."

> — Scott O. Shaffer, very thankful member of Foundation for Critical Thinking Study Group

"With her educational background in psychology and decades of work in the field of critical thinking, Dr. Linda Elder is eminently qualified to apply the Paulian framework for critical thinking to the broad field of mental health in this seminal work. Individuals seeking self-actualization, educators in the field of psychology, and current practitioners in mental health will benefit from Elder's work in *Critical Thinking Therapy: for Happiness and Self-Actualization*. Elder's melding of critical thinking theory with practical applications to one's mental health is a novelty in the field of psychology and brings new hope to those experiencing debilitating thinking patterns and the potential for lasting happiness to those willing to do the work of thinking deeply about themselves through this new lens.

> — Kathy Goddard, Associate Professor of Education (Retired), Southern Adventist University

"In *Critical Thinking Therapy for Happiness and Self-Actualization* Dr. Elder takes us on a significant, transformative journey into the realm of critical thinking therapy. Elder offers practical tools and activities to enhance our critical thinking abilities and navigate the complexities of life. A must-read for anyone seeking to take command of their rational potential in order to make effective decisions and take effective actions. This book presents a pathway to intellectual empowerment resulting in personal genuine happiness. The insights provided bridge past approaches to therapy with new and more comprehensive, and therefore more effective, approaches; they are a roadmap to a more discerning, fulfilling life."

> — Dr. Paul Bankes, Foundation for Critical Thinking Scholar and Consultant

"I have reviewed Dr Elder's new Critical Thinking Therapy book from my perspective as a health professional academic and clinician. I have 40 years' experience teaching clinical reasoning in postgraduate physiotherapy (Masters in Advanced Clinical Physiotherapy) with over 90 publications, including three editions of the text "Clinical Reasoning in the Health Professions" and two editions of the text "Clinical Reasoning for Musculoskeletal Practice". The Paul-Elder Framework for Critical Thinking had a significant impact on my teaching of clinical reasoning and to my personal development. I have taught cognitive behavioural therapy to physiotherapists working with patients in chronic pain and experienced first-hand the benefits of integrating the principles of critical thinking to the assessment and analysis of patients' thinking and to the therapists' ability to facilitate clinically relevant change.

I highly recommend this text to individuals seeking change in their lives and to therapists and health professionals tasked with facilitating change. While there is explicit relevance to mental health, there is a broader relevance to personal development across all parts of life including: professional life, intimate relationships, sexuality, parenting, friendships, physical health, self-development, finances, religion, ecology and relationship with nature, psychological health, social, civic and ethical responsibility.

Dr Elder provides a thorough summary of critical thinking concepts clearly articulated and visually portrayed in diagrams, to be accessible to the lay person and the therapist unfamiliar with the Paul-Elder Framework of Critical Thinking. A holistic definition of "genuine mental health" is provided that goes beyond simple notions such as being stress-free and coping with life's challenges to encourage a broader self-actualizing "honesty to oneself, consideration for others, and desire to achieve positive, creative self-expression". Activities throughout the book promote excellent application of critical thinking theory covered in the respective chapter to the reader's individual context and circumstances, facilitating reflection, analysis, reanalysis, and planning."

> — Mark Jones, Adjunct Senior Lecturer, Physiotherapy, Allied Health & Human Performance Academic Unit, University of South Australia

"*Critical Thinking Therapy: for Happiness and Self-Actualization* is grounded in relevant and significant methods and offers the reader a clear path to improve their critical thinking and, ultimately, mental health. Unlike many self-help or pop psychology books, this book refuses to be trite, simplistic, or superficial. This book is practical, deep, and accessible.

Critical Thinking Therapy: for Happiness and Self-Actualization provides the reader with an important foundation in the Paul-Elder Framework for Critical Thinking, which is the basis for the overall approach and activities addressing mental health. Framing the relationship between thoughts, feelings, and desires, the book highlights commonly acknowledged aspects of human nature and behaviour. What is less common, however, is the clarity with which this information is presented because such clarity is rarely modelled in other mental health or therapy publications. Elder's work insists on acknowledging other important writers in the field of psychology and mental health therapy and encourages the reader to broaden their own understanding through reading a breadth of resources. The book helps the reader to think through the breadth of perspectives in the field and points to significant writers and theorists, such as Sigmund Freud, Albert Ellis, Erich Fromm, Judith Beck, and Vickor Frankl; however, Elder's writing offers a breadth of perspective in the field that is refreshing. For example, the book's attention to the problems in thinking is unique. Focusing on the ways that egocentrism and sociocentrism are very real hurdles to fair-minded critical thinking, the book gives the reader hope that they are not alone and provides straight forward strategies to challenge and to change these problematic habits of mind. Elder also demonstrates the ways that these barriers to fair-minded thinking are the key to addressing bias and prejudice. The book emphasizes that critical thinking is foundational to emotional intelligence, which is yet another way that this book is significant. While Emotional Intelligence and Cultural Intelligence are buzzwords in contemporary academic and corporate contexts, publications and training sessions tend to simply identify the outcome of one's thinking and fail to provide a clear process of how to improve the quality of one's own thinking. Elder's book rectifies this gap.

The practicality of this book also extends to its discussion of the ways that problems within relationships, such as bullying, superiority, and manipulation, impact mental health. Rather than simply reminding the reader of the frequency of these problems that manifest in sexism, racism, and other power imbalances in personal and professional contexts, the book highlights how these behaviours betray a problematic pattern of thinking that is not limited to a specific category or group of people. In doing so, the book not only invites the reader to confront these mental habits, but also offers a plethora of activities and practices to help the reader to analyze and to assess their thoughts and to create new, more fair-minded habits of mind.

What truly sets this book apart within the field is its honesty. There are no "quick fixes" or naïve and idealistic promises; instead, the reader is encouraged to think deeply and to reframe their own thinking. Although clear in method, the book is not prescriptive. In giving the reader essential tools for thinking critically about their own mental health, the book facilitates the reader's intellectual freedom to radically reshape the quality of one's thinking and, therefore, the quality of one's life."

— Linda Tym, PhD, Associate Professor of English, Oakwood University

CRITICAL
THINKING
THERAPY

For Happiness and
Self-Actualization

LINDA ELDER

Treely Green
Publishing

Book Production and Layout: Kathy Abney
Proofreading: Jon Kalagorgevich

The image depicting a metal statue of a woman thinking is entitled "la Pensadora" by José Luis Fernández in Oviedo, Asturias, Spain, ca. 1968/1976, and is used in the activity sections throughout the book: Wá (https://commons.wiki.media.org/file:A-woman-thinking.jpg), "A woman thinking", https://creativecommons.org/licenses/by-sa/3.0/legalcode

Published by Treely Green Publishing Company
Treelygreenpublishing.com

Treely Green Publishing Company uses 100% recycled paper throughout the entire book. A tree is planted for each book published. No virgin trees were cut down to produce this book.

Library of Congress Cataloging-in-Publication Data
  Elder, Linda
  Critical thinking therapy: for happiness and self-actualization
  Linda Elder
  ISBN 10-digit: Ebook: 1-63234-002-X Print: 1-63234-001-1
    13-digit: Ebook: 978-1-63234-002-3 Print: 978-1-63234-001-6   (alk. paper)
  1. therapy 2. mental health 3. critical thinking 4. cognitive behavior therapy 5. rational emotive behavior therapy
  6. psychotherapy 7. psychoanalysis
  2021947013

Printed in the United States of America.

BOOKS BY LINDA ELDER:

Liberating the Mind: Overcoming Sociocentric and Egocentric Thinking
Critical Thinking Therapy for Happiness and Self-Actualization

BOOKS AND THINKER'S GUIDES COAUTHORED BY RICHARD PAUL AND LINDA ELDER:

Critical Thinking: Tools for Taking Charge of Your Professional & Personal Life
30 Days to Better Thinking and Better Living through Critical Thinking
Critical Thinking: Tools for Taking Charge of Your Learning and Your Life
Critical Thinking: Learn the Tools the Best Thinkers Use
The Thinker's Guide to the Nature and Functions of Critical and Creative Thinking
The Aspiring Thinker's Guide to Critical Thinking
A Glossary of Critical Thinking Terms and Concepts
The Thinker's Guide to Analytic Thinking
The Thinker's Guide to Intellectual Standards
The Thinker's Guide to the Human Mind
The Thinker's Guide to the Art of Asking Essential Questions
The Miniature Guide to Critical Thinking Concepts and Tools
A Critical Thinker's Guide to Educational Fads
The Thinker's Guide for Students on How to Study & Learn a Discipline
The Thinker's Guide to How to Write a Paragraph: The Art of Substantive Writing
The Thinker's Guide to How to Read a Paragraph: The Art of Close Reading
The Thinkers Guide to Fallacies: The Art of Mental Trickery and Manipulation
*The Thinker's Guide for Conscientious Citizens on
How to Detect Media Bias & Propaganda*
The Thinker's Guide to the Art of Socratic Questioning
The Thinker's Guide to Understanding the Foundations of Ethical Reasoning
A Thinker's Guide for Those Who Teach on How to Improve Student Learning
A Guide for Educators to Critical Thinking Competency Standards
Student Guide to Historical Reasoning w/ Meg Gorzycki
Historical Guide for Instructors w/ Meg Gorzycki
The Instructor's Guide to Critical Thinking
The Thinker's Guide to Scientific Thinking
The Thinker's Guide to Clinical Reasoning w/ David Hawkins
The Thinker's Guide to Engineering Reasoning

ACKNOWLEDGMENTS

First, it is important for readers to be aware that the foundations of critical thinking as detailed in this book come from what is now termed *Paulian Critical Thinking*^{TM}, or the *Paul-Elder Framework for Critical Thinking*^{TM}, of which the late Richard Paul was the originator and which has been further developed primarily by Richard Paul, myself, and Gerald Nosich over several decades. Due to its foundational nature, much of the core critical thinking content in this book comes from or has been modified from the coauthored works of Richard Paul and myself. All scholars in our tradition presuppose these foundations. I regret that Richard was not with me as I worked through the contextualizations of critical thinking in this book and to see this project come to fruition, for he was keenly aware of the essential relationship between vigorously applying critical thinking to one's life and living as an emotionally well person. And he recognized that sane and just societies require sane and just people.

I also want to thank Dr. Nosich for reviewing and giving feedback on several chapters in this book, and to Jon Kalagorgevich for his excellent editing of the book. Kathy Abney, my long-term friend and colleague, has once again provided the graphic work and layout for this book, always bringing sunshine and light to the process. I would not be able to count how many rounds of editing she has patiently gone through with me. An immense thank you to Gerald, Jon, and Kathy for their help in getting this book through to publication.

Finally, I owe a debt of gratitude to the many scholars who carefully reviewed this book and offered their excellent feedback, many of whom also wrote endorsements for the book. Thank you all for giving of your time to advance critical thinking in mental health therapy. Any mistakes or faults, of course, I claim as my own.

DEDICATION

This book is dedicated to Patricia Campbell Plumridge, my mother, who provided throughout my life all the love a mother can give a child and who continues to be my best friend. There are no topics or issues of importance we cannot discuss with relish and vigor until we exhaust ourselves.

I also thank her for allowing me to use part of her happiness journal to lay the groundwork for the activities in Chapter One of which she is a coauthor.

This book is for those people who are not at the moment under the crippling pressure of feeling suicidal, and this book can in no way substitute for professional help. If you are having any thoughts at all that might lead you to contemplate suicide, reach out immediately to someone for help.

Public Service for Suicide Prevention in the US: Dial 988 National Suicide Prevention Lifeline at 1-800-273-TALK (1-800-273-8255) or text HOME to 741741 at the Crisis Text Line.

Internationally: International Association for Suicide Prevention: http://www.iasp.info/contact/

Also check: https://en.wikipedia.org/wiki/List_of_suicide_crisis_lines

The degree to which people can improve their lives by improving their thinking entirely depends on the unique make up of every individual person, which itself depends on many variables. Whatever your situation or background, if you believe that you are able to improve your life by improving your thinking, you may greatly benefit from this book.

CONTENTS

CHAPTER TWO | 73
THE TOOLS OF CRITICAL THINKING: THE BIG PICTURE

CHAPTER THREE | 99
UNDERSTAND HOW THOUGHTS, FEELINGS, AND DESIRES ARE INTERTWINED

CHAPTER FOUR | 119
DEVELOP YOUR RATIONAL CAPACITIES; DIMINISH YOUR IRRATIONAL TENDENCIES

CHAPTER FIVE | 161
DEVELOP INTELLECTUAL VIRTUES THAT WILL LEAD TO HIGHER LEVELS OF MENTAL WELL-BEING

CHAPTER EIGHT | 237
EXAMINE YOUR REASONING: GOING DEEPER INTO THE ELEMENTS OF REASONING

CHAPTER NINE | 323
EXPLORE EVERY DIMENSION OF YOUR LIFE THROUGH POWERFUL QUESTIONS

CHAPTER TEN | 347
ASSESSING EXISTING MENTAL HEALTH THERAPIES AND THERAPISTS

APPENDIX A
THE LOGIC OF RATIONALITY, EGOCENTRICITY AND SOCIOCENTRICITY | 383

APPENDIX B
IMPROVE YOUR MENTAL HEALTH BY READING CLASSIC LITERATURE | 393

PREFACE

The quality of your life is determined fundamentally by the quality of your reasoning. When you reason poorly, you make poor decisions, and your mental health is diminished. When you make poor decisions, you and others around you are likely to suffer. If you want to achieve mental well-being, you must recognize that **it is your current reasoning that determines the quality of your life today**, whatever your life conditions or past experiences. To take command of your emotional life, to achieve happiness, and to become self-fulfilled requires taking command of the reasoning that drives you to do the things you do.

Of course, happiness is a state of mind that can be achieved, not every minute of every day, not at every time of life, of course, but as an overall orientation to life. In its fullest sense it is based on systematically cultivating rational thoughts. It entails feelings of pleasure, contentment, and joy. And it is tied to higher purposes worth achieving and worth living for.

There are degrees of happiness and sometimes happiness is just not possible. For instance, when experiencing grief, you cannot expect to feel happy until the grief subsides after some period of time—which differs for everyone and depends on circumstances. When enduring heavy grief, you may experience only moments of relief from the pain. If you are caught up in war, there can be little to no happiness. When you consider the destruction of the earth's resources or the many pathological ways in which people and societies live, it is easy to become depressed, whatever your natural temperament. If you think of yourself mired in a world of largely arbitrary rules, regulations, traditions, and taboos, it may seem that you are not free to live as you choose. The fact is that each of us faces the challenge of sustaining our own mental and emotional well-being in a highly imperfect world, throughout our lives and through countless circumstances.

Notwithstanding difficult realities you may face, it is reasonable to seek an overall sense of contentment based in self-realization and self-fulfillment. This is entirely possible, despite the dysfunctionalities in the world and the people around you. When happiness or sense of contentment does not come naturally to you, you will need to think critically about your life to determine how to achieve higher degrees of happiness, which includes pursuing your own needs and desires while being concerned with contributing to the lives of others as well as the common good.

Though we should never seek to reduce critical thinking to a single definition capable of explaining and entailing all of its complexities, we can begin with this conception:

> Critical thinking is a way of living in which you routinely examine your thinking for quality before acting on that thinking. It entails the ability to explicitly take your reasoning apart and examine each part for quality through intellectual standards (such as *clarity, accuracy, relevance, breadth, depth, logicalness, fairness, significance*, and *sufficiency*). It includes the intellectual virtue of *fairmindedness*, since critical thinkers strive to consider relevant viewpoints in good faith, and it necessitates working toward the embodiment of additional intellectual virtues such as *intellectual empathy, intellectual humility, intellectual integrity, intellectual courage, intellectual perseverance, confidence in reason*, and *intellectual autonomy*.
>
> Critical thinking implies understanding your own particular egocentric and sociocentric tendencies, and actively combating these tendencies throughout your daily life. Critical thinking requires understanding the intimate relationship between thinking, feelings, and desires. It involves a creative dimension that enables you to improve your thinking, thereby improving the quality of your decisions, your circumstances, and your life overall. Critical thinking provides explicit principles for commanding your mental health and is required if you are to achieve self-fulfillment and self-actualization. Critical thinking also enables you to accurately assess the reasoning of others and, where needed, to protect yourself from them.

Critical thinking can help you achieve your potential and lead a satisfying, rewarding life only through complete honesty with yourself. This requires not hiding from yourself things you do not want to face about yourself or others. It means identifying when you are deceiving yourself, and it requires investigating within your own mind precisely *why* you are deceiving yourself.

If you want to improve the quality of your life without looking for problems in your thinking and without facing unpleasant realities you are avoiding, you will inevitably either limit your potential or fail entirely. The only way to achieve your capacities is to face down your demons through disciplined self-scrutiny (but not self-punishment). Only in this way can you identify and transform your faulty assumptions and ideas. This is something your mind will try to avoid.

But through routine practice in examining and reworking your thinking, you can take command of your thinking and therefore the quality of your life. Once you have committed yourself to the practice of developing your critical thinking abilities as a vehicle toward mental well-being, you should find that you are better at intervening in your thinking with better thinking, and you should find that more satisfying emotions follow from these changes in your thinking. You will unearth the thinking that guides your actions; you will do so regularly, on an everyday basis, many times a day. This routine practice is required to understand the role of thinking in your life and raise the overall quality of your thoughts, feelings, and desires.

As you work through this book, you will learn skills of deep internal reflection, so you can better answer questions like:

- What are the most pressing problems I face?
- What can I do to improve my attitude and outlook on life? What can I change about myself or my circumstances so I am happier and more fulfilled?
- How can I fit myself into a society that is frequently superficial or pathological, without losing my identity? What can I contribute to such a world?
- How can I get outside my merry-go-round thinking (like worrying) and create new options for myself?
- What are the barriers to my achieving what I could achieve? How can I reach my potential and become self-actualized?
- Am I satisfied with my job/profession? Do I need to pursue a different career path?
- Can I continue to live with the people I have been living with?
- Is something about my work or home life causing me to be mentally unwell? What can I do about my conditions to improve them?
- How can I take the important questions I need to reason through, one by one, and reason through them at the highest level possible?
- What are my real options? What are my best options?

To achieve your potential and experience contentment, you will need to take command of your answers to the questions above. This will require you to actively work to improve your thinking every day.

If you are in therapy now, don't attempt to lean on the therapist to do your thinking for you. However skilled or unskilled, no therapist can change what is happening in your mind; this you must do yourself. No therapist can center yourself in yourself so that you see yourself as a whole and worthy individual. No one can give you self-esteem. Of course, the more knowledgeable your therapist is in critical thinking, and the more explicit the emphasis is on critical thinking in the therapy process, the better the therapist can help you take command of the reasoning controlling your life. Always keep this in mind: Any person trying to help you can offer a leg up, but no more. Only you can change your thinking; and this is required for improving your mental health.

INTRODUCTION

A great number of books and resources are now available for those who struggle to find happiness or contentment in the world we humans have crafted. Throughout the past half-century or more, a tremendous mass of literature has been developed to help humans become satisfied and fulfilled. The problems of depression, anxiety, and related emotional states are increasingly in focus through this literature. And yet, with all our knowledge and wisdom, with all our books and guides and videos, and with all the scientific promises, humans are still doing a relatively poor job of alleviating the suffering caused by depression, anxiety, and similar tormenting states of mind. Similarly, we have yet to effectively deal with the irritability, defensiveness, irrational anger, and self-justifying behavior that, though they may not lead to depression or anxiety, keep people from relating intimately with others and developing their innate capacities. And even those who do not experience pervasive negative emotions will yet rarely achieve self-realization or self-actualization, which is the most fulfilling level of thinking and living; this requires achieving the skills and abilities, and embodying the virtues, of the fairminded critical thinker. And it is self-actualized people, unfettered by nagging negative emotions, who can potentially make the greatest contributions to improving human life, as well as our treatment of the earth and its sentient creatures.

To understand why achieving mental well-being is difficult for you and for many others, you should understand a few things about the human mind itself. Perhaps first, the human animal is highly complex. Each of us is unique, while we share the following basic tendencies, which are manifest at various times, at varying levels of degree, and within differing circumstances: selfishness, narrowmindedness, groupishness and group-neediness,[1] reasonability and

---

1 By groupishness I am referring to group selfishness. This term refers to group pursuit of its interests without sufficient regard for the rights and needs of those outside the group; its counterpart is selfishness, which refers to individual pursuit of one's interests without sufficient regard for the rights and needs of others. Note that this use of the term "groupish" differs from the way in which evolutionary biologists use the same term. Their use generally refers to the fact that members of a group are aware of their group membership and are aware that there are others (like them) in the group. The term group-needy refers to a person's desire (which seems like a need) to be validated by group members in order to feel well emotionally.

rationality. Humans are both self-oriented and group-oriented, with the innate need to develop our individual selves while being part of human groups. Our self-orientation has an egocentric dimension, leading us to be frequently selfish and/or intellectually arrogant (trapped within a limited viewpoint). Our need for group contact has a sociocentric dimension, leading us to be frequently groupish (participating in group selfishness) and/or uncritical conformists (going along with a given group without questioning its motives and practices). In short, all human beings have, by their very nature, innate tendencies that cause problems for themselves and others. These tendencies lie at the heart of common mental health problems such as chronic depression, anxiety, discontentment, anger, and irritability. Yet, you can command your egocentric and sociocentric tendencies through the development of your rational capacities. This will become more clear as you learn the tools of critical thinking.

Second, the human mind is fundamentally *linguistic.* This means we largely live in the ideas we develop in our minds as we age; we are influenced by all manner of conditioning that influences the ideas we accept or reject. Our ideas are the concepts we have mentally formulated in order to make sense of the world. Our "accepted" ideas become formed into ideologies, or belief systems, which we then attempt to live in accordance with (and frequently force onto others). However, these ideas, which we naturally believe to be correct and sound, often defy logic, such as how people frequently conceptualize love to mean getting something from another person, or security, or romance. Many of our ideas are distorted due to the many prejudices, stereotypes, delusions, illusions, and other pathologies we are potentially taught by parents, teachers, religions, social groups, clubs, peers, and indeed anyone who has had influence over us, coupled with our innate ability to deceive ourselves into believing what we wish to believe. The human child may begin life without pathological ideologies, but all children soak up unsound ideas from those around them (since all children are highly dependent on others for their survival). Children also develop ideas in accord with their unique propensities and personality traits (such as being naturally shy, outgoing, aggressive, inquisitive, etc). It is these ideas that then guide our actions as we become adults, and it is these ideas you must unearth and begin to examine outside of the groups to which you belong.

Further, because humans create and maintain copious incompatible belief systems, it can be very difficult to find connection with other humans who share your belief systems to the degree that you want to be associated with them, much less trust them, much less be intimate with any one of them. This is especially true when you attempt to live outside of societies' pathologies, rather than indiscriminately following the crowd. Most people, having uncritically accepted the belief systems of their cultures and countries, neither question the status quo nor *know how* to do so. Those that do question societal views, though they may be well meaning, frequently lack the critical insights required to see through and break out of the irrationalities encouraged by human societies.

Some people struggle more than others to accept the rules, institutions, customs, and taboos of their culture. They perceive themselves as not able to assimilate into society without losing their sense of identity. These people, often more insightful than those who mindlessly accept the conventional views and customs, and yet also frequently lacking critical thinking abilities and virtues, may experience mental health problems. They reject the irrational views of society but are not sure what to replace these views with. They correctly perceive the principles of society to be frequently lacking, but may not know how to exchange these principles for more worthy principles. Perhaps you are one of these people.

Another key to your growth, then, is to learn to connect with others in meaningful ways while developing intellectual autonomy and achieving your potential in a sometimes brutal, sometimes fulfilling world. Another is to understand how ideas, or language, guide your reasoning. If taken seriously, this book will lead you to deep understandings about yourself and the ideas you use every day, about the world you live in, about the decisions you have made and are making, and about the consequences of those decisions; it will help you understand and face down your own irrationality, connect reasonably with others, and improve everything you desire to, and can, improve about yourself and your life.

Chapter One offers a series of guided activities designed to help you begin to unearth shortcomings in your thinking that cause your emotional problems. Chapters Two through Eight begin to detail a theory of critical thinking that will help you further improve your reasoning and gain lifelong tools for continual improvement. In addition to learning the fundamentals of critical thinking theory as it relates to therapy or self-therapy, there are potentially many important domains of human thought (such as parenting, intimate relationships, professional life, etc.) within which you will need to learn to reason if you are to enjoy the highest degrees of mental health. Primary domains of thought are therefore discussed in Chapter Nine, with questions to guide your thinking provided within each domain. Chapter Ten offers additional strategies for improving your mental health and provides suggestions for finding a mental health therapist, should you require or desire one. Recommended readings at the back of the book are provided for you to go deeper into many of the ideas discussed throughout the book. Appendix B offers suggestions and readings to further develop your intellect through continued learning.

By diligently working through this book, you should come to appreciate the tools of criticality you need to function in our complex world, the irrationalities of human thought to which all humans fall prey as well as those to which you particularly are vulnerable, and the domains of life especially important to you personally in achieving your potential. You should come to appreciate and then seek out the best thinking that has been done throughout history to address how best to live today—individually and collectively—as you forge the best path for your self-fulfillment and your achievement at the highest levels of which you are capable.

A BEGINNING CHECKLIST FOR HEALTHY LIVING

If you are to take your mental health seriously, you will need to adhere to the following principles, and internalize the following understandings. You have likely seen at least some of these before in some form—***do not try to skip any of these, however obvious they may seem***. Note that all of these require critical thinking. Taking the following guidelines seriously will require willingness to examine some of the most fundamental problems in your thinking. If any of these guidelines illuminate problems in your way of life, target and write about them in the activities throughout the book. In some cases, you may be limited in your ability to engage in any one of these recommendations due to your specific circumstances. In the end you will need to be the judge of which of these you need to take more seriously and which you may not be able to adhere to for any number of reasons.[2] For each one, you may need to do further research to delve into the general recommendation being made. The purpose here is to introduce you to basic understandings. (Also see the recommended readings.)

1. **If at all possible, maintain a dedicated exercise routine** that includes aerobic activity, stretching and weight or resistance training, and various forms of movement. Research shows a clear link between physical exercise and positive mental health. Find what works best for you, which might include tennis, swimming, or dancing, or any number of other interesting physical activities combined.

2. **Take your diet seriously.** We all know that most people need a healthy diet with plenty of whole fruits and vegetables and quality protein to function at a high level physiologically. Many people have food allergies and sensitivities they must consistently consider. Figure out the best diet for your physical body (if you can) and stick to that diet. Since your physiology affects your psychology, studies are increasingly showing that the way you eat may affect your mental health, including your level of depression.

---

2 Some people will undoubtedly argue against some of the points from 1-7 by giving examples of people who do not adhere to these but are still mentally healthy. While it is quite true that some people can get away with having, for instance, a poor diet and still not be depressed, research shows clear links between most of these points and lower levels of depression and other related emotional states. In other words, because some people can get away with a poor diet, poor exercise habits, poor sleep habits, and so forth, and still perceive themselves to be mentally well, it does not follow that you can do so.

3. **Get 7-9 hours of sleep every night and during the same time frame.** Most people require this routine to function properly. Otherwise, you may be irritable, run down, and/or depressed.

4. **Take the sun and the earth seriously.** The Stoics appreciated the importance of the human connection with nature. We have of course largely lost this connection which is one reason why many people seem increasingly given to feelings of hopelessness. But it is not too late for you to join with nature—by regularly getting out in nature and doing what you can to help preserve the earth. As for the sun, research shows (for many people) a direct link between getting proper amounts of sun exposure (especially in the morning) and improved mental well-being, no matter the temperature. If you live in an area where you cannot get sun exposure, find the best sunlamp available. And, of course, do not overexpose yourself to the sun, since our ozone layer is no longer able to keep harmful rays from us.

5. **Reduce or eliminate your alcohol intake.** Alcohol is unmistakably linked to depression and other negative emotional states. If you have a drinking problem, you have very little chance of improving your thinking and life conditions until you face and deal with this problem.

6. **Be aware of all the ways in which any medications or drugs you take affect you personally,** which includes both your physical and mental health. Observe and be aware of all the drug interactions that are happening in your body and eliminate any unnecessary or dangerous drugs from your system that you possibly can. Rethink the chemical imbalance theory if you believe your mental problems are caused merely by a biological deficiency in your brain that can easily be dealt with through medication (see Chapter Ten and Recommended Readings).

7. **Consider how the condition of your physical body affects your mental health.** Many people experience chronic pain. This pain can lead to depression and feelings of hopelessness. Each one of us must face our specific physiological fragilities and realities over which we may have little or no control. Your focus should be on what you can control about your health, environment, life conditions, and attitude. What eases the pain? What helps you forget you are in pain? How can you design your life so the pain is as little an impediment as possible? Do you need a skilled health professional to help you? If so, how will you find this help? These are questions you will need to ask, and answer with your best judgment.

8. **Understand that DNA and conditioning are intertwined.** Perhaps you believe you were born with tendencies toward depression, anxiety, or any other negative mental state, or in other words that by DNA you are highly predisposed to your challenging mental state. It is important to recognize that your DNA as well as conditioning *and your own will* combine and

interact to determine how you function in the world. Notwithstanding genetic predispositions toward depression, should they exist, *it doesn't follow that you need be a depressed or anxious person.* The brain affects the mind, and the mind affects the brain. Through critical thinking therapy we work to retrain the mind, because it is your mind that *you yourself* have direct access to and control over. The mainstream psychiatric approach to mental health seems on the whole to be still holding fast to brain-based answers to depression, anxiety, and other mental health problems. The brain-based chemical imbalance theory, with the prescribing of pharmaceutical drugs, is still sadly the first line of defense against most so-called mental illnesses. And it is these drugs themselves that frequently lead to many long-term forms of mental and physical illness, if not death.

9. **Have a reasonable conception of happiness.** When the term happiness is referred to throughout this book, it must be understood that achieving happiness means maintaining a hopeful, appreciative, contributory, and generally positive attitude toward life and the future. Again, remember that no one can possibly be happy all the time. You may suffer over the loss of a loved one or important relationship. In moments of extreme suffering, it is unrealistic to expect to "be happy" in the sense of having pleasant feelings, or even feeling that hopeful, especially if the pain is deep. But this must always be considered a temporary emotional state.

10. **Don't trap yourself in labels like** "mentally ill person," "depressed person," "anxious person," "psychotic person," even though mental health professionals may either deliberately or inadvertently encourage such labeling. Experiencing negative feelings is a normal part of living. Everyone at times will feel emotional pain—when experiencing the loss of a loved one, when dealing with ungrateful children, when faced with hostility at work, and in many other circumstances. Accept this fact and reject the tendency to label yourself as someone not capable of effectively handling normal everyday stress.

11. **Understand that you, like all humans, were born into a world filled with both the beautiful and the horrifying.** At birth you were thrust into worlds within worlds of ideologies you had no choice but to accept and participate in. These ideologies have influenced, and may have greatly hampered, your development. Cultures that humans have created entail, at one and the same time, potential for both happiness and misery. Some people have more difficulty mindlessly accepting social rules, customs, and taboos laid down by society. It is no wonder that many intelligent people have difficulty fitting into this curious species called homo sapiens. Your primary aim should be to find the best ways to have your needs met, fulfill your capacities, and contribute to the common good, while dodging cultural pathologies. The

better you understand the dysfunctionalities of human cultures, and the more autonomous you become as a thinker, the more mentally well you will be.

12. **Accordingly, you must find your own meaning that leads to a fulfilling life and includes commitment to the common good.** You cannot be mentally well if you are not developing yourself and pursuing purposes and projects you find personally meaningful and important. You cannot be mentally well if you impose on other people and live simply to gratify yourself. You may experience a façade of emotional well-being by doing so (sham mental health), but not genuine well being. Genuine mental health entails respecting the rights and needs of other sentient or feeling creatures, since we live in community with others.

13. **Be reasonable about your commitments and schedule.** If you overextend yourself by committing to too many projects or people, you are not being realistic and will suffer the consequences. The fast-paced world we have created increasingly prods us to go beyond our human capacities. This must be avoided. You cannot possibly be mentally well when you are daily frazzled. If others, such as your family, impact your schedule, together you need to establish a reasonable overall schedule that does not diminish your, or others', mental health. Incessant appointments and activities must be curtailed to that which is necessary and that which enhances your life.

14. **Come to terms with capitalism and how it affects you personally.** Most people in human societies will need to be responsible about money matters, since economics play such a tremendous role in our lives, like it or not. Whatever amount of money you bring in will need to be properly managed so you do not overspend. Getting into debt frequently leads to feelings of worry, depression or sense of hopelessness. You cannot be mentally well while constantly worrying about anything, including money. This can be very difficult with limited income and given that the cost of living is now excessive in many places. We can lament the cold hard world that our form of capitalism has cultivated. We can fight against its inequities over the long run. But this will not change the fact that whatever else may be true, you are still required somehow to make ends meet in the economic world you live in today.

15. **Give up blaming other people for your problems.** And learn to control your memories. Many people spend a lifetime blaming their parents for their problems and constantly revisiting bad memories. It is true that many people are traumatized during childhood by other people they could blame. If this is true for you, an essential question is: yes, but what can you do about it now? Of course, it would be irresponsible to underestimate the power of human conditioning. Many people become stuck in their traumatic experiences. If

this seems true for you, how can you stop actively repeating these memories again and again? This is what you yourself will have to figure out. But do realize that every time you "remember" a traumatic or negative experience, you are making the active decision to re-create that memory right then and there in the present moment? In other words, you are making the decision to actively create that idea again in your mind. But this you may choose not to do. Mentally healthy people do not torture themselves by recreating negative thoughts from the past. *You can control your memories and stop blaming others*, should you choose to.

16. **Do not overly isolate yourself from society.** All people need human connection even if they are loners. Seek out people to connect with who understand you, who you can laugh with, who you can share your concerns with, who you can meet with regularly for emotional nourishment.

17. **At the same time, designate time in each day just for yourself.** It is entirely possible to be overly social to the degree that you are not able to center yourself within yourself. Consider 1-2 hours a minimum amount of time to be alone each day in which you read, develop hobbies, meditate, or whatever helps you keep yourself from being overwhelmed by the people and circumstances around you.

18. **See yourself as you are, envision yourself as you want to be, and work every day to fulfill your capacity.** To achieve self-fulfillment requires clearly understanding and facing your weaknesses while also recognizing and celebrating your strengths. It is just as important for you to accurately recognize your achievements and contributions as it is for you to look for problems in your thinking. Depressed people are often woefully unskilled at accurately articulating their strengths and contributions. Practice accurately stating what you are good at and what you have done that deserves your own acknowledgment. Once you are successfully doing this, you can more accurately and with less fear and anxiety face the weaknesses in your thinking which are holding you back.

19. **Don't be a whiner and complainer.** Instead focus on your strengths and developing your own self. Nothing could be easier than focusing on and complaining about all the bad things happening in the world and in your life. But there is no use in doing this, and it will serve as a poison in your life. It gets you nowhere and saps your precious and limited energy. Spreading your negativity only makes you feel worse and affects others who have to tolerate it.

20. **Be a person who builds things up, rather than tears things down.** Though you may not and need not be a leader, support projects that lead to positive outcomes. Do not be a person who goes about destroying people and

projects, because you have little of your own accomplishments to feel positive about. Do not act from the point of envy, greed, or resentment. Throw your energy into creative self-expression that contributes significantly to your life and/or to the broader good. Believe in the power of your own mind. Work to achieve your capacities.

21. **Limit your time spent in virtual reality.** The internet, gaming, social networking, and all forms of virtual reality, as all things, should be engaged in deliberately through active choice, not passive participation. Examine how much time you spend in these activities, and determine what positive influence, if any, they have in your life.

22. **Strive to live always with a sense of equilibrium.** Living a human life means dealing with daily stress. People will do things that seem irritating to you. You may feel you are being verbally attacked from time to time. Do not allow yourself to become irrational when others around you are irrational. Do not reduce yourself to their level. For your emotional well-being, you must maintain the highest level of calm and composure in your daily communications. And again, it is essential to organize your life to keep stress to a minimal level.

In the next chapter, you can immediately begin to challenge your ways of thinking and living, those that caused you to open this book. Dive into the activities, which are designed to help you come to know yourself better, what you need in life to be fulfilled, and what you need to change about yourself or your circumstances to achieve that fulfillment. The checklist above helps illuminate some parts of yourself you may want to analyze and improve through these activities.

If at any time as you are working through the book's activities, you find yourself confused as to how to answer, or even what the activity entails, skip that activity and come back to it when you finish the book. As the theory builds throughout the book, and as you increasingly internalize critical thinking foundations, your ability to complete the activities as an aid in your transformation should also improve. Above all, be patient with yourself and give yourself time and room to develop.

CHAPTER ONE
FIGHT YOUR DEMONS, ACHIEVE CONTENTMENT, REACH TOWARD HAPPINESS
AUTHORED WITH PATRICIA CAMPBELL PLUMRIDGE

In this chapter, you will find a series of critical thinking activities which, if worked through truthfully and routinely, can significantly help you fight depression, anxiety, and other debilitating or destructive emotional states that may now control you. These exercises can help you cultivate confidence in your ability to take command of your life. They can help you achieve greater contentment, a happier outlook, and a sense of fulfillment.

Move around in the exercises in this chapter as you wish, but do not skip this chapter. It is only by working through these activities that you will begin to see things in your thinking you have never seen before. Work through each of these exercises again and again until you have mastered, as far as you are able, the problem or idea being focused on in each one. Write out your answers in detail—in a journal or on your computer. Come back to these again and again in the future as a basis for your journal entries. Note that several of these activities contain multiple exercises.

Chapter Two introduces the critical thinking theory underlying these activities; throughout the book you will find more activities to help you gain greater and fuller command of your life.[3]

---

3 The activities in this chapter were initiated by Patricia Campbell Plumridge in what was to be a Happiness Journal, which she has graciously allowed me to use. I have extensively developed these activities and the assignments, bringing in more critical thinking elements. But the original issues and problems come from Plumridge's journal.

ACTIVITY ONE: WORK TOWARD GREATER HAPPINESS BY EXAMINING YOUR GOALS

Consider the level of your happiness as you think across the parts of your life. When was the last time you felt happy, contented, joyful? What were you doing? Were you alone or with someone? In what parts of your life are you more satisfied? In what parts are you less satisfied? Write out your answers with details.

What do you want to experience most in your life? In other words, what are your most significant purposes? For example, perhaps . . .

- A meaningful intimate relationship
- A more fulfilling job or career
- Financial freedom
- Peace within yourself
- Contributing to an important cause

Considering the examples above, write down what you want to experience in your life—something currently missing but important to you:

1. _____
2. _____
3. _____
4. _____
5. _____

For each of your identified purposes above, complete the following:

1. What I really want to experience is . . . In other words, my purpose is to achieve . . .

2. The reason(s) I have not achieved this purpose to this point is/are . . .

3. The thinking I've been doing that has held me back from achieving this purpose is [BE HONEST] . . .

4. The thinking I need to do to achieve this purpose is as follows . . .

5. Based on this analysis, I intend to . . .

ACTIVITY TWO: STOP OBSESSING OVER NEGATIVE THOUGHTS: MAKE A GRATITUDE LIST AND RE-READ IT REGULARLY

Happier, more contented people are grateful for and enjoy the things they have, rather than obsessing over what they do not have or the unpleasant experiences that come their way. They also enjoy life's simple pleasures, like a walk in the park, a bicycle ride, or a book that transports them to new ideas. To be happy, you cannot harbor unproductive negative thoughts (i.e., negative thoughts that fail to motivate you toward positive action —and remember that even "productive" negative thoughts can be dwelled upon unproductively). If you continue these harmful patterns, they will make it difficult or impossible to appreciate the positive things in your life, and they may well consume you. Your negative thoughts may lead you to habits of negativity that, though "comfortable" in their familiarity, keep you from being happy, and from sharing happiness with others. Of course, being grateful does not mean denying cold hard realities in the world, but it does help keep things in perspective as you deal with those realities.

To experience happiness, try *seriously focusing* on the good things in your life, and routinely (every day, twice a day) reminding yourself of them.

Make a "gratitude list." List three things you are grateful for at this moment:

1. _____
2. _____
3. _____

Add to this list every day and carry it with you. When you feel down in the dumps and are focusing just on the negative things in your life, take out this list, read it, and believe it. Keep reading it until your emotional state changes for the positive. Don't just glance at the list, "agree" with it, and then dismiss it, only to retreat into negative rumination. Focus on the list line by line until you believe each point. You will know you have spent enough time on this when your feeling-state begins to change from negativity, insecurity, and/or depression to calm reasonability.

Make a short list of things you can do to add more simple pleasures to your life, or of things you already enjoy that you can spend more time doing, such as walking in nature, taking an art class, going to a play, listening to good music, or adding a garden to your home. Then carry through with your plans to enjoy the simple things in life.

ACTIVITY THREE: ELIMINATE RESENTMENT IN YOUR LIFE; DO YOU RESENT SOMEONE NOW?

Resentment is one of the many destructive emotions experienced by humans. All humans experience brief episodes of resentment, including when they have indeed been mistreated. But whatever may be its origins, when allowed to continue past a few minutes, resentment may grow like a cancer in your mind—easily engulfing you and impeding any chance you may have of being happy. Resentment may cause you to act out towards other people, to sabotage them, to harm them.

Resentment comes from thinking that somebody has done something to you that they had no right to do, or in other words, that they have wronged you. It is not irrational to be disappointed and even angry when someone has mistreated you. In many such cases, the person who has wronged you can be given the chance to redress the wrong. Some cases are more complicated, such as when the wrong is egregious (at which point your best option may be to avoid that person in the future), or when the person who has mistreated you cannot make amends (such as a deceased parent). Of course, you may also feel resentment based on your own faulty reasoning about another person's behavior or motives. In such a case, your misunderstanding of the other person's intentions leads you to a misplaced and destructive feeling of resentment. Critical thinkers take command of their feelings by understanding the thinking underlying those feelings, throughout every day, as they move through varied contexts and circumstances. They then correct any detected faulty thinking that leads to negative emotions, such as resentment.

One common example of resentment occurs when you stay in a relationship in which you perceive your partner to treat you without respect, consideration, or love, and you continually blame the other person for wronging you (whether he or she has or not). You may be in the habit of repeating to yourself, again and again, phrases like, "This is so unfair. How can he be so inconsiderate and selfish? Why do I have to put up with this? If he really loved me, he would never treat me like this." Ironically, *it is in fact your own mind which is wronging you the most*. If you decide to stay in a relationship in which you feel you are not treated as well as you wish, at least *understand* that you are making the active decision to stay in the relationship. If you then harbor the negative emotion of resentment while in the relationship, you should recognize that you are actively deciding to be resentful, though you know your partner's limitations. Is it possible to leave the relationship? Do you want to leave the relationship? What are you getting from the relationship that keeps you from leaving? Do the positives outweigh the negatives in the relationship? If this is an important issue in your life, write out in detail your answers to the questions above.

ACTIVITY THREE: CONTINUED

Think about the last time you experienced resentment. Complete these statements:

1. The situation was as follows . . .
2. I felt resentment because . . .
3. In other words, I do not like when I am treated as follows . . .
4. The thinking I am doing which is causing this resentment is . . .
5. The thinking I am doing that is problematic in this situation is . . .
6. I need to change my thinking to the following . . .
7. Once I change my thinking, my behavior should change as follows . . .

As you move through this week, check in with yourself routinely to make sure you are not harboring the feeling of resentment. Each time you experience resentment, complete the statements above for that situation. Do this until you no longer feel resentment as a powerful emotion in your life. Remember, if you cannot change your situation, *you can change your mind*. You can control how you think about the situation.

ACTIVITY FOUR: TARGET UNREASONABLE THOUGHTS THAT CAUSE YOU TO SUFFER EMOTIONALLY

Emotions come from, and influence, our thoughts. Many unreasonable thoughts are recurring and become habitual, causing you pain, frustration, and any number of other negative emotions. Unreasonable thoughts are based in selfish, self-denigrating, hypocritical, prejudicial, biased, conformist, and/or otherwise narrowminded or illogical reasoning.

While unreasonable thinking frequently leads to negative, destructive thinking, reasonable or sensible thoughts should lead to more positive and productive emotions, and to a higher level of overall contentment. Reasonability is based to a large degree on the routine application of intellectual standards to one's reasoning—standards such as accuracy, logicalness, breadth, depth, significance, and fairness (introduced in Chapter Six). Of course, some situations in which humans find themselves are horrifying. It would be extremely difficult to employ critical thinking about one's emotions while being tortured, for example. But as a general principle, in terms of mundane everyday life concerns, the more reasonably, logically, and openmindedly you think, the more satisfying will be your emotional life.

Continued...

ACTIVITY FOUR: CONTINUED

To eliminate or at least diminish your negative, unproductive thoughts requires first becoming conscious of them. Here is a routine exercise you can engage in to effectively deal with your negative emotions by uncovering the thinking that causes them. **Whenever you experience a negative feeling, immediately pause all your actions (where possible) and see if you can identify the thinking leading to this feeling**. What precisely is the thinking that leads to this feeling? Is it reasonable or unreasonable? If it is reasonable, and if the situation is the actual problem, you will need to change your life circumstances where possible. This will require you to change your thinking; if there is nothing you can do in unpleasant circumstances, correct your thinking with a more realistic way of looking at the situation. Facing the situation directly is the first step to changing it, or even knowing if you should. But do not hide from the truth about the thinking underlying your emotions.

Imagine, for instance, that you ruminate over the notion that you are not loved by a given person to whom you have given your love and who you have depended on for a long-term intimate relationship. This person has left you for good now. You feel you can't "stand it." You feel that you can't tolerate the situation because you must be loved by that person who has left you. Through this way of thinking, you have left yourself no choice but to be miserable.

You need not think this way at all; you have the choice to simply look at the situation logically and realize that this is the way it is, and you need to move on to creating your future. Consider: Is this person the only person in the world you can love? Of all the many thousands of people you might meet in your lifetime, is this the only person on the planet for you? Are you unworthy of love simply because one person does not love you (or your parents didn't love you)? And even if you never find the great love of your life (and most people do not), aren't there many ways to give and receive love?

Obsessing over not being loved by a given person or persons is unreasonable in several ways. First, it presupposes that your well-being depends on what someone else feels toward you—a way of thinking that is bound to lead to pain, since each of us will at times be rejected. Second, it presupposes that love is based on getting your way rather than understanding and respecting the needs of the one who is loved. If the person you love believes he or she must move on from your relationship to grow and develop in her or his own way, the reasonable way to show your love is by letting that person go, however much pain it may cause you. By acting out, throwing a tantrum, following the person around, or talking down about the person, you only demonstrate immaturity and lack of self-command. And you prove that you do not in fact love that person, but are instead irrationally dependent on her or him.

ACTIVITY FOUR: CONTINUED

All your negative emotional states should be examined and analyzed in a way similar to the analysis in the example above. With this in mind, **complete these statements for each negative emotion you had today, or this past week:**

1. The negative emotion I experienced was . . .

2. This thinking underlying this emotion was . . .

3. This thinking is a problem because. . .

4. I need to replace this thinking with the following realistic thinking . . .

5. Based on this analysis, I intend to change in the following ways . . . [Again, note that you may just need to change your thinking in the situation to be more realistic or reasonable, like when you feel you have been rejected when you have not. Alternatively, you may need to get out of a situation or relationship that is causing these recurring negative thoughts. Either way, you have to first change your thinking.]

See more on the relationship between thoughts and emotions in Chapter Three.

ACTIVITY FIVE: TARGET THE MAJOR STRESSORS IN YOUR LIFE THAT LEAD TO ANXIETY AND DEPRESSION

If you want to see your life change for the better, you will need to change the way you think and react to ordinary, everyday events in your life that you perceive as stressful. Again, you may need to change something about how you are living to remove this stress, or you may need to change the way you are perceiving the situation. Realize that dealing with complexities is simply part of living a human life. To eliminate them is impossible. The question is, how can you deal with the issues you face and the people around you without becoming unnecessarily stressed, worried, anxious, drained, or fatigued?

Some people more easily deflect unpleasant experiences and realities than others. They handle these circumstances as "water off a duck's back," which means not upsetting themselves about circumstances and people over which they have no control. Others must struggle to achieve this perspective on life; many never do. But all of us are capable of moving towards it by retraining our minds. This requires intellectual autonomy, or in other words, the willingness to stand alone in your beliefs while adhering to the principles of ethical

Continued. . .

ACTIVITY FIVE: CONTINUED

critical thinking. It means keeping things in perspective and commanding your reactions and responses. Of course, in dire circumstances, it may or will be impossible not to be affected by life's dark side; even then, and in every context, we want to be as little stressed over external circumstances as possible. Through this perspective, you are better able to use your energy to solve the problems that you face, both personally and in terms of contributing to a more civilized society.

Would you say you frequently feel stressed and tense? If so, write out in detail why this is so:

1. I feel stressed _____% of the time.

2. The primary conditions in my life that lead to this stress are . . .

    a. _____

    b. _____

    c. _____

    d. _____

3. The specific things I am doing to cause me to feel stressed are . . .

    a. _____

    b. _____

    c. _____

    d. _____

4. I need to change the following things in my thinking and my life to reduce my stress level . . .

    a. _____

    b. _____

    c. _____

    d. _____

5. Based on this analysis, I plan to make the following changes right away . . .

    a. _____

    b. _____

    c. _____

    d. _____

ACTIVITY FIVE: CONTINUED

Be keenly aware of what situations lead you to high levels of stress. To help target specific causes of stress In these situations, **work through the following activity each time you feel excessive stress:**

1. Today the following situation happened in which I felt stressed . . .

2. I reacted as follows . . .

3. I realize now I could instead have reacted in the following way . . .

4. If I had reacted in this more reasonable way, I would have been happier because . . .

Come up with a long-term plan to keep from becoming overly stressed. Do you need new amusements or outlets for your stress? See Chapter Ten for alternative therapies for funnelling your energy into fulfilling activities.

ACTIVITY SIX: DON'T ACT HELPLESS; DON'T LET OTHERS CONTROL YOU; EXERCISE YOUR POWER

There are times in your life when you may feel powerless. During these times, it may seem that others have all the power and you have none. But is this true? Are you letting others determine your happiness by allowing them to dictate how you think and act? Do you allow other people too much influence and control over your thinking? Do you spend too much time and energy trying to please others, thereby giving them power over you? Can you think of no fruitful ways to use your power?

Mentally well people do not allow others to control them. They do not see themselves as helpless, vulnerable, or defenseless. They think for themselves, while seeking and considering the views of other *reasonable* people. They take responsibility for their decisions, their actions, and all aspects of their lives.

If you often feel helpless, complete the following statements:

1. The following event happened today, or recently, in which I felt helpless [e.g., I thought my supervisor criticized me unfairly] . . .

2. Because of this criticism I had the following thoughts and feelings . . . [For example, I was upset because I don't like being criticized. My supervisor is always picking on me. My supervisor is a bully, and I am not taking this anymore.]

Continued...

ACTIVITY SIX: CONTINUED

3. Based on these thoughts, I reacted as follows . . .

4. I now see the thinking underlying my emotions was reasonable/unreasonable because . . .

5. I now realize I could have instead thought and behaved as follows . . . [For example, I could have considered that my supervisor is under pressure from her supervisor, that I had mischaracterized her behavior as being offensive when she meant no harm, or that there may be truth in her critique of my behavior. Or—if I cannot continue to live with the situation because I can't be happy and fulfilled in this job—I could have recognized that acting irritable or angry is not rational, and that I should remain civil until I can get another job.]

6. Based on this analysis, I intend to make the following changes in my thinking or my life circumstances . . .

For the next week, **practice reminding yourself of this important truth:**

> *My power comes from within;* **I therefore have power over my thoughts and my life. I will take control of my thoughts in every situation and will be responsible for my thoughts and actions in every circumstance.** I will use my power in the most advantageous ways possible, while still respecting the rights and needs of others. I will not pretend to have power when and where I have none, nor will I dwell negatively on the power I don't have.

ACTIVITY SEVEN: INTERVENE IN YOUR BAD HABITS OF THOUGHT

If you want to be happy, you must routinely monitor your thoughts throughout every day. This will help you stop falling prey to the same bad habits of thought you have developed in your lifetime. These bad habits keep you trapped in cages created by your own mind. They cause your feelings of frustration and unhappiness. They lead people to harm others while thinking they are the ones being harmed. It is only when you monitor and change these thoughts that you can experience contentment. But altering a habit of thought will take much commitment in the form of practice, since it is an unconscious, long-running mental pattern or process that naturally repeats itself.

ACTIVITY SEVEN: CONTINUED

For the next twenty-four hours, actively observe your thoughts and then evaluate them as follows:

1. **Today I had the following powerful thoughts that seem to be habits with me** [perhaps disturbing thoughts, perhaps empowering thoughts, perhaps destructive thoughts] . . .

    a. _____

    b. _____

    c. _____

    d. _____

    e. _____

2. I realize that these thoughts are largely determining my level of happiness and contentment. After evaluating these thoughts, I see that most of them are [realistic or unrealistic, empowering or debilitating, etc.] . . .

3. I uncovered the following irrational thoughts that I need to change because these thoughts are causing problems for me . . . [For example, I thought mainly about my past mistakes, or I worried most or a lot of the time about what bad things might happen tomorrow or next week, or I was frustrated with the same person over and again when that person seems incapable of being reasonable, or I thought other people were leaving me out or not appreciating me.]

4. I need to replace these thoughts with the following reasonable thoughts . . .

5. I frequently have trouble changing my unreasonable or illogical thoughts to more reasonable thoughts, because . . .

6. However, when I permanently change these thoughts, I am certain to experience the following positive outcomes . . .

7. Therefore, I intend to . . .

ACTIVITY EIGHT: GET CONTROL OF YOUR ANGER

Anger, like all feelings, *comes from the thinking you are doing* in a situation. Others cannot make you angry. You alone make yourself angry and therefore you should take command of your anger. Some anger is, of course, rational. It is rational to be angry about all the injustices and suffering in the world. But what can you do about these injustices and this suffering? Can you step in and help in some specific ways? If so, you have a positive way to deal with your negative emotion of anger by helping someone else in need. Alternatively, if you have no control in the situation, what good will it do to let the anger overwhelm you?

Anger can result from many situations and ways of thinking in those situations. As mentioned, it may be rationally based, but it can alternatively be based in unreasonable thinking. For instance, fear is often expressed through anger and vindictiveness. Is your anger coming from fear? Is it coming from feeling that you are being mistreated? What is the root of your anger? How frequently are you angry?

If you are angry because you feel someone has treated you unjustly, you will need to identify the root of that problem through your thinking. To experience mental well-being requires that you understand your reasons for feeling anger, and that you step in to control yourself (your thoughts) when you are feeling angry. If your perceptions or memories of experiences from your past are the source of your anger, what good is this anger doing you now? Why do you continue to let your past control you by being angry today about something that happened long ago? Are there lingering consequences of these past experiences that you need to do something about now? If so, what do you need to do?

Complete these statements about your anger:

1. I am frequently angry in the following situations . . . and with the following people . . .

2. I am angry about the following things that have happened to me in the past, and I keep carrying this anger forward . . .

3. The thinking I am doing that is leading to my anger is as follows . . .

4. After uncovering the thinking leading to my anger, I now realize . . .

5. I plan to change in the following ways, to eliminate this anger in my life . . .

ACTIVITY NINE: ACCEPT THE FACT THAT YOU WILL MAKE MISTAKES!

If you want to be mentally well, you will need to accept the fact that you are not perfect, and that you will sometimes fail at what you attempt. In other words, one thing you can be sure of is that you will sometimes make mistakes, even with best intentions. The best thinkers and most accomplished people realize they make mistakes. They work to decrease the number of mistakes they make, and most importantly, they do not let their mistakes stand in the way of future successes and achievements.

How do you react when you make mistakes? How do you feel when you make a mistake? Do you feel worthless and depressed? If you feel depressed, is it because you think others won't like you or accept you if you make a mistake? What changes do you need to make within yourself to avoid making the same mistakes in the future? How do you need to change your thinking to accept yourself as a fallible creature who will never be perfect (no matter how much you beat yourself up for being imperfect)?

Complete these statements:

1. **The last time I made a mistake, this is what happened** ...

2. I reacted to the mistake in the following way ...

3. In the situation, I felt ...

4. To better deal with this kind of situation in the future, I intend to ...

5. This means changing my thinking in the following ways ...

ACTIVITY TEN: STOP OBSESSING ABOUT PAST MISTAKES

If you want to be mentally well, you will need to not only realize that you will make mistakes, but you also must stop worrying or obsessing about all your past mistakes. You must move forward by focusing on building a new, productive life. You will need to realize there is absolutely nothing you can do to change the past; to continue spending time and energy wishing you had done things differently (beyond what is useful in determining how you might act differently in the future) is a complete waste.

Again, all humans make mistakes and later wish they had made different decisions. However, the past is gone; no matter how much you wish you had acted differently, obsessing over this wish will only reduce the quality of your life. So, it is time to move on, to create positive experiences in the present and future.

Learn from the past; live for the present; plan for the future. Remember that in worrying over your past mistakes, you suffer at least twice, and perhaps many times—once for the time you made the mistake, and again for each time you obsess over it.

Make a list of situations you seem unwilling or unable to forget because you think they are unforgivable mistakes you have made:

1. _____

2. _____

3. _____

4. _____

For each one of these mistakes, complete these statements:

1. The situation in which I made a big mistake was as follows . . .

2. The mistake I made was . . .

3. I can't seem to forgive myself for this mistake because . . .

4. If I want to move forward, I need to realize that instead of forever feeling bad about my mistake and perpetually beating myself up about it, I should . . .

5. In other words, I intend to put this mistake behind me by thinking . . .

ACTIVITY ELEVEN: PURSUE HAPPINESS IN PRODUCTIVE, REALISTIC WAYS—THE ONLY WAYS THAT WORK

We humans often seem to harbor the idea that all we need is to feel positive, and then we will be happy in the long run. Frequently, we try to chase happiness through the wrong means, like being accepted by our peers who may get us into trouble, shopping for clothes we don't need, attempting to be popular, having glamorous automobiles or houses, drinking alcohol or taking drugs, etc. It may seem, at times, that we get what we want by chasing these fancies, but they will not fulfill our needs as humans or make us happy in the long run. In other words, many people engage in activities they believe will make them happy, but which are actually empty, superficial, or dangerous. Some of these activities may seem to make you happy, but only for the moment; the happiness doesn't last. These empty or dangerous activities need to be replaced with meaningful ones such as reading classic works, engaging in artistic endeavors, cultivating a garden, volunteering at a nonprofit organization with a noble goal, or pursuing lasting relationships.

Happiness is ultimately gained only through self-development, through our contributions to a better world, through compassion and love, and through a realistic attitude towards life, oneself, and others. It requires recognizing that life entails realities we may not like, but which we must deal with as best we can in the circumstances.

Think about a time when you acted in a superficial or dangerous way to make yourself feel good and find meaning—for example, by impressing others with a new outfit or car, purchasing things you didn't need, or gossiping with a "friend." Did you achieve the feeling you wanted? How long did that feeling last? Was this feeling truly one of happiness and contentment, or was it just a fleetingly pleasurable distraction?

Complete these statements:

1. **On the following occasion, I pursued something that I incorrectly thought would bring me happiness** . . .

2. My positive feelings lasted for approximately . . . [How much time?]

3. I now realize I was after a goal that was not in my best interest, because . . .

4. Instead of chasing this goal, I would have been better off doing the following . . .

5. In the future, instead of going after superficial ideals, I will . . .

Explore your idea of happiness: If you were asked what you wanted most right now—at this moment—to make you happy, what would your answer be?

Continued . . .

ACTIVITY ELEVEN: CONTINUED

Complete the statements:

1. **My definition of happiness is** . . .

2. This idea of happiness is/is not reasonable, because . . .

3. To this point, I have been pursuing happiness in the following ways [or not at all] . . .

4. I need to change the following things in my life to be happy in a reasonable way . . .

5. At the same time, I intend to be grateful for the following things in my life . . . [Again, re-read the list of things you are grateful for in your life, and see if you've thought of anything to add to it.]

To examine your routine behaviors, complete the following:

1. **I routinely engage in the following activities which do not make me happy,** but which substitute for deeper meanings [e.g., shopping, gambling, drinking alcohol, superficial socializing] . . .

2. My thinking underlying these activities is . . . [Answer separately for each behavior.]

3. Right after I engage in these activities, I feel [e.g., exhilarated, less worried about my problems, etc.) . . .

4. But after some time goes by, I feel the following about the activity and my behavior in it . . .

5. Therefore, I need to eliminate or significantly reduce the following behaviors from my life to be more fulfilled . . .

6. I need to replace empty activities with the following [e.g., reading, volunteering for some good purposes, exercising, writing, creating, singing, art, etc.) . . .

7. Based on this analysis, I intend to make the following changes in my life . . .

ACTIVITY TWELVE: LET GO OF THE NEED TO ALWAYS BE RIGHT

The thought that you need to be right and show everyone else you are right in every situation, despite evidence to the contrary, will get in the way of your development and your ability to experience authentic happiness. This is an expression of intellectual arrogance and is a common problem in human thinking; every person routinely engages in it, because every person frequently falls prey to believing that they know more than they actually do know in a given situation. It leads to all kinds of mistakes in reasoning and problems in life. It keeps you from opening your mind to many possible ways of perceiving situations and experiences. It keeps you from hearing what other people may be able to contribute to the conversation, and from empathizing with them when they do speak. It impedes your ability to deeply experience intimate relationships or to love another being.

Identify a time recently in which you held onto the perceived "need" to be right, while in fact you were being unreasonable.

Complete the following statements:

1. A recent situation in which I held on to the "need" to feel I was right (when really there was more than one way to look at the situation, or in fact I was wrong) was as follows . . .

2. I held onto this "need" to feel I was right because . . .

3. I now feel as follows about the encounter [e.g. disappointed, embarrassed, etc.]. . .

4. I feel this/these thing(s) about the encounter because . . .

5. I would have been more reasonable in the situation if I had acted and thought as follows . . .

6. I see that by insisting on being right, I caused myself to feel unhappy. In a similar situation in the future, instead of insisting on being right, I will . . .

ACTIVITY THIRTEEN: CHANGE YOUR BELIEFS THAT LEAD TO POOR DECISIONS

If you want to be happy, you will need to identify and then improve upon the beliefs you have used to this point which have led you to make poor decisions.

Consider this metaphor: the entirety of your thoughts can be compared with a garden containing beautiful, robust flowers, but mixed with considerable weeds. Maintaining and improving the garden of your mind requires you to meticulously examine each part and find the weeds (which are problems in your thinking). You must then pull out or eliminate the undesirable weeds in your thoughts, one by one, and replace them with desirable flowers (thoughts that will allow you to thrive through skilled decision-making). And remember that your garden cannot thrive with one analysis and one weeding. Without constant vigilance over the garden of your thoughts, more weeds can easily grow, and even begin choking out your cultivated flowers.

In other words, though difficult, you will need to identify and closely examine your thinking with the goal of throwing out unsound beliefs. These beliefs cause you to make poor decisions and therefore to experience negative emotions; you will need to actively replace them with reasonable, productive beliefs which will elevate you to higher-quality decisions.

Complete these statements for each important poor decision you made recently:

1. One poor decision I made recently was . . .

2. This decision resulted from the following thinking . . .

3. This thinking [was/was not] irrational in the circumstances because . . .

4. Based on this analysis, I plan to . . .

ACTIVITY FOURTEEN: COME TO TERMS WITH THE NEGATIVE THINKING CAUSING YOUR NEGATIVE EMOTIONS

If you frequently ruminate over negative thoughts, you will frequently, or even perpetually, experience negative emotions. And in this way, you can never achieve happiness. Again, bad things happen. You may be unlucky, as many people are. People commonly do terrible things to each other and to other sentient creatures. Some of these things may happen to you, and it is always easy to focus on the negative experiences that come your way.

It is vital for each of us to do what we can to contribute to a more reasonable world, insofar as we are capable, given our life conditions. Beyond that, there is simply no point in ruminating over all the bad things that have happened or might happen. Doing so adversely affects your mental well-being. Ensconcing yourself in negativity exhausts your energy, weakens you, and reduces your power. You need this energy for your development and your contributions.

Realize that you become what you spend most of your time thinking about; therefore, *by continually thinking negative thoughts, you become a negative person.* **What is at the root of all this negativity?** Why keep going over the same ground again and again? Take action to get out of the loop of negativity in which your mind is tormenting you. Move toward something productive and satisfying for you personally.

Complete the following statements:

1. **I spent a lot of time today [or recently] thinking negative thoughts as follows** . . .

2. Ruminating over these negative thoughts caused me to feel . . .

3. The issue(s) I need to deal with that are causing these perpetual negative thoughts are . . .

4. Instead of ruminating over these destructive or unhelpful thoughts, I need to take the following actions to deal with, or divert from, these issues that are dragging me down . . .

5. I also realized that I need to replace these negative thoughts with the following more realistic thoughts . . .

If a dystopian orientation is at the root of your negativity, see the section entitled "Implications of Dystopian Thinking" in Chapter Eight.

ACTIVITY FIFTEEN: BE NOT AFRAID, UNLESS FOR GOOD REASON

Many people are unable to achieve happiness because they are in an almost constant state of fear. There are some conditions, of course, in which people are fearful for good reason. They may be under threat of attack, for instance. But if there is no good reason for your fear, then the fear is based in unreasonable thought processes, which this book can help you conquer.

If you are frequently fearful, or if you live in a generalized state of fearfulness, this fear may come from experiences in the past in which you felt vulnerable. Perhaps you were very small when you felt this fear. Perhaps it resulted from being mistreated by people in the past.

You must now embrace the belief that you are not a small child, but a powerful adult with the ability to command your thinking. People in the past that caused you fear should not be controlling you today. To the extent that you allow them to cause you to feel fearful today, you are not in command of your thinking. To the extent that you allow beliefs or experiences from the past to control you, you lack command of your thinking. To achieve happiness, it is essential to reject any thoughts that come into your mind that cause you irrational fear, even if those thoughts made sense in your past when you were a vulnerable child.

If you feel irrational fear, write out your answers to the following statements, and follow up by actively fighting against your debilitating fears:

1. **The irrational fear that I experience comes from the following thoughts** . . .

2. The source of these thoughts is . . .

3. Even if these thoughts come from past experiences, I now realize it is unreasonable to hold onto them so they destroy my happiness today. Therefore, the thoughts I allow into my mind today will be under my command.

4. I intend to replace my fearful thoughts based in irrationality with the following courageous thoughts based in reasonability . . .

5. When I do so, my behavior will change in the following ways . . .

6. And my future will change in the following ways . . .

ACTIVITY SIXTEEN: LEARN TO LISTEN TO REASONABLE OTHERS

If you want to become more reasonable, and therefore more content, you will likely need to find one or a few reasonable friends who can help you in this effort by sharing thoughts in a mutually beneficial relationship. This is especially important for being exposed to, and then entertaining, fruitful ideas that can help you improve your thinking. This requires enhancing your ability to listen to new ideas; the importance of listening cannot be underestimated if you are going to move forward with your growth and your goal of being happy.

Have you ever thought about the importance of listening? As you listen, is your mind open to new ideas being presented? Do you find it difficult to listen carefully and thoughtfully to others? If so, why?

Instead of listening during a conversation, do you find yourself thinking about how you are going to respond while the other person is talking? Do scattered, distracting thoughts come into your mind? Productive, meaningful communication entails giving your full attention to what the other person is saying. By instead focusing on how you might respond, it is difficult to fully hear, and reasonably interpret, what the other person is saying.

Practice active listening on a daily basis. You can do this in the following ways:

1. **Practice simply listening to what others say to you without prejudging what they are saying. Then say back to them what you heard them saying, to clarify and correct your understanding of what they said. Try in good faith to enter their viewpoints. For instance, you can say:**

a. This is what I understand you to be saying . . . Is this correct?

b. Let me try to enter your point of view. Here is what I think you mean . . .

c. Have I done a good job of clarifying your views?

d. Have I distorted any of your views?

e. Now you speak from my point of view [using the prompts above].

f. What have we learned from entering each other's viewpoints?

2. **Complete the following statements, based on a situation in which you focused your full attention on understanding what another person was saying before you responded:**

a. What I heard this person saying is as follows . . .

Continued...

ACTIVITY SIXTEEN: CONTINUED

b. Because I was critically listening, I was able to understand the following about what the person was saying, or about the person him or herself . . .

c. While I was listening, I found that my mind [was/was not] open to the ideas being expressed by the other person.

d. I believe this because . . .

e. What I have learned from this experience that I can take with me moving forward is . . .

During the following week, evaluate whether you are actively and openmindedly listening to what others are trying to communicate to you. Write out your observations of your own critical listening abilities each day.

ACTIVITY SEVENTEEN: REACH FOR MORE EFFECTIVE COMMUNICATION TO IMPROVE YOUR LIFE

To have meaningful and deeply fulfilling relationships, it is important to realize that all such relationships require open, honest, forthright, objective, and deeply fulfilling communication in which all parties are acting in good faith.

Of course, every relationship you have is unique, and how you relate to the other person will differ to some degree in each relationship. But open, civil, considerate communication skills are necessary for fulfilling relationships, whatever they may be—between parent and child, intimate partners, work colleagues, friendships, etc.

Beyond intimate relationships where communication skills are essential, because we are social creatures, we cannot avoid being in relationships with at least some people. These relationships also require effective communication if they are to be effective or rewarding. Therefore, it is important to learn to communicate effectively, and to work at doing so in all circumstances. In short, expressing your feelings openly, in a respectful way, is important in every relationship and essential to close relationships. If you are in a relationship wherein the other person is unwilling or unable to so communicate, this means trouble; you will either both need to learn to communicate productively with one another, or you may need to part. Otherwise, you may be continually frustrated. Do not expect your partner to want to

Continued . . .

ACTIVITY SEVENTEEN: CONTINUED

communicate effectively—some people do not have the will or the developed capacity. Do not expect your partner to change in any way—realize that you can only change yourself. If you can happily work together for better communication, this is the ideal situation. But both people must be committed to communicating as effectively as possible if the relationship is to be ultimately fulfilling.

Through the tools of critical thinking, we learn the importance of being clear and precise in our communications. We also learn the importance of being accurate, and we avoid distorting the facts to "score points" on the other person. We realize we are frequently egocentric, and that our egocentricity can easily get in the way of honest exchange. We face up to our irrationality wherever and whenever we find it.

Now consider how well you communicate with important others in your life. Complete these statements:

1. When I think about my manner and patterns of communication, I realize I [am/am not] usually clear in how I communicate . . .

2. I [am/am not] generally satisfied with the way I communicate with others for the following reasons . . .

3. I tend to be [honest/not so honest] in my communications, because . . .

4. I tend to be [respectful/disrespectful] in my communications because . . .

5. I could improve my communications with [name an important person in your life] by doing the following . . .

6. Based on this analysis, I intend to make the following changes in the way I communicate . . .

ACTIVITY EIGHTEEN: TO IMPROVE YOUR FUTURE, FIRST EXAMINE WHERE YOU ARE NOW

If you want to be happy, it is important to first face your present situation, just as it is at this moment. What do you like about your current way of living? What do you want to change about your current way of living? Do you continually complain about your circumstances? If so, this only keeps your thinking focused on what you don't like about your situation, instead of on what you want to achieve and experience.

Imagine that a genie has appeared in your life and has given you three wishes. Complete the following activities, being both realistic and reasonable:

1. **If I could, I would change the following about my situation/life** . . .

    a. _____

    b. _____

    c. _____

2. **To change these things in my life, I would need to** . . .

    a. _____

    b. _____

    c. _____

3. The following barriers will get in the way of changing what I need to change in my life to achieve happiness . . .

4. Based on this analysis, I plan to make the following changes in my life to achieve a higher degree of happiness . . .

ACTIVITY NINETEEN: EXPRESS EMOTIONS IN A HEALTHY WAY; STOP HOLDING A GRUDGE

If you want to be happy, you will need to learn to express your emotions and feelings in healthy, non-threatening ways. This is especially important if you are holding a grudge against others. Remember that being continually resentful of someone you think has wronged you might seem like a good idea, but only because it is comfortable to your ego. In fact, this feeling comes from the thinking you are doing in the situation. Resentment will not go away until you change the thinking that causes it. Before then, you may feel comfortable, and to some degree satisfied, by holding a grudge. But in the final analysis, these thoughts and feelings are always harmful; holding onto resentments does not help you.

Even in situations where you may have good reason to resent someone, resentment may operate as a disease, keeping you in your own mental prison and holding you back from your potential. If someone causes you significant harm, again, the best way forward may be to figure out how to avoid that person. But if you are harboring irrational resentment, expecting another person to have knowledge or insight they simply do not or cannot have, your problem lies with your own thinking.

Learning to examine your feelings (such as resentment) to determine the thinking leading to them, and to state your desires and express your feelings to others in forthright, considerate ways are vital to your well-being as a developing person. Can you honestly express them to yourself?

Complete the following activities:

1. **I have difficulty expressing my feelings about the following issues** ... to the following person(s) ...

2. The thinking underlying my feelings is as follows ...

3. The problems in my thinking are ...

4. I need to replace this problematic thinking with the following thinking ...

5. To express my feelings in a healthy way, I need to ...

6. Today, I will practice expressing my feelings in a non-threatening way by doing the following ...

ACTIVITY TWENTY: ENTERTAIN NEW IDEAS; OPEN YOUR MIND TO BETTER WAYS OF VIEWING SITUATIONS

If you want to be mentally well, you will need to open your mind to new ways of looking at things. Are you unwilling to consider better ways of looking at a situation when others suggest them? Are you locked into narrowminded views that keep you from growing and developing as an engaged, productive person?

Complete the following statements, focusing on a situation in which you were unable to consider a reasonable alternative way of looking at a situation:

1. The situation was as follows …

2. I was narrowminded in the situation, so I reacted as follows …

3. I felt as follows in the situation …

4. I could have reacted more reasonably as follows …

5. If I had reacted more reasonably, my thinking would have been more openminded in the following ways …

6. Based on this analysis, in a similar situation in the future, instead of being narrowminded, I will …

ACTIVITY TWENTY-ONE: STOP HARMING YOURSELF THROUGH YOUR UNREASONABLE THOUGHTS

Unless you are in command of your thinking, you may easily fall prey to harming yourself through unhealthy thoughts, whether physically or emotionally. But you can choose to intervene and take charge of your thinking by ferreting out your thoughts that lead to self-harm. Complete the following statements:

1. **I acknowledge that I hold the following thoughts that are harmful to me** …

2. These thoughts harm me in the following ways …

3. I need to replace these irrational thoughts with the following more reasonable thoughts …

4. When I replace my harmful thoughts with these more reasonable thoughts, I will experience the following changes in my actions and feelings …

ACTIVITY TWENTY-TWO: STOP ALLOWING OTHERS TO HARM YOU THROUGH YOUR UNREASONABLE THOUGHTS

Unless you are in command of your thinking, you may easily fall prey to avoidable harm from others. It seems obvious that some people go about the world using and manipulating others as a matter of course, and without regard to the rights and needs of the people they harm. If you happen to be around such persons, you may need to protect yourself. This may necessitate getting away from certain persons entirely (including family members), which could require you to change your thinking in the situation.

Do you live with someone who is or may be harming you? Have you been programmed or brainwashed by someone in ways that have distorted your views or are against your interests? Have you been so brainwashed to believe certain distorted views about yourself or others that you are unaware of even how you have been brainwashed? **Are you confused as to whether someone in your life is harming you?** If so, complete the following statements (but you will likely want to make sure the person you are writing about does not read your answers).

1. **The situation I am in that is (or may be) harmful to me is** . . .

2. I believe the harm being done to me is . . .

3. The problem(s) in the thinking of the person harming me are . . .

4. The problem(s) in my thinking in this situation are . . .

5. I need to replace these thoughts with the following more reasonable thoughts . . .

6. Based on this analysis, I intend to . . .

If you feel confused about whether you have been brainwashed or are being controlled, speak with your therapist or trusted friend who can help explore this situation with you in a safe place.

CHAPTER TWO
THE TOOLS OF CRITICAL THINKING—
THE BIG PICTURE

In the previous chapter, you worked through a number of activities that should have, at least to some degree, lifted your spirits by helping you gain better command of your thoughts, decisions, and actions. Hopefully you now think more consciously and conscientiously about your thinking, and remember that small amounts of success are to be expected during the first phases of Critical Thinking Therapy.

Embedded in the activities you have been working through are critical thinking concepts and principles. But these structures have mainly not yet been made explicit. In this and the next few chapters, you will be introduced to an integrated, comprehensive approach to critical thinking. This approach provides critical thinking tools that will help you further improve your mental health through your reasoning (again, if you are willing to do the work required). We will expand our definition of critical thinking and consider, in brief, its opposite. The following critical thinking theory will be introduced to help you improve your mental health and your ability to reach your potential:

1) **The interrelationships between thinking, feelings, and desires**, which includes how thoughts, feelings, and desires continually influence one another, and how it is through commanding your thinking that you command your feelings and desires. Without command of your thoughts, feelings, and emotions, you cannot command your mental health.

2) **Egocentric and sociocentric thinking as intertwined barriers to critical thinking** and mental health, to which all humans fall prey by varying degrees in differing circumstances.

3) **Intellectual virtues that form one's core character**, which must be the focus of your attention if you are to develop as a self-fulfilled, ethically sensitive person.

4) **Reasonable criteria for determining which ideas to accept and which to reject** in a world that is often pathological, where people frequently lie and

deceive one another, and which can be very confusing due to its complexities.

5) **The elements of thought present in all reasoning**, which provide explicit tools for entering, analyzing, and reconstructing faulty reasoning that leads to poor life decisions (and hence contributes to poor mental health).

As you read these next few chapters, note the integrated nature of robust critical thinking concepts. Each conceptual set in critical thinking forms clusters of essential ideas that are interrelated and, when deeply internalized, form pathways for reasoning at the highest levels of quality, to achieve greater degrees of mental well-being. It is in commanding and strengthening these pathways that you command the quality of your thinking and, hence, your life. Internalizing the tools of criticality requires active and dedicated practice through years of study and application. If you think you have it by completing a few activities, think again. No one can come to understand powerful ideas over a brief period of time, no matter how intense the learning is during that time. The key is life-long commitment to critical thinking concepts, which should lead to increasing degrees of self-awareness, self-control, and sense of well-being. The tools explicit in critical thinking should become your most important weapons in fighting mental and emotional problems, for it is ultimately by commanding your reasoning that you will achieve mental health.

WHY CRITICAL THINKING IS ESSENTIAL TO YOUR MENTAL HEALTH

Almost everything you do as a human involves thinking. Your thinking tells you what to believe, what to reject, what is important, what is unimportant, what is true, what is false, who your friends are, who your enemies are, how you should spend your time, what jobs you should pursue, where you should live, who you should marry, how you should parent. Everything you know, believe, want, fear, and hope for, your thinking tells you.

It follows, then, that the quality of your life and mental health are primarily determined by the quality of your thinking. Your thinking has implications for how you go about doing everything you do. The quality of your work is determined by the quality of your thinking as you reason through the problems you face as you work. The quality of your relationships is determined by the thinking you do in those relationships. The quality of anything and everything you do is determined by the thinking you do while engaging in every one of those things. Critical thinking provides the standards for thought you need if you are to effectively solve your problems and thereby improve the quality of your life. This is something only you can do for yourself, using your own reasoning. Therefore, critical thinking should be at the heart of any mental health therapy you consider.

WHAT IS MENTAL HEALTH?

To experience mental well-being means maintaining an overall sense of fulfillment and self-worth, based in cultivating your capacities, while contributing to the lives of others. It entails confidence in your ability to effectively navigate within the realities of a complex world. To be a mentally well person requires commanding your emotional life through reasonable thinking, and developing the will to contribute something of value within your capacities.

It is important to distinguish between two distinctly different uses of the term "mental health," or what it means to be mentally healthy. Both imply positive feeling states, but one is genuine and the other is a sham. *Genuine mental health* is based on honestly to oneself, consideration for others, and the desire to achieve positive, creative self-expression. It is based in understanding your own need to grow and develop in your own right. It entails respecting the rights of others and having concern for the common good. Genuine well-being requires that you appreciate your vulnerabilities and uniquenesses, while attempting to respond reasonably in all situations, and engaging in opportunities that lead to self-realization.

Sham mental health refers to those people who lack the ability to empathize with the feelings of others, but who experience positive feeling states themselves. These people may range from those who can learn to empathize, to those frequently referred to as sociopaths, who are presumably incapable of empathizing or sympathizing with others. These include people who lack a developed sense of what it means to be an ethical person, but who see themselves as entirely justified in their actions.

To be genuinely mentally healthy in our complex and frequently hostile world requires a relatively high level of command of your own reasoning and of how that reasoning leads to your actions. It means coming to terms with what you can and cannot control. It means realizing your power and using it for the good. It entails achieving your unique capacities even while working against unreasonable social customs and ideologies. Mentally healthy people who rely on explicit tools of criticality are able to consistently and accurately assess their own reasoning as well the reasoning of others—politicians, writers, family members, great thinkers, indeed, anyone they choose and in any context they choose.

WHAT IS CRITICAL THINKING?

You will recall from our introduction that critical thinking is the disciplined art of ensuring that one uses the best reasoning one possibly can in any set of circumstances; this entails adhering to intellectual standards (again, such as logicalness, accuracy, fairness), understanding reasoning and how reasoning can go wrong (one's own reasoning as well as the reasoning of others), developing ethical character that embraces and contributes to community while cultivating one's individual potential, and embodying critical thinking virtues such as intellectual empathy, intellectual humility, intellectual integrity, intellectual perseverance, and confidence in reason.

Through developed critical capacities, you can take command of the thinking that commands you. No matter what your circumstance or goals, no matter where you are or what problems you face, you are better off if you are in control of your thinking. As a professional, parent, citizen, lover, friend, colleague—in every realm and situation of life—skilled thinking is needed. Poor thinking, in contrast, inevitably causes problems, wastes time and energy, and engenders frustration and pain. Poor thinking frequently leads to or exacerbates mental pathologies,[4] and keeps you from achieving your potential as a unique individual.

Becoming a critical thinker requires that you learn to observe, monitor, analyze, assess, and reconstruct thinking of many sorts in many dimensions of human life. It has implications for every act that takes place in your mind. It requires a special form of dedication and perseverance, and of honesty and integrity.

Critical Thinking Therapy, as illuminated in this book, shows you how to use your mind to improve your mind. Each of the activities and essential ideas in this book can help you take command of the mind that controls your thoughts, emotions, desires, and behavior. My hope is to lay a foundation for your future that is firmly situated in intellectual, ethical, creative and emotional growth. Critical thinking does not provide a quick fix, but rather explicit tools for the process of self-development and self-actualization. When you take your intellectual growth seriously, using these tools, you will begin to see payoffs in every part of your life.

First, you must wake up your mind. You must begin to understand your mind, to see when it causes you and others problems. You must learn how to intervene in your thinking when it tries to hide from itself (using one of the many forms of self-deception at which humans are naturally skilled). You must discover and face the

---

4 The term *pathology* used throughout this book in reference to mental health is not in any way being used in a medical sense. Some medical professionals argue that the term *pathological* should be confined to concerns connected to the physical body. Some mental health professionals argue that the use of the term leads to the medicalization of the mind (which is an abstract set of processes). While these concerns are valid, the uses of the term *pathology* related to the mind and to human societies are also valid and important. The human mind can sometimes be said to be sick or pathological. Human cultures and groups are frequently filled with sick, or pathological features. These are proper uses of the term and need not be abandoned. The term neurosis has mainly been avoided in this book since it has largely fallen out of use. See the glossary for a brief discussion of the uses of the terms *pathological* and *neurotic* in reference to mental health.

nonsense you have unknowingly taken into your mind during years of passive absorption—to which all of us are subject.

Only through thinking can you change whatever it is about your life that needs changing (including the parts you don't yet know need changing). Only through thinking can you take command of your future.

Humans routinely (you might say almost constantly) think. For certain, thinking is one of the primary things we do. From the minute you wake up in the morning, you begin thinking. During all of your waking hours, you are thinking. You cannot escape your thinking, even if you want to.

Right now, you are thinking about whether to take seriously what you are reading. Your thinking structures your feelings, shapes your desires, and guides your actions. The way you think about your mental health problems determines how you deal with them, or avoid dealing with them. The way you think about your financial situation determines your financial decisions. The way you think when you are at work determines how you function on the job. The way you think about your relationships determines the power you give other people over your life. The same is true for everyone.

The problem is that human thinking—your thinking—is often flawed. Most, if not all, of your regrettable actions emerge from faulty reasoning. In fact, problems in thinking lead to more problems in life than perhaps any other single variable. Yet, most people are content with their thinking. Because critical thinking typically is not valued in human societies, people don't tend to trace the problems in their lives, including their emotional problems, to problems in their thinking. Instead, they blame others, they blame circumstances, and they often live the whole of their lives without recognizing the leading role that their thinking plays in it.

To significantly improve the quality of your life, and pull yourself out of depression, anxiety, or any other negative emotional state, requires taking your thinking seriously. This means systematically observing your thinking and looking more closely at the consequences of your actions. It necessitates disciplining your thinking through knowledge of thinking, and practicing using that knowledge (of thinking) daily. It involves routinely analyzing your thinking, accurately assessing your thinking, and a commitment to improving your thinking. It also requires skill in seeing problems in others' thinking so as to protect yourself from others who may manipulate or harm you. In short, to improve your emotional life requires commanding your thinking, and all of the tools of critical thinking are relevant to that process.

INTERNALIZE THE IDEA: THINK ABOUT THE THINKING UNDERLYING YOUR BEHAVIOR

Write out some thinking, any thinking, you have done in the past week which you think may not be reasonable. Complete these statements:

1. The situation was as follows...

2. I behaved in the following way(s) in the situation...

3. I wish I had not behaved in this way because...

4. The thinking I was doing that led to my behavior was...

5. In a similar situation in the future I plan to think in the following way... which will lead to the following behavior...

THE FLAWED NATURE OF HUMAN REASONING

To begin to take thinking seriously, you must first recognize the frequently flawed nature of human thought in its "normal" state. Put another way, without active intervention, human thinking often develops problems. For example, humans are prejudiced. We stereotype one another. We are often hypocritical. We sometimes justify in our own minds policies and practices that result in stealing, killing, and torture. We often ignore important problems that we could, with determination and good thinking, solve—problems such as world hunger, poverty, and homelessness, as well as problems related to our own mental health. We allow ourselves to be manipulated, taken advantage of, or otherwise harmed by others. We get stuck in irrational patterns of thought and suffer as a result.

What is more, when we behave irrationally, our behavior typically seems reasonable to us. When challenged, the mind says (to itself), "Why are these people giving me a hard time? I'm just doing what makes sense. Any reasonable person would see that!" In short, we naturally think that our thinking is fully justified. As far as we can tell, we are only doing what is right and proper and reasonable. Any fleeting thoughts suggesting that we might be at fault typically are overcome by more powerful self-justifying thoughts: "I don't mean any harm. I'm just! I'm fair! It's the others who are wrong!"

It is important to recognize this self-justifying tendency of the human mind as its natural state. In other words, humans don't have to learn self-serving, self-deceptive thinking and behavior. These patterns are innate in every one of us to varying degrees. How does self-deception work in the mind? How can it be that we can see ourselves as right even when readily available evidence proves us wrong? One powerful reason is the mind's native ability (through self-deception) to represent unreasonable thoughts as perfectly reasonable. Indeed, this is perhaps the most significant reason that humans fail to recognize their own irrationality. And it is a primary cause of mental illness.

Consider, for instance, the man who thinks his wife should do all the housework while also working full-time. As he looks back at his childhood, he remembers his mother always doing the housework, and never his father. He selectively forgets his wife's persistent attempts to communicate her need for help with the housework. He is then devastated when one day she walks out, fed up with doing more than her fair share. He may become distraught, fall into depression, hunt down his wife and even kill her for leaving, or develop any number of other mental problems when his picture of reality is shattered.

The material point is that unreasonable, narrowminded thinking appears to the mind as dispassionate, unprejudiced, impartial thinking. We don't see ourselves as wrong. Rather, we see ourselves as right, as doing what is most reasonable in the situation, even when we are dead wrong.

Such is the power of self-deception. Welcome to human nature. We are all, to varying degrees, prejudiced. We all stereotype and deceive ourselves. We see ourselves as possessing the truth. In short, we all fall prey to human egocentricity—although not to the same degree. None of us will ever be a perfect thinker, but we can all be better thinkers, for greater sense of emotional well-being and a greater chance of achieving self-actualization and contributing to a better world.

To take command of your mind and hence your life, you need to work daily to bring what is unconscious in your thinking to the level of consciousness. You need to discover the problems that exist in your thinking and face them. Only then can you make significant improvements in your thinking and life. Inherent in human nature is the capacity to rise above native egocentric patterns of thought. You can learn to use your mind to become emotionally stable and come closest to achieving your potential in a world of limitations and hardships. You can "remake" or "transform" yourself to achieve emotional well-being in the long term.

INTERNALIZE THE IDEA: CONTINUING TO UNEARTH YOUR IRRATIONAL THINKING

Reread the example a few paragraphs above about the man and his wife. Can you think of an example in your own life in which your unreasonable, narrowminded thinking led you to have unreasonable expectations of another person?

1. The situation was as follows...

2. I behaved in the following way(s) in the situation...

3. I wish I had not behaved in this way because...

4. The thinking I was doing that led to my behavior was...

5. In a similar situation in the future I plan to think in the following way... which will lead to the following behavior...

Thinking can go wrong in many ways, including the following, all of which can may lead to mental health problems. Our thinking gets us into trouble because we often:

- are unclear, muddled, or confused
- jump to conclusions
- fail to think through implications
- lose track of our goals
- are unrealistic
- focus on the trivial
- fail to notice contradictions
- accept inaccurate information
- ask vague questions
- give vague answers
- ask loaded questions
- ask irrelevant questions
- confuse questions of different types
- distort data and present it inaccurately
- make inferences not justified by our experience
- fail to notice our inferences

- fail to notice our assumptions
- fail to distinguish inferences from assumptions
- answer questions we are not competent to answer
- come to unreasonable conclusions
- give vague answers
- form confused ideas
- form superficial concepts
- misuse words
- ignore relevant viewpoints
- confuse issues of different types
- are unaware of our prejudices
- think narrowly
- think imprecisely
- think illogically
- think one-sidedly
- think simplistically
- think hypocritically
- think superficially
- think sociocentrically
- think egocentrically
- think irrationally
- fail to reason well through problems
- make poor decisions
- are poor communicators
- lack insight into our ignorance
- come to conclusions based on inaccurate or irrelevant information
- ignore information that does not support our view
- cannot see issues from points of view other than our own

INTERNALIZE THE IDEA: EXEMPLIFY WHEN YOUR THINKING HAS LEAD YOU TO TROUBLE

Reread the bulleted list on the previous page which details some of the many ways in which our thinking gets us into trouble (note that this applies to all of us). Complete the following statements:

1. In reading through this list, the following problems listed are significant in my own thinking...

2. Focusing on just one of them, here's an example which shows this as a serious problem in my thinking...

3. To elaborate (in a few sentences)...

4. Focusing on another one of these problems, here's another example that shows this as a serious problem in my thinking...

5. To elaborate (in a few sentences)...

6. I plan to do the following to begin eliminating these serious problems in my thinking...

MENTAL HEALTH REQUIRES WORK AND PERSEVERANCE

Most people recognize that a no-pain, no-gain attitude is necessary for physical fitness; yet, those same people often give up at the first sign of mental discomfort when working on their minds. If you are unwilling to persevere through intellectual discomfort, you will limit your development as a thinker and fail to gain command over your mental well-being. Without some stress, the condition of the mind, like the body, will not improve.

Therefore expect some mental tension and discomfort as you work to take command of your mind. When the discomfort comes, learn to face it and work through it. You must come to realize that the most important ideas humans need to learn are often among the most difficult for the mind to understand and accept (like the fact that you yourself may be closeminded at any given moment). You must come to recognize that your mind, by nature, resists change—especially change that would force you to see yourself in an unfavorable light. So, as you begin to internalize critical thinking concepts, and feel frustrated, uncomfortable, or discouraged, keep pushing forward. Celebrate the fact that you are beginning to take command of your emotions and behavior, that you are growing, rather than—like most people—standing still or regressing. Look forward to the improved quality of your life that will occur in the long run. Realize that you must stretch and work your mind if you are to achieve mental well-being.

INTERNALIZE THE IDEA: PERSERVERING THROUGH DIFFICULITIES

Learning to persevere through difficulties is essential to developing as a mentally healthy person. Many people do not come into the world with a high degree of perseverance. Many of us have to learn to work through difficulties, complexities, and confusions. To what degree are you perseverant? To what degree do you easily give up when your problems or issues are difficult to work through? Complete the following statements:

1. I would say that I am/I am not generally a perseverant person.

2. To the degree that I lack perseverance, I experience the following problems in my life...

3. The thinking I am doing that is leading to this lack of perseverance is...

4. The thinking that I must do to become more perseverant is...

5. Therefore, I plan to do the following in order to become more perseverant...

BUILD YOUR CONCEPTION OF CRITICAL THINKING

Hopefully you are continuing to see changes in your life as you actively work through the activities in this book and apply the ideas learned, but to go further, you need explicit tools for intervention. These tools must emerge from a rich, substantive approach to the mind and to human reasoning, not one that is simplistic or superficial. Using these tools, you have a framework for reasoning skillfully and ethically through the many complex problems you will and do face. You should also be better at understanding the complexities in the human mind itself, and in disciplining and guiding your own mind according to those complexities.

You need to build in your reasoning a concept of critical thinking that helps you overcome or minimize your destructive tendencies. This includes theory, for instance, that helps you deal with the forces within you that lead you to seek uncritical approval from others (if, like many people, this is a problem for you).

You need principles of critical thinking that help you live more successfully in all parts of your life, which entail adhering to reasonable standards for thought—standards like clarity, accuracy, relevance, depth, breadth, logicalness, sufficiency, justifiability, and fairness. You need a concept of critical thinking that helps you systematically take your thinking apart and examine each part for quality. All of these critical thinking abilities, and more, are essential to your mental health.

The introductory diagrams on the following pages will give you a further sense of critical thinking concepts, and the problems in reasoning that critical thinking can address. The ideas in these diagrams will be developed in the next few chapters.

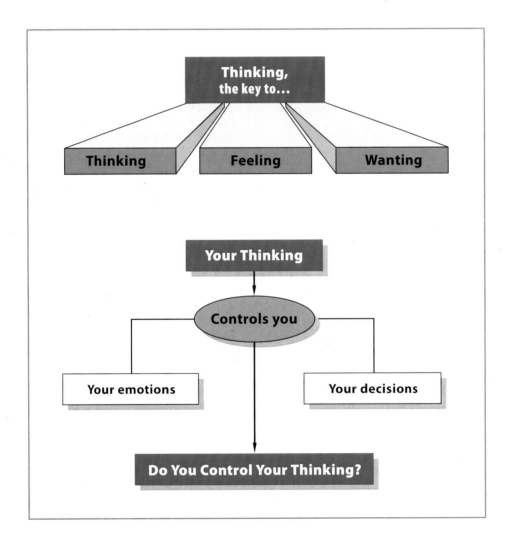

THREE TYPES OF CHARACTER SIMPLIFIED

THE NAÏVE THINKER	THE SELFISH CRITICAL THINKER	THE FAIRMINDED CRITICAL THINKER
The person who doesn't care about, or isn't aware of, his or her thinking	The person who in some ways is good at thinking, but is unfair to others	The person who is not only good at thinking, but is also fair to others

Fairminded critical thinkers consistently seek their own happiness and tranquility while contributing to a better world. Selfish critical thinkers spend their energy seeking more for themselves, and naive thinkers are easily manipulated by the selfish and power-hungry thinkers. Neither of these latter states of mind are healthy. Each of us may sometimes be a naïve thinker, sometimes a selfish critical thinker, and sometimes a fairminded critical thinker.

THE CORE OF CRITICAL THINKING

The concept of critical thinking includes the disciplined analysis and assessment of reasoning as one cultivates intellectual virtues in one's self. This process entails concern for two primary barriers to criticality—egocentric and sociocentric thinking—which are prevalent and widespread in human thought and life.

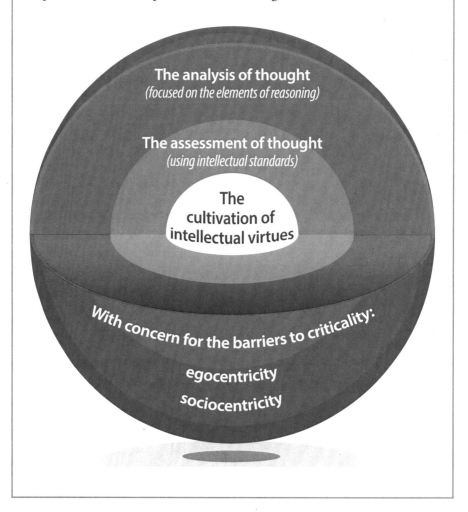

The analysis of thought
(focused on the elements of reasoning)

The assessment of thought
(using intellectual standards)

The cultivation of intellectual virtues

With concern for the barriers to criticality:

egocentricity

sociocentricity

CRITICAL THINKERS ROUTINELY APPLY INTELLECTUAL STANDARDS TO THE ELEMENTS OF REASONING IN ORDER TO DEVELOP INTELLECTUAL VIRTUES

Those who adhere to relevant intellectual standards when reasoning through issues in the essential parts of human life develop intellectual virtues increasingly over time.

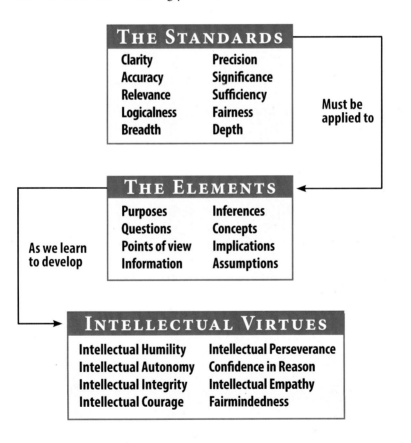

THE STANDARDS

Clarity	Precision
Accuracy	Significance
Relevance	Sufficiency
Logicalness	Fairness
Breadth	Depth

Must be applied to

THE ELEMENTS

Purposes	Inferences
Questions	Concepts
Points of view	Implications
Information	Assumptions

As we learn to develop

INTELLECTUAL VIRTUES

Intellectual Humility	Intellectual Perseverance
Intellectual Autonomy	Confidence in Reason
Intellectual Integrity	Intellectual Empathy
Intellectual Courage	Fairmindedness

THE ELEMENTS OF THOUGHT

Eight basic structures are present in all thinking: Whenever we think, we think for a purpose within a point of view based on assumptions that lead to implications and consequences. We use concepts, ideas, and theories to interpret data, facts, and experiences in order to answer questions, solve problems, and resolve issues.

Thinking, then:

- generates purposes
- raises questions
- uses information
- utilizes concepts
- makes inferences
- makes assumptions
- generates implications
- embodies a point of view

Eight Elements Define All Reasoning

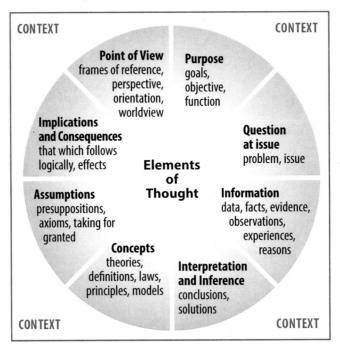

Critical thinkers use the elements of reasoning with sensitivity to universal intellectual criteria, or standards, such as clarity, precision, accuracy, relevance, significance, depth, breadth, logicalness, sufficiency, and fairness.

WE TAKE OUR THINKING APART TO FIND PROBLEMS IN OUR THINKING — AND SOLVE THEM

HERE ARE THE PARTS:

Points of View we need to consider

Purpose of our thinking

Implications and Consequences of our thinking

Questions we are trying to answer

Parts of Thinking

Assumptions we are taking for granted

Information needed to answer the question

Concepts or key ideas we are using in our thinking

Inferences or conclusions we are coming to

©2025 Linda Elder

CRITICAL THINKING STANDARDS HELP YOU THINK BETTER

The best thinkers don't believe any and everything they hear or read. They use intellectual standards to decide what to believe. They use intellectual standards to keep their thinking on track. In this book, we focus on some of the important ones. When you use them every day, your thinking improves.

Be <u>clear</u>! — Can you state what you mean?
Can you give examples?

Be <u>accurate</u>! — Are you sure it's true?

Be <u>relevant</u>! — Is it related to what we are thinking about?

Be <u>logical</u>! — Does it all fit together?

Be <u>fair</u>! — Am I considering how my behavior might make others feel?

Be <u>reasonable</u>! — Have we thought through this problem thoroughly and with an open mind?

If everyone in the world regularly used critical thinking standards, we could solve most of our big problems.

SOME ESSENTIAL CRITICAL THINKING STANDARDS AND QUESTIONS RELATING TO EACH

Clarity — Could you elaborate further? Could you give me an example? Could you illustrate what you mean?

Accuracy — How can I check on that? How can I find out if that is true? How can I test or verify that?

Precision — Could you be more specific? Could you give me more details? Could you be more exact?

Relevance — How does this information help me solve my problem? How does this statement bear on the question? How does that help me with the issue?

Depth — What factors make this a difficult problem? What are some of the complexities in this question? What are some of the difficulties I need to deal with?

Breadth — Do I need to look at this from another perspective? What other viewpoints do I need to consider? In what other reasonable ways might I look at this situation?

Logic — Does all of what she has said make sense together? Does my lifestyle make sense given the realities I face? Does what he is saying follow from the evidence?

Significance — What is the most important problem I need to work through? Is this the central idea I should be focused on, or is something else more important? Which of these facts are most important?

Fairness — Am I being fair in this situation, or am I distorting something to fit my desires? Am I being selfish? How can I sympathetically represent the viewpoints of others?

Sufficiency — Do I have sufficient information to answer the question? Am I unfairly leaving out information I would rather not consider in order to get more for my group while ignoring or downplaying the rights and needs of others?

©2025 Linda Elder

BECOMING A FAIRMINDED CRITICAL THINKER

Intellectual virtues form the character of the ethical thoughtful person; they are central to any reasonable conception of critical thinking and to a self-actualizing lifestyle. Here is a brief introduction to some essential intellectual virtues.

Intellectual Integrity

Act towards others the way you want people to act towards you. Respect others in the same way you want to be respected. Don't expect others to act better than you are willing to act yourself. Consider the feelings of others in the same way you want your own feelings to be considered. Because you don't want others to be rude to you, avoid being rude to others. Because you don't want to be harmed by others, be careful not to harm others.

Intellectual Independence

Do your own thinking. Figure things out for yourself. It is good to listen to others to find out what they think, but you must do your own thinking to decide who and what to believe. Of course *don't* just believe what you want to believe. Use intellectual standards to decide standards like accuracy, relevance, significance and fairness.

Intellectual Perseverance

Don't be a quitter. When you begin to think you can't learn something, remind yourself that *you can.* If reading is hard for you, stick to it (because it is important to learn to read well). When writing is hard, keep trying so you can learn to write better. Don't be afraid to work hard when you feel like giving up. Remember that no matter how good you are at thinking, you can always improve. And no matter how much you struggle with learning, keep trying. *Never give up!* Be the captain of your own ship. Chart your own course in life.

Intellectual Empathy

Always try to understand how other people think and feel. Whenever you disagree with someone, try to see things from that person's point of view. When you do try to see things from other people's viewpoints, you will often find that there are some things you are right about and some things other people are right about. Being able and willing to imagine how others think and feel is very important in life. If everyone did this a lot, the world would be much better for everyone. There would be a lot less pain and suffering.

Intellectual Humility

Recognize that you don't know most things. There is a lot that you don't know (and will never know). Don't say something is true *when you don't know for sure that it is*. Lots of things you *think* are true may not be. Lots of things people say are true are actually not true, and lots of things you read or see on TV or online are not true. Always ask, "How do I know that? How do you know that?"

Intellectual Courage

Be ready to speak up for what you think is right, even if it is not popular with your friends or the people around you. Of course, sometimes speaking up can be dangerous. Use your best thinking to figure out when it makes sense to speak up and when you should just keep your thoughts to yourself. When you do speak up, try always to show respect for others. But don't ever be afraid to disagree in the privacy of your own mind. And don't be afraid to question your beliefs, to figure out what makes best sense. Develop the courage to look inside your own mind and figure out what is really going on there. Even if you have held a belief for a long time, you still need to be willing to question it, to use the tools of critical thinking to recheck it.

Confidence in Reason

The best chance we have to create a fair and just world is if we use our best thinking, all of us, together, living on the planet. When people disagree, they need to overcome disagreements by looking at the facts, at the evidence. We need to work together to come to the most defensible conclusions. Use intellectual standards in working through problems. For example, make sure you use information that is *accurate* and *relevant* to the problem you are trying to solve. Look for the complexities in deep issues. Avoid superficial answers to complicated problems, as they almost never work. Think about problems from different points of view. Trust evidence, facts, and credible reasoning. Distrust blind faith, jealousy and fear.

Fairmindedness

Try to figure out what is most fair in every situation. Think about everyone involved, not just about yourself. Don't put your desires and needs above those of others. You should even be willing to give things up to help other people when their needs are much greater than yours. Try to imagine what it would be like to think and feel as other people do, to be in their shoes. Don't act until you have done this. Think before you act. Don't act before you think.

CRITICAL THINKERS SEEK
BETTER WAYS OF DOING THINGS

There's always a better way and I can find it.

I can figure out anything I need to figure out.

Critical Thinkers Believe in
The Power of Their Minds

DISTINGUISHING RATIONAL FROM EGOCENTRIC AND SOCIOCENTRIC MOTIVES

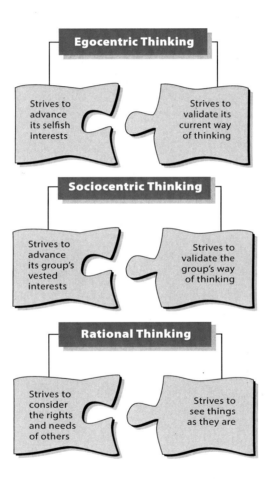

Egocentric Thinking

Strives to advance its selfish interests

Strives to validate its current way of thinking

Sociocentric Thinking

Strives to advance its group's vested interests

Strives to validate the group's way of thinking

Rational Thinking

Strives to consider the rights and needs of others

Strives to see things as they are

Essential Idea: Though egocentric, sociocentric and rational thought may be complex, we can capture their basic motives.

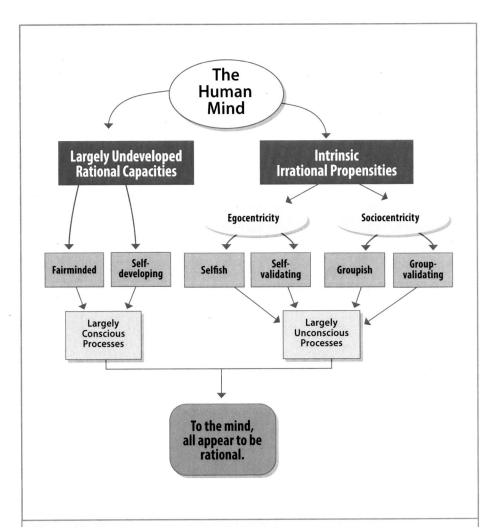

Essential Idea: All humans are innately egocentric and sociocentric. Humans also have (largely undeveloped) rational capacities. Humans begin life as primarily egocentric creatures. Over time, infantile egocentric self-centered thinking merges with sociocentric group-centered thinking. All humans regularly engage in both forms of irrational thought. The extent to which any of us is egocentric or sociocentric is a matter of degree and can change significantly in various situations or contexts. While egocentric and sociocentric propensities are naturally occurring phenomena, rational capacities tend to require deliberate study and practice over the long term. It is through the development of rational capacities that we combat irrational tendencies and develop as mentally well persons.

HUMANS OFTEN DISTORT REALITY THROUGH IRRATIONAL LENSES

When engaging in irrational pursuits, the mind must deceive itself; it relies on pathologies of thought to do so. Pathologies of thought can be pictured as a set of filters or lenses that:

- cause or "enable" us to see the world according to our perceived interests, without regard to others;
- distort reality so we can get what we want;
- lead us to ignore relevant information to paint a favored picture of the world based on our vested interests.

These pathologies allow us to deceive ourselves into believing what we want to believe (in order to get what we want or maintain our viewpoint). Pathologies of thought, hence, serve their master: self-deception. They are manifest in both egocentric and sociocentric thought.

CHAPTER THREE
UNDERSTAND HOW THOUGHTS, FEELINGS, AND DESIRES ARE INTERTWINED

Everyone thinks. It is our nature to do so. But remember that much of our thinking left to itself is biased, distorted, ill-founded, or prejudiced. Our thinking can easily lead to problems in our lives, including mental health problems. Our thinking can also cause problems for others, through disrespect, negligence, and cruelty, for instance. Of course, the mind doesn't just think, it also feels and wants. What is the connection? Our thinking shapes and determines how we feel and what we want. When we think well, we are motivated to do things that make sense and to act in ways that help rather than harm ourselves and others. At the same time, emotions or desires may influence our thinking, helping or hindering how well we think in a situation.

At any given moment, our minds (that complex of inner thoughts, feelings, and desires) can be under the sway of our irrational or rational capacities. Our thoughts, feelings, and desires may be either mentally healthy or unhealthy. When we are ruled by our irrational tendencies, we see the world from a narrow or self-serving perspective. We may have difficulty perceiving how our behavior affects others. We are fundamentally concerned with getting what we want and/or with validating our beliefs and views. These dysfunctional ways of thinking limit our ability to experience positive, satisfying emotions, and lead us to do things that cause suffering to ourselves and/or others.

A key to understanding human thought, then, and to becoming mentally healthy, is to understand the essential duality of your mind: 1) its intrinsic tendencies toward irrationality (i.e., being trapped in egocentric and/or sociocentric thought with their attendant self-delusions, rationalizations, and other dysfunctional processes) and, 2) its capacity for reasonability (freeing itself from self-delusion, paranoia, depression, myth, illusion, etc.). You will read more on this in the next chapter.

Though thinking, feeling, and wanting are, in principle, equally important, it is only through your thinking that you can take command of your mind. It is through your thinking that you figure out what is going wrong with your thinking. It is through your thinking that you figure out how to deal with your destructive emotions. It is through your thinking that you change unproductive desires to productive ones. It is fairminded reasonability that frees you from intellectual slavery and group conformity. If you understand your mind and its functions, if you face the barriers to your development caused by egocentric and sociocentric thought, if you work on your mind through daily, disciplined practice, you may find a clear pathway to mental well-being and self-actualization.

THE MIND'S THREE DISTINCTIVE FUNCTIONS

The mind has three basic functions: thinking, feeling, and wanting.

- **Thinking** is the part of the mind that figures things out. It makes sense of life's events. It creates the ideas through which we define situations, relationships, and problems. It continually tells us: "This is what is going on." "This is what is happening." "Notice this and that."
- **Feelings*** are created by thinking—evaluating whether the events of our lives are positive or negative or somewhere in between. Feelings continually tell us such things as: "This is how I should feel about what is happening in my life. I'm doing really well." Or, alternatively, "Things aren't going well for me."
- Our **desires** allocate energy to action, in keeping with what we define as desirable and possible. They tell us, for instance: "This is worth getting. Go for it!" Or, conversely, "This is not worth getting. Don't bother."

---

* Though the terms "feelings" and "emotions" might be used in some cases to refer to different phenomena, these terms are used interchangeably in this book.

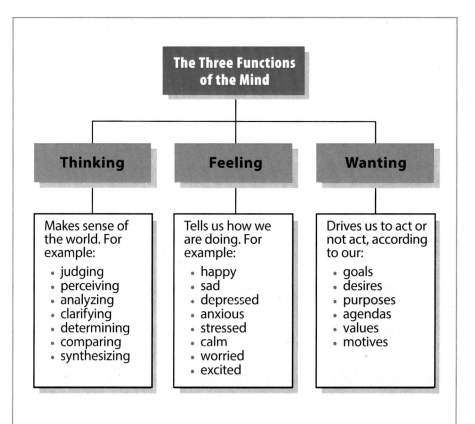

Essential Idea: Your mind is continually communicating three kinds of things to you:

1) what is going on in life (thinking),

2) feelings (positive or negative) about those events, and

3) things to pursue, where to put your energy (in light of 1 and 2).

THE DYNAMIC RELATIONSHIP BETWEEN THINKING, FEELING, WANTING

There is an intimate, dynamic interrelation between thinking, feeling, and wanting. Each is continually influencing the other two.

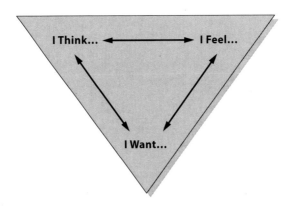

For example, when we think we are being threatened, we feel fear, and we inevitably want to flee from or attack whatever we think is threatening us. When we feel depressed, we think there is nothing we can do to improve our situation, and we therefore lack the motivation to do anything about our situation. When we want to improve our eating habits, it may be because we think that our diet is causing us harm, and we therefore feel dissatisfied with our diet.

Though we can consider the functions of the mind separately (to better understand them), they can never be absolutely separated. Imagine them as a triangle with three necessary sides: thoughts, feelings, and desires. Eliminate one side of the triangle and it collapses. Each side depends on the other two. In other words, without thinking there can be no feelings or desires; without feelings, no thoughts or desires; without desires, no thoughts or feelings. For example, it is unintelligible to imagine thinking that something is threatening you and might harm you, wanting to escape from it, yet feeling nothing in relationship to what you think and want. Because you think you might be harmed and you want to flee, you necessarily feel something like fear, or at least extreme concern.

INTERNALIZE THE IDEA: THINKING, FEELING, WANTING

Write out your understanding of the relationship between thoughts, feelings, and desires. Complete the statements:

1. My understanding of the relationship between thoughts, feelings, and desires is as follows…
2. An example in my own life of thoughts I have had that have led to certain feelings and desires is as follows…

YOUR BEHAVIOR COMES FROM YOUR THINKING, FEELINGS, AND DESIRES

Thoughts, feelings, and desires continually interact and produce behavior as a result of that interaction.

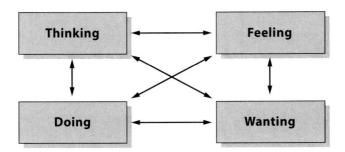

To understand this, consider the example on the previous page about eating habits. Suppose you feel dissatisfied with your diet. You want to improve your diet because you think that by doing so you will improve your health. You therefore behave in the following ways:

1. read about different diets (behavior),
2. come to conclusions about the best diet for you, then change your diet accordingly.

After a few weeks you notice that you feel better physically and are losing weight. You now feel satisfied. You think that your diet is improving your health. You therefore want to continue with the new diet.

But then after a few more weeks you think: "I don't want to eat any more salads and tasteless foods. I can't keep this up for the rest of my life! There must be a diet available that is not boring." You therefore act on that thinking. Again you consider different dieting possibilities, finally deciding upon a new diet. The process begins again, with your thoughts, feelings, and desires continually shaping your behavior.

INTERNALIZE THE IDEA: THINKING, FEELING, WANTING, BEHAVIOR

Add to your understanding of the relationship between thoughts, feelings, and desires by adding the behavioral dimension. Complete the statements:

1. My understanding of the relationship between thoughts, feelings, desires, an behaviors is as follows...

2. An example in my own life of thoughts I have had that have led to certain feelings, desires and behavior is as follows...

Though thoughts, feelings, and desires play equally important roles in the mind, continually influencing and being influenced by one another, thinking is the key to commanding feelings and desires. To change a feeling is to change the thinking that leads to the feeling. To change a desire is to change the thinking that underlies the desire.

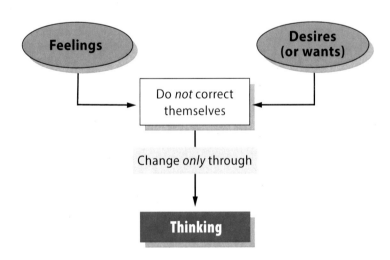

If you feel angry because your child is behaving disrespectfully toward you, you can't simply replace your anger with a feeling of satisfaction, for example. To change the anger to a more positive emotion, *you must change the thinking you are doing* in the situation. Perhaps you need to think about how to teach your child to behave respectfully towards you, and then behave in accordance with that new thinking. Perhaps you need to think about the influences in your child's life that might be causing the rude behavior and then try to eliminate or reduce those influences. In other words, you get control of your emotional state and are able to change your feelings through your *thinking*.

Similarly, a desire cannot change without changing the thinking that causes the desire. Suppose two people, Jan and Enrique, have been in a romantic relationship, but Enrique has broken off the relationship. Yet, Jan still wants to be in the relationship. Suppose her desire comes from thinking (that may be unconscious) that she needs to be in the relationship to be emotionally stable, that she won't be able to function without Enrique. Clearly this thinking is the problem. Jan must therefore change her thinking so she no longer wants a relationship with Enrique. In other words, until she thinks that she does not need Enrique to be content within herself, that she can function satisfactorily without him, that she doesn't need to be in a relationship with a person who doesn't want to be with her, she will hanker after the failed relationship with Enrique. And she may engage in any manner of irrational or destructive behaviors to get him back. In short, unless her thinking changes, her desire won't change. She must defeat the thinking that is defeating her.

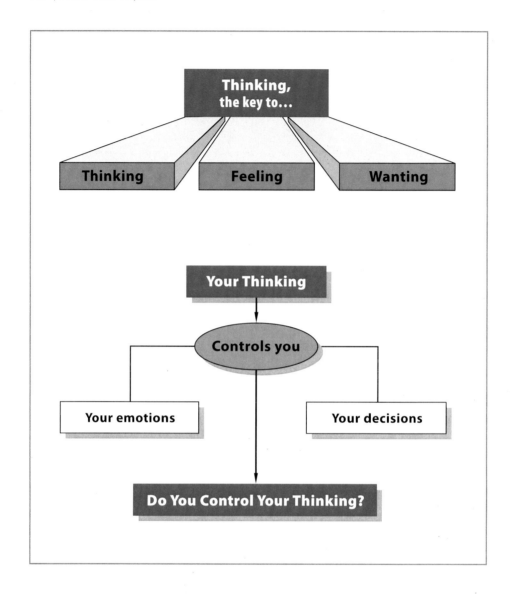

INTERNALIZE THE IDEA: TO WHAT DEGREE DO YOU CONTROL YOUR THINKING?

Since your thinking controls your emotions, desires, and behavior, it is essential to take command of your thinking. To what degree do you control the thinking that is controlling your feelings? Think of a situation you were in recently in which your emotions seemed out of your control. Complete the following statements:

1. The situation was as follows. . .

2. My feelings were as follows. . .

3. The thinking I was doing that led to these feelings was. . .

4. I now realize that my thinking was irrational in the following ways. . .

5. I plan to replace this irrational thinking with the following thinking. . .

6. When I do this, my life should improve in the following ways. . .

To become mentally well requires taking command of your thoughts, feelings, and desires through practice in understanding their interrelationships.

YOUR THINKING IS THE KEY TO COMMANDING YOUR FEELINGS AND DESIRES

Each of the activities in this book offers a strategy for applying critical thinking understandings on a routine, daily basis. To gain command of your mental health, regularly work through these activities until you are actively using them as strategies throughout your life. This chapter has introduced the relationships between these three interrelated and interdependent functions of the mind: thinking, feeling, and desiring, or wanting. Here is one powerful strategy you can use every day: Whenever you find yourself experiencing what may be irrational emotions or desires, figure out the thinking generating these emotions and desires. Then develop reasonable thinking with which to replace the unreasonable thinking you have been using in the situation. Whenever you feel the irrational negative emotions, rehearse the reasonable thinking you now intend to use. Use this format:

1. Explicitly state your feelings and desires.

2. Figure out the irrational thinking leading to them.

3. Figure out how to transform the irrational thinking into thinking that makes sense in context. Precisely state (with details) the new, reasonable thinking.

4. Whenever you feel the negative emotion, repeat to yourself the reasonable, logical thoughts you developed—to replace the irrational thoughts—until you convince yourself of the new reasonable thinking. This is when you should feel the rational emotions that accompany reasonable thinking.

5. Do not allow yourself to slip back into your original irrational thoughts, which may only take you back into the go-nowhere merry-go-round thinking that causes you to experience negative, self-defeating emotions and keeps you from taking command of your emotional life.

Again, each of the activities you work through in this book represents a strategy you can go back to again and again to work the ideas into your thinking until you begin to experience positive change in yourself.

As with all forms of personal development, development of thinking means transforming deeply ingrained habits. This can happen only when you take responsibility for your own growth. Learning to think strategically to target bad habits of thought must become a lifelong habit. It must replace the habit most of us have of thinking impulsively, of allowing our thinking to gravitate toward its own, typically unconscious, egocentric or sociocentric agendas.

If you want command of your life, ask these questions:

- Am I willing to make self-reflection a lifelong habit?
- Am I willing to become a strategic thinker—to identify and get rid of problems in my thinking?
- Am I willing to unearth the unreasonable thoughts, feelings, and desires that lurk in the dark corners of my mind?
- Am I willing to develop a compassionate mind that respects the rights and needs of others while also attending to my own needs and desires?

This type of strategic thinking has two primary components:

1. The ability to figure out when your thinking is illogical, unjustifiable or otherwise flawed.

2. Actively challenging the flawed acts of your mind through the tools of critical thinking.

This requires figuring out:

1. What is actually going on in the situation.

2. Your options for action.

3. Justifiable reasons for choosing the option you are perceiving as the "best" in the situation.

4. Ways of reasoning with yourself when you are being unreasonable, or in other words, ways of reducing the power of your irrational state of mind

---

INTERNALIZE THE IDEA: UNEARTHING YOUR IRRATIONAL THINKING

Identify an area of your personal or professional life in which you use, or have used, thinking that is possibly irrational. If you are having trouble, think of a situation in which you felt a powerful negative emotion and had difficulty dealing with it. Write out the answers to these questions:

1. What is/was actually going on in the situation as it stands? Elaborate on the details.

2. What are/were your options for action?

3. Which option seems/seemed best? How do you know? Can you view the situation in any other ways?

4. Construct the reasoning you need to rehearse when you are again in this situation or a similar one.

If you have trouble doing this activity, read the example in the next section.

FIND THE THINKING UNDERLYING YOUR POWERFUL EMOTIONS AND URGES

Sometimes you may find yourself struggling with emotions or passions that seem disconnected from thought. At least, you may not know what thinking is leading to or connected with the emotion. Whatever the exact thought is, it seems unconscious, primitive, and powerful. For example, suppose a woman feels a powerful urge to have sex with a person other than her spouse, and suppose further that this urge becomes very intense when alone with that person. The urge may be experienced as irresistible at the moment. How do we reconstruct the primitive thinking at the root of such urges? No doubt the thinking will differ according to divergent sexual patterns among people. The common denominator might be suggested by the primitive desire to prove our sexual attractiveness and therefore reinforce feelings of being "masculine" or "feminine." The material point is that no matter how primitive your urges may be, thinking always informs and interacts with those urges, though it may feel as if no thinking is involved and the experience is entirely emotional. Look beneath the surface of your desires and behaviors to find your thinking.

As Freud demonstrated, the thinking of the unconscious mind may be very hard to plumb. It may take years to uncover and bring to consciousness deeply primitive unconscious thoughts. Even then it may be hard to be sure you are correct in your analysis. Your unconscious thoughts are those that lie beneath the surface of your thinking, that you have limited or no access to, and that you may be motivated to avoid facing. Perhaps you are trying to avoid seeing something in yourself. Perhaps you are trying to avoid seeing something in another person or a situation. If an urge results in consequences harmful to another person, making the harm as explicit as you can to yourself should help you face up to your unethical behavior. Keep this ethical principle before you at all times, like a mantra: "It is wrong to harm another person for my pleasure." Then discipline yourself to behave at all times in accordance with this principle. If you are unable to control your urges that harm other people, seek help.

If obeying an urge does not result in any negative consequences other than to violate a social convention, then the solution may be to act on the urge, but only in private or in a supportive environment. In many societies of the past, throughout our history as humans, many dissenters have violated social norms and conventions in private. *Indeed, sometimes this may be required for your sanity.* For instance, though cross-dressing may be more accepted in some societies today than in the past, men who may be inclined to dress in women's clothing are still frequently made to feel uncomfortable when doing so in public.

In short, no matter what urges, desires, or emotions you have, whether they lie at the conscious, subconscious or unconscious level, it is essential to realize that there will always be thinking you are doing that affects or directs those urges or desires. Your thinking can be affected by your urges and emotions as well. Remember that by understanding the intertwined nature of your thoughts, feelings, and desires, and specifically uncovering the thinking leading to your emotions and desires, you are better able to intervene in your behavior when you are off course.

INTERNALIZE THE IDEA: ANALYZE AND COMMAND YOUR URGES

Stop a minute and think about your urges. Do they get you into trouble? If so, why? Are they unacceptable to society for no good reason?

Complete these statements, but not in writing if they could be used against you:

1. One urge that I have which is not acceptable to people but causes no harm is...
2. This urge is frowned upon because...
3. I can best handle this urge by... [make sure to work out a reasonable solution]
4. Therefore I intend to...

---

1. One urge that I have which is not acceptable to people because it causes harm is...
2. The problem with this thinking is that it violates someone else's rights. My urge causes actual harm in the following ways...
3. I therefore realize I cannot act upon this urge under any conditions.
4. I can best handle this urge by... [make sure to work out a reasonable solution]
5. Therefore I intend to...

TO SUMMARIZE: THOUGHTS, FEELINGS, AND DESIRES ARE INTERDEPENDENT

As has been the focus of this chapter, it is important to recognize that the mind is composed of three functions: thinking, feeling, and desiring (or wanting). Wherever one of these functions is present, the other two are present as well. And these three functions are continually influencing and being influenced by one another. Your thinking influences your feelings and desires. Your feelings influence your thinking and desires. Your desires influence your thinking and feeling. You cannot immediately change your desires or feelings. It is only thinking that you have direct access to. It makes no sense for someone to order you to feel what you do not feel or to desire what you do not desire. You do not change feelings by substituting other feelings, or desires by substituting other desires. But someone can suggest that you consider a new way to think about a situation. You can role-play new thoughts, but not new emotions or desires. It is possible to reason within a point of view with which you do not agree. By rethinking your thinking, you may change it. And when your thinking changes, your feelings and desires will shift in accordance with your thinking.

EMPLOYING THE KEY IDEA: THOUGHTS, FEELINGS, AND DESIRES ARE INTERDEPENDENT

With a basic understanding of the interrelation among thoughts, feelings, and desires, you should be able to routinely notice and evaluate your feelings. If, for example, you experience a degree of anger that you suspect *may* be unreasonable, you should be able to determine whether the anger is or is not rational. You should be able to evaluate the rationality of your anger by evaluating the thinking that gave rise to it. Has someone truly wronged you, or are you misreading the situation? Was this wrong intentional or unintentional? Are there ways to view the situation other than the ways you are viewing it? Are you giving a fair hearing to these other ways? By pursuing these questions, you can come closer to a reasonable view of the situation.

Even if your way of viewing the situation is justified, and you do have good reason to feel some anger, it does not follow that you have acted reasonably, given the full facts of the situation. You may have good reason to feel angry, but this will not justify your acting irrationally as a result of that anger. Following up from the activity on p. 109, actively employ this process:

1. Identify a feeling you have experienced that you suspect might be irrational (a feeling such as irritability, resentment, arrogance, or depression).

2. What thinking were you doing that would account for the feeling? There may be more than one possibility here. If so, figure out which possibility is most likely.

3. Determine the extent to which your thinking was reasonable in the situation. Pay close attention to the reasons you give to justify your thinking. Is it possible that these are not your actual reasons? Can you think of any other motives you might have? Consider alternative interpretations of the situation—don't hide from the truth, whatever you do.

4. If you conclude that the feeling was irrational, express precisely why you think so.

For example, suppose you read an article about a fatal disease and come to the conclusion, from reading the symptoms, that you probably have the disease. You then become depressed. Late at night, you think about how you will soon be dead, and you therefore feel more and more depressed as a result. Clearly, the irrational feeling is the depression you are experiencing. It is irrational because, until a doctor examines you and confirms a diagnosis, you likely have no good reason for believing that you actually have the disease in question. Your irrational thinking is something like this:

I have all the symptoms described in the article. So I must have this awful disease. I am going to die soon. My life is now meaningless. Why is this happening to me? Why me?

In the same situation, rational thinking would be something like this:

Yes, it is possible that I have this disease, given that I seem to have symptoms of it, but very often the same symptoms are compatible with many different bodily states. Given this, it is not likely that I have this rare disease, and, in any case, it will do me no good to jump to conclusions. Still, as a matter of prudence and for peace of mind, I should go to the doctor as soon as possible to get a professional diagnosis. Until I get this diagnosis, I should focus my thinking on other, more useful things.

Whenever you find yourself feeling depressed about what the article said, rerun the rational thinking through your mind and give yourself a good talking-to:

"Hey, don't go off the deep end. Remember, you will see the doctor on Monday. Don't put yourself through unnecessary pain. Remember, there are probably a lot of possibilities to account for your symptoms. Come back down to earth. Remember the Mother Goose rhyme, "For every problem under the sun, there is a solution or there is none. If there be one, seek till you find it. If there be none, never mind it." Don't wallow in misery when it doesn't do any good and only diminishes the quality of your life today. And now, how about scheduling some tennis for this afternoon, and a good movie for tonight?

INTERNALIZE THE IDEA: FOCUSING ON THE RELATIONSHIP BETWEEN THOUGHTS, FEELINGS, AND DESIRES PART I

Focusing on another negative feeling you sometimes or often experience, go through the four-point strategy outlined in the section you just read, writing out your answers in detail.

A similar approach can be taken to changing unreasonable behavior grounded in unreasonable desires or motivations:

1. Identify the questionable behavior (behavior that is getting you in trouble, causing problems for you, or causing problems for someone else).

2. Identify the precise thinking leading to that behavior. What is the thinking that is motivating you to act in this manner?

3. Analyze the extent to which the thinking is justified, without leaving out any significant relevant information.

4. If the thinking is irrational, develop thinking that would be reasonable in this situation.

5. Actively attack the unreasonable thinking with reasonable thinking.

We might use many examples to illustrate our point. But let's choose one that deals with a large segment of irrational human behavior. Here we are thinking of the many times when people abandon a commitment to change a bad habit because they are unwilling to work through the pain or discomfort that accompanies changing habits. Here's how the irrational behavior arises:

1. You notice that you have developed some bad habit that you would like to end. You realize, quite reasonably, that you shall have to make a change in your behavior. This could involve giving up any of the following habits: smoking, drinking too much alcohol, eating foods that are not good for you, not exercising enough, spending too much time on the internet, spending too much money, not studying until just before an examination, and so on.

2. You make a resolution to change your bad habit.

3. For a short time, you do change your behavior, but during that time you experience pain or discomfort. These negative emotions discourage you, so you give up.

In this situation, the feelings of pain or discomfort are to be expected. These feelings must be worked through if you are to reach higher, more rational ground. The irrational feeling, then, is not the discomfort that comes from most significant mental growth, but rather the discouragement that emerges from the discomfort and causes us to give up our resolution to change. This feeling is a result of irrational thinking (probably unconscious), which can be put into words roughly as follows.

> I should be able to change my behavior without experiencing any pain or discomfort, even if I have had this habit for years. This pain is too much. I can't stand it. Furthermore, I really don't see how my changed behavior is helping much. I just don't see much progress given all of the sacrificing I am doing. Forget it. It's not worth it.

This thinking makes no sense. Why should you expect to experience no pain or discomfort when changing a habit? Indeed, the reverse is true. Discomfort or pain of some kind is an essential by-product of going through a process of withdrawal from almost any habit. The appropriate rational thinking is something like this:

> Whenever I am trying to change a habit, I must expect to feel discomfort and even pain. Habits are hard for anyone to break. And the only way I can expect to replace the habit with rational behavior is to endure the

necessary suffering that comes with change. If I'm not willing to endure the discomfort that goes hand in hand with breaking a bad habit, I'm not really committed to change. Rather than expecting no pain, I must welcome it as a sign of real change. Instead of thinking, "Why should I have to endure this?" I rehearse this thinking: "Enduring this is the price I must pay for success." I must apply the motto, "No pain, no gain."

INTERNALIZE THE IDEA: FOCUSING ON THE RELATIONSHIP BETWEEN THOUGHTS, FEELINGS, AND DESIRES PART II

Focusing on some questionable behavior you sometimes engage in, go through the five-point strategy as outlined in the section you just read and write out your answers in detail. As soon as you have a chance, experiment with making some change in your behavior that you have wanted to make. See if you can succeed now with new thinking at your disposal. Don't forget the essential ingredient of predicting, and accepting, discomfort or pain as a likely hurdle in the process of change.

Here again is the strategy:

1. Identify the questionable behavior (behavior that is getting you in trouble, causing problems for you, or causing problems for someone else).

2. Identify the precise thinking leading to that behavior. What is the thinking that is motivating you to act in this manner?

3. Analyze the extent to which the thinking is justified, without leaving out any significant relevant information.

4. If the thinking is irrational, develop thinking that would be reasonable in this situation.

5. Actively attack the unreasonable thinking with reasonable thinking.

POPULAR MISUNDERSTANDINGS OF THE MIND

It is common to erroneously believe that:
- Emotion and reason often conflict with each other.
- Emotion and reason function independently of each other.
- It is possible to be an emotional person and hence do little reasoning.
- It is possible to be a rational person and hence experience little emotion.
- Rational persons are cold and mechanical, like Mr. Spock.
- Emotional persons are lively, energetic, and warm, but are poor reasoners.

In These Mistaken Views:
1. One must give up the possibility of a rich emotional life if one decides to become a rational person.
2. One must give up rationality if one is to live a passionate life.

These Misunderstandings:
- Lead us to think of thought and emotion as if they were oil and water rather than inseparable functions of mind.
- Lead us away from realizing the thinking underlying our emotions and the emotions that influence our thinking
- Lead us to think that there is nothing we can do to control our emotional life.

EMOTIONAL INTELLIGENCE AND CRITICAL THINKING

Emotion: A state of consciousness having to do with the arousal of feelings. Refers to any of the personal reactions, pleasant or unpleasant, that one may have in a situation.

Intelligence: The ability to learn or understand from experience or to respond successfully to new experiences; the ability to acquire and retain knowledge. Implies the use of reason in solving problems and directing conduct effectively.

Emotional Intelligence: Bringing intelligence to bear upon emotions. Guiding emotions through high quality reason. Implies that high quality reasoning in a situation will lead to more satisfactory emotional states than low quality reasoning.

Critical Thinking provides the link between:

Intelligence ⟵⟶ Emotion

Critical Thinking:

- brings your intelligence to bear upon your emotional life
- enables you to take command of your emotions
- enables you to make good judgments
- provides you with a satisfactory emotional life

Essential Idea: When your thinking is of high quality, rational emotions follow. When you develop rational emotions, you think reasonably.

CHAPTER FOUR
DEVELOP YOUR RATIONAL CAPACITIES; DIMINISH YOUR IRRATIONAL TENDENCIES

The three functions of the mind—thoughts, feelings, and desires—discussed in the last chapter, can be guided or directed either by one's irrational propensities or rational capacities (potentially changing from moment to moment given changing situations or circumstances).

In human thought, irrational tendencies function automatically and largely unconsciously. Rational tendencies tend to arise from active self-development and are largely conscious. Irrationality can be principally categorized according to whether and to what degree it is egocentric and/or sociocentric in nature. Therefore, root causes of problems in human thought can be understood in terms of these two sets of tendencies, both of which are "natural" and "comfortable" to the human mind:

    1) egocentrism, or narrowminded, selfish thought, and
    2) sociocentrism, or narrowminded, "groupish" thought.

Egocentric thought is the native propensity to see things from one's own narrow, self-serving, self-validating perspective. It leads people to uncritically accept that which makes them feel good and serves their selfish desires. To understand egocentric thinking is to begin with the assumption that the human mind is frequently and quite naturally trapped in pathological ways of looking at the world. Instead of being openminded, we humans (naturally) tend to be narrowminded. Instead of seeing situations fairmindedly, we (naturally) tend to see them from our own selfish perspectives. Instead of recognizing that complex issues require complex reasoning, we (naturally) oversimplify them.

Human egocentricity, then, can be organized in terms of two primary tendencies. One is to see the world in self-serving terms, i.e., to seek what makes "me" feel good—what I selfishly want—without regard to the rights and needs of others. The second is the desire to maintain "my" beliefs. This latter tendency entails rigidity of thought. When I am rationalizing my irrational beliefs, I see them as obviously reasonable.

The first tendency, selfishness, is intuitive to most people. It makes sense that I would intrinsically want to get what I think is "best" for me, what serves me, what I like and want. The second tendency may seem less intuitive. Why would the mind be intrinsically rigid? Look at it this way: All the beliefs you have taken in or generated through the years of your life seem to make perfect sense to you—yes? Otherwise, you would have changed them. And no doubt you have changed many of your beliefs. But the beliefs you now hold seem correct to you. This would be true for any given period of your life. Egocentrically, you want to "protect" beliefs you now hold. People frequently would far rather hold onto their beliefs (however irrational) than deal with the discomfort that accompanies changing them. We are all creatures of mental habit, at least to some degree.

In short, to the extent that we protect our beliefs out of sheer habit, and to the extent that we are closed to new ways of looking at things, we are rigid egocentric thinkers. One caveat to this is that when people are being egocentric, they may be skilled at flexible thought in certain narrow ways to serve their selfish interests. (Highly successful business people and politicians are often paradigm cases of this point.) In other ways they would be narrowminded, or intellectually arrogant.

Sociocentric thinking may be conceptualized as an extension of egocentric thinking—or as a pathological orientation that interlocks directly with egocentricity. This is evidenced in the fact that sociocentric thought seems to operate in parallel with at least two primary tendencies of egocentric thought:

1. Seeking to get what the group wants without regard to the rights and needs of others.
2. Maintaining a rigid belief system that serves (or is perceived as serving) the group's interests.

Sociocentric thought is the native human tendency to see the world from narrow, biased, group-centered perspectives—to operate within the world through subjective and partial group beliefs, group influences, group rules, and group interests. It seems intimately connected with the human "need" for validation, which is the innate need to be accepted and esteemed by others.

Starting at a very young age, humans begin fitting themselves into groups. They do so not by their own choice, but out of instinct, and primarily to survive. For the most part, young children lack the skills to properly critique the beliefs thrust upon them by these various groups—to determine group practices that make sense to accept, to identify those that need modification, and to abandon those that should be rejected. Thus, from a very young age, humans tend to uncritically accept the beliefs of family, school, religion, peers—indeed, any group in which they become members. Then they frequently spend their lives defending and building on views they have uncritically accepted as children. As we age, we don't naturally become less sociocentric, just perhaps more sophisticated in our groupthink tendencies.

Of course, many beliefs given to us through group membership make perfect sense to accept (such as treating others the way you would want to be treated); many of them help us survive (such as proper ways to drive a car). But many are based in dangerous ideologies (such as harsh drug laws or laws against homosexuality). And we don't inherently distinguish the one from the other.

There are many situations in which people need to work together as a cohesive unit. For this to happen, some level of agreement is necessary. That people function in groups is not the problem; this is only natural. But how they function in groups often is a problem—whether and to what extent blind obedience is required or expected, whether and to what extent reasoned dissent is allowed and encouraged, etc. These realities determine, to a large degree, the extent to which any group can be said to be reasonable or rational.

Thus, it is important to distinguish dysfunctional group-centered thought and behavior from that which is either productive and useful, or neutral. Healthy groups can and do exist, though every group can potentially fall prey to groupthink, prejudice, bias, distortion in thought, and so on.

EGOCENTRICITY

Egocentricity exists in two forms: skilled and unskilled. Both pursue selfish, or at least what appear to be, self-serving ends. Highly skilled egocentric persons use their intelligence to effectively rationalize gaining their selfish ends at the expense of others. They skillfully distort information to serve their interests. They are often articulate in arguing for their selfish ends (which they typically cover with language that implies they are well-meaning). They hide their prejudices well. Naïve others often fail to see their selfish core (masked, as it is, in a seemingly considerate façade). They often succeed in moving up the social ladder and gaining prestigious jobs and honored positions. Skilled egocentric persons may favor either domination or submission to get what they want, but often combine both in effective ways. For example, they may successfully dominate persons "below" them while they are subtly servile to those "above" them. They know how to tell people what they want to hear. They are consummate manipulators and often hold positions of power.

Unskilled egocentric persons are unsuccessful in pursuing their selfish ends because many see through them and do not trust them. Their prejudices and narrowness are more obvious and less sophisticated. They often have blatantly dysfunctional relationships with others. They are often trapped in negative emotions they do not understand. Unskilled egocentric persons may prefer either domination or submission as a means of getting what they want, but whichever they use, they are usually unsuccessful at either. Sometimes they are overtly cruel or play the victim in openly self-pitying ways.

SOCIOCENTRICITY

As humans, we are all born centered in ourselves. As part of our native egocentricity, we feel directly and unavoidably our own pain and frustration, our own joy and pleasure. We largely see the world from a narrow, self-serving perspective. But, as mentioned, we humans are also social animals. We must interact with others to survive as beings in the world. In interacting with others in groups we form complex belief systems. These belief systems often reflect various forms of intellectual blindness as well as intellectual insights. In living a human life, we develop world views that are a mixture of self-serving, group-serving, and rational thought.

Our social groups not only provide us with ways and means of surviving, they also impose on us relatively narrow ways of looking at the world. And they powerfully influence our thoughts and actions. Our intrinsic narrowness of perspective, focused on our own needs and wants, merges with our group views as we are increasingly socialized and conditioned, over time, to see the world, not only from our own point of view but from the perspective of our groups: family, gender, peers, colleagues, ethnic group, nationality, religion, profession, and so forth.

Sociocentric thought, then, is the native human tendency to see the world from narrow and biased group-centered perspectives, to operate within the world through group rules and group interests. It is intimately connected with the human "need" for validation—the innate need to be accepted and esteemed by others. It leads to conformity in ways that may have powerful negative consequences for your mental health.

RATIONALITY

Rationality is properly thought of as a way of thinking and acting in which intelligence and sound reasoning are used to advance and cultivate oneself, in which thinkers adhere to the same standards by which they judge others and do not need to rationalize or project a fake front to impress others. Successful, powerful people are often intelligent, unreasonable, and unethical—all in one. They often cannot openly admit the games they play to obtain social and economic success. They often suppress evidence that puts them in a bad light. Reasonable people, on the other hand, respect the rights and needs of others, are flexible, open-minded, and just. They embody intellectual integrity as well as intellectual humility and intellectual perseverance. They have confidence in reason and therefore follow the facts wherever they lead. They are able to enter empathically into others' viewpoints. They do not misuse language to gain advantage. They say what they mean and mean what they say. They are continually on the lookout for problems in their reasoning—to correct mistakes in their thinking and improve how they are perceiving situations and experiences. They believe in their abilities to successfully function in the world and they actively refuse to let past experiences get in the way of their present and future successes. They continually work to create a powerful voice of reason within themselves, which seeking to contribute to a better world while taking care of and developing themselves to the fullest.

In this book, the terms *rational* and *reasonable* are often used synonymously. The term *rationality* may go beyond how people typically think of reasonability in that when we refer to thinking as being fully rational, we mean not only that the reasoning is logical and justifiable in context, or in other words, reasonable, but that it meets additional criteria. These criteria include embodiment of intellectual virtues (as mentioned above), and the active pursuit of self-development while showing compassion for others. In this book, when you read the term *rational*, think of it in this richer sense.

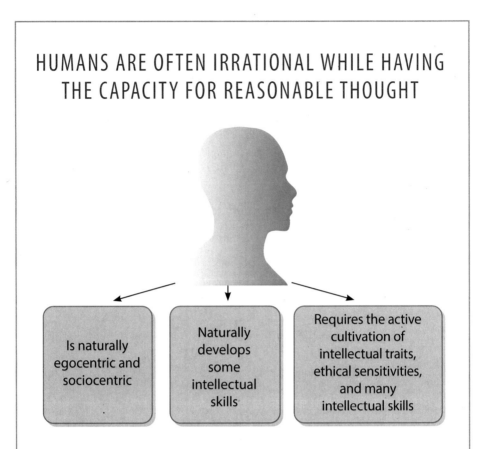

HUMANS ARE OFTEN IRRATIONAL WHILE HAVING THE CAPACITY FOR REASONABLE THOUGHT

Is naturally egocentric and sociocentric

Naturally develops some intellectual skills

Requires the active cultivation of intellectual traits, ethical sensitivities, and many intellectual skills

Essential Idea: All humans are innately egocentric and sociocentric. Humans also have (largely undeveloped) rational capacities. Humans begin life as primarily egocentric creatures. Over time, infantile egocentric self-centered thinking merges with sociocentric group-centered thinking. All humans regularly engage in both forms of irrational thought. The extent to which any of us is egocentric or sociocentric is a matter of degree and can change significantly in various situations or contexts. While egocentric and sociocentric propensities are naturally occurring phenomena, rational capacities must be largely developed. It is through the development of rational capacities that we combat irrational tendencies and cultivate emotional well-being.

DISTINGUISHING RATIONAL FROM EGOCENTRIC AND SOCIOCENTRIC MOTIVES

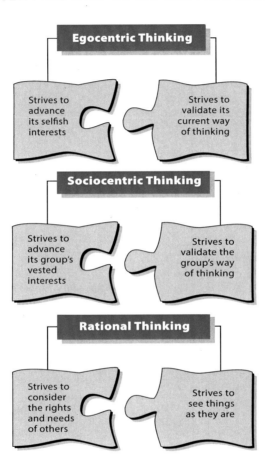

Egocentric Thinking

Strives to advance its selfish interests

Strives to validate its current way of thinking

Sociocentric Thinking

Strives to advance its group's vested interests

Strives to validate the group's way of thinking

Rational Thinking

Strives to consider the rights and needs of others

Strives to see things as they are

Essential Idea: Though egocentric, sociocentric, and rational thought may be complex, we can capture their basic motives.

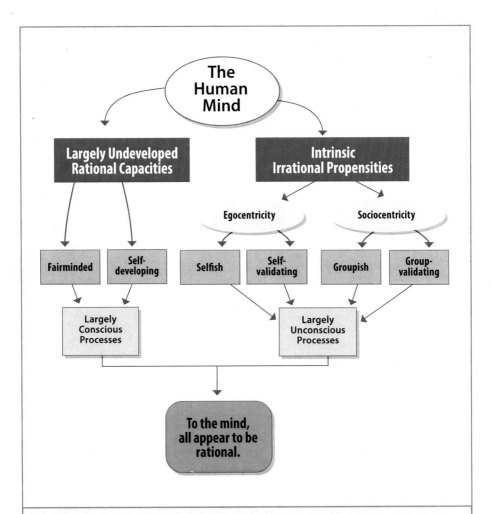

Essential Idea: There is always an unconscious dimension to irrational thinking. Through self-deception, we delude ourselves into believing that our views are correct even when glaring evidence would prove us wrong. If rational thinking appears in your mind to be rational, and irrational thinking appears in your mind to be rational, how difficult do you think it will be to find the problems in your thinking that lie at the unconscious level and cause you to behave in unreasonable ways?

HUMANS OFTEN DISTORT REALITY THROUGH IRRATIONAL LENSES—WHAT ARE YOUR SPECIFIC DISTORTING LENSES?

When pursuing irrational goals, the mind must deceive itself; it relies on pathologies of thought to do it. The pathologies of thought can be pictured as a set of filters or lenses that:

- cause or "enable" you to see the world according to your perceived interests, without regard to others,
- distort reality so you can get what you want,
- lead you to ignore relevant information to paint a favored picture of the world, or to pursue your selfish or vested interests.

These pathologies allow you to deceive yourself into believing what you want to believe (in order to get what you want or maintain your viewpoint). Pathologies of thought, hence, serve their master—self-deception. They are manifest in both egocentric and sociocentric thought. Everyone, no matter how well developed as a thinker, frequently falls prey to these pathologies.

BECOME KEENLY AWARE OF FEELINGS THAT ACCOMPANY EGOCENTRISM

These are some of the many feelings that might accompany egocentric thinking. They often occur when egocentric thinking is "unsuccessful." Note that some of these emotions may come from rational thought—depending on the context and particulars in a given case.

Essential Idea: When egocentric thinking is successful in getting what it wants, positive feelings accompany it. But when egocentric thinking is not able to achieve its purposes, negative feelings result.

INTERNALIZE THE IDEA: IDENTIFY YOUR NEGATIVE IRRATIONAL EMOTIONS

Think of some negative irrational emotion you have or do experience as seen in the diagram on the previous page. Complete these statements:

1. The negative emotion I frequently experience is...

2. I feel this negative emotion in the following situation or types of situations...

3. This emotion is coming from the following thinking that I am doing in the situation...

4. To change this emotion, I need to change my thinking in the following way(s)...

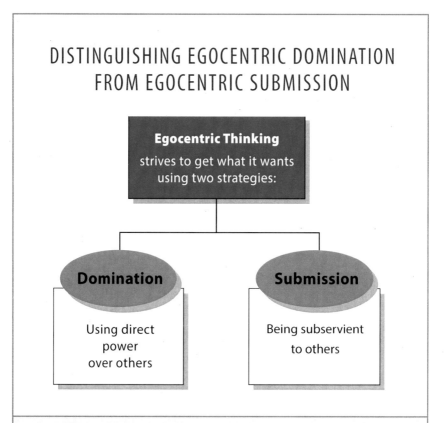

DISTINGUISHING EGOCENTRIC DOMINATION FROM EGOCENTRIC SUBMISSION

Egocentric Thinking strives to get what it wants using two strategies:

Domination
Using direct power over others

Submission
Being subservient to others

Essential Idea: These two distinct forms of egocentric thinking are commonly used when the egocentric mind is trying to get what it wants:

1) The art of dominating others (a direct means to getting what you want by using unconcealed power and control).

2) The art of submitting to others (an indirect means to getting what you want by being irrationally subservient).

Insofar as you are thinking egocentrically, you seek to satisfy your desires either directly or indirectly, by exercising power and control over others, or by submitting to those who can act to serve your interests. To put it crudely, egocentric behavior either bullies or grovels. It either threatens those weaker or subordinates itself to those more powerful, or oscillates between these approaches in subtle maneuvers and schemes. Manipulation may be involved in both forms of irrational behavior.

WE OFTEN PURSUE POWER THROUGH DOMINATING OR SUBMISSIVE BEHAVIOR

When thinking irrationally or egocentrically, the human mind often seeks to achieve its goals by either or submissive behavior. Put another way, when under the sway of egocentrism, we try to get our way either by dominating others or by gaining their support through outward submission to them. Bullying (dominating) and groveling (submitting) are often subtle in nature, but they are nonetheless common in human life.

Power is not bad in itself. We all need some power to rationally fulfill our needs. But in human life it is common for power to be sought as an end in itself or used for unethical purposes. One of the most common ways for egocentric people and sociocentric groups to gain power is by dominating weaker persons or groups. Another way is by playing a subservient role toward a more powerful other to get what they want. Much of human history could be told in terms of the use of dominating and submissive behavior. Much individual and group behavior can be understood by assessing the presence of these two patterns.

Though everyone tends to use one of these behavioral patterns more than the others, everyone uses both to some extent. Some children, for example, play a role of subservience toward their parents while abusively bullying other children. Of course, when a bigger and tougher bully comes along, the weaker bully often becomes subservient to the stronger one.

When we are egocentrically dominating or submissive, we do not readily recognize we are doing so. For example, people presumably attend rock concerts to enjoy the music. But members of the audience often act in a highly subservient (adoring, idolizing) way toward the musicians. Many people literally throw themselves at the feet of celebrities or take their own definition of significance from distantly attaching themselves to a celebrity, if only in their imaginations. In like manner, sports fans often idolize and idealize their heroes, who appear bigger than life to them. If their team or their hero is successful, they vicariously feel successful and more powerful. "We really whipped them!" translates as, "I am important and successful just as my hero is."

Rational people may admire other people, but do not idolize or idealize them. Rational people may form alliances, but not ones in which they are dominated by others. They expect no one to submit to them blindly. They blindly submit to no one. Although none of us fully embodies this rational ideal, critical thinkers continually work toward it in all their relationships.

Using another example, in the past traditional male and female sex-role conditioning entailed the man dominating the woman and the woman playing a submissive role toward her man. Women were to gain power by attaching themselves to powerful men. Men displayed power in achieving domination over women. These traditional roles are far from dead in present romantic relationships.

If you realize the prominent role that egocentric domination and submission play in human life, you can begin to observe your own behavior to determine when you are irrationally dominating or submitting. When you understand that the mind naturally uses numerous methods for hiding its egocentrism, you recognize that you must scrutinize your own mental functioning carefully to locate dominating and submissive patterns. With practice, you can begin to identify your own patterns of domination and submission. At the same time, you can observe others' behavior, looking for similar patterns. You can look closely at the behavior of your supervisors, friends, spouse or partner, children, parents, and indeed anyone, noticing when they tend to irrationally dominate and/or submit to the will of others.

In short, the more you study patterns of domination and submission in human life, the more you can detect them in your own life and behavior. And when you become adept at detecting them you can take steps toward changing them.

INTERNALIZE THE IDEA: WHEN ARE YOU DOMINATING OR SUBMISSIVE? HOW CAN YOU CHANGE THIS IRRATIONAL BEHAVIOR?

Reread the diagram on page 130 and complete these statements:

1. I tend to be egocentrically (or irrationally) dominating in the following types of situations...

2. The problem with my thinking in these situations is...

3. To become less dominating I need to...

4. Therefore I plan to make the following changes in my thinking and in my behavior...

1. I tend to be egocentrically (or irrationally) submissive in the following types of situations...

2. The problem with my thinking in these situations is...

3. To become less submissive I need to...

4. Therefore I plan to make the following changes in my thinking and in my behavior...

EGOCENTRIC PATHOLOGIES COMMON IN HUMAN LIFE

An array of interrelated pathological dispositions are inherent in native egocentric thought. To significantly develop as a rational person, you must identify these tendencies in your life, determining which of them cause you the most problems. As you read through these pathologies, make note of one or more examples from your own thinking in each category.

- **egocentric memory:** the natural tendency to "forget" evidence and information that do not support your thinking and to "remember" evidence and information that do
- **egocentric myopia:** the natural tendency to think in an absolutist way within an overly narrow point of view
- **egocentric righteousness:** the natural tendency to see yourself in possession of "The Truth"
- **egocentric hypocrisy:** the natural tendency to ignore flagrant inconsistencies—between what you profess to believe and the actual beliefs your behavior implies, or between the standards you apply to yourself and those you apply to others
- **egocentric oversimplification:** the natural tendency to ignore real and important complexities in the world in favor of simplistic notions when considering those complexities would require you to modify your beliefs or values
- **egocentric blindness:** the natural tendency not to notice facts and evidence that contradict your favored beliefs or values
- **egocentric immediacy:** the natural tendency to over-generalize immediate feelings and experiences, so that when one, or only a few, events in your life seem highly favorable or unfavorable, all of life seems positive or negative to you
- **egocentric absurdity:** the natural tendency to fail to notice when your thinking has "absurd" implications

CHALLENGING YOUR EGOCENTRIC DISPOSITIONS

It is not enough to recognize abstractly that your mind has predictable pathologies. You must take concrete steps to correct them. This requires you to develop the habit of identifying these tendencies in action, which occurs only over time and with deliberate practice.

Correcting egocentric memory. You can correct your natural tendency to "forget" evidence and information that do not support your thinking and to "remember" evidence and information that do, by overtly seeking evidence and information that do not support your thinking and directing explicit attention to them. What information about yourself would you rather not know, or are hiding from yourself?

Correcting egocentric myopia. You can correct your natural tendency to think in an overly narrow point of view by routinely thinking within points of view that conflict with your own. Are you reading (in good faith) works of significant writers who offer studied and important views in opposition to yours? Are you able and willing to place yourself in the thinking and feelings of others and imagine how their perceptions may differ from yours?

Correcting egocentric righteousness. You can correct your natural tendency to feel superior in light of your confidence that you possess the truth by regularly reminding yourself how little you actually know. For example, you can explicitly state the unanswered questions that surround whatever knowledge you may have in a given area. Do you frequently act and feel as if you more or less know the answer to everything? Do you often make assertions when you lack the facts to support your views? Do you routinely overgeneralize?

Correcting egocentric hypocrisy. You can correct your natural tendency to ignore flagrant inconsistencies between what you profess to believe and the actual beliefs your behavior implies, and to ignore inconsistencies between the standards to which you hold yourself and those to which you hold others. You can do this by regularly comparing the criteria and standards by which you are judging others with those by which you judge yourself. Do you often say one thing and do its opposite? Do you tell your children to act in one way while you act in a contrary manner? Do you expect more from others than you do from yourself?

Correcting egocentric oversimplification. You can correct your natural tendency to ignore real and important complexities in the world by regularly focusing on those complexities, formulating them explicitly in words, and targeting them. Do you often oversimplify problems and issues? If so, where does this lead you? Do you find yourself frustrated because you try to deal with complex issues in superficial ways?

Correcting egocentric blindness. You can correct your natural tendency to ignore facts or evidence that contradict your favored beliefs or values by explicitly seeking out those facts and evidence. Egocentric blindness is similar to egocentric memory as in both cases you are ignoring evidence you would rather not have to consider. In what parts of your life are you unwilling to look at the evidence beyond what serves your current viewpoint, or the way you prefer to see things, or your narrow vision?

Correcting egocentric immediacy. You can correct your natural tendency to over-generalize immediate feelings and experiences by getting into the habit of putting positive and negative events into a larger perspective. You can temper the negative events by reminding yourself of how much you have that many others lack. You can temper the positive events by reminding yourself of how much is yet to be done, of how many problems remain. You know you are keeping an even keel if you find that you have the energy to act effectively in either negative or positive circumstances. You know that you are falling victim to your egocentricity if and when you are immobilized by it. Do you tend to blow things out of proportion in terms of your overall view of things—to see things in terms of either "life is great," or "life is horrible"? How will you maintain a more realistic, objective view of things as they happen day to day, living in the moment rather than exaggerating situations?

Correcting egocentric absurdity. You can correct your natural tendency to ignore thinking that has absurd consequences by making the consequences of your thinking explicit and assessing them for their realism. This requires that you frequently trace the implications of your beliefs and their consequences in your behavior. For example, you should frequently ask yourself: "If I really believed this, how would I act? Do I really act that way?" We frequently act in ways that are "absurd"—given what we insist we believe in.

INTERNALIZE THE IDEA: CHALLENGING YOUR EGOCENTRIC DISPOSITIONS

Read through the pathological dispositions and ways to correct them on the previous pages. Complete these statements:

1. After reading these dispositions, I see that the following are especially a problem for me...
2. I intend to correct these pathologies in the following ways...

DEFENSE MECHANISMS OF THE MIND

As has been discussed, the human mind routinely engages in unconscious processes that are egocentrically motivated, and that strongly influence our behavior. When functioning egocentrically, we seek to get what we want. We see the world from a narrow self-serving perspective. Yet we also see ourselves as driven by purely rational motives. We therefore disguise our egocentric motives as motives that appear rational. This disguise necessitates self-deception.

Self-deception is manifest in many ways, including through defense mechanisms. The concept of defense mechanisms was first originated by Sigmund Freud and then developed by Anna Freud. Defense mechanisms overlap and interrelate with the intellectual pathologies described on the previous pages. Here are some common defense mechanisms:

Denial: When a person refuses to believe undisputable evidence or facts in order to maintain a favorable self-image or favored set of beliefs. A basketball player, for example, may deny that there are any real flaws in his game in order to maintain an image of himself as highly skilled at basketball. A "patriot" may deny—in the face of clear-cut evidence—that his country ever violates human rights or acts unjustly. You may deny that there are any problems in your thinking, and that it is always "the other person's fault" when things go wrong.

Identification: When a person takes to herself those qualities and ideals she admires in other people and institutions. Through sociocentric identification she elevates her sense of worth. Examples: a football fan experiencing an inner sense of triumph when her team wins, a parent experiencing a triumph in the success of her children, a citizen feeling elevated by the triumph of her nation's armed forces.

Projection: When a person attributes to another person what he or she feels or thinks in order to avoid unacceptable thoughts and feelings. A wife who doesn't love her husband may accuse him of not loving her (when he really does) in order to unconsciously deal with her own dishonesty in the relationship.

Repression: When thoughts, feelings or memories unacceptable to the individual are prevented from reaching consciousness. The person repressing these thoughts is unable to face something about himself, his past, or about anything he does not want to deal with. This often occurs when memories are considered too painful to remember. It can also be a form of "forgetting" because the person doesn't want to remember something unpleasant (such as a dental appointment). Repression is not the same as acknowledging painful memories and then actively refusing to let those memories cause pain today.

Rationalization: When a person gives reasons (sometimes good reasons) for his behavior, but not the true reasons, because his actions result from unconscious motives he cannot consciously accept. The father who beats his children may rationalize his behavior by saying he is doing it for his children's "own good," so they will become more disciplined, when the true reason is that he has lost control of his behavior.

Stereotyping: When a person lumps people together based on some common characteristic, forming a rigid, biased perception of the group and its members. One form of stereotyping comes from cultural bias wherein the person assumes that practices and beliefs in his culture are superior to those in other cultures simply by virtue of being part of his culture. People frequently take their group to be the measure of all groups and people.

Scapegoating: When a person attempts to avoid criticism of herself by blaming another person, group or thing for her own mistakes or faults.

Sublimation:[5] When a person diverts instinctive, primitive or socially unacceptable desires into socially acceptable activities (or activities that appear so). The sexually unfulfilled drill sergeant may sublimate his sexual energy through aggressive and dominating behavior toward new recruits.

Wishful Thinking: When a person unconsciously misinterprets facts in order to maintain a belief. Wishful thinking leads to false expectations and usually involves seeing things more positively than is reasonable in the situation.

INTERNALIZE THE IDEA: IDENTIFY YOUR PRIMARY DEFENSE MECHANISMS

Read through the list of defense mechanisms above and complete these statements:

1. I tend to use the following defense mechanisms to avoid seeing something I do not want to see or facing something I do not want to face…
2. Problems in my thinking when I use these mechanisms include…
3. In order to stop using these defense mechanisms, I intend to do the following…

BECOME SENSITIVE TO THE EGOCENTRISM OF THOSE AROUND YOU

Because human beings are by nature egocentric, and few are aware of how to exercise control over their egocentric thinking, it is important that you develop the ability to recognize egocentrism in the thinking of those around you. You must recognize, though, that even highly egocentric people sometimes act rationally, so be careful not to stereotype. Nevertheless, it is reasonable to expect that everyone will behave irrationally sometimes, so you must learn to evaluate behavior in an openminded, yet realistic, way. When you understand the logic of egocentrism, when you become adept at identifying its self-serving patterns, you can begin to master it.

---

5 Unlike the other defense mechanisms mentioned here, sublimation can be handled appropriately or inappropriately. An example of appropriate sublimation might be, lacking an intimate relationship a person gives and receives love by helping animals, other people and/or the earth.

It is important that you draw a distinction between attacking your own irrationality and attacking that of others. Often with others you must bite your tongue, as it were, and distance yourself from people who are fundamentally irrational. Or, at least, you must learn to deal with their egocentrism indirectly. Few people will thank you for pointing out egocentrism in their thinking. The more egocentric people are, the more resistant they are to owning it. The more power egocentric people have, the more dangerous they are. As a developing rational person, then, you are hopefully learning to better deal with the irrationality of others rather than be controlled or manipulated by it.

When thinking irrationally, people find it difficult to think within the perspectives of others. They unconsciously refuse to consider information that contradicts their ego-centered views. People frequently and unconsciously pursue purposes and goals that are not justifiable. They use assumptions in their thinking that are based in their own prejudices and biases. Unknowingly, people frequently engage in self-deception to avoid recognizing their egocentrism in operation.

Another problem relevant to dealing with the egocentric reactions of others will be your own egocentric tendencies. When you interact with others who are relating to you egocentrically, your own irrational nature may be easily stimulated into action, or, to put it more bluntly, "your buttons may be easily pushed." When others relate to you in an ego-centered way, violating your rights or ignoring your legitimate needs, your own native egocentrism will likely assert itself. Ego will meet ego in a struggle for power. When this happens, everyone loses. It is essential therefore to anticipate your own egocentric reactions in advance of any confrontation and come up with appropriate reasonable thinking to deal with it.

Once you are aware that humans are naturally egocentric, and that most people are unaware of their native egocentrism, you can conclude that, in any given situation, you may well be interacting with the egocentric rather than the rational dimensions of those persons' minds. You therefore can question whether they are presenting rational ideas and pursuing rational purposes, or whether they are operating with irrational motives of which they are unaware. You should not take for granted that others are relating to you in good faith. Rather, observe their behavior carefully to determine what their behavior actually implies.

Moreover, because you know that your irrational nature may be easily activated by irrationality in others, you can carefully observe and assess your own thinking to ensure that you do not become irrational in dealing with others who are egocentric. Be on the lookout for your own ego-centered thinking, and when you recognize it, take steps to "wrestle it down" and refuse to be drawn into irrational games—whether initiated by others or by your own egocentric tendencies. When you realize you are dealing with an irrational person, do not let that person's irrationality summon your irrational nature. Refuse to be controlled by the unreasonable behavior of others.

Strategically, the best thing to do is to avoid contact with highly egocentric people whenever possible. When you find yourself deeply involved with that sort of person, seek a way to disengage yourself when possible. When disengagement is not possible, minimize contact or act in such a way as to minimize stimulating their ego.

You can minimize stimulating a person's ego by recognizing the conditions under which most highly egocentric reactions take place—namely, when people feel threatened, humiliated, or shamed, or when their vested interest or self-image is significantly involved. By getting into the habit of reconstructing in your own mind the point of view of others, and therefore of frequently thinking within the perspective of others, it is possible to anticipate many of the egocentric reactions of those around you. You then can choose a course of action that sidesteps many of the land mines of human egocentrism.

INTERNALIZE THE IDEA: DEALING WITH THE EGOCENTRISM OF OTHERS

Think of a recent situation in which you believed someone you were interacting with became irrational in his or her response to you. Complete these statements:

1. The situation was. . .

2. What I did/said was. . .

3. The reaction of this person was. . .

4. I believe this person's thinking was. . .

5. I think this reaction/thinking was egocentric because. . .

6. The best response I could have made to this egocentric behavior would have been. . .

7. I might have been able to avoid stimulating an egocentric response in the first place by. . .

INTERNALIZE THE IDEA: RECOGNIZING WHEN ANOTHER PERSON'S EGOCENTRISM BRINGS OUT YOUR OWN EGOCENTRISM

Think of a recent situation in which you felt yourself becoming irrational in reaction to someone else's irrationality. Complete these statements:

1. The situation was...
2. I reacted in the situation by...
3. In thinking through the situation, I realize that a more rational way to respond to the other person would have been...
4. Therefore, in future similar situations I intend to...

THE MIND TENDS TO GENERALIZE BEYOND THE ORIGINAL EXPERIENCE

One of the important truths that Jean Piaget, the noted child psychologist, discovered about children is that they tend to overgeneralize their immediate feelings. If something good happens to them, the whole world looks good to them. If something bad happens to them, the whole world looks bad to them. He called this phenomenon egocentric immediacy. What Piaget did not emphasize, however, is that the same reaction patterns are found in much adult thinking. It is fair to say that everyone has some difficulty putting the ups and downs of daily life into a long-range perspective. It is not easy to keep things in proper perspective, given the strength of our immediate (emotional) reactions.

Once you begin to interpret situations or events in your life as negative, you may also tend to generalize that negativity and even allow it to cast a gloom over your whole life. A broad-based pessimism or a foolish optimism can come to permeate your thinking when negative or positive events happen to you. You may move rapidly from thinking of one or two events in your life as negative (or positive) to thinking of everything in your life as negative (or positive). Egocentric negative thinking easily leads to indulgent self-pity. And egocentric positive thinking easily leads to an unrealistic state of complacent comfort.

Consider an everyday problem for many people who tend to see the world in largely negative terms. They wake up in the morning and must deal with a few unexpected minor problems. As the day progresses, and as they deal with more "problems," everything in their lives appears negative. The snowball of bad things happening gets bigger and bigger as the day passes. By the end of the day, they are unable to see any positive things in their lives. Their thinking (usually tacit of course) is something like this:

> Everything looks bad. Life isn't fair. Nothing good ever happens to me. I always have to deal with problems. Why does everything bad happen to me?

Controlled by these thoughts, they lack the ability to counteract unbridled negativity with rational thoughts. They can't see the many good things in their lives. Their egocentric mind is shielding them from the full range of facts that would change their way of thinking so they could see things in a more realistic and, in this case, a more positive light.

If you intervene with rational thoughts when egocentric negativity begins, before it completely pervades your mind's functioning, you have a better chance of reducing or overthrowing it. The first step requires that you become intimately familiar with the phenomenon of egocentric immediacy. Then, begin to identify instances of it in your own life as well as the lives of those around you.

The second step requires that you develop a rich and comprehensive list of the facts of your life. It is important that you develop this list not when you are in the throes of an egocentric "fit," but, instead, when you are viewing the world from a reasonable perspective.

You also want to develop a long-range perspective to call upon when necessary to give the proper weight to individual events, whether positive or negative. Work toward establishing in your mind the values most important to you. Frame a long-range historical perspective about the quality of your life overall. Bring those values and this perspective strongly before your mind when lesser values and the distortions of egocentric immediacy begin to dominate your thoughts and feelings. When you have a well-established "big picture" in your mind, you will be more likely to keep things in proper perspective. Small events will remain small, not blown out of proportion.

When you perceive that your thinking is tending toward egocentric immediacy, you can actively undermine it through comprehensive rational thinking. This involves reasoning with yourself, pointing out flaws in your thinking, identifying and presenting relevant information you may be ignoring, pointing out information you may be distorting, checking your assumptions, and tracking the important implications of your thinking. By developing a deep and comprehensive big picture in your mind and keeping this perspective at the center of your thinking, you can minimize your tendencies toward egocentric immediacy. You can become skilled in recognizing what truly is small and large in your life.

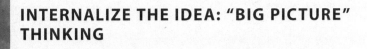

INTERNALIZE THE IDEA: "BIG PICTURE" THINKING

Think of a situation you were recently in where you felt an intense negative emotion that generated a chain reaction of further negative states in your mind, leading to a generalized feeling of negativity. At that moment, your life looked bleak and unforgiving. Figure out the "big picture" thinking that was missing from your mind as you fell prey to egocentric immediacy. Complete these statements:

1. The objective situation was as follows...
2. I irrationally responded to the situation by blowing out of proportion the following...
3. I felt these negative emotions...
4. The "big picture" thinking that I needed but was not able to bring to mind at the time is something like the following...
5. The information I was failing to consider in my thinking was...
6. I can best avoid this type of situation in the future by...
7. I now realize...

EGOCENTRIC THINKING APPEARS TO THE MIND AS RATIONAL

A primary reason why human beings have difficulty recognizing egocentric thinking is that it appears to the mind as perfectly reasonable. No person says to himself or herself, "I shall now think irrationally for a while." When we are most under the sway of irrational states (for example, in a state of irrational rage), we typically feel quite indignant and unfairly put-upon. Egocentric thinking blinds us in a variety of ways. We deceive ourselves.

When we are irrational, we feel rational. Our perceptions seem perfectly justified. And, not recognizing any flaws in our thinking, we see no reason to question those thoughts. We see no reason to behave differently. The result is that there is little or no chance of overriding the dysfunctional behavior that is dominating us. This is especially true when our egocentric thinking is working to get us what we want.

Strategic Idea

Once you recognize that egocentric thinking appears in the human mind as rational thinking and can exemplify this truth with specific examples from your own life, you are potentially in a position to do something about it. You can learn to anticipate egocentric self-deception. For one thing, you can educate yourself on the signs of it. You look for signs of shutting down—not really listening to those who disagree with you, stereotyping those who disagree with you, ignoring relevant evidence, reacting in an emotional manner, and rationalizing your irrational behavior (thinking of justifications for your behavior that have little to do with your actual motivations).

Consider the following examples:

Situation 1. You are driving to work. You fail to notice that the off-ramp of your exit is near. You recognize it at the last moment. You cut off someone to get to the off-ramp. He blows his horn at you and shouts. You shout back. You then are cut off by yet another car in a few minutes, and you blow your horn and shout at him.

During these events you feel an inner sense of "rightness." After all, you had to get to work on time. You didn't mean to cut anyone off, but the other guy clearly had no right to cut you off. We often use this kind of simplistic thinking when we deceive ourselves. We ignore evidence against our view. We highlight evidence for our view.

We experience negative emotions accordingly. And we easily feel an acute sense of righteousness about how we think, feel, and act.

Situation 2. You come home after a bad day at work. Your teenage son is playing music loudly and singing in the kitchen. You say, "Could we please have some peace and quiet around here for once?" Your son says, "What's bugging you?" You stomp out of the room, go to your room and slam the door. You stay there for an hour, feeling depressed and angry. You come out and your children and spouse are chatting in the kitchen. They ignore you. You say, "Well, I can see that no one needs me around here!" You walk out, slamming the door.

Sometimes in cases like this you may recover from your egocentric immediacy after you cool off. But during the actual events that set you off, you feel righteous in your anger and justified in your negativity. You have no trouble thinking of reasons to feed your righteousness or intensify your anger. You can dig up grievances from the past. You can go over them in your mind, blowing them up as   much as you care to. You may do this with no sense of your own self-deception.

In principle you are capable of learning to catch yourself in the process of engaging in deception or distortion. You can develop the habit of doing the following:

1. Looking at all events from the point of view of those you disagree with, as well as from your own. If you are in a conversation, you can check yourself by repeating to the person your understanding of what he or she is saying, and why.

2. Becoming suspicious of your accounts of things whenever you seem completely correct to yourself while those you disagree with seem completely wrong.

3. Suspending judgment of people and events when you are in the throes of intensive emotions. Reserving judgment for moments when you can quietly question yourself and review facts with relative objectivity.

INTERNALIZE THE IDEA: RECOGNIZING AND REPLACING IRRATIONAL THINKING

Think of a situation you were in recently when you thought at the time that you were perfectly rational, which you now realize consisted of self-deception. Complete these statements:

1. The situation was as follows...

2. I behaved in the situation by...

3. At the time, I thought I was rational because...

4. Now I think I may have been irrational because...

5. I rationalized my behavior by telling myself...

6. The real reason I behaved the way I did is...

THE EGOCENTRIC MIND IS AUTOMATIC IN NATURE

Egocentric thinking, unlike rational thought, operates in a highly automatic, unconscious, and impulsive manner. Based in primitive, often "childish," thought patterns, it reacts to situations in programmed and mechanistic ways. You must recognize, therefore, that it often will spring into action before you have a chance to sidestep or prevent it. It fights. It flees. It denies. It represses. It rationalizes. It distorts. It negates. It scapegoats. And it does all of these in the blink of an eye, with no conscious awareness of its deceptive tricks.

Because you now know that the irrational mind operates in predictable, preprogrammed, automated ways, you can become an interested observer of the egocentric mechanisms of your own mind. You can begin to observe the mechanistic moves your mind makes. Rather than allowing thoughts to operate strictly at the unconscious level, you can actively strive to raise them to conscious realization, as Piaget put it. You can work to bring them into full consciousness. This typically will be after the fact—especially in the beginning of your development as a critical thinker. After a time, when you become keenly aware of how your personal ego functions, you can often forestall egocentric reactions by the prior activity of rational thought.

For instance, as mentioned, you can begin to recognize when your mind rationalizes in patterned ways. You also can become familiar with the kinds of rationalization your mind tends to use. For example, "I don't have time to do this!" may be a favorite rationalization. You could limit its use by remembering the insight, "People always have time for the things most important to them." You then are forced to face the truth about what you are doing: "I don't want to make room in my priorities for this," or, "Since I continually say this is important to me, I'm only deceiving myself by saying, 'but I don't have time for it.'"

Over time and with practice, you will increasingly notice when you are denying some important truth about yourself. You can begin to see when you are refusing to face some reality rather than dealing with it openly and directly. You can begin to recognize when you are automatically thinking in a dishonest way in attempting to avoid working on a solution to a problem.

In principle, then, you can study the tricks and stratagems of your mind to determine its automated patterns. Furthermore, and most important, you can learn to intervene to disengage irrational thought processes—if necessary after they have begun to operate. In short, you can refuse to be controlled by primitive desires and modes of thinking. You can actively work to replace automatic egocentric thinking with reflective reasonable thinking.

INTERNALIZE THE IDEA: FOCUSING ON DENIAL AS A MECHANISM OF IRRATIONALITY

Although the egocentric dimension of the mind uses many defense mechanisms to maintain its self-centered view, just one will be singled out for this activity: denial. Think of a relationship you are in now in which you have a selfish interest in seeing things a certain way, although the facts probably don't support your view. Let's say you want to believe that your spouse really loves you, even though his or her actual behavior toward you indicates that he or she is probably using you (perhaps as a vehicle of his or her self-gratification).

As another example, let's say that you want to believe you are treating your spouse respectfully, though the facts show that you often treat him or her with little respect and consideration. Admitting the truth would be painful to you. Complete these statements:

1. The situation is...

2. What I have denied accepting in this situation is...

3. I have avoided the truth by telling myself the following untruth...

4. I realize I have denied looking at the truth in the situation because...

5. Some implications that have followed from my denial about this situation are...

HUMANS ARE NATURALLY SOCIOCENTRIC ANIMALS

Not only are humans naturally egocentric, but we are also easily drawn into sociocentric thinking and behavior. Groups offer us security to the extent that we internalize and unthinkingly conform to their rules, imperatives, and taboos. Growing up, we learn to conform to many groups. Peer groups may dominate our life. Our unconscious acceptance of the values of the group leads to the unconscious standard: "It's true if we believe it." There seems to be no belief so absurd that some group of humans will irrationally accept it as rational.

Not only do we accept the belief systems of the groups to which we belong, but also most importantly, we act on those belief systems. Groups may expect their members to adhere to any number of dysfunctional behaviors. Many groups are anti-intellectual in nature. For example, some youth groups expect members to abuse outsiders verbally and physically (as proof of power or courage). And some groups who share lunch together during the workweek engage in malicious gossip about others in the same workplace.

In addition to face-to-face groups we are in, we are influenced indirectly by large-scale social forces that reflect our membership in society at large. For example, in capitalist societies, the dominant thinking is that people should strive to make as much money as possible, though this form of thinking, it might be argued, encourages people to accept a large gap between the haves and have-nots as right and normal.

Or consider this: Within mass societies the nature and solution to most public issues and problems are presented in sensationalized sound-bytes by the news media. As a result, people often come to think about complex problems in terms of simplistic media-fostered solutions. Many people are led to believe that expressions such as "Get tough with criminals!" and "Three strikes and you're out!" represent plausible ways to deal with complex social problems.

What is more, the portrayal of life in movies, on TV and in social media exerts a significant influence on how we conceptualize our problems, our lives, and ourselves. Sociocentric influences are at work at every level of social life in both subtle and blatant ways.

You must take possession of the idea that, because you are a member of social groups, your behavior reflects the imperatives and taboos of the groups to which you belong. Like everyone, you, to a greater or lesser degree, uncritically conform to the rules and expectations of the groups of which you are a member. When you recognize this, you can begin to analyze and assess that to which you conform. You can actively analyze the rules and taboos of your peer groups and those you are aligned with. You can rationally think through the groups' expectations to determine the extent to which these expectations are reasonable.

When you identify irrational expectations, you can refuse to adhere to those requirements. You can shift your group memberships from those that are flagrantly irrational to those that are more rational. Indeed, you can actively create new groups, groups that emphasize the importance of integrity and fairmindedness, groups that encourage their members to develop independence of thought and work together in that pursuit. Or you can minimize the groups you belong to—except for those you cannot escape. With respect to the large-scale sociocentric influences to which you are subjected by the mass media, you can develop an ongoing critical sensitivity that minimizes your falling prey to group influences. In short, by understanding your personal relationship to sociocentric thinking, you can begin to take charge of the influence that groups have over you. You can significantly reduce that influence.

INTERNALIZE THE IDEA: ANALYZE THE REQUIREMENTS AND TABOOS IN ONE OF YOUR GROUPS

Identify a group to which you belong. It can be a small group of colleagues at work, friends, a club, a religious group, or a large non-face-to-face cultural group of which you are a part. Complete the following statements:

1. The group I am focused on is...

2. The taboos or behaviors not allowed within the group are...

3. The injunctions or requirements are...

4. In analyzing my behavior in this group, I realize ... about myself.

5. After analyzing this group's taboos and injunctions, I think it is/is not in my interest to be involved in this group, for these reasons...

PRIMARY FORMS OF SOCIOCENTRIC THOUGHT

Now that we have focused briefly on the problem of egocentric thinking and some of its primary manifestations, let us dig deeper into the problem of sociocentric thinking. Consider four distinct forms of sociocentric thought. These forms function and are manifest in complex relationships with one another; all are destructive and can lead to mental health problems.[6] They can be summarized as follows:

1. *Groupishness*[7] *(or group selfishness)*—the tendency on the part of groups to seek the most for the in-group without regard to the rights and needs of others, in order to advance the group's biased interests. Groupishness is almost certainly the primary tendency in sociocentric thinking, the foundational driving force behind it (probably connected to survival in our dim dark evolutionary past). Everyone in the group is privileged (in-group); everyone outside the group is denied group privileges and/or seen as a potential threat (out-group). This happens, for instance, when some members of the family take more family resources for themselves than is reasonable, denying adequate resources to others in the family.

2. *Group validation*—the tendency on the part of groups to believe their way to be the right way and their views to be the correct views; the tendency to reinforce one another in these beliefs; the inclination to validate the group's views, however dysfunctional or illogical. These may be long-held or newly-established views, but in either case, they are perceived by the group to be true and in many cases to advance its interests. This tendency informs the world view from which everyone outside the group is seen and understood and by which everything that happens outside the group is judged. It leads to the problem of in-group thinking and behavior—everyone inside the group thinking within a collective logic; everyone outside the group being judged according to the standards and beliefs of the in-group. The need to be validated is at the heart of many mental health problems. Finding strength from within and developing

---

6 The term sociocentric thought is being reserved for those group beliefs that cause harm or are likely to cause harm. Group thought that is reasonable, useful, or helpful would not fall into this category. In my view, it is important to see sociocentric thought as destructive because otherwise the mind will find a variety of ways to rationalize it. By recognizing it as irrational, we are better able to identify it in our thinking and take command of it.

7 By groupishness I mean group selfishness. This term refers to group pursuit of its interests without sufficient regard for the rights and needs of those outside the group; its counterpart in egocentric thinking is selfishness, which refers to individual pursuit of one's interests without sufficient regard for the rights and needs of others. Note that this use of the term "groupish" differs from the way in which evolutionary biologists use the same term. Their use generally refers to the fact that members of a group are aware of their group membership and are aware that there are others (like them) in the group.

self-confidence are essential to avoiding the tendency to seek validation in unhealthy ways.

3. *Group control*—the tendency on the part of groups to ensure that group members behave in accordance with group expectations. This logic guides the intricate inner workings of the group, largely through enforcement, ostracism, and punishment in connection with group customs, conventions, rules, taboos, mores, and laws. Group control can also take the form of "recruitment" through propaganda and other forms of manipulation. It is often sophisticated and camouflaged. There are many forms and patterns of group control, for instance, in the work world. Powerful group members ostracizing those who do not agree with them in order to maintain control of the overall group is one example.

4. *Group conformity*—a byproduct of the fact that to survive, people must figure out how to fit themselves into the groups they are thrust into or voluntarily choose to join. They must conform to the rules and laws set down by those in control. Dissenters are punished in numerous ways. Group control and group conformity are two sides of the same coin—each presupposes the other. People tend to conform within groups in any number of ways which are not healthy. Many people are not comfortable if they are not part of a group, going along with the group and believing in the ideas of the group. By implication, they are unable to establish their own unique identity.

These four sociocentric tendencies interrelate and overlap in any number of ways and thus should be understood as four parts of an interconnected puzzle.

Again, sociocentric tendencies largely lie at the unconscious level. It isn't that people are aware of these tendencies and consciously choose to go along with them. Rather, these dispositions are, at least to some extent, hidden by self-deception, rationalization, and other native mechanisms of the mind that keep us from seeing and facing the truth in our thoughts and actions. The mind tells itself one thing on the surface (e.g., we are being fair to all involved) when in fact it is acting upon a different thought entirely (e.g., we are mainly concerned with our own interests). In most instances, the mind can find ways to justify itself—even when engaging in highly unethical acts.[8]

---

8 It should be pointed out that there are many circumstances where rational behavior might be confused with sociocentric behavior. For instance, group members may well validate among themselves views that are reasonable. And groups should expect group members to behave in ethical ways. There may also be many other conditions under which it would make sense for an individual to conform to group expectations (e.g., to keep from being tortured or to contribute to the well being of the planet).

INTERNALIZE THE IDEA: IDENTIFY YOUR SOCIOCENTRIC TENDENCIES

Complete these statements:

1. In reading through the sociocentric tendencies above, I see that one problem in my thinking is...

2. This is a problem because...

3. I intend to address this problem in the following ways...

INTERNALIZE THE IDEA: EXAMINE THE SOCIOCENTRIC GROUPS YOU BELONG TO

Consider the primary groups you belong to now or have belonged to in the past. Focus on those that exemplify one or more of the four primary forms of sociocentric thought (and that you have not previously written about while working through this book; these groups may include family, peer groups, religious groups, professional groups, sports groups, etc.). For each group, complete these statements:

1. This group demonstrates groupishness (or group selfishness) in the following ways...

2. This group validates its narrow views as follows...

3. People in the group are controlled in the following ways...

4. People in the group are required to conform to the following rules...

5. The following behaviors or thoughts are considered taboo in this group. Dissenters are punished in the following ways...

6. As a result of this analysis, I now realize...

ONE COMMON PATHWAY FOR SOCIOCENTRIC THINKING

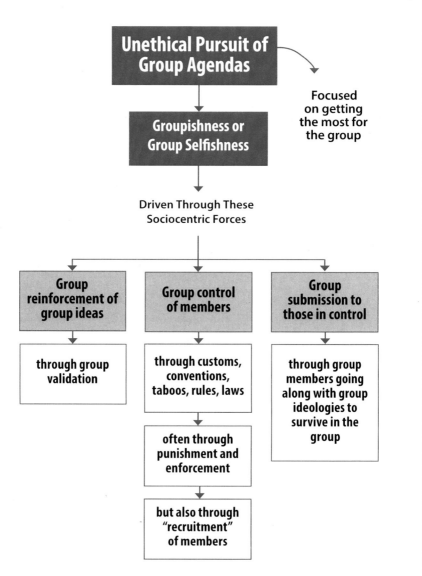

Groupishness, to be effectively "achieved," requires group reinforcement, group control, and group submission; this diagram begins to illuminate the complex relationships between and among the four primary forms of sociocentric thought. Which of these sociocentric ways of thinking do you most fall prey to?

SOCIOCENTRIC DISPOSITIONS ARE PARALLEL WITH EGOCENTRIC DISPOSITIONS

There are multiple interrelated sociocentric dispositions that are parallel with egocentric tendencies. All of us, insofar as we are sociocentric, embody these pathological dispositions (as well as others that cluster with them). Critical thinkers are keenly aware of these tendencies and consistently seek to counter them with fairminded reasoning. As you read through these dispositions, think of examples from your own thinking and behavior that fit into each category:

- **sociocentric memory**: the natural group tendency to "forget" evidence and information that does not support the group's thinking, and to "remember" evidence and information that does.
- **sociocentric myopia**: the natural group tendency to think in an absolutist way within a narrow "groupish" viewpoint.
- **sociocentric righteousness**: the natural group tendency to feel that "our group" is superior in light of our confidence that "we" inherently possess the truth.
- **sociocentric hypocrisy**: the natural group tendency to ignore flagrant inconsistencies between what a group professes to believe and the actual beliefs implied by its members' collective behavior, or inconsistencies between the standards to which they hold their group members and those to which they expect other people to adhere.
- **sociocentric oversimplification**: the natural group tendency to ignore real and important complexities in the world in favor of simplistic, group interested notions when considering these complexities would require the group to modify its beliefs or values.
- **sociocentric blindness**: the natural group tendency not to notice facts and evidence that contradict the group's favored beliefs or values.
- **sociocentric immediacy**: the natural group tendency to over-generalize immediate group feelings and experiences so that when one significant event (or a few such events) is experienced by the group as highly favorable or unfavorable, this feeling is generalized to the group's overall outlook on the world (or view of other groups).
- **sociocentric absurdity**: the natural group tendency to fail to notice group thinking that has absurd consequences or implications.

CHALLENGE YOUR SOCIOCENTRIC DISPOSITIONS

It is not enough to recognize abstractly that the human mind has predictable sociocentric pathologies. If you want to live a rational life, you must take concrete steps to correct these pathologies in yourself (in ways similar to dealing with your egocentric pathologies). Routinely identifying these tendencies in action needs to become habitual for you. Those who take this challenge seriously recognize that it is a long-term process, never complete. Therefore, each of the following admonitions should not be taken as simple suggestions that any group could immediately, and effectively, put into action, but rather as guiding concepts for group mental health. Every group can perform these corrections, but only over time and with considerable practice. You will need to determine what role you can play in these group corrections. Or you may need to leave a group you deem too sociocentric for your mental health.

Correcting sociocentric memory. We can take steps to correct the natural tendency of our group to "forget" evidence that does not support our group's thinking and "remember" evidence that does. We can do this by overtly seeking evidence and information that does not support the thinking of the group, and by directing explicit attention to that information. We should especially seek information and evidence that does not place our group in a positive light—information the group would rather forget or not be faced with. How do the groups you belong to tend to remember events and situations from its past? Are these memories in any way distorted; if so how?

Correcting sociocentric myopia. We can take steps to correct our natural group tendency to think in an absolutistic way within an overly-narrow group point of view. We can do this by routinely thinking within points of view that conflict with our group's viewpoint. For example, if we are "liberals," we can read books by insightful conservatives. If we are "conservatives," we can read books by insightful liberals. If we are North Americans, we can study a contrasting South American point of view, or a European, Far-Eastern, Middle-Eastern, or African point of view. In what ways are your group's views narrow and confined? What are some important limitations in your culture's viewpoint?

Correcting sociocentric righteousness. We can take steps to correct our natural sociocentric tendency to feel superior in light of our confidence that our group possesses *the truth*. We can do this by regularly reminding ourselves of how little our group actually knows. To do so, we can explicitly state the unanswered questions that our group has never openly reasoned through (though our past group behavior would imply that we have *the truth* in answer to those questions). In what ways is any of your groups arrogant about their knowledge? What are the limits of your group's knowledge? When and how do the people in your group tend to step beyond these limits, pretending to know what they do not know?

Correcting sociocentric hypocrisy. We can take steps to correct the natural tendency of our group to ignore flagrant inconsistencies between what it professes to believe and the actual beliefs its behavior implies. We can uncover inconsistencies between the standards we impose on group members and those we require of those outside the group. We can do this by regularly comparing the criteria and standards by which we judge others with those by which we judge our own group. To what extent do any of your groups profess what they do not live up to? Do your groups expect more from those outside the group than they do of those inside the group, or are they harder on those outside the group?

Correcting sociocentric oversimplification. We can take steps to correct our group's natural tendency to ignore real and important complexities in the world by regularly focusing on those complexities, formulating them explicitly in words, and targeting them. We can look for instances when it is in our group's interest to simplify the complex in order to maintain a particular view, or to pursue some particular group interest. To what extent do your groups oversimplify complex issues? What does this lead to? What are some complexities your group may be missing?

Correcting sociocentric blindness. We can take steps to correct our natural tendency to ignore facts or evidence that contradict our group's favored beliefs or values. We can do this by explicitly seeking out those facts and that evidence. We can look for situations when it is in our group's interest to ignore information it would rather not see or have to face. What are some facts any of your groups would rather ignore? What are some consequences of your group ignoring important information?

Correcting sociocentric immediacy. We can help correct our natural tendency to overgeneralize our group's immediate feelings and experiences by developing the habit of putting them into a larger perspective. We can look for examples of times in the past when our group has overgeneralized some event or set of events, whether positive or negative, and then examine the consequences of our group's having done so. We can consider the implications of our doing so again, should we face similar events in the future. We can strive to avoid group distortions of any kind. Does your group tend to overgeneralize beyond the immediate situation by perceiving the whole as good or bad, rather than perceiving nuances in situations?

Correcting sociocentric absurdity. We can take steps to correct our natural tendency to ignore groupthink that has absurd implications. We can do this by making the important implications of our group's thinking explicit, then assessing these implications for their desirability and realism. This requires that we frequently trace the implications of our group beliefs and the consequences of our group's behavior. For example, we should frequently ask ourselves, "If we really believed this, how would we act? Do we really act that way? Do we want to act that way? Is it ethical for us to act that way?"

GROUPS ROUTINELY USE SOCIOCENTRIC DEFENSE MECHANISMS

Sociocentric thought is connected to a number of well-established defense mechanisms. Defense mechanisms tend to be understood in terms of individual thought—the individual person as in denial, the individual as engaging in identification, projection, repression, and so on. But defense mechanisms that apply to individual thought are commonly used in pathological group thought as well. All are connected with "in-group deception"; they interact with the sociocentric pathological tendencies described in the last section (as well as possibly with egocentric thinking).

Consider the following **sociocentric defense mechanisms:**

sociocentric denial: when a group refuses to believe indisputable evidence or facts in order to maintain a favorable group image, or a favored set of group beliefs. Members of a basketball team, for example, may deny that they collectively have significant weaknesses which the opposing team lacks. "Patriots" in a given country may deny—in the face of clear-cut evidence—that their country ever violates human rights or acts unjustly. A set of parents may deny ever being unjust to their children.

sociocentric identification: when people within a group accept, as their own, the values and ideals of the group. Through connection with the group, its members elevate their sense of worth. For instance, football fans often experience an inner sense of triumph when "their" team wins; parents often experience a sense of "puffed up" success when their children perform well (or even relatively well) at something; citizens often feel smug when their nation's armed forces make a "clean sweep" or assassinate someone.

sociocentric projection: when, to avoid unacceptable thoughts and feelings, a group attributes to another group what they themselves are doing. By avoiding these thoughts and feelings, they can successfully avoid facing their own actions and changing them. For instance, a family may falsely accuse its neighbors of being loud and disrespectful (perhaps when their music is slightly elevated), when the family itself is the one actually being loud and disrespectful (with routine playing of very loud music).

sociocentric repression: when thoughts, feelings, or memories unacceptable to the group are prevented from reaching consciousness. This often occurs when groups do not want to face something disagreeable they have done or are doing. For hundreds of years in the United States, for instance, the government repressed the fact that Christopher Columbus engaged in egregious acts against native peoples during the "discovery" of the Americas (and is therefore not the hero he is often portrayed to be). In the United States today, the often horrific treatment of native peoples during "colonialism" is still, to a large extent, repressed (as are its accompanying consequences that last to this day). The same is true regarding our historical treatment of black people.

sociocentric rationalization: when members of a group give reasons (sometimes good ones) for their behavior—but not the real reasons, because they cannot consciously face their actions. Farmers who don't care about the effects of dangerous pesticides on animals and people rationalize their behavior by arguing that they have no reasonable alternatives to control pests (when, in fact, they usually do).

sociocentric stereotyping: when a group lumps together people or other sentient creatures outside the group based on some perceived common (usually negative) characteristics. The in-group forms a rigid, biased perception of the out-group. One form of stereotyping comes from cultural bias, wherein people assume the practices and beliefs in their culture to be superior to those in other cultures. They take their group to be the measure of all groups and people. For instance, those who argue for public-nudity rights are sociocentrically stereotyped by many western cultures as perverted and unethical, whereas in many cultures throughout history this practice has seemed only natural. In what ways do your groups stereotype those outside the group?

sociocentric scapegoating: when groups attempt to avoid criticism of their practices by blaming persons outside their group, or blaming the circumstance, etc., for their own mistakes or faults. A group of teachers criticized for failing to foster critical thinking in the classroom may try to avoid responsibility for this failure through scapegoating—by blaming the school system, the parents, or the curriculum—when in fact they could do far more to foster critical thinking. Similarly, parents who do not live up to their duty to teach their children responsibility and citizenship often blame the schools and society for what they themselves have failed to do.

sociocentric sublimation: when groups inappropriately divert instinctive, primitive, or socially unacceptable desires into socially acceptable activities. A group of sexually unfulfilled prison guards may well sublimate their sexual energy through aggressive and dominating behavior toward prisoners, and they may encourage one another in this egregious behavior. A pair of sexually frustrated parents may unconsciously take their mutual sexual frustrations out on their children through harsh punishment.

sociocentric wishful thinking: when those within a group unconsciously misinterpret facts in order to maintain their beliefs. Wishful thinking leads to false expectations, and usually involves seeing things more positively than is reasonable in a given situation. Parents who ignore relevant data that implies that their child has little chance of success in a traditional college setting, and who send their child to college anyway (while merely hoping for the best), are engaging in sociocentric wishful thinking.

HUMANS ARE INFLUNCED BY GROUPS WITHIN GROUPS

Because humans are intrinsically social creatures, we form groups for almost every imaginable purpose. Any given person will belong to numerous groups in a lifetime. These groups will each have their own sets of social rules, expectations, and taboos. Many groups will overlap with others; some will operate more independently. Some people will be more autonomous, allying themselves with fewer groups. And each of us, whether we like it or not, belongs to a broader culture or society that imposes rules on its members.

To put this another way, everyone is part of a number of groups, each of which has its own influence and many of which influence one another. Any given individual is usually influenced first by the family, each member of which has in turn been influenced by the groups he or she has been a member of. Then, as we go through life, the groups we become members of (either voluntarily or involuntarily), with their various ideologies and belief systems, influence our thoughts and actions in many ways.

In a typical pattern of group influence, the views of the family are thrust upon the child—views on "the family," on marital relations, sibling relations, intimacy, parenting, sexuality, health and well-being, and so forth. If the family is religious, the child is likely expected to uncritically accept the same religious beliefs. When the child goes to school, the views of teachers are inculcated into the mind of the child. At the same time, peers can have significant influence on the child's developing mind. As the child moves through childhood and adolescence, there are many influencing parties—teachers and peers, neighbors and clergy, and still the parents and siblings—each having varying degrees of sway at different ages. Religion, sports, TV, other media, extracurricular activities, and other agencies contend for the child's attention. The young adult may attend college and be carried along by various crowds in various directions, then move into the world of work, and of professions with their varied influences. Add to all of these the many cultural ideologies trickling down through each group and manifested, again, in media sources like TV, newspapers, radio, and the internet.

Given these many group influences, from birth throughout life, one can hardly imagine what one's life or views would be, or would have been, without them. Importantly, these influences cause us to form ideas and assumptions almost before we have the benefit of conscious reasoning, and certainly before we have developed critical capacities for discerning what to accept and what to reject. When we do develop these capacities, to the extent that we do, we still are often overly influenced by groups and cultures—by groups within groups that affect the way we think and live.

When significant contradictions arise between and among groups to which we belong, we often (if not typically) compartmentalize, rather than resolve the contradictions. Take, for example, the wealthy college student whose parents have taught him not to socialize with people of lower economic status. Let's imagine that this student has uncritically accepted the view of his parents—that people of a lower economic class are "beneath" him. Then, while attending college, he is thrown into a social group comprised of people from differing economic levels, and he befriends someone less wealthy than his family. In so doing, he has two choices: he rejects (either in the long- or short-run) his parent's views as narrow and dogmatic, or he makes an exception in this particular case (again, either short- or long-term). Very likely he will do the latter, having been indoctrinated into his parents' views before he could reasonably critique the validity of these beliefs. This is a common way of dealing with contradictions in the mind—maintain the original beliefs while making an exception.

Critical thinkers recognize that they have been influenced by all of the groups in which they have been members. They examine their beliefs to understand how, and to what extent, these beliefs have been guided by group assumptions and ideologies. They understand that the differing agendas and convictions of the groups to which they belong often conflict with one another. They try, whenever possible, to deal directly and forthrightly with these conflicts and contradictions. Insofar as possible, they join only those groups that function with a critical spirit. Recognizing that all groups may fall prey to irrational thought, they are ever on the lookout to tease apart the reasonable from the unreasonable views and actions within a given group.

CHAPTER FIVE
DEVELOP INTELLECTUAL VIRTUES THAT WILL LEAD TO HIGHER LEVELS OF MENTAL WELL-BEING

DEVELOPING INTELLECTUAL CHARACTER

As you take better command of your mind, it is essential to work towards developing the intellectual habits or characteristics you see in the diagram below. When you embody critical thinking principles, these habits define how you live your life—how you work through issues, how you communicate, how you treat other people, how you allow other people to treat you, how you see the world and your place in it. Before reading about these virtues, consider the three types of thinkers in the diagram on the next page, and ask yourself which one of these you are most like. Perhaps you are sometimes a naïve thinker, sometimes a fairminded critical thinker, and sometimes a selfish critical thinker.

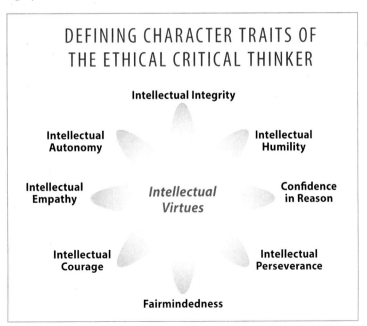

DEFINING CHARACTER TRAITS OF THE ETHICAL CRITICAL THINKER

Intellectual Integrity

Intellectual Autonomy

Intellectual Humility

Intellectual Empathy

Intellectual Virtues

Confidence in Reason

Intellectual Courage

Intellectual Perseverance

Fairmindedness

©2025 Linda Elder

THREE TYPES OF CHARACTER SIMPLIFIED

THE NAÏVE THINKER

THE SELFISH CRITICAL THINKER

THE FAIRMINDED CRITICAL THINKER

The person who doesn't care about, or isn't aware of, his or her thinking

The person who in some ways is good at thinking, but is unfair to others

The person who is not only good at thinking, but is also fair to others

Fairminded critical thinkers consistently seek their own happiness and tranquility while contributing to a better world. Selfish critical thinkers spend their energy seeking more for themselves, and naive thinkers are easily manipulated by the selfish and power-hungry thinkers. Neither of these latter states of mind are healthy. Each of us may sometimes be a naïve thinker, sometimes a selfish critical thinker, and sometimes a fairminded critical thinker.

THE FAIRMINDED CRITICAL THINKER

Fairminded critical thinkers work to improve their thinking whenever they can. They want things for themselves, but they aren't selfish. They want to help other people. They want to help make the world better for everyone. They are willing to give things up to help others (when it makes sense to); they also know the importance of taking care of themselves. They don't always have the right answers, but they work to improve their thinking and actions over time. They don't sit back and hope for a better future; instead they take daily steps to achieve within their capacities. They have a zest for life. They appreciate and actively build the power of their own minds as they reach toward self-actualization.

HERE IS THE VOICE OF THE FAIRMINDED CRITICAL THINKER...

"I think a lot. It helps me learn. It helps me figure things out. I want to understand the thinking of other people. I want to understand myself and why I do things. Sometimes I do things I don't understand. It's not easy trying to understand everyone and everything. Lots of people say one thing and do another. You can't always believe what people say. You can't believe a lot of what you see on TV and the internet. People often say things they don't mean because they want things and are trying to please you.

"I would like to make the world a better place. I want to make it better for everyone, not just for me and my friends. To understand other people you have to look at things as they do. You have to understand their situation and what you would feel like if you were them. You have to put yourself in their shoes. I think about people who don't have what I have, like people who are starving or homeless. I want to help create a world where everyone has enough to eat and somewhere to live.

"It isn't easy to be fair. It's a lot easier to be selfish and just think about yourself. But the world isn't a nice place to be if people are selfish."

THE SELFISH CRITICAL THINKER

Selfish critical thinkers are people who use their thinking to get what they want, without considering how their actions might affect other people. They are good at some aspects of thinking, and they know it. But they are also very selfish. They may be greedy and unkind as well.

HERE IS THE VOICE OF THE SELFISH CRITICAL THINKER...

"I think a lot! It helps me get what I want. I believe whatever I want to believe as long as it gets me what I want. I question anyone who asks me to do what I don't want to do. I figure out how to get other people to do what I want them to do. I even figure out how to avoid thinking if I want.

"Sometimes I say 'I can't!' when I know I could but don't want to. You can get what you want from people if you know how to manipulate them. Just the other night, I talked my brother into lending me his car, even though I lost my driver's license recently. What do I care about laws that get in my way of doing what I want?

"It helps to tell people what they want to hear. Of course, sometimes what they want to hear isn't true, but that doesn't matter because you can't get what you want when you tell people what they don't want to hear. You can always trick people if you know how. You can even trick yourself into believing almost anything you want, if you know how."

THE NAÏVE THINKER

Naïve thinkers don't see why it is important to work on their thinking. They don't want to be bothered with developing their minds. These people are easily manipulated and controlled by selfish and self-centered people. If you tend to be a naïve thinker, you are at risk for believing and following people who are not well-meaning and are unconcerned with your well-being. These may be family members, colleagues, supervisors, people you consider to be your friends, people you meet through social media, indeed, anyone who can use you to serve their selfish interests. This book provides the tools you need to move away from naïve thinking and toward fairminded critical thinking so you can become the master of your life, rather than allowing others to be.

HERE IS THE VOICE OF THE NAÏVE THINKER...

"I don't need to think! I understand everything without thinking. I just do whatever occurs to me to do. I believe most of what I hear. I believe most of what I see on TV and what I read on the internet. I don't see why I should question the messages that come at me on TV shows and the internet. I don't think they affect me that much anyway.

"And I don't need to waste a lot of time trying to figure things out. If I need to find the answer to a problem, I just ask someone else or rely on social media. Other people can figure things out better than I can, so why should I try to figure things out for myself? It's a lot easier to say 'I can't!' than to do a lot of work. A lot of times trying to figure things out takes too much time. And sometimes it's just too hard for me, so why bother?

"I mostly go along with whatever people are doing. It's just easier that way. I do what I'm told, keep my mouth shut, and go along with whatever other people decide. I don't like to make waves. Thinking gets you into trouble."

INTERNALIZE THE IDEA: WHICH TYPE OF CHARACTER ARE YOU?

Study the diagrams and information on the previous pages about the three types of characters as thinkers; be aware that all people are sometimes uncritical thinkers, sometimes self-serving critical thinkers, and sometimes fairminded critical thinkers. To what extent do you fall into either of these categories?

Complete the following statements:

1. I would say that I am mostly a... [naïve person/self-serving critical person fairminded critical person].

2. I would prove that I am such a person with the following evidence...

3. Other people who know me well would say I am...

4. As I think about my future and molding myself to become what I want to become, I need to do the following to become a more fairminded critical person...

HOW TO BECOME A FAIRMINDED CRITICAL THINKER: DEVELOP INTELLECTUAL VIRTUES

To become a fairminded, self-developing emotionally well critical thinker, actively work toward embodying these characteristics:

Intellectual Integrity

Act towards others the way you want people to act towards you. Respect others in the same way you want to be respected. Don't expect others to act better than you are willing to act yourself. Consider the feelings of others in the same way you want your own feelings to be considered. Because you don't want others to be rude to you, avoid being rude to others. Because you don't want to be harmed by others, be careful not to harm others.

Intellectual integrity consists in holding yourself to the same standards you expect others to honor (no double standards). Questions that foster intellectual integrity include:

• Do I behave in accordance with what I say I believe, or do I tend to say one thing and do another?

• To what extent do I expect the same of myself as I expect of others?

• To what extent are there contradictions or inconsistencies in my life?

• To what extent do I strive to recognize and eliminate self-deception in my life?

Intellectual Autonomy

Do your own thinking. Figure things out for yourself. It is good to listen to others to find out what they think, but you must do your own thinking to decide who and *what* to believe. Of course, don't just believe what you want to believe. Use intellectual standards to decide—standards like accuracy, relevance, significance and fairness.

Intellectual autonomy is thinking for oneself while adhering to standards of rationality. It means thinking through issues using one's own thinking rather than uncritically accepting the viewpoints of others. Questions that foster intellectual autonomy:

• To what extent am I a conformist? Do I depend on others for my mental health? Must I be accepted by others to feel whole within myself?

• To what extent do I uncritically accept what I am told by my government, the media, my peers, my spouse?

• Do I think through issues on my own, or do I merely accept the views of others?

• Having thought through an issue from a rational perspective, am I willing to stand alone despite the irrational criticisms of others?

Intellectual Perseverance

Don't be a quitter. When you begin to think you can't learn something, remind yourself that you can. If reading is hard for you, stick to it (because it is essential to read important works). When writing is hard, keep trying so you can learn to write better. Don't be afraid to work hard when you feel like giving up. Remember that no matter how good you are at thinking, you can always improve. And no matter how much you struggle with learning, keep trying. Never give up! Be the captain of your own ship. Chart your own course in life.

Intellectual perseverance is the disposition to work your way through intellectual complexities despite frustrations inherent in the task. Questions that foster intellectual perseverance include:

• Am I willing to work my way through complexities in an issue, or do I tend to give up when I experience difficulties?

• Can I think of a complex problem in which I have demonstrated patience and determination in working through its difficulties?

• Do I have strategies for dealing with complex problems?

• Do I expect my mental well-being to be easy, or do I recognize the importance of persevering to change my bad habits of thought that cause me pain?

Intellectual Empathy

Always try to understand how other people think and feel. Whenever you disagree with someone, try to see things from that person's point of view. When you do try to see things from other people's viewpoints, you will often find that there are some things you are right about and some things other people are right about. Being able and willing to imagine how others think and feel is very important in life. If everyone did this a lot, the world would be much better for everyone. There would be a lot less pain and suffering.

Intellectual empathy is awareness of the need to actively entertain views that differ from your own, especially those you strongly disagree with. It is to accurately reconstruct the viewpoints and reasoning of your opponents and to reason from premises, assumptions, and ideas other than your own. Questions that foster intellectual empathy include:

• To what extent do I accurately represent viewpoints I disagree with?

• Can I summarize the views of my opponents to their satisfaction? Can I see insights in the views of others and prejudices in my own?

• Do I sympathize with the feelings of others in light of their thinking differently than me?

Intellectual Humility

Recognize that you don't know everything. There is a lot you don't know (and never will). Don't say something is true when you don't know for sure that it is. Lots of things you think are true may not in fact be true. Lots of things people say are true are actually not true, and lots of things you read or see on the internet are not true. Always ask, "How do I know that? How do you know that?"

Intellectual humility entails knowledge of your own ignorance and therefore sensitivity to what you know and what you do not know. It means being aware of your biases, prejudices, self-deceptive tendencies, and the limitations of your viewpoint. Questions that foster intellectual humility include:

• What do I really know (about myself, about the situation, about another person, about my nation, about what is going on in the world)?

• To what extent do my prejudices or biases influence my thinking?

• To what extent have I been indoctrinated into beliefs that may be false?

• How do the beliefs I have uncritically accepted keep me from seeing things as they are?

• Does my uncritical acceptance of ideas lead me to illogical behavior or cause me frustration?

Intellectual Courage

Be ready to speak up for what you think is right, even if it is not popular with your friends or the people around you. Of course, sometimes speaking up can be dangerous. Use your best thinking to figure out when it makes sense to speak up and when you should just keep your thoughts to yourself. When you do speak up, try always to show respect for others, but don't ever be afraid to disagree in the privacy of your own mind. And don't be afraid to question your beliefs, to figure out what makes best sense. Develop the courage to look inside your own mind and figure out what is really going on there. Even if you have held a belief for a long time, you still need to be willing to question it, to use the tools of critical thinking to recheck it.

Intellectual courage is the disposition to question beliefs you feel strongly about. It includes questioning the beliefs of your culture and groups to which you belong, and a willingness to express your views even when they are unpopular (in safe situations).

Questions that foster intellectual courage include:

- How do the beliefs I have uncritically accepted keep me from seeing things as they are?
- To what extent have I analyzed the beliefs I hold?
- To what extent have I questioned my beliefs, many of which I learned in childhood?
- To what extent have I demonstrated a willingness to give up my beliefs when sufficient evidence is presented against them?
- To what extent am I willing to stand up against the majority, even though people might ridicule me?

Confidence in Reason

The best chance we have to create a fair and just world is if we use our best thinking, all of us, together, living on the planet. When people disagree, they need to overcome disagreements by looking at the facts, at the evidence. We need to work together to come to the most defensible conclusions. We need to use intellectual standards in working through problems. For example, make sure you use information that is accurate and relevant to the problem you are trying to solve. Look for the complexities in deep issues. Avoid superficial answers to complicated problems, as they almost never work. Think about problems from different points of view. Trust evidence, facts, and reasoning. Distrust blind faith, jealousy, and fear.

Confidence in reason is based on the belief that one's own higher interests and those of humankind and all sentient creatures are best served by giving the freest play to reason. It means using standards of reasonability as the fundamental criteria by which to judge whether to accept or reject any belief or position. Questions that foster confidence in reason include:

- Am I willing to change my position when the evidence leads to a more reasonable one?
- Do I adhere to principles of sound reasoning when persuading others, or do I distort matters to support my position?
- Do I deem it more important to "win" an argument, or do I instead see the issue from the most reasonable perspective?
- Do I encourage others to come to their own conclusions, or do I try to force my views on them?

Fairmindedness

Try to figure out what is most fair in every situation. Think about everyone involved, not just about you. Don't put your desires and needs above those of others. You should even be willing to give things up to help other people and sentient creatures when their needs are greater than yours. Try to imagine what it would be like to think and feel as other people or sentient creatures do, to be in their circumstances. Don't act until you have done this. Think before you act; don't act before you think.

Fairmindedness is having a consciousness of the need to treat all viewpoints alike, without reference to one's own feelings or vested interests, or to the feelings or vested interests of one's friends, community, nation, or species. It implies adherence to intellectual standards without reference to one's own advantage or the advantage of one's group.

- To what extent do self-interests or biases tend to cloud my judgment?
- How do I tend to treat relevant viewpoints? Do I tend to favor some over others? If so, why?
- To what extent do I appropriately weigh the strengths and weaknesses of all significant relevant perspectives when reasoning through an issue?
- What personal interests do we have at stake here, and how can we ensure that we don't favor our own interests over the common good?

INTERNALIZE THE IDEA: INTELLECTUAL HUMILITY I

Name a person you think you know fairly well. Make two lists. In the first list include everything you know for sure about the person. In the second list include everything you know you don't know about him/her. For example: "I know for sure that my spouse likes to garden, but I'm also sure that I have never really understood what her fears and personal desires are. I know many superficial things about her, but about her inner self I know little." Support what you claim by writing out an explanation of your thinking.

INTERNALIZE THE IDEA: INTELLECTUAL HUMILITY II

Think of a situation you were in recently wherein you stated something to be true which you in fact were not sure of. Analyze the situation using this format:

1. The situation was as follows...

2. In the situation, I said...

3. What I really should have said (which would have been more accurate) is...

INTERNALIZE THE IDEA: TO WHAT DEGREE DO YOU EMBODY INTELLECTUAL VIRTUES?

Read through each of the intellectual virtues again, and this time write out your answers to the questions in each section. Repeat this activity frequently to remind yourself of the virtues you are striving toward.

INTERNALIZE THE IDEA: INTELLECTUAL COURAGE

Try to think of a circumstance in which either you or someone you knew defended a view that was unpopular in a group to which you belonged. This may be your family or work colleagues, for instance. Describe the circumstances and especially how the group responded. If you can't think of an example, what does this tell you about yourself?

INTERNALIZE THE IDEA: INTELLECTUAL EMPATHY

Try to reconstruct the last argument you had with someone (a supervisor, colleague, friend, or intimate other). Reconstruct the argument from your perspective and that of the other person. Complete the statements below. As you do, watch that you do not distort the other's viewpoint. Try to enter it in good faith, even if it means you have to admit you were wrong. (Remember that healthy thinkers want to see the truth in the situation.) After you have completed this activity, show it to the person you argued with to see if you have accurately represented that person's view.

1. My perspective was as follows (state and elaborate your view):

2. The other person's view was as follows (state and elaborate the other person's view):

INTERNALIZE THE IDEA: INTELLECTUAL INTEGRITY

Write about a dimension of your life that you suspect holds some inconsistencies or contradictions (where you probably are not holding yourself to the same standard to which you hold those whom you dislike or disagree with). Think of a situation where your behavior contradicts what you say you believe. This might be in your relationship with an employee or a spouse, for example. Explain what inconsistencies may be present in your behavior. For instance, you may routinely tell your spouse that you love her or him while at the same time routinely mistreating her or him.

INTERNALIZE THE IDEA: INTELLECTUAL PERSEVERANCE

Most people have more physical perseverance than intellectual perseverance. Most are ready to admit, "No pain, no gain!" when talking about the body. Most give up quickly, on the other hand, when faced with a frustrating mental problem that requires their best thinking. Thinking of your own responses, in your work or your personal life, how would you evaluate your own intellectual perseverance on a scale of 0 to 10? Complete these statements:

1. In terms of intellectual perseverance, I would rate myself as follows...

2. I say this because (support your position with evidence)...

3. I could develop intellectual perseverance by routinely doing the following...

INTERNALIZE THE IDEA: CONFIDENCE IN REASON

Think of a recent situation in which you felt yourself being defensive. You now realize you were not able to listen to an argument you did not agree with, though the argument had merit. In this situation, you apparently could not be moved by good reasons. (Realize that this happens to everyone, and perhaps often.) Briefly write what happened in the situation. Then write the reasonable arguments against your position that you were not willing to listen to. Why weren't you able to give credit to the other person's argument? Complete these statements:

1. The situation was as follows...

2. The argument I did not want to hear was as follows...

3. I did not want to hear this argument because...

4. In future similar situations, to be more open to good reasoning as a guiding force in my life, I intend to...

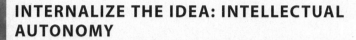

INTERNALIZE THE IDEA: INTELLECTUAL AUTONOMY

Briefly consider some of the variety of influences to which you have been exposed in your life (influences of culture, company, family, religion, peer groups, media, personal relationships, etc.). See if you can discriminate between those dimensions of your thought and behavior in which you have done the least thinking for yourself and those in which you have done the most. What makes this activity difficult is that we often believe we are thinking for ourselves when we are actually conforming to others. What you should look for, therefore, are instances of your actively questioning beliefs, values, or practices to which others in your "group" were, or are, conforming. Use this format:

1. In the following areas of my life, I have done at least a fair job of figuring out the important influences on my thinking...

2. I support this view with the following evidence...

3. In the following areas of my life, however, I have not really thought critically about the influences on my thought and action...

4. Some implications of my failure to think critically in these areas of my life are...

INTERNALIZE THE IDEA: IN WHICH PARTS OF YOUR LIFE DO YOU MOST EMBODY INTELLECTUAL VIRTUES?

Each of us does a better job of reasoning within some parts of our lives than in others. Consider, for instance, these parts of life:

1. your mental health
2. your physical well-being
3. parenting
4. intimate relationships
5. friendships
6. your professional or work domain
7. civic and political life
8. any other part of your life...

Focusing on each important part or domain of your life separately, complete these statements for each one:

1. In this part of my life (e.g. my intimate relationship), I most embody these intellectual virtues...

2. This is evidenced in these actions on my part (give clear and accurate examples)...

3. In this part of my life, I most lack development of the following intellectual virtues...

4. This is evidenced in these actions on my part (again, give clear and accurate examples)...

5. Other people I communicate with within this domain of my life would/would not agree with my reasoning as detailed in numbers 1-4 above.

6. This is because...

7. After completing this analysis, I now think the following... and therefore I intend to make the following changes in my life... (if changes are needed).

©2025 Linda Elder

ESSENTIAL INTELLECTUAL VIRTUES

The diagram facing this one points out the opposites of these intellectual virtues, which form the core character of the self-actualizing person. In the mind and life of the ethical critical thinker, these virtues operate in constellation with other intellectual virtues such as intellectual responsibility and intellectual discipline.

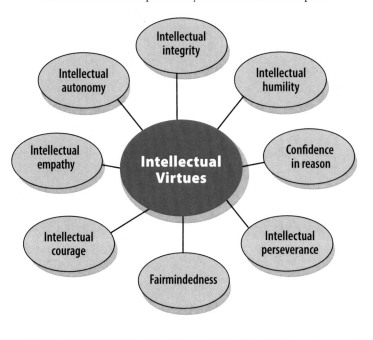

INTELLECTUAL VICES

Intellectual vices are the opposites of intellectual virtues. They occur naturally in the mind and are countered by deliberately cultivating intellectual virtues. Here are some primary intellectual vices:

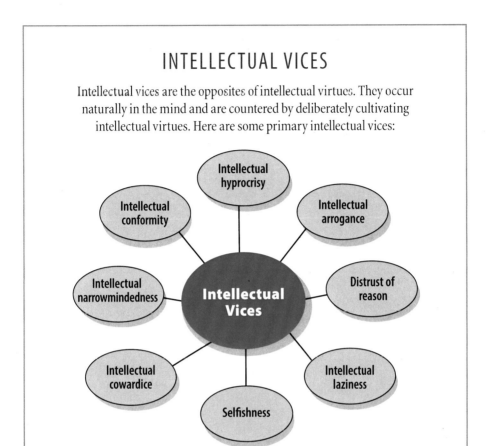

INTELLECTUAL VICES CAUSE MENTAL SUFFERING

When you actively strive toward intellectual virtues, you enjoy an explicit pathway toward a life in which it is possible to achieve peace and contentment while realizing your unique potential as an individual (even within our human-induced pathological world). Whatever your background, whatever your past, developing these characteristics of mind is a central part of your development toward mental and emotional well-being. And for all of homo sapiens, far greater movement toward these intellectual virtues is essential to our development as a species. By actively working to embody intellectual virtues, you develop mental pathways for countering your specific irrational tendencies and achieving your capacities.

Yet remember that *striving* toward intellectual virtues is all any of us can do. It is impossible to embody intellectual virtues at every moment, even under the best of conditions and in the most enriching situations. In other words, intellectual virtues are achieved and embodied only imperfectly, never fully and completely. In addition to the fact that all humans are given to making honest mistakes, all of us have egocentric and sociocentric tendencies that stand as barriers to our personal development and to our achievements (yes, this applies even to the most brilliant achievers). And you will recall that these irrational tendencies always have a strong unconscious dimension. For example, when you are being narrowminded, you likely see yourself as being reasonable. Therefore, a big part of your challenge is to bring your unreasonable thinking to the surface. By doing so you can then examine what is keeping you from embodying intellectual virtues.

When, instead of intellectual virtues, you personify their opposites—intellectual vices or character deficits—you are unable to achieve your potential. Further, these vices probably cause you and/or others in your life much mental suffering. Again, every person succumbs to intellectual vices to some degree—how frequently and to what degree you do so will depend upon you.

Let us consider some of the primary intellectual vices—those that oppose the intellectual virtues introduced earlier in this chapter. In each section below, you will find several questions designed to help you contemplate how frequently you employ a given intellectual vice. It is vital that you be honest in answering these questions. (Note that these questions dovetail with the intellectual virtues questions in the previous section.) When doing so, consider two important overarching questions in each case: *How does my behavior, which demonstrates that I use this intellectual vice, affect my mental well-being, including my opinion of myself? How does this intellectual vice keep me from achieving my potential?* If you struggle with this, a useful inroad may be to start with these questions: "What advice would I give other people who regularly exhibited this character defect? What would I tell them about their behavior? What would be clear to me if I noticed another person engaging in this vice, but would be hidden from me if I were engaging in it?"

Intellectual Narrowmindedness (Opposite of Intellectual Empathy)

Consider people who, instead of being able to understand and empathize with other people's situations and feelings, are chiefly stuck in their own point of view (displaying *narrowmindedness*). They are unwilling to consider any reasoning except their own. They are unable to enter other viewpoints and learn from them. They are unable to read and gain deep and transformative ideas from literature worthy of their attention. They are unaware even of what literature is worthy of their attention. Their mental space is highly constricted; they see everything according to their limited vision. They are therefore unable to actively internalize ideas beyond, or contrary to, those they already harbor, cherish, and protect. They feel secure in their beliefs, though they have rarely (if ever) honestly and objectively examined these beliefs.

It should be easy to see how intellectual narrowmindedness leads to mental suffering. When the world does not behave according to your prearranged way of thinking, how do you react? Do you open your mind to the possibility that you may be wrong? When a reasonable colleague, friend, or partner points out a problem in your thinking to help you improve, how do you react? Are you able to immediately consider the possibility that you may be wrong, or do you resist undertaking such consideration? Can you think of occasions where you accepted that you may be wrong, and where this resulted in improved mental wellness? Can you think of other occasions where you missed opportunities for greater contentment because your ego prevented the reasonable consideration of what others were saying? Do you employ defense mechanisms such as projection—for example, by accusing another person of being narrowminded when it is actually you who is entrenched in narrow beliefs, or diverting from the issue, or engaging in any number of other mechanisms to avoid changing your thinking? Do you lose control of your emotional state by shouting, stomping off, throwing things, putting your fist through walls, hitting people, or kicking innocent creatures? How far out of control do you allow yourself to go when your narrow views are crossed? What are the limits of your irrationality when others disagree with you? Do you humiliate others? Do you allow yourself to harm people emotionally or even physically when they don't agree with you?

Intellectual Arrogance (Opposite of Intellectual Humility)

When people are unable to accurately distinguish what they know from what they do not know, yet at the same time perceive themselves to be correct in all their beliefs, they are engaging in intellectual arrogance. This is, along with the other intellectual vices, a significant problem in human life. All people, at times, believe themselves to know more than they do know in a given situation; even experts make this mistake. The danger in this can be seen in such drastic cases as people being killed while engaging in extreme sports when they were fully confident they could safely handle the extreme conditions.

It is very easy to be overly confident in your beliefs, especially when you are unaware of the ever-present possibility that you may be wrong, and when you live in a culture that encourages false bravado and the constant pretense that you know more than you do know. The problem of intellectual arrogance connects with intellectual hypocrisy (see below). Think of typical job interview advice in which people are advised never to reveal their weaknesses, and to instead not only discuss their strengths but embellish the truth in doing so. Look at how far some individuals go in the professional world or politics by misrepresenting their knowledge and abilities—not only to others, but to themselves. People may get away with these prevarications for years without getting caught. Or they may not. Either way, living a life of dishonestly can only lead to sham mental health, never authentic mental health.

Do you know the limits of your knowledge? In each context or situation, can you clearly delineate what you do know from what you do not know? What do you really know about your spouse? What do you really know about your children? What do you really know about the subjects you studied in school? What do you really know about climate change? What do you really know about how much pollution is in the waterways in your country? What do you really know about how to raise children in a complex world? How truly aware are you of the many varied influences on your mental health, and of how each one affects your thinking, emotions, and behavior? If you are a therapist, what do you really know about the human mind? If you are a medical doctor, what are the limits of your knowledge within your medical specialty or field? Do you see how in any situation you can ask these questions: "What do I know right now for certain? What do I think is true, but may not be true? What do I need to question about my prior beliefs in this context?"

Intellectual Hypocrisy (Opposite of Intellectual Integrity)

When people assert a set of beliefs, but behave in ways contrary to their words, they lack intellectual integrity. Their words cannot be trusted, and therefore, they themselves cannot be trusted. Instead of being persons of integrity, they embody *intellectual hypocrisy.* This may be found in the form of lying to others and/or to oneself. Or it may take the form of expecting more of others than you expect of yourself.

If you grew up in a family or culture that encourages lying, you may have developed the habit of lying early in your life. If so, you will likely face great challenges in overcoming this habit. You will need to first become committed to living a life of truthfulness. You will then need to be vigilant in detecting situations in which you are dishonest with yourself or others.

Are you being completely honest in your relationships? Are you hiding behind lies? Would people say of you that you are a person of integrity? What pain and suffering are caused by your dishonesties with yourself and/or others? Have you developed habits of lying? How deeply engrained are these habits? When did they begin, and why? Why do you maintain them now? Did past circumstances (such as an abusive environment in childhood) encourage lying as a defensive habit? If so, do your present circumstances also incentivize self-protective dishonesty? If they do, can you change your situation so you can live more honestly? Do you treat others the way you want to be treated, or do you expect others to treat you better than you treat them? If everyone acted the way you do towards others, what would the world be like?

Intellectual Cowardice (Opposite of Intellectual Courage)

When people are unwilling to examine their beliefs, they lack intellectual courage and are instead employing *intellectual cowardice*. This keeps them from seeing their irrational or otherwise unwarranted beliefs. Most people can rarely, if ever, bring themselves to rationally assess the ideas they have accumulated through life—ideas from their childhood, from the groups they have belonged to, from broader society, etc. They fear having to admit that they have been wrong, perhaps for many years or even decades. They are more comfortable holding onto inaccurate, frequently harmful beliefs than they are in honestly examining those beliefs, and therefore facing the strong possibility that they have been wrong in the past. Ironically, this feeds into their own sense of inadequacy—the very feelings which they attempt to avoid by not examining and assessing their beliefs.

Another aspect of intellectual cowardice is an unwillingness to present ideas to others for fear of rejection. This does not apply to situations where it is genuinely unsafe to present one's ideas; rather, it happens when people are insecure in their beliefs, and therefore are unable or unwilling to discuss them publicly, or even privately. They cannot abide the possibility that someone might contradict them, ask them to further explain their thoughts, or request examples of the reasoning in question.

What beliefs are you afraid of examining? What keeps you from honestly doing so? What precisely are you afraid of as you consider exploring and questioning any part of your beliefs? If you scrutinize your marriage, might you see something you would prefer not to see? If you examine your parenting patterns and habits, will you see something about your parenting that upsets you? If you ponder your career path, what might you have to face? If you review what you said in the last argument you had with someone, what might you discover about yourself that you need to face, and change? What pain and suffering do you experience because you are unwilling to examine some beliefs you have been harboring? What pain and suffering do you cause others because you are unwilling to reconsider your beliefs? Why have you determined that refusing to reflect on your beliefs is worth these harms done to yourself and others? What about the current version of yourself is so beneficial that it outweighs the damage you are doing to yourself? Can you think of times when, despite your fears and concerns, you nevertheless spoke up about your views, and positive consequences resulted from your courage? What stops you from doing this? Is it fear of rejection? Is it fear you may have to face you are wrong? Is it the need to always be right in every situation?

Intellectual Conformity (Opposite of Intellectual Autonomy)

Are you always in search of someone to tell you how wonderful and great you are? Do you need acceptance from others to feel that you are a worthy person? Of course, it is natural to have connection and, in some cases, intimacy, with other people. But how do you go about finding healthy ways of finding connection and intimacy? This is one of the most significant questions we personally face as humans. One way of doing this is to proactively seek groups that are pursuing rational and uplifting purposes.

When people are unwilling to stand alone in their beliefs and are instead in constant need of validation from one person or another, they lack intellectual autonomy and instead rely on *intellectual conformity* to get by. This means they cannot find meaning and purpose in charting their own paths, because they have always relied on others. They have not developed the character traits required to make their own decisions and cultivate their own ideas. They waste precious time and energy seeking validation from others, so they have little time left to determine and build their own dreams and accomplishments. They may spend tremendous amounts of time in front of the TV, on social media, playing videogames, on the telephone, or chatting. Through social media, they may become involved in the drama and dishonesty prevailing there. They may become obsessed with playing video games with others doing the same. They may frequent gaming sites while losing reems of money. They may set up their mobile phones so they are constantly bombarded with messages from everywhere and sundry to feel part of a group.

Some of this behavior is merely a waste of precious time. But some conformity can be extremely harmful. Do you drop into dark and dangerous websites where people are propagating and conforming to noxious, destructive ideas? It is easy for naïve thinkers to be carried along by bizarre or perilous ideologies when they perceive they are part of a group that will accept them. Do you fall prey to any of these practices? If so, what will you do to extricate yourself from these harmful behavior patterns?

Do you conform to others' ideas and behaviors to be accepted? Are you always in search of someone to validate you? Do you conform to others' ideas and behaviors to be accepted? Do you conform to family members' thinking and habits, although you detect problems in the ways they live? Are you afraid to stand up to one or more of your family members? If so, precisely why?

Does someone threaten your physical or emotional well-being? If you have good reason to be fearful, you are advised to take immediate steps to protect yourself. You should conform to another person's irrational demands only long enough to protect yourself and get out of the situation, never in a prolonged, habitual self-induced way. Your intellectual conformity may have kept you mired in a toxic living or work situation to this point, but your fear today may be justifiable if you are subject to people who may harm you. If you are threatened by your minor children, who have gained emotional or physical power over you, you may need to take immediate steps to protect yourself from them—for instance, finding a new living situation for them.

Do you hang out with people who do not have your best interest at heart, just so you can feel accepted by them? Do you keep quiet when you disagree so as not be ostracized from a group? Have you decided that conformity is the best way to survive? What experiences led to this decision, and how did you interpret these experiences to arrive at your beliefs about conformity? Were those interpretations reasonable, or can you see flaws in them? Even if they were reasonable within a specific context (for example, when trying to avoid unreasonable consequences for non-conformity in childhood), do you see that you can now largely control the contexts of your life? How can you develop greater intellectual autonomy by taking command of these contexts? What else must you do to break out of your conformist habits? How would developing intellectual autonomy improve your emotional life? If you persist with the same degree of intellectual conformity as you have to this point, what important negative consequences will continue? How might these consequences lead to further negative consequences? How can you intervene in your intellectual conformity to free yourself from craving the false security blanket of acceptance?

Selfishness (Opposite of Fairmindedness)

When people do not value fairminded thinking, they are, in essence, selfish people. They seek primarily to get what they want without fully and in good faith considering the rights and needs of others. They see their wants, desires, and urges as above all else in importance. They may do some things for others, or appear to do so, but only to get something for themselves. They may be dominating, submissive, or otherwise manipulative to get what they want.

All humans are selfish to some degree. All of us sometimes value our desires over the rights and needs of others. This includes not checking to see how we may be violating someone else's rights while pursuing our goals. If you purchase a shirt made in a sweatshop, without questioning how and under what conditions it was produced, you exemplify the point. You may excuse yourself with rationalizations such as: "I can't think through every little decision I make and how it might affect someone else. I can't help it if some people live in poverty and must work in sweatshops. Look, if people like me didn't buy their shirts, they wouldn't have a job and then where would they be? At least this way they can eat. So, when you look at it this way, people who work in sweat shops are lucky."

As we see from this example, our selfishness may cause distress to others. But it also impacts our own well-being, even when our selfishness seems to get us what we want in the short term. Selfish people tend to be so wrapped up in their own egos that they have little or no concern for the well-being of those around them. Other people frequently notice this and decide to avoid such selfish people. Children raised by fundamentally selfish parents frequently turn their backs on their parents in adulthood to avoid being further subjected to their selfishness. On the other hand, children who are intentionally taught to be selfish, or who otherwise indulge their selfishness, often become some of the worst human specimens, as they inflict their selfishness onto others both in childhood and throughout adulthood. Selfish supervisors may "successfully" dominate their employees at work while finding themselves ostracized from after work employee-get-togethers.

To what degree are you a selfish person? In what specific ways do you tend to be selfish, and in what contexts? Do you pretend to be a fairminded person at the office, while your true selfish nature is evidenced when you are at home with your family? Can you readily see selfishness in other people while failing to see it in yourself? Do you think you are "getting away" with selfish behavior, or do you think other people can see it? For every person who has directly pointed out your selfish acts, how many may have noticed and simply refrained from confronting you? How might this have affected their behavior towards, around, and regarding you? How might such people be undermining you without your knowledge, and how might this be affecting your life in ways that outweigh whatever benefits your selfishness has achieved? Do you know people who are fairminded? How do they behave, in comparison with the way you behave? If selfishness is a problem for you, how can you begin to transform yourself into someone who cares about the welfare of others as well as your own welfare? As you work to develop fairmindedness, what steps can you can take to improve relationships that have been damaged by your selfishness?

To what degree are others in your life selfish? Who are these people and how are they selfish? How do you allow their selfishness to affect you? Do you feel depressed when you are around these people? Do you feel taken advantage of? Do you engage in greater selfishness when people around you are selfish? Do you rationalize your own selfishness as a self-defense against another person's selfishness? Do you need to get away from a selfish person in your life?

Again, if you tend toward selfishness, can you see how working toward fairmindedness and away from selfishness will improve your sense of self-worth and emotional wellness? Can you see how removing yourself from the influence of selfish people can you improve your well-being?

Distrust in Reason (Opposite of Confidence in Reason)

When people are unwilling to follow evidence and fully consider the facts in a situation, and when they do not want to understand what makes sense to believe and do in a given situation given the facts, they embody *distrust in reason* rather than confidence in reason. These persons value their own opinions or those of their group above the truth and above conclusions reached through high-quality reasoning. They do this however wrong their thinking might be, and whatever negative consequences may emerge from their willful ignorance.

People who harbor mob mentality, for example, distrust facts and logical reasoning—except where such facts and reasoning happen to align with their own views, in which cases their acceptance of reality is based not on demonstrable accuracy, but on validating their egos, emotions, and the groups to which they belong. Such individuals frequently whip up public emotions by distorting information and mislabeling falsehoods as "facts." But facts are not determined by human minds; they are determined by the questions at issue embedded in situations and realities. These facts must be examined objectively as they relate to the questions at issue. When people are motivated to believe whatever they or their friends want to believe, if they feel self-righteous in their beliefs, and if they come to believe ideas that are dangerous, this is likely to lead to harmful actions.

People who value ego-validation, group-validation, or emotional validation above rationality may or may not realize they are advancing irrational lines of reasoning; to the extent that they are aware, they seek ways to rationalize the shortcomings in their thinking. Again, this reasoning is at the unconscious level, at least to some degree.

Are you willing to follow facts and sound reasoning wherever they take you, or do you fear doing so? What will happen if you open your mind to truth and rational judgement instead of believing what you would prefer to believe? Can you tell the difference between a fact and misinformation parading as a fact? Do you know how to assess a line of reasoning by holding it to reasonable intellectual standards like clarity, logicalness, precision, depth, fairmindedness, and so forth (see the next chapter)? How do you go about figuring out the relevant and important facts in a situation, or analyzing and evaluating an idea or claim? Do you rely on others to figure this out for you and trust their answers, or do you verify the facts and assess the reasoning for yourself?

For instance, imagine that in a therapy situation, your therapist suggests a technique for simulated "rebirthing" (to deal with past emotional trauma). This technique involves rolling in a blanket tightly bound around your body, including your head, and you perceive that the process may cause you to suffocate. Do you go along with it because your therapist is to be implicitly trusted, or do you question the sanity of such a practice?

Or imagine that your therapist recommends that you and your partner or spouse use plastic bats to repeatedly hit each other in the "therapeutic" setting to release your frustrations. Do you question this technique as potentially harmful and unlikely to improve your relationship? Or do you relish whacking your partner with a bat in what it appears to be an authorized setting?

Often you can see that what people say, or suggest, is irrational because the facts and reasoned judgement would not support it. Do you trust yourself in these situations to question what is being suggested, or do you say, "Well, these people are authorities, so they are probably correct?"

Can you think of occasions where you voluntarily went along with something that didn't make sense to you, and the consequences were harmful to your mental well-being? How could you have handled these situations differently, in ways that might have improved your mental wellness? Do these past experiences suggest to you certain principles or other ideas that will help you act more reasonably when you next encounter similar circumstances?

Can you see how learning the tools of critical thinking are necessary to developing confidence in reason?

Intellectual Laziness (Opposite of Intellectual Perseverance)

When people are unwilling to persevere through difficulties in problems and they easily give up when faced with complexities in working through issues or projects, they exhibit *intellectual laziness*. Its opposite, intellectual perseverance, is required for working through problems as you develop your mind. The mind, being habitual by nature, is in some ways loath to change unless it values and develops the habit of self-reflection and self-discipline (or, egocentrically, if it needs to change to get what it selfishly wants).

Nothing is easier than giving up when faced with difficulties. Those who prevail in life are not those who lack any difficulties to work through, but those who persist through the difficulties they face. This is true because achieving anything of value entails enduring complexities that require the mind to alter its habits and develop new ones. This can only be done through deliberation, practice, and a willingness to work through confusions, perplexities, uncertainties, and frustrations with equanimity.

To become mentally well requires facing patterns of quitting in your thinking and life. You can never achieve your capacities if giving up is a common pattern for you. You can never have a healthy relationship if you cannot tolerate disagreement and reasonable critique. You will have great difficulty completing important projects if you collapse under the pressure typically entailed in them.

In terms of intellectual perseverance, some people are naturally proficient in one or more parts of their life, while failing miserably in others. For instance, a person may be an excellent mathematician at work, highly esteemed by his colleagues, even a Nobel prize winner, while at the same time experience great angst in dealing with complexities in family life. Working through mathematical complexities does not threaten the person, and/or the work happens to come easily to him, while in family life he is incompetent and family life itself feels threatening. This person may lash out at family members, or retreat inside himself and participate only partially in the family, when complexities arise. By constantly reminding himself of how smart and intelligent he is in his profession, he hides from his inability to persevere through familial difficulties. Therefore, he cannot be an integral member of his family. Such a person excels professionally but fails as a family member.

Do you easily give up at the first sign of difficulties in reasoning through a complicated situation or question? Can you think of a time in your life when you worked through a difficult issue or situation, even though you felt frustrated during the process? Have you ever experienced positive feelings of achievement, relief, and pride in your efforts? If so, when precisely?

How do you perceive difficulties when you face them? Do you see yourself as incapable of working through them? Do you tell yourself that if you wanted to work through these complexities, you could certainly do so, but since you don't want to, you'll just give up instead (and maybe do it later)? Do you tell yourself that when you get around to it you will certainly accomplish something great? Do you present yourself as brilliant? What evidence do you have to support this claim, if so? What have you in fact accomplished? What can you do to accomplish what you know you're capable of accomplishing? How will you take the first steps that you have been avoiding? How will you face the truth about yourself when it comes to intellectual perseverance?

Have you ever achieved something of importance by taking one step at a time toward a set goal? Would you rather give up easily than accomplish something of importance in your life? Do you expect others to carry all the weight in developing ideas and solutions needed to improve life on earth, while you sit back and say you are not capable of doing much to help (or that nothing can be done so there's no point)? If so, how does this affect the way you see and feel about yourself? What benefits do you perceive in avoiding or abandoning intellectual struggle? And do these benefits truly amount to greater feelings of emotional wellness than those found in even modest day-to-day achievement?

INTERNALIZE THE IDEA: AVOID INTELLECTUAL VICES, THE OPPOSITES OF INTELLECTUAL VIRTUES

For each of the intellectual vices discussed above, complete these statements:

1. I would define this bad habit of mind as follows . . .
2. In other words . . .
3. Some examples of when I have behaved in accordance with this intellectual vice include . . .
4. Behaving in this way has been a problem for me or others in my life because . . .
5. After working through this activity, I now understand . . .
6. To avoid this intellectual vice moving forward, I intend to . . .

INTELLECTUAL VIRTUES ARE ESSENTIAL TO YOUR MENTAL HEALTH

It should now be clear that your mental health depends on your ability to embrace and embody intellectual virtues that will give you the ability and strength to:

- follow the facts and good reasoning wherever they lead you, including when it means having to change something about yourself;
- face the limits of your knowledge in any given situation, distinguishing your knowledge from what you simply "feel" is true;
- examine the beliefs that are causing your mental health problems, and change those that are inaccurate or illogical;
- persevere through any difficulties you face, across all important parts of your life;
- actively enter points of view that differ from your own in good faith, rather than fearing them as threats;,
- openly state your examined views when it is safe and productive to so;
- avoid group conformity so that you can stand alone in your studied beliefs against mob thinking;

- say what you mean and mean what you say, rather than saying one thing and behaving contrary to what you are saying (in other words, hiding the truth or lying);
- think in a fairminded way about all ethical issues.

It should now be more obvious to you how your own intellectual vices may be root causes of your mental suffering. Only you can determine the extent to which this is true.

INTELLECTUAL VIRTUES ARE REQUIRED FOR SELF-ACTUALIZATION

The concept of self-actualization is rarely used today, but it is a concept worth considering if you are to take command of your mind and achieve the highest level of self-fulfillment. Self-actualization and intellectual virtues go hand in hand. In the 1940s, Abraham Maslow conducted a private study of individuals (personal acquaintances and friends, public and historical figures) as well as one college student who fit his developing criteria. In 1956, Maslow detailed his conception, saying,

> It [self-actualization] may be loosely described as the full use and the exploitation of talents, capacities, potentialities, etc. Such people seem to be fulfilling themselves and to be doing the best that they are capable of doing… all subjects felt safe and unanxious, accepted, loved and loving, respectworthy and respected…. (pp. 161-162)

From his studies, Maslow suggests that self-actualizing people embody the following characteristics:

- "… an unusual ability to detect the spurious, the fake, and the dishonest in personality and, in general, to judge people correctly and efficiently." (p. 165)
- "In art and music, in things of the intellect, in scientific matters, in politics and public affairs, they seemed as a group to be able to see concealed or confused realities more swiftly and more correctly than others." (p. 165)
- "A superior ability to reason, to perceive the truth, to come to logical conclusions and to be cognitively efficient, in general." (p. 166)
- "… distinguish far more easily than most the fresh, concrete, and idiosyncratic from the generic, abstract, and 'rubricized.' The consequence is that they live more in the real world of nature than in the man–made set of concepts, expectations, beliefs, and stereotypes which most people confuse with the real world." (p. 167)
- "They are therefore more apt to perceive what is 'there' rather than their own wishes, hopes, fears, anxieties, their own theories and beliefs, or those of their culture or group." (p. 166)

- "… are uniformly unthreatened and unfrightened by the unknown, being therein quite different from average men. They accept it, are comfortable with it, and, often are even more attracted by it than by the known… they can tolerate the ambiguous." (p. 167)

- "Since for healthy people the unknown is not frightening, they do not have to spend any time laying the ghost, whistling past the cemetery, or otherwise protecting themselves against imagined dangers." (p. 167)

- "They do not neglect the unknown, or deny it, or run away from it, or try to make believe it is really known… they do not cling to the familiar, nor is their quest for truth a catastrophic need for certainty, safety, definiteness, and order… they can be, when the objective total situation calls for it, comfortable disorderly, anarchic, chaotic, vague, doubtful, uncertain, ambiguous, indefinite, proximate, inexact, or inaccurate (all, at certain moments in science, art, or life in general, quite desirable)." (p. 167)

- "… find it possible to accept themselves and their own nature." (p. 168)

- "… tend to be good and lusty animals, hearty in their appetites and enjoying themselves mightily without regret or shame or apology." (p. 169)

- "Closely related to self-acceptance and to acceptance of others is (a) their lack of defensiveness, protective coloration, or pose (b) and their distaste for such artificiality in others. Cant, guile, hypocrisy, 'front,' 'face,' playing a game, trying to impress in conventional ways: these are all absent in themselves to an unusual degree." (p. 169)

- "… what healthy people do feel guilty about (or ashamed, anxious, sad, or defensive) are (a) improvable shortcomings, e.g., laziness, thoughtlessness, loss of temper, hurting others; (b) stubborn remnants of psychological ill health, e.g., prejudice, jealousy, envy; (c) habit, which though relatively independent of character structure, may yet be very strong, or (d) shortcomings of the species or of the culture or of the group with which they have identified. The general formula seems to be that healthy people will feel bad about discrepancies between what is and what might very well be or ought to be." (p. 170)

- "… his unconventionality is not superficial but essential or internal. It is his impulses, thought, consciousness that are so unusually unconventional, spontaneous, and natural. Apparently recognizing that the world of people in which he lives could not understand or accept this, and since he has no wish to hurt them or to fight with them over every triviality, he will go through the ceremonies and rituals of convention with a good-humored shrug and with the best possible grace." (p. 170)

- "The self-actualizing person practically never allows convention to hamper him or inhibit him from doing anything that he considers very important or basic." (p. 171)

- "… these people have codes of ethics which are relatively autonomous and individual rather than conventional. The unthinking observer might sometimes believe them to be 'unethical' since they can break not only conventions but laws when the situation seems to demand it. But the very opposite is the case. They are the most ethical of people even though their ethics are not necessarily the same as those of the people around them." (p. 171)

- "Their ease of penetration to reality, their closer approach to an animallike or childlike acceptance and spontaneity imply a superior awareness of their own impulses, desires, opinions, and subjective reactions in general. Clinical study of this capacity confirms beyond a doubt the opinion, e.g., of Fromm, that the average 'normal,' 'well-adjusted," person often hasn't even the slightest idea what he is, what he wants, what is own opinions are." (p. 172)

- "… are in general strongly focused on problems outside themselves. In current terminology they are problem-centered rather than ego-centered. They generally are not problems for themselves and are not generally much concerned about themselves; i.c. as contrasted with the ordinary introspectiveness that one finds in insecure people. These individuals customarily have some vision in life, some task to fulfill, some problem outside of themselves which enlists much of their energies… these tasks are nonpersonal or 'unselfish,' concerned rather with the good of mankind in general, or of a nation in general, or of a few individuals in the subject's family." (pp. 173-174)

- "Our subjects are ordinarily concerned with basic issues and eternal questions of the type that we have learned to call by the names philosophical or ethical. Such people live customarily in the widest possible frame of reference. They work within a framework of values which are broad and not petty, universal and not local, and in terms of the century rather than the moment…[They are] above small things, [They have] a larger horizon, a wider breadth of vision." (p. 174)

- "They seem to be able to retain their dignity even in undignified surroundings and situations. Perhaps this comes in part from their tendency to stick by their own interpretation of the situation rather than to rely upon what other people feel or think about the matter." (p. 175)

- "Self-actualizing people have deeper and more profound interpersonal relations than any other adults… Their circle of friends is rather small… Partly this is for the reason that being very close to someone in the self-actualizing style seems to require a good deal of time." (p. 180)

- "[Their] 'love' does not imply lack of discrimination. The fact is that they can speak realistically and harshly of those who deserve it, and especially of the hypocritical, pretentious, the pompous, or the self-inflated. But the face-to-face relationship even with these people does not show signs of realistically low evaluations." (p. 181)
- "… they find it possible to learn from anybody who has something to teach them – No matter what other characteristics he may have." (p. 182)
- "… these individuals are strongly ethical, they have definite moral standards, they do right and they do not do wrong. Needless to say, their notions of right and wrong are often not the conventional ones." (p. 183)

Maslow goes on to say, "The neurotic is not only emotionally sick, he is cognitively wrong (p. 166)." What is clear from this list of characteristics of the self-actualized person is its relationship with characteristics of the fairminded critical thinker. This will be made more clear as the explicit tools of critical thinking are further revealed in this and subsequent chapters.

INTERNALIZE THE IDEA: TO WHAT DEGREE ARE YOU SELF-ACTUALIZED?

Reread Maslow's list on the previous pages, which details some of the characteristics of the self-actualized person. Complete the following statements:

1. After reading the bullet points detailing the characteristics of people who are self-actualized, I would say that I am/am not self-actualized.
2. I believe this because is…
3. One thing I can do to move closer to being self-actualized is…
4. A second thing I can do to move closer to being self-actualized is…
5. A third thing I can do to move closer to being self-actualized is…
6. Based on this analysis, I intend to make the following changes in my thinking…

INTERNALIZE THE IDEA: TO WHAT DEGREE ARE YOU SELF-ACTUALIZED? — GO DEEPER...

Go through each point again from Maslow's list and for each bullet point, complete these statements:

1. I would state this point using my own words in the following way...
2. I do/do not typically embody this characteristic in my daily life [give examples].
3. I can more frequently embody this characteristic by doing the following...
4. Therefore, I intend to...

INTERNALIZE THE IDEA: CONSIDER THE RELATIONSHIPS BETWEEN SELF-ACTUALIZATION AND INTELLECTUAL VIRTUES

Read through each point again from Maslow's self-actualization list and write out connections you see between these points and the intellectual virtues described in this chapter.

CHAPTER SIX
USE SOUND CRITERIA TO DECIDE WHAT TO BELIEVE

Humans live in a world of thoughts. We accept some thoughts as true. We reject others as false. But the thoughts we perceive as true are sometimes false, unsound, or misleading. And the thoughts we perceive as false and trivial are sometimes true and significant.

The mind doesn't instinctively grasp the truth. We humans don't naturally see things as they are. We don't automatically sense what is reasonable and what is unreasonable. Our thought is often biased by our agendas, interests, and values. We typically see things as we want to. We twist reality to fit our preconceived ideas. Distorting reality is common in human life. It is a phenomenon to which we all unfortunately fall prey.

Each of us views the world through multiple lenses, often shifting them to fit our changing feelings. In addition, much of our perspective is unconscious and uncritical and has been influenced by many forces —including social, political, economic, biological, psychological, and religious influences. Social rules and taboos, religious and political ideologies, biological and psychological impulses, all play a role, often unconscious, in human thinking. Selfishness, vested interest and parochialism are deeply influential in the cognitive and emotional lives of most people.

To improve the quality of your life, you need a system for intellectual intervention, a method for pre-empting bad thinking. You need to take rational command of your cognitive processes to reasonably determine what to accept and what to reject. In short, you need standards for thought, standards that guide you to consistently excellent thinking—standards you can count on to keep your thinking on track, to help you mirror in your mind what is happening in reality, to reveal the truth in situations, to enable you to determine how best to live your life.

In other words, to live reasonably, you need to construct your thinking so as to be clear, precise, accurate, relevant, significant, logical, deep, broad, fair, sufficient and so forth. You also need to clarify the thinking of others, to check for accuracy, logic, significance and so on. Routine use of these intellectual standards is essential to thinking well within every domain of human life.

Your fundamental objective in this chapter is to begin to internalize intellectual standards in order to improve your thinking across the complexities of your life. Without explicit standards for thinking, the quality of your reasoning and your actions is left to chance, intuition, or some other automatic mode of functioning.

By way of introduction, we will begin with a core group of essential intellectual standards. We will also refer to these as critical thinking standards, and will use the two terms interchangebly.

SOME ESSENTIAL CRITICAL THINKING STANDARDS

We postulate that there are at least ten intellectual standards important to reasoning well and living an emotionally healthy life. These are, again, clarity, precision, accuracy, relevance, depth, breadth, logicalness, significance, sufficiency, and fairness. The importance of these standards is given in the need to avoid their opposites. In other words, it stands to reason that you will experience significant problems in your life if your thinking is routinely unclear, inaccurate, imprecise, irrelevant, narrow, superficial, illogical, trivial, insufficient, and unfair. These standards come from a much broader list of standards that are used by skilled reasoners.

TO EVALUATE THINKING WE MUST UNDERSTAND AND APPLY CRITICAL THINKING STANDARDS

Reasonable people judge reasoning by intellectual standards. When you internalize these standards and explicitly use them in your thinking, your thinking becomes more clear, more accurate, more precise, more relevant, deeper, broader and more fair. Again the focus here is on a selection of standards. Among others are credibility, sufficiency, reliability, and practicality. Some primary questions that employ these standards are listed on the following page.

Clarity:
understandable; the meaning can be grasped

Accuracy:
free from errors or distortions; true

Precision:
exact to the necessary level of detail

Relevance:
relating to the matter at hand

Depth:
containing complexities and multiple interrelationships

Breadth:
encompassing multiple viewpoints

Logic:
the parts make sense together; lacking contradictions

Significance:
focusing on the important; not trivial

Fairness:
ethically justifiable; not self-serving or one-sided

Sufficiency:
all relevant information and viewpoints have been fully considered; all parts of the question have been adequately reasoned through.

SOME ESSENTIAL CRITICAL THINKING STANDARDS AND QUESTIONS RELATING TO EACH

Clarity
Could you elaborate further? Could you give me an example? Could you illustrate what you mean?

Accuracy
How can I check on that? How can I find out if that is true? How can I test or verify what this person is saying?

Precision
Could you be more specific? What other details are needed? Could you be more exact?

Relevance
How does this information help me solve my problem? How does this statement bear on the question? How does that help me with the issue?

Depth
What factors make this a difficult problem? What are some of the complexities in this question? What are some of the difficulties I need to deal with?

Breadth
Do I need to look at this from another perspective? What other viewpoints do I need to consider? What other potential ways are there to look at this?

Logic
Does all of what she has said make sense together? Does my lifestyle make sense given the realities I face? Does what he is saying follow from the evidence?

Significance
Is this the most important problem to consider? What is the central idea I should be focused on? Is something else more important? Which of these facts are most important?

Fairness
Am I being fair in this situation, or am I distorting something to fit my desires? Am I being selfish? How am I sympathetically representing the viewpoints of others?

Sufficiency
Do I have sufficient information to answer the question? Am I unfairly leaving out information I would rather not consider in order to get more for myself while ignoring or downplaying the rights and needs of others?

WHERE DO CRITICAL THINKING STANDARDS COME FROM?

Critical thinking standards ultimately derive from the nature of thought itself and what we characteristically need thinking to do. Failure to internalize and regularly use these standards frequently leads to irrational thoughts, which can result in mental health issues. For instance, failing to focus on what is significant in human life can lead you to a life of superficiality such as performing for others and constantly needing other's approval instead of cultivating your unique capacities. Failing to be logical or failing to thinking fairly in your relationships may lead to your failing in those relationships.

- Thus, the intellectual standard of clarity derives from the fact that we want or need to communicate a certain meaning to others, and unclear language undermines or defeats that purpose.

- The intellectual standard of accuracy derives from the fact that we are trying to understand or communicate things as they actually are, without any distortions. Inaccurate thought defeats that purpose.

- The intellectual standard of precision derives from the fact that we often need details and specifics to accomplish our purpose. Imprecision, or the failure to provide details and specifics, undermines that purpose.

- The intellectual standard of relevance derives from the fact that some information—however true it might be—does not bear upon a question to which we need an answer. Irrelevant information, thrust into the thinking process, diverts us from the information and viewpoints pertinent to answering the question at hand.

- The intellectual standard of depth derives from the fact that some issues involve complexities, and thinking that ignores these complexities is necessarily inadequate.

- The intellectual standard of breadth derives from the fact that some issues can be dealt with only by reasoning within multiple points of view. Thinking that is one-sided when many-sidedness is called for cannot be adequate.

- The intellectual standard of logic derives from the fact that reasoning that is inconsistent and self-contradictory necessarily lacks intelligibility.

- The intellectual standard of fairness derives from the fact that humans commonly ignore relevant facts and insights when they are not in line with one's interest or agenda.

- The intellectual standard of sufficiency derives from the fact that it is possible to gather detailed and vast information that is relevant and accurate, but that is still not sufficient to answer the question at issue or solve the problem at hand.

To generalize, it would be unintelligible to say, "I want to reason well, but I am indifferent as to whether my reasoning is clear, precise, accurate, relevant, logical, consistent, or fair."

©2025 Linda Elder

CRITICAL THINKING STANDARDS HELP YOU THINK AND FEEL BETTER

The best thinkers don't believe any and everything they hear or read. They use intellectual standards to decide what to believe and to keep themselves mentally well. They use intellectual standards to keep their thinking on track. In this book, we focus on some of the important ones. When you use them every day, your thinking improves.

Be <u>clear</u>! —   Can you state what you mean?
                       Can you give examples?

Be <u>accurate</u>! —   Are you sure it's true?

Be <u>relevant</u>! —   Is it related to what we are thinking about?

Be <u>logical</u>! —   Does it all fit together?

Be <u>fair</u>! —   Am I considering how my behavior might
                       make others feel?

Be <u>reasonable</u>! — Have we thought through this problem
                       thoroughly and with an open mind?

If everyone in the world regularly used critical thinking standards, we could solve most of our big problems.

BE CLEAR: DON'T CONFUSE PEOPLE

You are confused when you are not clear.

You are clear when you understand:

- what you are saying
- what you are hearing
- what you are reading
- what you are seeing

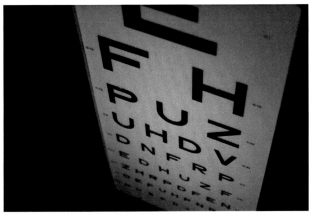

Ideas can be fuzzy or clear, like letters on an eye chart.

THINGS YOU CAN SAY AND QUESTIONS YOU CAN ASK WHEN YOU WANT TO BE CLEAR:

- Let me tell you what I mean. Let me give you an example.
- Could you tell me what you mean?
- Could you say that in other words?
- I'm confused. Could you explain what you mean?
- Let me tell you what I think you said. Tell me if I'm right.
- How can I clarify the goals I set for myself?

BE ACCURATE: MAKE SURE IT'S TRUE

Something is accurate when it is true or correct, when it is not distorted.

When you aren't sure whether something is true, check to see if it is.

When you need to be accurate you want to hit your bull's-eye exactly. You don't want your thinking to be distorted in any way.

QUESTIONS YOU CAN ASK TO MAKE SURE YOU ARE ACCURATE:

- How could we find out if this is really true?
- How can we check this?
- How can we test this idea to see if it is true?
- How do I know if what I am saying is true?
- How do I know that what I read on the internet is true?
- How do I know that the information in this book is true?
- How do I know that what my friends say is true?
- How can I find out for myself if "X" is true?
- What important truths do I want to live by?

BE RELEVANT: MAKE SURE YOU STAY ON TRACK

Something is relevant when it relates directly to:

- the problem you are trying to solve.
- the question you are trying to answer.
- whatever you are talking about or writing about.

All instruments in a cockpit are *relevant* to flying the airplane, but they are not relevant to riding a bicycle.

QUESTIONS YOU CAN ASK WHEN YOU ARE NOT SURE WHETHER SOMETHING IS RELEVANT:

- How does what you say help us solve this problem?
- How does this information relate to the question I need to focus on?
- What will help me solve this important problem which I have been to this point unable to solve?
- How does what you say relate to what we are talking about?
- Am I staying on track, or allowing my mind to wander to other, irrelevant things which keep me from achieving my goals?

BE LOGICAL:
MAKE SURE EVERYTHING FITS TOGETHER

Thinking is logical when everything fits together, when everything makes sense together.

QUESTIONS YOU CAN ASK WHEN YOU ARE NOT SURE WHETHER SOMETHING IS LOGICAL:

- This doesn't make sense to me. Can you show me how it all fits together?
- The way I am thinking about parenting is not logical since my children are not showing me respect. What do I need to change about my thinking in this situation?
- What you are saying doesn't sound logical. How did you come to your conclusions? Explain why this makes sense to you.
- The messages I am getting from this TV show don't seem sensible. Should I follow along with these ideas, or should I reject them?

BE FAIR: MAKE SURE YOU CONSIDER OTHERS

When you consider the rights and needs of others before you do something, you are being fair.

There are many problems in the world because people often aren't fair to others.

It is important to be fair, both to yourself and to others.

QUESTIONS YOU CAN ASK WHEN YOU ARE NOT SURE WHETHER YOU, OR SOMEONE ELSE, IS BEING FAIR:

- Am I being selfish right now?
- Am I allowing someone's selfish behavior to harm me? If so, how can I stop this harm to me?
- Am I considering the thinking of others?
- Am I considering the feelings of others?
- Do I need to get out of this relationship and seek another relationship in which I would be treated fairly?

CRITICAL THINKERS SEEK BETTER WAYS OF DOING THINGS

There's always a better way and I can find it.

I can figure out anything I need to figure out.

Critical Thinkers Believe in The Power of Their Minds

INTERNALIZE THE IDEA: LEARN TO CLARIFY THINKING

Our own thinking usually seems clear to us, even when it is not. Vague, ambiguous, muddled, deceptive, or misleading thinking are significant problems in human life. If you are to develop as a thinker, you must learn the art of clarifying your thinking—of pinning it down, spelling it out, and giving it a specific meaning. Here's what you can do to begin. When people explain things to you, summarize in your own words what you think they said. When you cannot do this to their satisfaction, you don't truly understand what they said. When they cannot summarize to your satisfaction what you have said, they don't truly understand what you said.

To improve your ability to clarify your thinking (in your own mind, when speaking to others, or when writing, for example), use this basic strategy:

• I think [state your main point]...

• In other words [elaborate on your main point]...

• For example [give an example of your main point]...

To clarify other people's thinking, ask any of the following questions:

• Can you restate your point in other words? I didn't understand you.

• Can you give an example?

• Let me tell you what I understand you to be saying. Do I understand you correctly?

As you begin to use these strategies, as basic as they seem, note how seldom others use them. Notice how often people assume that others understand them when what they have said is, in fact, unintelligible, muddy, or confusing. Note how, very often, the simple intellectual moves are the most powerful. (For example, saying to someone: "I don't understand what you are saying. Can you say that in other words?") Be aware that mentally healthy people openly and clearly communicate their views when possible. And they want to understand the views of others.

INTERNALIZE THE IDEA: IS THE THINKING RELEVANT?

When thinking is relevant, it is focused on the main task at hand. It selects what is germane, pertinent, and related. It is on the alert for everything that connects to the issue. It sets aside what is immaterial, inappropriate, extraneous, or beside the point. That which directly bears upon (helps solve) the problem you are trying to solve is relevant to the problem. When thinking drifts away from what is relevant, it needs to be brought back to what truly makes a difference. Undisciplined thinking is often guided by associations ("this reminds me of that, that reminds me of this other thing") rather than what is logically connected ("if he said this, he might also mean..."). Disciplined thinking intervenes when thoughts wander and it concentrates the mind on the things that help it figure out what it needs to figure out.

If you find your thinking digresses, try to figure out why. Is your mind simply wandering? If so, you probably need to intervene to get it back on track. Or, perhaps you realize that you need to deal with a different issue before addressing the one you were originally focused on. If so, by all means address the issue your mind has surfaced. But most importantly, know precisely, at any given moment, the issue you are addressing, and then stick to that issue until you have either reached resolution or made an active decision to revisit the issue later. Do not allow your mind to wander aimlessly from idea to idea, issue to issue, without direction or discipline.

Ask these questions regularly to make sure your thinking is focused on what is relevant:

• Am I focused on the main problem or task?

• How are these two issues connected, or are they?

• How is the problem raised intertwined with the issue at hand?

• Does the information I am considering directly relate to the problem or task?

• Where do I need to focus my attention?

• Am I being diverted to unrelated matters?

• Am I failing to consider relevant viewpoints?

• How is my point relevant to the issue I am addressing?

• What facts will actually help me answer the question? What considerations should be set aside?

• Does this truly bear on the question? How does it connect?

INTERNALIZE THE IDEA: BE REASONABLE

A hallmark of critical thinkers is the disposition to change their minds when given a good reason to do so. Good thinkers want to change their thinking when they discover better thinking. In other words, they can and want to be moved by reason. Yet, comparatively few people are reasonable in the full sense of the word. (Reasonability is another critical thinking standard.) Few are willing to change their minds once set. Few are willing to suspend their beliefs to hear the views of those with whom they disagree. This is true because the human mind is not always reasonable. Although we routinely come to conclusions, we don't necessarily do so reasonably. Yet we typically see our conclusions as reasonable. We then want to stick to our conclusions without regard for their justifiability or plausibility. To put it another way, and as you should already be learning, the mind is frequently rigid. People often shut out good reasons readily available to them and refuse to hear arguments that are perfectly reasonable (when those reasons contradict what they already believe).

To become more reasonable, open your mind to the possibility, at any given moment, that you might be wrong and another person might be right. Be willing to change your mind when the situation or evidence requires it. Recognize that you don't lose anything by admitting you are wrong; rather, you gain in overall sense of empowerment and mental well-being.

Strategies for becoming more reasonable:

• Notice how seldom people admit they are wrong. Notice, instead, how often they hide their mistakes. Many people would rather lie than admit to being wrong. Decide that you do not want to be such a person.

• Say aloud, "I'm not perfect. I make mistakes. I'm often wrong." See if you have the courage to admit this during a disagreement, "Of course, I may be wrong. You may be right."

• Practice saying in your own mind, "I may be wrong. I often am. I'm willing to change my mind when given good reasons." Then look for opportunities to make changes in your thinking.

• Ask yourself, "When was the last time I changed my mind because someone gave me better reasons for his or her views than I had for mine? To what extent am I open to new ways of looking at things? To what extent can I objectively judge information that refutes what I already think?"

Continued...

INTERNALIZE THE IDEA: BE REASONABLE: CONTINUED

• Realize you are being unreasonable if:

    a. You are unwilling to listen to someone's reasons.

    b. You are irritated by reasons people give you (before thinking them through).

    c. You become defensive during a discussion.

When you catch yourself being closedminded, analyze your thinking by completing the following statements in your journal (remember that the more details you write in your journal entries, the better able you should be to change your thinking in future similar situations):

a. I was being closedminded or narrowminded in this situation because...

b. The thinking I was trying to hold onto is...

c. Thinking that is potentially better is...

d. This thinking is better because...

INTERNALIZE THE IDEA: RECOGNIZING ILLOGICAL THINKING

Identify a situation at work where decisions made seemed to be based on illogical thinking—thinking that didn't make sense to you:

1. What was the situation?

2. What was the thinking in the situation that you consider to be illogical? Why do you think it was illogical?

3. What were some consequences that followed from the illogical thinking?

INTERNALIZE THE IDEA: FOCUSING ON SIGNIFICANCE IN THINKING

Think about your life in terms of the amount of time you spend on significant versus trivial things. As you do so, write the answers to these questions:

1. What is the most important goal or purpose you should focus on at this point in your life? Why is this purpose important? How much time do you spend focused on it?
2. What are the most trivial or superficial things you spend time focused on (things such as your appearance, impressing your friends or colleagues, spending money on things you don't need, chatting about insignificant things on social media or at parties, and the like)?
3. What can you do to reduce the amount of time you spend on the trivial and increase the amount of time you spend on the significant?

INTERNALIZE THE IDEA: ARE YOU ALWAYS FAIR?

Most of us want to see ourselves as imminently fair. Yet because we are by nature self-serving, we are not always able to consider the rights and needs of others in equivalent terms as we do our own. Indeed, one of the most difficult things for people to do is identify times when they are unfair. Yet highly skilled thinkers, aware of this human tendency, routinely search for problems in their thinking.

In the spirit of this idea, try to think of several times in the past few weeks when you were not fair. You are looking for situations where your behavior was selfish or self-serving and as a result, you negated another person's desires or rights. You placed your desires first. Remember that the more examples you can think of, the better. Also remember that, because of our native egocentrism, we are highly motivated to hide our unfair thoughts and behavior. Try not to fall into this trap. Also realize that some people are more naturally (or by conditioning) prone to selfishness. Where do you fall along the selfishness continuum?

PEOPLE OFTEN USE EGOCENTRIC STANDARDS FOR DETERMINING WHAT TO BELIEVE

Because people are largely egocentric, they often use egocentric standards to determine what to accept and what to reject. At the same time, they are unrealistically confident that they have fundamentally figured out *the way things actually are*, and that they have done so objectively. They naturally *believe* in their *intuitive perceptions*—however inaccurate. Here are the most commonly-used egocentric standards in human thinking:

"IT'S TRUE BECAUSE *I* BELIEVE IT." *Innate intellectual arrogance:* I assume that what I believe is true, even though I have never questioned the basis for many of my beliefs or carefully examined them.

"IT'S TRUE BECAUSE I *WANT* TO BELIEVE IT." *Innate wish fulfillment:* I believe what "feels good," what supports my other beliefs, what does not require me to change my thinking (or my life) in any significant way, and what does not require me to admit that I have been wrong. I believe in accounts of behavior that put me in a positive rather than a negative light, even though I have not seriously considered the evidence for more negative accounts.

"IT'S TRUE BECAUSE I *HAVE ALWAYS* BELIEVED IT." *Innate self-validation:* I have a strong desire to maintain beliefs I have long held, even though I have not seriously considered the extent to which those beliefs are justified, given the evidence.

"IT'S TRUE BECAUSE IT IS *IN MY SELFISH INTEREST* TO BELIEVE IT." *Innate selfishness:* I hold fast to beliefs that justify my getting more power, money, or personal advantage, even though these beliefs are not grounded in sound reasoning or evidence.

INTERNALIZE THE IDEA: IDENTIFY YOUR EGOCENTRIC THINKING

For each of the egocentric standards above which are commonly used by humans, write out examples from your own life in each category:

1. "IT'S TRUE BECAUSE I BELIEVE IT." Some examples from my own life of me using this standard are...

2. "IT'S TRUE BECAUSE I WANT TO BELIEVE IT." Some examples from my own life of me using this standard are...

3. "IT'S TRUE BECAUSE I HAVE ALWAYS BELIEVED IT." Some examples from my own life of me using this standard are...

4. "IT'S TRUE BECAUSE IT IS IN MY SELFISH INTEREST TO BELIEVE IT." Some examples from my own life of me using this standard are...

PEOPLE OFTEN USE SOCIOCENTRIC STANDARDS FOR DETERMINING WHAT TO BELIEVE

Just as humans use egocentric standards to determine what to believe (as you read on the previous page), they use sociocentric standards as well. Consider the following parallels between egocentric and sociocentric "standards" of thought. These pathological standards are routinely used in human life:

Egocentric standard: "It's true because I believe it."

Related sociocentric standard: "It's true because we believe it." *Innate group intellectual arrogance*: We assume our group beliefs to be true, even though we have never questioned the basis for many of them.

Egocentric standard: "It's true because I want to believe it."

Related sociocentric standard: "It's true because we want to believe it." *Innate group wish fulfillment*: We believe what "feels good" to our group, what supports our other beliefs, what does not require us to change our thinking in any significant way, and what does not require us to admit we have been wrong. We believe in, for example, accounts of behavior that put our group in a positive rather than a negative light, even though we have not seriously considered the evidence showing that our group may be wrong.

Egocentric standard: "It's true because I have always believed it."

Related sociocentric standard: "It's true because we have always believed it." *Innate group-validation*: We have a strong desire to maintain beliefs we have long held, even though we have not seriously considered the extent to which those beliefs are justified, given the evidence.

Egocentric standard: "It's true because it's in my selfish interest to believe it."

Related sociocentric standard: "It's true because it's in our vested interest to believe it." *Innate groupishness*: We hold fast to beliefs that justify our group getting more power, money, or personal advantage, even though these beliefs are not grounded in sound reasoning or evidence.

Given the four forms of sociocentric thought you read about on page 212, we can add these two sociocentric standards for thought:

"It's true because those of us in control say so." *Innate group control*: Those of us in control of the group expect group members to uncritically accept our beliefs and values. We controllers are the "dominators" in the group.

"It's true because our leaders have said so." *Innate group conformity*: Those of us who conform to the ideologies of the group as laid down by the dominators, and therefore uncritically accept group beliefs, norms, customs, and taboos. We are the "submitters" in the group who blindly follow authority figures.

All of these pathological standards naturally lie at the unconscious level of human thought. They illuminate some of the parallels that exist between egocentric and sociocentric thought, at least to some degree. Just as individuals deceive themselves through egocentric thinking, groups deceive themselves through sociocentric thinking. Just as egocentric thinking functions to serve one's selfish interest, sociocentric thinking functions to serve groupish interests. In the same way that egocentric thinking operates to validate the uncritical thinking of the individual, sociocentric thinking operates to validate the uncritical thinking of the group. All of these unhealthy ways of thinking can negatively affect your mental health.

IDENTIFY YOUR SOCIOCENTRIC USE OF STANDARDS

For each of the sociocentric standards above which are commonly used by humans, write out examples from your own life in each category:

1. "IT'S TRUE BECAUSE WE BELIEVE IT." Some examples from my own life of me using this standard are...

2. "IT'S TRUE BECAUSE WE WANT TO BELIEVE IT." Some examples from my own life of me using this standard are...

3. "IT'S TRUE BECAUSE WE HAVE ALWAYS BELIEVED IT." Some examples from my own life of me using this standard are...

4. "IT'S TRUE BECAUSE IT IS IN OUR VESTED INTEREST TO BELIEVE IT." Some examples from my own life of me using this standard are...

5. "IT"S TRUE BECAUSE THE DOMINATORS IN MY GROUP SAY SO." Some examples from my own life of me using this standard are...

CHAPTER SEVEN
LEARN TO ANALYZE THE PARTS OF YOUR THINKING

To be mentally healthy means commanding the reasoning that is commanding your mind, your life, and your decisions. To command reasoning requires understanding reasoning—what it entails and how it goes wrong—and how to correct poor reasoning. In this chapter, you will begin to learn how to take command of your reasoning by taking it apart and assessing it for quality, using the critical thinking standards introduced in the last chapter.

ALL HUMANS USE THEIR THINKING TO MAKE SENSE OF THE WORLD

The words *thinking* and *reasoning* are used in everyday life as virtual synonyms. Reasoning, however, has a more formal flavor. This is because it highlights the inference-drawing capacity of the mind.

Reasoning occurs whenever the mind draws conclusions on the basis of reasons. We draw conclusions whenever we make sense of things. The result is that whenever we think to make sense of things, we reason. Usually we are not aware of the full scope of reasoning implicit in our minds.

We begin to reason from the moment we wake up in the morning. We reason when we figure out what to eat for breakfast, what to wear, whether to make certain purchases, whether to go with this or that friend to lunch. We reason as we interpret the oncoming flow of traffic, when we react to the decisions of other drivers, when we speed up or slow down. One can draw conclusions, then, about everyday events or, really, about anything at all: about poems, microbes, people, numbers, historical events, social settings, psychological states, character traits, the past, the present, the future.

By reasoning, then, we mean making sense of something by giving it some meaning in our mind. Virtually all thinking is part of our sense-making activities. We hear scratching at the door and think, "It's the dog." We see dark clouds in the sky and think, "It looks like rain." Much of this activity operates at a subconscious level.

For example, all of the sights and sounds around us have meaning for us without our explicitly noticing that they do. Most of our reasoning is unspectacular. Our reasoning tends to become explicit only when someone challenges it and we have to defend it ("Why do you say that Jack is obnoxious? I think he is quite funny"). Throughout life, we form goals or purposes and then figure out how to pursue them. Reasoning is what enables us to come to these decisions using ideas and meanings.

On the surface, reasoning often looks simple, as if it had no component structures. Looked at more closely, however, it implies the ability to engage in a set of interrelated intellectual processes. By learning to take your thinking apart and routinely analyze these eight elements, you are in a better position to take command of the reasoning guiding your emotional and intellectual life.

YOU NEED TO TAKE YOUR THINKING APART TO FIND PROBLEMS IN YOUR THINKING — AND SOLVE THEM

HERE ARE THE PARTS:

Points of View we need to consider

Purposes of our thinking

Implications and Consequences of our thinking

Questions we are trying to answer

Parts of Thinking

Assumptions we are taking for granted

Information needed to answer the question

Concepts or key ideas we are using in our thinking

Inferences or conclusions we are coming to

©2025 Linda Elder

TO ANALYZE THINKING YOU MUST LEARN TO IDENTIFY AND QUESTION ITS PARTS

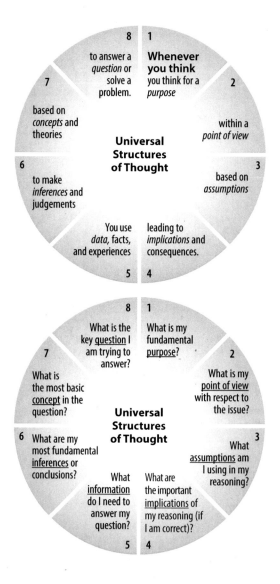

Be aware: When you have internalized the structures of thought, you ask important questions implied by these structures.

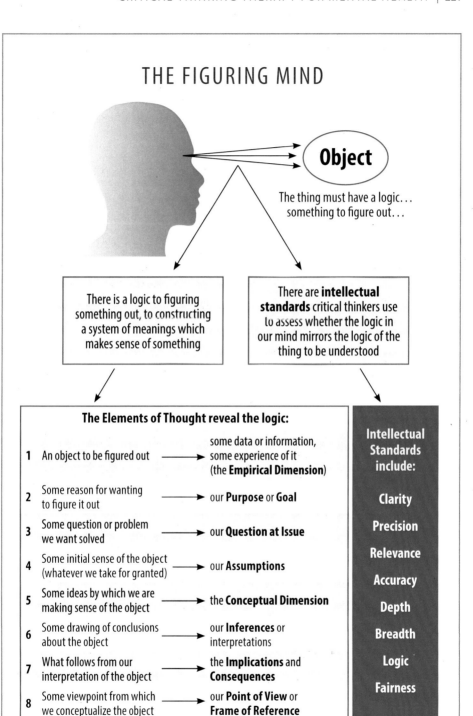

THE FIGURING MIND

Object

The thing must have a logic...
something to figure out...

There is a logic to figuring something out, to constructing a system of meanings which makes sense of something

There are **intellectual standards** critical thinkers use to assess whether the logic in our mind mirrors the logic of the thing to be understood

The Elements of Thought reveal the logic:

1 An object to be figured out → some data or information, some experience of it (the **Empirical Dimension**)

2 Some reason for wanting to figure it out → our **Purpose** or **Goal**

3 Some question or problem we want solved → our **Question at Issue**

4 Some initial sense of the object (whatever we take for granted) → our **Assumptions**

5 Some ideas by which we are making sense of the object → the **Conceptual Dimension**

6 Some drawing of conclusions about the object → our **Inferences** or interpretations

7 What follows from our interpretation of the object → the **Implications** and **Consequences**

8 Some viewpoint from which we conceptualize the object → our **Point of View** or **Frame of Reference**

Intellectual Standards include:

Clarity

Precision

Relevance

Accuracy

Depth

Breadth

Logic

Fairness

©2025 Linda Elder

THINK ABOUT PURPOSE

Your purpose is what you are trying to achieve or make happen. By taking command of your purposes, you take better command of your mental health.

Good athletes stay focused on their goals. Good thinkers do too.

QUESTIONS YOU CAN ASK TO TARGET PURPOSE:

- What is my purpose in doing what I am doing?
- Am I fully in command of my purposes or do I let other people choose my purposes for me?
- Do I allow myself to be carried along by the crowd, which leads me to derail from my purposes, or do I stand firm in my purposes?
- What are my husband/wife's purposes? Are our purposes compatible or not? If not, what, if anything, can be done to improve the relationship?
- What is my primary purpose in my work? Is that purpose fulfilling?
- What purposes do I want guiding my life?
- Have I thought deeply about my purposes?

STATE THE QUESTION

The question lays out the problem and helps you understand what you need to do to solve it.

Good thinkers are clear about the questions they are pursing answers to, and they take command of the questions guiding their lives.

Good thinkers spend time figuring out the questions they need to ask.

QUESTIONS YOU CAN ASK ABOUT THE QUESTION:

- What question am I trying to answer?
- Is my question clear?
- Should I be asking a different question?
- What question are you asking me?
- What questions have I been asking which have not helped my mental health? What questions do I need to ask and answer to be more mentally well?
- Am I guided by my own questions, or is someone else guiding my questions for me?

GATHER THE INFORMATION

The information is the facts, evidence, or experiences you use to figure things out.

You are bombarded by information every day — from the internet, TV, radio, friends, relatives, therapists… Watch out! <u>Lots of information is not accurate</u>.

QUESTIONS YOU CAN ASK ABOUT INFORMATION:

- What information do I need to answer this question?
- Do I need to gather more information?
- Is this information relevant to my purpose?
- Is this information accurate? How do I know it is?
- What information am I leaving out? Why am I leaving out this information? Is it because I am trying to avoid seeing something or changing my view?
- Am I vulnerable to believing information that is untrue? If so, under what conditions and why?

CHECK YOUR INFERENCES

Inferences are conclusions you come to. It's what the mind does in figuring something out. You make inferences every day. (Tara is my friend, so I infer I can trust her.)

Realize that every time you make an inference, you might make a different, more logical one.

An inference is a step of the mind which happens when the mind says "'X' is true, therefore 'Y' is true."

For example, "My child is misbehaving; therefore I should try to get to the root of the problem."

QUESTIONS YOU CAN ASK TO CHECK YOUR INFERENCES:

- What conclusions am I coming to in this situation?
- Are there other conclusions I should consider?
- Is my inference logical?
- Is this other person's inference logical or am I being led astray by someone?
- Are my illogical inferences leading me to suffer unnecessarily? If so, how can I reformulate these inferences so they are more logical?

QUESTION YOUR ASSUMPTIONS

Assumptions are beliefs you take for granted.
("I assume that so-and-so loves me.") We don't usually
question our assumptions, but we should.

Assumptions are usually unconscious in the mind. We don't
know they are there. But we use them to figure things out.

We need to dig them up, examine them, and
see if they make sense or not.

QUESTIONS YOU CAN ASK TO IMPROVE
YOUR ASSUMPTIONS:

- What am I taking for granted?
- Am I assuming something I shouldn't?
- What assumption is leading me to this conclusion?
- What is this other person assuming?
- What have I been assuming about my mental health that needs to be questioned? Am I assuming that someone else will make me happy? Am I assuming that I can blame others for my poor mental health?
- What does my significant other assume about me? Are these assumptions justifiable?

CLARIFY YOUR CONCEPTS

Concepts are ideas you use in thinking to understand what is going on and to figure out how to act in a situation.

Good thinkers are aware of the key ideas they are using in their thinking.

What is your concept of "healthy foods"? What is your concept of "unhealthy foods"?

QUESTIONS YOU CAN ASK TO CLARIFY CONCEPTS:

- What is the main concept guiding my behavior in this situation?
- What ideas come into my mind when I hear the words intimacy, happiness, friend, therapy, peace, mental health, work, _____? Are these ideas based in reasonable thinking?
- What ideas am I using to improve my life?
- Do my ideas cause problems for me or for others?
- Am I willing to consider new ways to conceptualize myself and my life so I am more self-fulfilled?

UNDERSTAND YOUR POINT OF VIEW (AND THE POINT OF VIEW OF OTHERS)

Point of view is what you are looking at and the way it looks to you.

Keep in mind that people have different points of view, especially when they disagree.

You have a point of view. But can you understand other people's viewpoints?

QUESTIONS YOU CAN ASK ABOUT POINT OF VIEW:

- How am I looking at this situation?
- What am I looking at, and how am I seeing it?
- Is there another reasonable way to look at this situation?
- Does my point of view seem to be the only correct one? (Watch out if it does.)
- Do I try to enter and appreciate the point of view of others?
- Is my point of view keeping me from seeing something important in the situation?

THINK THROUGH THE IMPLICATIONS

Do you think through possible consequences before you act?

An implication is that to which your thinking is leading you, or what is implied in the situation or context.

When you say things, you imply certain other things. For example, if you make a promise, you imply that you will keep it.

Consequences result from something that occurred earlier. For example, if you are rude to someone, he might be rude back. If he is, it would be a consequence of your being rude first.

QUESTIONS YOU CAN ASK ABOUT IMPLICATIONS:

- If I decide to do "X," what things might happen?
- If I decide not to do "X," what things might happen?
- When I made an important decision in the past, what happened as a result? What were the consequences?
- What are some implications of trusting people I don't know?
- What are some implications of not acting to take command of my thinking?
- What are some implications of refusing to see my thinking for what it is?
- What are some important implications of following my therapist's advice?

ANALYZING PROBLEMS

Think of an important problem you are facing. Then analyze the problem by targeting the parts of thinking. Write out your answers. (Use this template repeatedly to work through significant problems in your life.)

THE PROBLEM IS THIS...
>   (Write out the problem clearly and precisely, with details. Write the problem in different ways until you get it perfectly clear in your mind.)

THIS IS AN IMPORTANT PROBLEM BECAUSE...

THE KEY QUESTION THAT NEEDS TO BE ANSWERED TO SOLVE THIS PROBLEM IS...
>   (Every problem has questions connected to it. Write out the most important question you need to answer to solve the problem. State it clearly and precisely. Being specific is very important.)

THE MAIN PURPOSE IN ADDRESSING THE PROBLEM IS...

THE FOLLOWING INFORMATION IS NEEDED TO ANSWER THIS QUESTION...
>   (Here you are looking for the facts that help you solve the problem.)

SOME IMPORTANT ASSUMPTIONS I AM USING IN MY THINKING ARE...
>   (Figure out what you are taking for granted. Make sure these assumptions are reasonable.)

THE KEY IDEAS (CONCEPTS) GUIDING MY THINKING AS I DEAL WITH THIS PROBLEM ARE... I WOULD DESCRIBE THIS IDEA IN THE FOLLOWING WAY...

(For example, if the issue is your mental health and how to improve it, one key idea is "mental health." Your concept of mental health is how you are defining it in your mind.)

THE POINTS OF VIEW RELEVANT TO THIS PROBLEM ARE... I WOULD ELABORATE THESE VIEWPOINTS IN THE FOLLOWING WAY...

(For example, in working to improve your mental health you would need to consider your own viewpoint as well as the viewpoints of others who you allow to affect your mental health—possibly the viewpoints of your children, parents, spouse, therapist, colleagues at work.)

IF THIS PROBLEM GETS SOLVED, SOME IMPORTANT IMPLICATIONS ARE...

(Here you are trying to figure out some important things that should happen if the problem gets solved.)

IF THIS PROBLEM DOES NOT GET SOLVED, SOME IMPORTANT IMPLICATIONS ARE...

(Here you are trying to figure out some important things that will probably happen if the problem does not get solved.)

AFTER THINKING THROUGH THE PARTS OF REASONING ABOVE, I THINK THE BEST SOLUTION TO THE PROBLEM IS...

AN EVERYDAY EXAMPLE: JONATHON AND NADINE

Let's now look at, and then analyze, a disagreement that might arise in everyday life—in this case, between lovers who come to different conclusions about a situation they both experienced.

Suppose Jonathon and Nadine, who are in a romantic relationship, go to a party, during which Jonathon spends most of the evening talking with Rosa. On their way back, Jonathon, sensing that Nadine is upset, asks, "What's wrong?"

After some hesitation, Nadine says, "I didn't appreciate your spending the whole night flirting with Rosa!"

Jonathon: Flirting … flirting, I was not flirting!

Nadine: What would you call it?

Jonathon: Being friendly. I was being friendly.

Nadine: When a man spends the whole evening focused on one woman, sits very close to her, looks at her in a romantic way, and periodically touches her in supposedly casual ways, he is engaged in what can only be called flirting.

Jonathon: And when a woman spends her whole evening watching everything her boyfriend does, collecting evidence as if preparing for a trial, a boyfriend who has always been faithful to her, she is engaged in what can only be called paranoia.

Nadine: Paranoid? How dare you call me that!

Jonathon: Well, how else can I describe your behavior? You're obviously distrustful and insecure. You're accusing me without a good reason for doing so.

Nadine: Don't act like this is the only time you flirted. I heard from your friends that you were quite a lady's man before we got together.

Jonathon: And I heard about your possessiveness and jealousy from your friends. I think you need to deal with your own problems before you cast stones at me. Perhaps you need counseling.

Nadine: You're nothing but a typical male. You think that women are to be measured by conquest. You're so focused on getting strokes for that male ego of yours that you can't see or admit what you're doing. If you can't see fit to change your behavior, I must question the wisdom of our having a relationship.

Jonathon: I agree. I, too, question our relationship, but I question it on the basis of your paranoia. I think I deserve an apology!

Analysis of the Example

Now let's analyze this exchange using the elements of thought:

Purpose. Both Jonathon and Nadine presumably seek a successful romantic relationship. That is their implied shared goal.

Problem/Question. They see a problem or issue standing in the way, a problem they conceptualize differently. To Jonathon, the problem is, "When is Nadine going to deal with her paranoia?" To Nadine, the problem is, "When is Jonathon going to take responsibility for his flirtatious behavior?"

Conclusions. Both Jonathon's and Nadine's inferences (conclusions) about the situation derive from the same behavior in the same circumstance, but they clearly see the behavior differently. To Jonathon, his behavior is to be understood as merely "friendly." To Nadine, Jonathon's behavior can be understood only as "flirtation."

Facts/Information. The raw facts of the situation include everything Jonathon actually said and did at the party. Other relevant facts include Jonathon's behavior toward other women in his past. Additional facts include Nadine's behavior toward former boyfriends and any other facts that bear on whether she is acting out of insecurity or "paranoia."

Assumptions. Jonathon is assuming that he is not self-deceived in his motivation with respect to Rosa and other women. Jonathon also is assuming that he is competent to identify paranoia in another person's behavior. Further, he is assuming that a woman could not behave in the way that Nadine did without being paranoid. Nadine is assuming that Jonathon's behavior is not compatible with ordinary friendliness. Both assume that what they have heard about the other from friends is accurate. Both assume themselves to be justified in their behavior in the situation.

Concepts. Key concepts in the reasoning are: flirtation, friendliness, paranoia, jealousy, intimate relationships.

Implications. Both Jonathon and Nadine imply by their reasoning that the other person is entirely to blame for any disagreement regarding Jonathon's behavior at the party. Both seem to imply that the relationship is hopeless.

Point of View. Both Jonathon and Nadine may be seeing the other through the bias of a traditional point of view. Both see themselves as a victim of the other. Both see themselves as blameless.

Given what we know about the dispute, it is not possible to assess who is correct and to what extent. To decide whose interpretation of the situation is most plausible, we would need more facts. There are a variety of subtle but observable behaviors that—if we could verify them in the behavior of Jonathon toward Rosa—might lead us to conclude that Nadine is correct, and that Jonathon was behaving flirtatiously. Or, if we heard the conversation firsthand, we might decide that Nadine's response is unjustified.

A CHECKLIST FOR REASONING

When we bring together the elements of reasoning with critical thinking standards, we have a checklist for reasoning, which can help guide our reasoning in any situation.

1) All reasoning has a PURPOSE.
- Can you state your purpose clearly?
- What is the objective of your reasoning?
- Does your reasoning focus throughout on your goal?
- Is your goal realistic?

2) All reasoning is an attempt to figure something out, to settle some QUESTION, to solve some PROBLEM.
- What question are you trying to answer?
- Are there other ways to think about the question?
- Can you divide the question into sub-questions?
- Is this a question that has one right answer or can there be more than one reasonable answer?
- Does this question require judgment rather than facts alone?

3) All reasoning is based on ASSUMPTIONS.
- What assumptions are you making? Are they justified?
- How are your assumptions shaping your point of view?
- Which of your assumptions might reasonably be questioned?

4) All reasoning is done from some POINT OF VIEW.
- What is your point of view? What insights is it based on? What are its weaknesses?
- What other points of view should be considered in reasoning through this problem? What are the strengths and weaknesses of these viewpoints? Are you fairmindedly considering the insights behind these viewpoints?

5) All reasoning is based on DATA, INFORMATION, and EVIDENCE.

- To what extent is your reasoning supported by relevant data?
- Do the data suggest explanations that differ from those you have given?
- How clear, accurate, and relevant are the data to the question at issue?
- Have you gathered data sufficient to reach a reasonable conclusion?

6) All reasoning is expressed through, and shaped by, CONCEPTS and THEORIES.

- What key concepts and theories are guiding your reasoning?
- What alternative explanations might be possible, given these concepts and theories?
- Are you clear and precise in using concepts and theories in your reasoning?
- Are you distorting ideas to fit your agenda?

7) All reasoning contains INFERENCES or INTERPRETATIONS by which we draw CONCLUSIONS and give meaning to data.

- To what extent do the data support your conclusions?
- Are your inferences consistent with each other?
- Are there other reasonable inferences that should be considered?

8) All reasoning leads somewhere or has IMPLICATIONS and CONSEQUENCES.

- What implications and consequences follow from your reasoning?
- If we accept your line of reasoning, what implications or consequences are likely?

CHAPTER EIGHT
EXAMINE YOUR REASONING: GOING DEEPER INTO THE ELEMENTS OF REASONING

In the previous chapter, the elements of reasoning were introduced. In this chapter, these elements are expanded with emphasis on their relevance to your mental health.

COMMAND YOUR *PURPOSES* TO IMPROVE YOUR LIFE

For your mental well-being, it is essential to think critically about the purposes that drive your behavior and the quality of your life. This requires deeply understanding your ultimate purposes as well as the role that purpose plays across human life. Without significant purposes that are self-chosen, it is very difficult, if not impossible, to be fulfilled. Most people do not actively choose their purposes, and where they do, they tend to choose some purposes well and others poorly. It is rare indeed for someone to actively choose and command all their important purposes, but this should be your goal.

Achieving mental well-being requires pursuing important goals while being realistic about the purposes available to you and your means for achieving important purposes. *Mental wellness is achieved through, among other things, a powerful internal will to realize your goals and make the most of your life.* It requires understanding and commanding your purposes in dealing with others, and in working through issues throughout your daily experience. It requires eliminating obstacles, internal and external, that would interfere with the achievement of your goals. Emotional well-being requires that you rationally control the story you tell yourself about your past, present, and future. It means understanding the limitations humans place on themselves and each other, including at the societal level, in terms of what purposes are even allowed. It entails understanding how your purposes may be affected by the pathologies of others.

Pursuing important purposes, or even being aware of one's purposes, does not come naturally to most people. Again, many, if not most, of our purposes are not consciously chosen. Instead, social belief systems tend to determine what purposes we consider appropriate, meaningful, and worthy of our attention. This is because humans are born into groups, with each group's belief system imposing purposes upon us long before we have developed the skills necessary for rejecting irrational or unreasonable purposes. As children, and throughout our lives, we tend to soak up the beliefs and purposes of groups and people around us. Consequently, we largely live within cultural constraints that define what jobs are available to us, how we should view intimate relationships, how we should parent, and most everything else in our lives.

In short, we choose many of our purposes in accord with societal beliefs, customs, and taboos. At the same time, we frequently deceive ourselves into believing that we deliberately choose the purposes that are dictated to us. For instance, the types of jobs most people choose are those available through current economic systems; people tend to confine themselves to these restricted work situations as defined by societal structures, yet they see themselves as independent agents making independent decisions.

For your mental well-being, it is essential for you to clearly understand and take command of your purposes—those you choose as well as those that have been thrust upon you by parents, supervisors, children, friends, neighbors, and any other groups to which you belong or persons you allow to influence you.

Deliberately Choose Your Ultimate Purposes, Even in a Dark World

The importance of deliberately choosing your important purposes in life has been the focus of some distinguished thinkers through the ages. For instance, in his book, *Man's Search for Meaning* (1959; 2006), Victor Frankl says:

> The greatest task for any person is to find meaning in his or her life . . .
> A person may remain brave, dignified and unselfish, or in the bitter fight for self-preservation he may forget his human dignity and become no more than an animal . . . Forces beyond your control can take away everything you possess except one thing, your freedom to choose how you will respond to the situation. You cannot control what happens to you in life, but you can always control what you will feel and do about what happens to you. (p. x)

Of course, remember that many things are under your control. We should be reminded that Frankl wrote these words after suffering horrifying conditions for years in one of the worst Nazi concentration camps.[9] His point is well taken, in that *many things are not under your control*, and these things must be accepted and sometimes suffered through as best you can. Frankl's view, which is in keeping with Stoic and critical thinking philosophy, is that what cannot be changed must be accepted. And yet even in the darkest times and the darkest places, we can often cultivate meaning through purposes we personally value and deliberately pursue.

9 This is the primary focus of his book, *Man's Search for Meaning* (see Recommended Readings), in addition to further detailing his philosophy, which he termed *Logotherapy*.

Frankl agrees: "Man's search for meaning is the primary motivation in his life . this meaning is unique and specific in that it must and can be fulfilled by him alone; only then does it achieve a significance which will satisfy his own will to meaning." (p. 99)

According to Frankl, therapeutic analysis should try

> . . . to make the patient aware of what he actually longs for in the depth of his being . . . Thus it can be seen that mental health is based on a certain degree of tension, the tension between what one has already achieved and what one still ought to accomplish, or the gap between what one is and what one should become. Such attention is inherent in the human being and therefore is indispensable to mental well-being . . . What man actually needs is not a tensionless state but rather the striving and struggling for a worthwhile goal, a freely chosen task. (p. 103)

Frankl argues that we need to be aware of

> … the detrimental influence of that feeling of which so many patients complain today, namely, the feeling of the total and ultimate meaninglessness of their lives. They lack the awareness of a meaning worth living for. They are haunted by the experience of their inner emptiness, a void within themselves; they are caught in that situation which I have called the "Existential Vacuum." (pp. 104-106)

More than half a century ago, Frankl lamented thus: "The existential vacuum is a widespread phenomenon of the 20th Century." He described this vacuum that exists within people's thinking as manifesting itself ". . . mainly in a state of boredom." Frankl points out that, unlike other animals, humans cannot rely on instinct to determine our meanings and purposes in life. He points out that traditions that have guided human behavior in the past have rapidly diminished; this means that people must increasingly make decisions for themselves, yet they frequently do so based on following other people's wishes and behavior. He contends that suicide can frequently be traced back to the existential vacuum: "Such widespread phenomena as depression, aggression and addiction are not understandable unless we recognize the existential vacuum underlying them." (pp. 106-107)

In emphasizing that our purposes must come from within, Frankl says, "Man should not ask what the meaning of his life is, but rather he must recognize that it is he who is asked. In a word, each man is questioned by life; and he can only answer to life by answering for his own life . . ." (p. 109)

In other words, only you can decide how you will achieve meaning in your own life, and this meaning is largely found in the purposes you set for yourself and actively pursue.

INTERNALIZE THE IDEA: CLARIFY YOUR THOUGHTS ON THE EXISTENTIAL VACUUM

Read again the excerpts above from Frankl's book, *Man's Search for Meaning*, focused on what he terms *the existential vacuum*. Complete the following statements:

1. My understanding of the *existential vacuum*, according to Frankl, is as follows . . .

2. I see the *existential vacuum* exemplified in the following ways in human societies and the people around me . . .

3. This [is/is not] a problem I personally experience. [If this is a problem for you, continue to numbers 4 and 5.]

4. To eliminate this existential vacuum in my life, I need to do the following . . .

5. Therefore, I intend to do the following . . . [Periodically reread your answer to #5 to make sure you are progressing. If you are unsure how you will eliminate the existential vacuum in your life, come back to this activity after you complete all the activities in this book.]

INTERNALIZE THE IDEA: EXPLORE YOUR IMPORTANT PURPOSES

Think seriously about the primary purposes you pursue as you go through your daily life. Make a list of each of these purposes and complete the following statements for each one. Go as far as you need to in this activity:

1. One primary purpose in my life is . . .

2. This purpose is important because . . .

3. I [do/do not] commit enough time to pursuing this purpose.

4. To pursue this purpose more assertively and productively, I need to . . .

5. Therefore, I intend to achieve this purpose more fully by doing the following . . . [Periodically reread your answer to #5 to make sure you are progressing.]

Reach for Significant Purposes While Critically Examining the Status Quo

As you work to pursue reasonable purposes, realize that it is a grave error to be naïve as to the world you face and the options available to you within the constraints of society. Again, the human world you inhabit creates parameters within which you are, to a large degree, forced to live. The highest-level thinkers work to expand those parameters or change them for the better, but all humans inhabit societies which require individuals to behave in given ways—whether these individuals want to or not, and whether it makes sense to or not. For instance, each of us is required to belong to some country and own proof of our nationality, especially if we want to travel internationally. Each of us is expected to adhere to our country's laws, whether the laws are fair or not. To be accepted into typical human groups, all of us must dress according to certain (often unwritten) guidelines within our cultures or groups, wear our hair according to arbitrary societal standards, and have the manners expected of us.

Some social customs and rules are harmless or even helpful; others cause suffering, as people and other sentient creatures become victims of unreasonable laws, customs, and taboos. Your mental health problems may stem from this very problem. Perhaps you have had difficulty fitting yourself into what you perceive to be unjust or nonsensical rules and customs of your society, family, or employer. As you analyze your situation, remember that it always might be you who is self-deceived; you may perceive something to be unreasonable when it is really your own thinking that is unreasonable. To develop your ability to determine whether it is you or someone else who is self-deceived in a given context, internalize and actively use the tools found in Chapter Four on the barriers to critical thinking and Chapter Six on intellectual standards.

Some problems caused by social ideologies, group think, or other forms of sociocentrism are far more significant than others. Some of your country's laws are more unfair than other laws, sometimes egregiously so (as in the cases, for instance, of slavery, clitorectomy, animal experimentation, the removal of native people from their lands, bullfighting, destroying animal habitat for human expansion, and governments spying on their own people without due process). Some of your society's customs are more distasteful or repulsive than others (such as requiring children to pledge allegiance to the flag, pressuring students to pray during football games, compelling the singing of the national anthem, or adulating a monarchy, the wealthy, or the famous). Some of the groups you belong to, and the people within those groups (such as family, friends, neighbors, social and religious groups, etc.), behave in more superficial or otherwise irrational ways than others.

To protect yourself from narrowminded people, institutions, and ideologies, it is essential that you learn to critique the customs, laws, traditions, and taboos of your society, and of all the groups and people who in any way have influence over you— including where you have allowed this influence. Being unaware of how society restricts you and impacts your purposes, needs, and desires can easily cause you to be mentally unwell.

INTERNALIZE THE IDEA: ELIMINATE PURPOSES YOU PURSUE THAT STEM FROM IRRATIONAL SOCIETAL INFLUENCE

Figure out which of your purposes are not adding to the quality of your life, and which you pursue uncritically due to societal influences. Concentrate on giving higher priority to the important purposes in your life. Complete these statements:

1. The purposes in my life that I pursue due to societal influence, but which are not healthy, include . . .

2. I get caught up in these purposes because . . .

3. Getting caught up in these purposes has caused the following problems in my life . . .

4. I plan to eliminate these societally-induced purposes by doing the following . . . [Periodically reread your answer to #4 to make sure you are progressing.]

Become a Free Agent

Every person lives as both an individual and a member of groups; we live within ourselves and in relationship with others. Some people have greater difficulty navigating between these two realities. R.D. Laing, a pioneer in understanding schizophrenia and chronic psychosis, writes in his book *The Divided Self* (1960), ". . . each and every man is at the same time separate from his fellows and related to them…our relatedness to others is an essential aspect of our being, as is our separateness, but any particular person is not a necessary part of our being." (p. 25)

This points to a special problem we face as humans. We need other humans if we ourselves are to survive (especially at the beginning of life) and if we are to experience emotional well-being (as we move through life). But any number of dysfunctionalities may occur in the process of relating to others; these dysfunctional ways of relating can then trigger further irrational thought patterns. Laing describes one of these irrational ways of thinking: *the mechanism of depersonalization.* He says:

> Depersonalization is a technique that is universally used as a means of dealing with the other when he becomes too tiresome or disturbing. One no longer allows oneself to be responsive to his feelings and may be prepared to regard and treat him as though he had no feelings . . . it is usual to cherish if not the reality, at least the illusion that there is a limited sphere of living free from this dehumanization. Yet it may be just [in] this sphere that the greater risk is felt, and the insecure person experiences this risk in highly potentiated form.
>
> The risk consists in this: if one experiences the other as a free agent, one is open to the possibility of experiencing oneself as an object of his experience and thereby of feeling one's own subjectivity drained away. One is threatened with the possibility of becoming no more than a thing in the world of the other, without any life for oneself, without any being for oneself.
>
> The issue is in principle straightforward. One may find oneself enlivened and the sense of one's own being enhanced by the other, or one may experience the other as deadening and impoverishing. (pp. 48-49)

All of us have been exposed to deadening and impoverishing people. Each of us has had the challenge of learning to operate as a free agent, rather than being used or manipulated by other people or groups to serve their interests. For some people the challenge has been greater, due to harsh or otherwise difficult circumstances and/or one's predispositions.

In his book, *To Have or to Be* (1976; 1988), Erich Fromm describes modern cultural pathologies resulting from the incorrect belief that one's identity is properly determined by egocentric desires and pursuits (that in fact can never be satisfied). He says, for instance,

> . . . our kind of "pursuit of happiness" does not produce well-being. We are a society of notoriously unhappy people: lonely, anxious, depressed, distracted, dependent – people who are glad when we have killed the time we are trying so hard to save . . . Ours is the greatest social experiment ever made to solve the question whether pleasure (as a passive aspect in contrast to the active aspect, well-being and joy) can be a satisfactory answer to the problem of human existence . . . In the industrialized countries the experiment has already answered the question in the negative.
>
> The . . . psychological premise of the industrial age, that the pursuit of individual egoism leads to harmony and peace, growth in everyone's welfare, is equally erroneous on theoretical grounds, and again its

fallacy is proven by the observable data . . . to be an egoist refers not only to my behavior but to my character. It means: that I want everything for myself; that possessing, not sharing, gives me pleasure; that I must become greedy because if my aim is having, I *am* more the more I *have*; that I must feel antagonistic toward all others: my customers whom I want to deceive, my competitors whom I want to destroy, my workers whom I want to exploit. I can never be satisfied, because there's no end to my wishes; I must be envious of those who have more and afraid of those who have less. But I have to repress all these feelings in order to represent myself (to others as well as to myself) as the smiling, rational, sincere, kind human being everybody pretends to be. (pp. xxvii-xxviii)

Fromm is highlighting the challenge, in today's capitalistic world, of becoming the best you can be and developing your character, when societal emphasis is on accumulating things and aggrandizing those who have wealth, power, and prestige. This is only one example of societal ideologies permeating human existence.

To be mentally well, you must recognize that you live as an individual within the privacy of your mind, while at the same time being obliged to fit yourself into at least some groups. The more pathological the groups you find yourself in, the more difficult it may be to find a reasonable path forward or a healthy plan for your life.

INTERNALIZE THE IDEA: EXAMINE THE PATHOLOGIES OF YOUR CULTURE THAT AFFECT YOUR PURPOSES

Consider some of the pathologies of your culture or the groups to which you belong that have affected you. Figure out the rules and customs these groups require of their members. Complete these statements:

1. One pathology of my culture that has affected me personally has been . . .

2. This societal sickness has affected me in the following ways . . .

3. My purposes have been negatively affected by these pathologies in the following ways . . .

4. I can avoid these pathologies, as much as is possible, by doing the following . . .

5. Therefore, I intend to . . .

Given the many dysfunctional ways in which human societies work, your challenge now is to find ways forward which enliven and enhance your development, whatever your past has been. To do this, you must:

- face the realities involved in being human,
- understand how human societies work,
- recognize when groups and people around you are pathological,
- recognize when and how the irrational behavior of others is affecting you,
- set and vigorously pursue your highest-level purposes within these realities, and
- learn to operate as a free, open-minded, enlightened person.

INTERNALIZE THE IDEA: BECOME A FREE, ENLIGHTENED PERSON

Answer the following questions based on the bullet points above. Give examples of each answer:

1. To what degree can you face the realities involved in being human?
2. To what degree do you understand how human societies work?
3. To what degree do you recognize when groups and people around you are pathological?
4. To what degree do you recognize when irrational people are affecting you?
5. To what degree are you setting and vigorously pursuing your highest-level purposes within these realities?
6. To what degree are you learning to operate as a free, enlightened agent? How would you live if you were a fully free and enlightened person?
7. What do you plan to change about yourself or your situation based on this analysis?

Realize and Command How Groups Affect Your Purposes

Because humans naturally form groups, and because humans develop and think within complex belief systems, we systematically affect one another through our beliefs and ideologies. As you have learned, every group has rules, taboos, and customs to which everyone in the group is expected to adhere. These belief systems affect the very purposes we will then think to pursue. Families, religious groups, school systems, clubs, special interest groups, political groups, peer groups, athletic programs, indeed, all groups impose rules, traditions, and taboos on the people within those groups. These impositions influence and affect your purposes.

INTERNALIZE THE IDEA: EXAMINE HOW IMPORTANT GROUPS AFFECT YOUR PURPOSES

Consider the groups you have been a member of—including being a member of your country. Examine how these groups have affected the very purposes you have pursued in your life. For each one, complete these statements:

1. One group that has significantly influenced my purposes is . . .

2. My purposes have been influenced in the following ways by this group's belief systems (due to their influence over me) . . .

3. Now that I'm examining this, I understand the following . . .

4. I need to make the following changes in my thinking based on this examination . . .

5. Therefore, I intend to . . .

Realize and Command How Capitalism Affects Your Purposes

A primary variable affecting the purposes of people across the world is, of course, capitalism, which has already been briefly touched upon. The effects of capitalism on each of our lives would be difficult to overestimate, so entrenched are we in its grasp. The need to survive economically is a difficult or even overwhelming reality for many. Overall, as a species, we appear to uncritically accept capitalism in its current form as if it were the only feasible economic system, as if it were handed down from on high; and since it seems set in stone, we must live in accord with it and suffer through its consequences. Of course, this way of thinking, being very narrow, confines us within a pathological world view that may negatively impact mental health.

Economics should not define who you are, nor control the human experience. Unbridled capitalism, which is the prominent form of economics today, has devastating consequences for the health of the earth, which in turn affects human mental well-being. In his writings, Erich Fromm (1976; 1988) stresses this problem and the increasing disconnection between humans and nature as we attempt to selfishly bend nature to our will. He says:

> ... the economic machine was supposed to be an autonomous entity, independent of human needs and human will ... The suffering of the workers as well as the destruction of an ever-increasing number of smaller enterprises for the sake of the growth of ever larger corporations was an economic necessity that one might regret, but that one had to accept as if it were the outcome of a natural law.
>
> The development of this economic system was no longer determined by the question: *What is good for man?* But by the question: *What is good for the growth of the system?* ... people's relations to nature became deeply hostile. Being "freaks of nature" who by the very conditions of our existence are within nature and by the gift of our reason transcend it, we have tried to solve our existential problem by giving up the ... vision of harmony between humankind and nature by conquering nature, by transforming it to our own purposes until the conquest has become more and more equivalent to destruction. Our spirit of conquest and hostility has blinded us to the fact that natural resources have their limits and can eventually be exhausted, and that nature will fight back against human rapaciousness. (pp. xxix-xxx)

Because we have all been thrust into a harsh economic system created by unbridled capitalism, it is essential to have a reasonable conception of money within the constraints of your own life, while also having the ability to critique how economics affect people and the earth itself. Humans have ethical responsibilities to the welfare of one another, to the planet, and to future life; this includes the responsibility to think critically about the destruction caused by unrestrained capitalism and the role money should play in human life.

To become mentally well requires being aware of how economic constraints affect you personally. It entails thinking critically about the economics of your own life and how you can safely function within the economic realities you face.

In short, money drives much of human thinking and behavior. For good or for ill, many of our purposes are directly connected with money. Of course, it is not easy to live within one's means in a world with exorbitant costs of living, in a climate that encourages people to accumulate debt, in a society where excessive waste is the norm, and in cultures that glorify what excessive money can buy. It is up to you to see through the pathologies built into a capitalist culture and, insofar as possible, to guard against these pathologies. And you should never allow money to define who you are, for you can never be mentally well if you do.

INTERNALIZE THE IDEA: EXAMINE HOW ECONOMICS AFFECTS YOUR PURPOSES

Clarify and examine how you think about money and how money influences the purposes you pursue. Answer these questions:

1. Do you worry about money?

2. Are you constantly thinking of money? How much of your time do you spend thinking about money? What precisely are you thinking?

3. Do you spend too much time thinking about money?

4. Do you like to show off what your money can buy? Do you try to buy friends with your money?

5. Do you have a healthy attitude about money, given that you must accept the economic realities you face?

6. Do you have a careless or irresponsible attitude toward money?

7. What messages do you get through your culture and country about how you should think about money?

8. What purposes do you pursue based on how you think about money?

9. What problems do you see money causing in your life and the lives of significant others?

10. How can you effectively deal with these problems?

11. How can you think and live differently based on this analysis?

Develop the Will to Achieve Your Purposes

Your purposes are directly connected to the will *within you*, or in other words, your own individually-motivated will. As you know, you may set purposes, but without the will to achieve those purposes, very little to nothing will be accomplished. How do you develop the will to achieve meaningful purposes? This question points up one of the great mysteries in understanding any individual human mind. Many variables can affect a person's will, including being born into impoverished conditions or being egocentrically predisposed to self-handicapping. Yet many people born into impoverished conditions achieve great things, as do many people who overcome their inborn irrational tendencies.

Whatever your past may have been, an immediate and palpable question for you is, "*How do I develop the will to achieve what would make me mentally well?*"

One thing to recognize is that there can be no will to achieve without the belief that you are able to achieve. If you carry voices in your head that constantly tell you that you are a failure, and if you do not counteract these voices, your fear of failure will always get in the way of your ability to achieve.

Therefore, you must first set realistic purposes and then systematically work toward achieving these purposes. Keep moving your thinking forward slowly and gradually, as you are hopefully now doing as you work through the exercises in this book. As you develop deeper understandings about the mind, you have greater control over the purposes you set for yourself. The key is to take individual steps, developing new understandings each day, completing the activities in this book, opening up your mind to new ways of looking at the world, and trusting that the process will lead to a more fulfilled life over time.

But if you have no will to change, you will continue to suffer emotionally.

INTERNALIZE THE IDEA: DO YOU HAVE THE WILL TO CHANGE AND IMPROVE?

Examine the barriers you create within your mind which keep you from achieving your highest purposes. Answer these questions:

1. To what degree do I command my own will?

2. Do I believe in the power of my own mind?

3. Do I believe in my ability to achieve within my capacities?

4. Do I continually tell myself illogical reasons as to why I cannot achieve?

5. What barriers stand in the way of achieving what I know I can achieve? Which of these barriers are simply created by me, within my own mind? Which of these barriers are created by others? Which of these barriers have I accepted from what other people have said about me, but which are not actual barriers?

6. How can I think and live differently based on this analysis?

Develop a Rich Set of Purposes to Improve Your Mental Well-Being

As you think more critically about your purposes, realize that you want to develop a rich set of purposes within all the important areas of your life. It is not enough to pursue high purposes in one part of your life while ignoring important purposes in other areas. For instance, many people think more critically about their professional purposes than their purposes within intimate relationships. This results in people's lives becoming impoverished by narrow focus over the long term; in this scenario, some parts of the mind are developed while other important parts are neglected.

For example, *to what degree do you think through and establish purposes for yourself that address your specific mental health concerns?* Perhaps you find your life so overwhelming that you believe you have no time to address your mental health. You may, for instance, have children who require most of your attention. Or you may be giving all your productive waking hours to your work. In such cases, it is essential to understand that *taking care of yourself comes before taking care of other people, and is more important than giving extra energy to professional goals.* You need to understand and pursue the types of activities that bring joy, happiness, and creativity into your life. For some people, music is essential to their mental health. Some people are writers and must write to be mentally well. Others enjoy playing an instrument or being part of a sports team. Still others may enjoy gardening, volunteering, dancing, attending theater, and any number of other activities that enhance their mental well-being.

One key to your mental health, then, is to know yourself—to know what types of purposes you personally need to pursue to achieve a sense of accomplishment and contentment. Only you can create this list; only you should choose your path. At the same time, all of us are responsible to contribute to the common good, since we do interrelate with, and therefore affect, one another. Hence, some of your goals should target contributing to others and to a better world, but not at the expense of your mental health.

Consider the following types of purposes that all humans should critically analyze (note that some of these will overlap):

1. The purposes you set for yourself to achieve and maintain physical health.

2. The purposes you set for yourself to develop your intellect and creativity.

3. The purposes you set for yourself to contribute to the common good.

4. The purposes you set for yourself to contribute to the welfare of your family and intimate friends.

5. Your professional purposes.

6. Your civic purposes.

7. Your social purposes.

8. The additional purposes you set for yourself that help address your specific mental health concerns.

INTERNALIZE THE IDEA: CRITICALLY ANALYZE YOUR PURPOSES

For each of the types of purposes above, complete these statements:

1. The purposes I have set for myself regarding point (one) above (to achieve and maintain physical health) include . . .

2. I [need to/do not need to] improve how I think about my physical health, because . . .

3. To improve my physical health, I need to pursue the following purposes . . .

4. Therefore, I intend to . . .

Clarify and Command Your Purposes in Relationship With Others

Many people pursue irrational purposes in their relationships with others. This can take such forms as pushing one's children to do things that are unrealistic or unachievable, nagging one's spouse to get him or her to change, or chasing someone romantically who does not reciprocate your romantic interest.

In relationships involving romance, intimacy, and raising children, it can be especially easy to slip into irrational thinking. Your will must be marshaled to deal with these situations in as reasonable a manner as possible, because this is when people tend to behave in unhealthy, destructive ways. It is essential, therefore, to be in command of your purposes in your relationships with others—especially the important ones—from the beginning. This requires clarifying and assessing your purposes using all the tools of reasonability in achieving your purposes. See the section on concepts (pp. 289-305) for a more detailed discussion on intimate relationships and parenting.

INTERNALIZE THE IDEA: CRITICALLY ANALYZE YOUR PURPOSES IN RELATIONSHIPS WITH IMPORTANT PEOPLE IN YOUR LIFE (AND CRITICALLY ANALYZE THEIR PURPOSES TOO)

Identify the primary purposes you have in relationships with the important people in your life. Complete these statements:

1. One important relationship in my life is . . .

2. My primary purposes in this relationship are . . .

3. These purposes [are/are not] reasonable because . . .

4. I believe the primary purposes of my partner in relation to me are . . .

5. I believe this because . . .

6. These purposes [are/are not] reasonable because . . .

7. Based on this analysis, I need to do the following . . .

Eliminate Obstacles That Interfere With Achieving Your Goals

To be mentally well requires that you eliminate all obstacles to your personal development that you possibly can. The obstacles to achieving your goals can come from those who have influence over you, or from inside your own mind. You must effectively deal with both types of barriers if you are to be mentally well.

You cannot avoid all unreasonable or annoying people, but you can limit the time you spend with them. And in many cases, you can entirely avoid them or remove yourself from their lives, so long as you believe you can.

You should also be aware by now that your egocentric and sociocentric tendencies (introduced in Chapter Four) can impede your ability to achieve your goals. It is essential for you to command the stories you tell yourself about yourself, about your past, and about your ability to achieve within your capacities. For instance, are you telling yourself that you are unable to achieve anything of worth because people in your past told you this and you believed them? Are you allowing past messages that you have received from people to hold you back from your development? To realize your capacities, you certainly must face down the dark inner voice of self-doubt, however you have developed this voice—whether from others' influence or from your own self-handicapping tendencies. Everyone faces the same challenges: 1) to see oneself as fully capable of realizing one's goals, within reason, and 2) to repel negative, destructive tendencies and people.

Recognize that worrying and obsessing may *seem* to advance your pursuit of productive purposes, but instead, they stand in the way of achieving your purposes. And they can have devastating consequences for your mental health. Worrying simply operates as a merry-go-round ad nauseum—your thinking goes around and around over the same ground, but never moves forward to any solutions (while all the while perceiving itself to be actually achieving something). This is the opposite of critical thinking, whereby we actively seek solutions and believe in our ability to do so. Again, remember the following rhyme:

> For every problem under the sun
> There is a solution, or there is none
> If there be one, seek till you find it
> If there be none, never mind it

When taken seriously, this simple rhyme can lead you to actively pursue solutions to the problems you face, while also helping you accept the limitations in your context and situation. Seeking reasonable solutions to your problems requires breaking out of the habit of worry.

Being overly introspective has a similar effect on the mind as worrying. Thinking about your thinking to improve it is essential to critical thinking, but ruminating over irrational thoughts, while thinking you are being reasonably introspective, is counterproductive. As with worrying, ruminating may seem to be getting you somewhere when it is only causing you more pain and suffering as you go over the same ground, again and again, thinking it out—or so it seems—but with no realizable solutions.

Likewise, obsessing over what you cannot have, no matter how hard your pursuit, can be as harmful to your mental health as worrying or any other bad habit of thought. In short, acceptance of reality is required for mental well-being.

Another barrier to your development is the pursuit of superficial, narrow, or limiting purposes which do not enrich your life, but instead distract you from the work involved in pursuing healthy purposes. For instance, excessively thinking about your dress, hair style, and your superficial effect on others will not help you develop into your capacities.

INTERNALIZE THE IDEA: ELIMINATE OBSTACLES TO ACHIEVING YOUR GOALS

Identify the primary purposes you would like to pursue, which you believe will make you more mentally healthy. Complete these statements:

1. The primary obstacles (internal or external) to achieving my goals are . . .

2. These obstacles have been a problem for me because . . .

3. I need to remove these obstacles by doing the following . . .

4. Therefore, I intend to do the following to eliminate these obstacles and to become more fulfilled . . .

It is usually possible to create reasonable and productive purposes, even in a world which seems, and often is, dismal and gloomy.

There are many healthy purposes you can pursue. You will need to pursue them through your own will.

THE QUALITY OF YOUR LIFE DEPENDS UPON THE QUALITY OF YOUR *QUESTIONS*

As you have learned, the quality of your thinking is driven by all the elements of your reasoning as they work together to form a whole. We have just focused on how your purposes drive your thinking and behavior, thereby illuminating the importance of commanding your purposes. How you formulate questions goes hand in hand with your purposes, because together your purposes and questions guide the specific directions in which your thinking must go to answer your questions. And even to determine your purposes, you need to ask questions like, "What is my purpose in this situation? Is this a reasonable purpose in these circumstances? What is this other person's true purpose?" Therefore, questions are essential to the healthy pursuit of your purposes.

What Questions Should You Be Asking?

Throughout the book to this point, we have pondered numerous important questions. Here are some additional essential questions that can help guide you to a higher quality of mental health:

- What exactly am I doing with my life?
- What goals am I pursuing? Where is the pursuit of these goals taking me?
- Are these the goals I need and want to be pursuing? Will these goals lead me to achieve my creative capacities? Will these goals help me contribute to a more rational and compassionate society? What can I contribute that would also give me a sense of fulfillment? If I accomplished these goals, would I actually feel happy as a result?
- Do I really want to stay in this relationship? Do I need to change the way I am behaving in this relationship? What precisely are the problems in this relationship? What do I need to do to change my thinking or behavior in this relationship?
- What creative outlets should I pursue for purposes of relaxation?
- What books can I read that will help me develop my intellectual and ethical capacities?
- What types of books do I most desire to read for sheer pleasure?
- How do I think about my physical being? Do I think critically about the foods I eat? Do I think critically about my exercise regime? Do I prioritize taking care of my physical body, or do I neglect this essential priority? Why do I neglect taking care of my needs?

INTERNALIZE THE IDEA

For the next several weeks, spend a few minutes each day answering the questions above in your journal. Keep coming back to these questions until you are completely satisfied with your answers, and with the questions you are now asking.

What Questions Are You Asking?

In contrast to asking the rich questions in the previous section, if you ask no questions, you demonstrate that there is little or nothing of interest you are pursuing. By asking no questions, you get no answers.

There are many ways you can improve the questions you ask, but you need to be aware of the pitfalls in formulating questions. For instance, if you ask vague questions, your thinking will have no clear direction; if you ask loaded questions, you have a hidden or unethical purpose; if you ask superficial questions, you will behave in superficial ways. If you ask inappropriate questions, you don't understand the circumstances within which you are operating. If you answer questions you do not understand, you can get into trouble. If you are continually guided by the questions of the people around you, rather than by your own questions, you are not an independent thinker. If you are not asking important questions in your intimate and family relationships, your lives together will be impoverished. It is important to be in control at all times of the questions you ask, and to be aware of the questions those around you are asking (and how their questions affect you).

Thinking is propelled forward when you actively pursue answers to important questions. Questions lay out the tasks you must fulfill to answer them. Therefore, after formulating your question, you must have the will to face the question and fulfill the tasks required by it.

For every concept in critical thinking, there are questions that emerge from your understanding of the concept. You have already been introduced to some of these in Chapters Three through Seven. Internalizing the elements of reasoning gives rise to questions focused on those elements; internalizing intellectual standards gives rise to questions focused on those standards; internalizing intellectual virtues gives rise to questions focused on those virtues; internalizing the problems of egocentric and sociocentric thinking gives rise to questions focused on these barriers to rational living. In the next few sections, you will find examples of these questions.

Asking Analytic Questions

Asking essential analytic questions is vital to your development. As you know, when we analyze, we break a whole into parts. We do this because problems in a "whole" are often a function of problems in one or more of its parts. Success in thinking depends, first of all, on our ability to identify the components of thinking by asking essential questions focused on those components. Here are some powerful questions you can ask that arise from understanding each of them.

1. Questioning Goals and Purposes. All thought reflects an agenda or purpose. Assume that you do not fully understand someone's thought (including your own) until you understand the agenda behind it. Questions that focus on purpose in thinking include:

- What is my central purpose in this relationship?
- What is the purpose of the comment I just made to my spouse?
- What is my main purpose in my professional life?
- What other goals do I need to consider to become more mentally well?
- What am I trying to persuade this other person to think or do?

2. Questioning Questions. All thought is responsive to a question. Assume that you do not fully understand a thought until you understand the question that gives rise to it. Questions that focus on questions in thinking include:

- I am not sure exactly what question you are raising. Could you explain it?
- Is this question the best one to focus on at this point, or is there a more pressing question I need to address?
- The question in my mind is this… Do you agree, or do you see another question at issue?
- Should we put the question (problem, issue) this way… or that…?

3. Questioning Information, Data, and Experience. All thoughts presuppose an information base. Assume that you do not fully understand the thought until you understand the background information (facts,

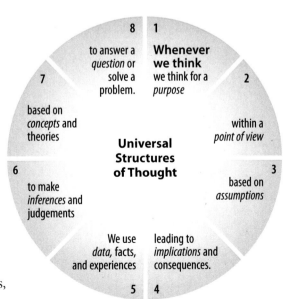

©2025 Linda Elder

data, experiences) that supports or informs it. Questions that focus on information in thinking include:

- On what information did I base my comment?
- What experience convinced me of this? Could my experience be distorted?
- How do I know this information is accurate? How could I verify it?
- Have I failed to consider any information or data that I need to consider?
- What are these data based on? Where do the data come from? Is my conclusion based on hard facts or someone's interpretations?

4. Questioning Inferences and Conclusions. All thought requires the making of inferences, the drawing of conclusions, the creation of meaning. Assume that you do not fully understand a thought until you understand the inferences that have shaped it. Questions that focus on inferences in thinking include:

- How did I reach that conclusion?
- Can I explain my reasoning? Can you explain your reasoning?
- Is there an alternative plausible conclusion I have not yet considered?
- Given all the facts, what is the best possible conclusion?

5. Questioning Concepts and Ideas. All thought involves the application of concepts. Assume that you do not fully understand a thought until you understand the concepts that define and shape it. Questions that focus on concepts in thinking include:

- What is the main idea I am using in my reasoning? Could I explain that idea?
- Am I using the appropriate concept or do I need to re-conceptualize the problem?
- Do I need more facts or do I need to rethink what I am labeling as facts?
- Is this question a legal, a theological, a social, or an ethical one?

6. Questioning Assumptions. All thought rests upon assumptions. Assume that you do not fully understand a thought until you understand what it takes for granted. Questions that focus on assumptions in thinking include:

- What exactly am I taking for granted here?
- Why am I assuming that? Should I rather assume … ?
- What assumptions underlie my point of view? What alternative assumptions might I make?

7. Questioning Implications and Consequences. All thought is headed in a direction. It not only begins somewhere (resting on assumptions), it also goes somewhere (has implications and consequences). Assume that you do not fully understand a thought unless you know the most important implications and consequences that follow from it. Questions that focus on implications in thinking include:

- What are you implying when you say … ? Are you implying … ?
- If I do this, what is likely to happen as a result?
- Are you implying that … ?
- Have I considered the implications of this behavior I am engaging in?

8. Questioning Viewpoints and Perspectives. All thought takes place within a point of view or frame of reference. Assume that you do not fully understand a thought until you understand the point of view or frame of reference that places it on an intellectual map. Questions that focus on point of view in thinking include:

- From what point of view am I looking at this?
- Is there another point of view I should consider? Is there an important viewpoint I am missing?
- Which of these possible viewpoints makes the most sense, given the situation?

ANALYTIC QUESTIONS IMPLIED BY THE ELEMENTS OF THOUGHT

Universal Structures of Thought

8 What is the key question I am trying to answer?

1 What is my fundamental purpose?

2 What is my point of view with respect to the issue?

3 What assumptions am I using in my reasoning?

4 What are the important implications of my reasoning (if I am correct)?

5 What information do I need to answer my question?

6 What are my most fundamental inferences or conclusions?

7 What are the most basic concepts in the question?

THREE KINDS OF QUESTIONS

In approaching a question, it is useful to figure out what type it is. Is it a question with one definitive answer? Is it a question that calls for a subjective choice? Or does the question require you to consider competing reasonable answers? Many problems in thinking occur because people do not understand the basic distinctions in these three types of questions:

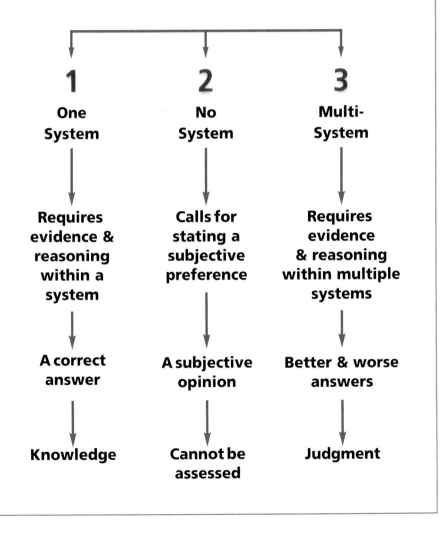

1	**2**	**3**
One System	**No System**	**Multi-System**
Requires evidence & reasoning within a system	**Calls for stating a subjective preference**	**Requires evidence & reasoning within multiple systems**
A correct answer	**A subjective opinion**	**Better & worse answers**
Knowledge	**Cannot be assessed**	**Judgment**

Asking One-System, No-System, and Conflicting-System Questions

There are a number of essential ways to categorize questions for the purpose of analysis. One such way is to focus on the type of reasoning required by the question. With **one-system** questions, there is an established procedure or method for finding the answer. With **no-system** questions, the question is properly answered in accordance with one's subjective preference; there is no "correct" answer. With **conflicting-system** questions, there are multiple competing viewpoints from which, and within which, one might reasonably pursue an answer to the question. There are better and worse answers, but no verifiable "correct" ones, since these are matters about which even experts disagree (hence the "conflict" from system to system).

Questions of Procedure (established- or one-system) - These include questions with an established procedure or method for finding the answer. These questions are settled by facts, by definition, or both. Examples:

- Are there enough bedrooms in this house for our family?
- Can we afford to purchase this house?
- How many jobs have you had in your life?
- Do you have any food allergies you are aware of?

Questions of Preference (no system) - Questions with as many answers as there are different human preferences (a category in which subjective taste rules). Examples:

- Which would you prefer, a vacation in the mountains or one at the seashore?
- How do you like to wear your hair?
- Do you like to go to the opera? Which is your favorite?
- What color scheme do you prefer in your house?

Questions of Judgment (conflicting systems) - Questions requiring reasoning, but with more than one arguable answer. These are questions that make sense to debate, questions with better-or-worse answers (well-supported and reasoned or poorly-supported and/or poorly-reasoned). Here you are seeking the best answer within a range of possibilities. Evaluate answers to these questions using universal intellectual standards such as clarity, accuracy, relevance, etc. These questions are predominant in the human disciplines (history, philosophy, economics, sociology, art…). Examples:

- How can I best manage my household budget?
- What can be done to help my son overcome his drug addiction?

- What can I do to help achieve sustainability of natural ecosystems?
- What is the best college for our child to attend?
- How can I arrange my life and my thinking so I am self-fulfilled?
- Should I have an abortion?

People tend to be better at figuring out answers to questions of fact or procedure than questions of judgment. People often want to simplify the thought process by looking for the "right" answer. But many of the important questions in life cannot be answered so easily. How does it make sense to parent this particular child? How can we best manage our child's destructive behavior? What is the best way to work with this difficult employee? What do I want in a marriage? Should I go out to a party tonight, or is my time better spent reading a good book or starting that art project? What can I personally do to help planet earth? All of these are questions of judgment and, as such, require us to reason within multiple, conflicting viewpoints.

As you go through your day, practice identifying these different types of questions. Identify them in your own thinking as well as in the thinking of others. Notice when you (erroneously) assert a factual answer to a question that is not a question of fact, but one requiring reasoned judgment. Notice the same tendency in others. When thinking through a question of judgment, identify all the important and relevant viewpoints and articulate those viewpoints as accurately as possible, especially those with whom you disagree.

Avoid Dogmatic Absolutism and Subjective Relativism

Some people, dogmatic absolutists, try to reduce all questions to matters of fact. They think that every question has one and only one correct answer. Others, subjective relativists, try to reduce all questions to matters of subjective opinion. They think that <u>no</u> question has correct or incorrect answers but that all questions whatsoever are matters of opinion: "I have my opinion and you have yours. Mine is right for me and yours is right for you." Neither absolutists nor relativists leave room for what is crucial to success in human life: matters of reasoned judgment.

Many important questions require our best judgment. It is required when we sit on a jury, when we assess a political candidate, when we take sides in a family argument, when we decide to support an educational reform movement, when we decide on how to raise our children, how to spend our money, or how much time to dedicate to our self development. Judgment based on sound reasoning goes beyond, but is never to be equated with, fact or opinion alone. When you reason well through conflicting-system questions, you do more than state facts. Furthermore, a well-reasoned position is not to be described as mere "opinion." All well-reasoned positions are based on relevant evidence and sound reasoning.

When questions requiring reasoned judgment are reduced to matters of subjective preference, counterfeit critical thinking occurs. Some people, then, come to uncritically assume that everyone's "opinion" is of equal value. Their capacity to appreciate the importance of intellectual standards diminishes, and we can expect to hear comments such as these: "What if I don't like these standards? Why shouldn't I use my own standards? Don't I have a right to my own opinion? What if I'm just an emotional person? What if I like to follow my intuition? What if I think spirituality is more important than reason? What if I don't believe in being rational?" When people reject questions calling for sound evidence and good reasoning, they fail to see the difference between offering legitimate reasons and evidence in support of a view and simply asserting the view.

Intellectually responsible persons, in contrast, recognize questions of judgment for what they are: questions requiring the consideration of alternative points of view. Put another way, intellectually responsible persons recognize when a question calls for good reasoning (from multiple points of view), and they behave in accordance with that responsibility. This means that they realize when there is more than one reasonable way to answer a question.

To determine which of these three types of questions you are dealing with (in any given case) you can ask the following question: Are there relevant facts I need to consider? If yes, then either the facts alone settle the question (and you are dealing with a question of procedure), or the facts can be interpreted in different ways (and the question is debatable). If there are no facts to consider, then it is a matter of personal preference. Remember, if a matter is not one of personal preference, then there must be some facts that bear on the question. If the facts settle the question, then it is a "one-system" procedural question.

Think Through Complex Questions

When addressing a complex question, realize that you need to figure out which domains of thought are embedded in the question. Does the question, for example, include a dimension focused on money? Does it include a parenting dimension, a biological, sociological, cultural, political, ethical, psychological, religious, historical, or some other dimension? For each dimension of thinking inherent in the question, formulate questions that force you to consider complexities you otherwise may miss. As you become better skilled at reasoning through complexities, the quality of your life should improve.

When focusing on domains within questions, consider such questions as:

- What are the domains of thinking inherent in this complex question?
- Am I dealing with all the relevant domains within the question?
- Am I leaving out some important domains?

- Within the main question, what are the sub questions which lay out the tasks I need to reason through before trying to answer the main question?

Think Through Complex Questions: An Example

Consider some of the domains of questions inherent in this complex question: What changes do I need to make in order to be mentally well? (See more on questions within important life domains in Chapter Nine.)

Economic
- What economic forces affect my mental health?
- What can I do to improve my economic situation?

Professional
- Am I satisfied in my choice of profession?
- Am I fulfilled in the job I now have? Am I achieving my capacity?
- Do I need to make a professional move to become more fulfilled?

Social/Sociological
- What social groups am I a member of? Do these groups help or harm me?
- What social groups can I join to improve my mental health?
- What people are in a role to influence me and what is their influence?
- Is anyone influencing me who I need to avoid in future?

Psychological
- How do factors such as stress, my unique personality, and the ways in which I view childhood traumas support affect my mental health?
- What role does irrationality play in my life?
- What am I doing to relax and appreciate life every day?
- What activities do I enjoy doing just for fun, like playing an instrument? Am I making sure I am actively pursuing these activities?

Biological/Physical
- How might genetics play a role in my mental health problems? How might I fight against these influences?
- What biological limitations do I have? Can I work around these to reach my goals?
- What do I need to do to stay physically fit, which should improve my mental health?
- What types of physical activities am I most likely to enjoy and persevere through?

Educational
- What do I need to learn in order to become mentally well?
- What education do I need to pursue in order to become more fulfilled?

Religious
- What religious views do I hold? Are these views based in sound reasoning?
- How do my religious views, or how does my religious upbringing, affect my mental health?

Cultural
- What cultural beliefs adversely affect my mental health?
- What cultural views am I unable to accept? How can I work around social customs in order to achieve self-fulfillment?

Ask Ethical Questions

Ethics is the study of what benefits or harms people and other creatures. Human behavior can be either ethically praised (if someone acts to benefit the welfare of others) or criticized (when someone acts so as to harm others). Ethics is not to be confused with social conventions, laws, or religious beliefs. Unethical acts deny another person or creature an inalienable right. Social conventions and laws, as well as religious beliefs, vary enormously along national and cultural lines. In contrast, all ethical questions are settled in accordance with ethical concepts and principles that do not so vary. Ethical questions can be either simple or complex. Without essential understandings in ethics, it is difficult to live the life of an ethical person, which is required for authentic mental health.

The following classes of harmful acts enable us to define universal rights:

- SLAVERY: Enslaving people, whether individually or in groups.
- GENOCIDE: Systematically killing with the attempt to eliminate a whole nation or ethnic group.
- TERRORISM: The use or threat of violence to achieve political aims, especially against civilians.
- TORTURE: Inflicting severe pain as an act of revenge or to obtain information from a person.
- SEXISM: Treating people unequally (and harmfully) by virtue of their gender.
- RACISM: Treating people unequally (and harmfully) by virtue of their race or ethnicity.

- MURDER: The premeditated killing of people for revenge, pleasure, or to gain advantage.
- ASSAULT: Attacking an innocent person with intent to cause grievous bodily harm.
- RAPE: Forcing an unwilling person to have intercourse.
- FRAUD: Intentional deception to cause someone to give up property or some right.
- DECEIT: Representing something as true which one knows to be false in order to gain a selfish end harmful to another.
- INTIMIDATION: Forcing others to act against their interests or deter from acting in their interests by use of threats or violence.
- Putting persons in jail without telling them the charges against them or providing them with a reasonable opportunity to defend themselves.
- Putting persons in jail, or otherwise punishing them, solely for their political or religious views.

Distinguish Among Questions of Ethics, Questions of Cultural Preference, and Questions of Religion

Ethical questions are often confused with questions from other domains—for example, social conventions, religion and the law. People commonly believe that social conventions, laws, and religious beliefs are self-evidently ethical. Yet social norms, religious theology, and laws all may advocate unethical behavior. People can be socially ostracized or imprisoned for behavior that is not ethically wrong. Many religions have been used to justify such ethically repugnant practices as racism and slavery.

The following examples highlight confusions of ethics with religion, law, or social conventions:

Confusing Ethics and the Law:

- Many sexual practices (such as homosexuality) have been unjustly punished with life imprisonment or death (under the laws of one society or another).
- Many societies have enforced unjust laws based on racist views.
- Many societies have enforced laws that discriminate against women.
- Many societies have enforced laws that criminalize unpopular beliefs.
- Many societies have made torture and/or slavery legal.

Confusing Ethics with Social Conventions:

- Many societies have created taboos against showing various parts of the body and have severely punished those who violate them.
- Many societies have created conventions denying women the same rights as men.
- Many societies have socially legitimated religious persecution.
- Many societies have socially stigmatized interracial marriages.

Confusing Theological Beliefs with Ethical Principles:

- Members of majority religious groups often enforce their beliefs on minorities.
- Members of religious groups often act as if their theological views (which are in fact debatable) are self-evidently true, scorning those who hold other views.
- Members of religious groups often fail to recognize that "sin" is a theological concept, not an ethical one. ("Sin" is defined theologically.)
- Divergent religions defend divergent views of what is sinful (but often expect their views to be enforced on all others as if a matter of ethics).

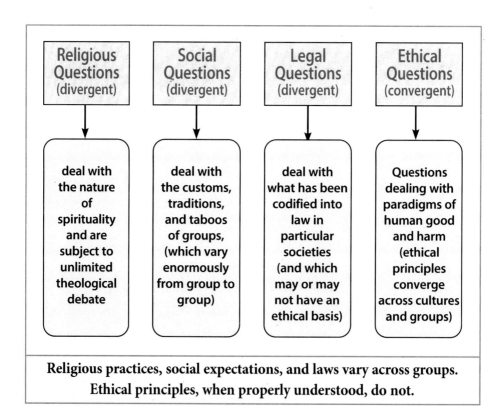

Religious Questions (divergent)	Social Questions (divergent)	Legal Questions (divergent)	Ethical Questions (convergent)
deal with the nature of spirituality and are subject to unlimited theological debate	deal with the customs, traditions, and taboos of groups, (which vary enormously from group to group)	deal with what has been codified into law in particular societies (and which may or may not have an ethical basis)	Questions dealing with paradigms of human good and harm (ethical principles converge across cultures and groups)

Religious practices, social expectations, and laws vary across groups. Ethical principles, when properly understood, do not.

Question Your Egocentrism

As you have learned, one of the primary barriers to the development of insightful thinking is the natural human tendency toward egocentric thought. And as you now know, to take command of your egocentric tendencies, you need to actively target these tendencies through questions. In other words, you need to routinely question your motivations and study your own selfishness and narrowmindedness.

Further, one of the natural motives of the human mind is the desire for power. All of us need some power. If you are powerless, you are unable to satisfy your needs. Without power, you are at the mercy of others. Hence, the acquisition of power is essential for human life. But you can pursue power through either rational or irrational means, and you can use power to serve rational or irrational ends. Power used irrationally is typically rationalized through egocentric (and sociocentric) thought.

Questions You Can Ask to Target Your Egocentrism

By focusing on the two motives of egocentric thinking, you can formulate questions that target your own egocentrism, questions specifically designed to uncover selfishness and self-validation. Here are some examples:

- Do I usually consider the views of those who disagree with me? Do I tend to assume that those who disagree with me are wrong?
- Do I tend to place my needs and desires over the needs and desires of others?
- When I have something personal to gain, does my fairness to others diminish?
- Will I personally gain something for myself in this situation if I ignore or distort some information or viewpoint?
- Am I usually willing to consider that I might be wrong?
- Do I tend to ignore information that would require me to rethink my position?
- Do I tend to assume that I know more than I actually do?
- Do I assert information to be true when I don't know for sure that it is?

You can also question the motives of others, through questions such as:

- Is this other person considering my rights and needs, or the rights and needs of others?
- Is he using me to serve his selfish interest?
- Is she distorting what I am saying? If so, why? Does she have something to gain by doing so?
- Is he trying to manipulate me?

- Is she honestly trying to understand what I am saying? Is she able to accurately state what I am trying to say?
- Is she willing to admit she might be wrong?
- Is he open to reason? Or is he close-minded?
- Is she refusing to consider relevant information in order to maintain her viewpoint?
- Is he assuming that he knows more than he does?
- Is she asserting something as true that may not be?

Question Your Sociocentrism

Sociocentric thinking, as you will recall, is egocentric thinking raised to the level of the group. It is as destructive as egocentric thinking, if not more so, as it carries with it the sanction of a social group. When sociocentric thinking is made explicit in the mind of the thinker, its unreasonableness is generally evident. However, just as individuals deceive themselves through egocentric thinking, groups deceive themselves through sociocentric thinking. Just as egocentric thinking functions to serve one's selfish interest, sociocentric thinking functions to serve groupish interests. Just as egocentric thinking operates to validate the uncritical thinking of the individual, sociocentric thinking operates to validate the uncritical thinking of the group.

Questions You Can Ask to Target Your Sociocentric Tendencies:

- What groups do I belong to and how do they influence my behavior when I am with the group? How do these groups influence my behavior when I am away from the group?
- Is it in my best interest to belong to these groups?
- What does this group require of its members (its demands)?
- What behaviors does this group forbid (its taboos)?
- What behaviors are allowed within the group (its range of free decision)?
- What would happen to me if I went against the taboos of the group or culture? Would I be ostracized? Would I be imprisoned? Would I be killed?
- How does my society influence my behavior?
- What is involved in thinking like an American (a German, a Japanese person)?
- Have I ever thought within the perspective of another culture?
- What beliefs and behaviors does my culture punish? Are these forbidden behaviors unethical, or are they culturally relative?
- What would happen to me if I violated any of the taboos of my culture?

TARGET *INFORMATION, ASSUMPTIONS,* AND *INFERENCES* TO IMPROVE YOUR MENTAL HEALTH

As you now recognize, the elements of reasoning interrelate. They continually influence and are influenced by one another. In this section, we will focus on the crucial relationships between three of the elements: information, inferences, and assumptions. Learning to distinguish among these three elements is an important skill in your ability to understand what is happening in the world, and therefore to living as a mentally healthy person.

We will begin with *information.* Humans continually use information in their reasoning. Some of this information is false, distorted, or misconstrued when presented to them. Some of this information they themselves misconstrue through their interpretations, and through their desire to see reality in a particular way.

It is impossible to reason without using some set of facts, data, or experiences. These facts and data should be accurate, and the ways in which you view your experiences should be based in facts. To experience mental well-being, you must be vigilant about the sources of information you accept and use. You must critically analyze how you perceive your own experiences. You may have heard that experience is the best teacher, but biased experience supports bias, distorted experience supports distortion, and self-deluded experience supports self-delusion. In other words, when you consider your experiences, realize you may be misremembering or misunderstanding what happened in the situation that you interpret as your experience. You should therefore not think of your experiences as sacred, but instead as one important dimension of thought that must, like all others, be critically analyzed and assessed.

Many problems exist in human life because people fail to understand the important role information plays in everything we do. You may, for example, fail to see that you are excluding important information from your thinking when reasoning through a complex problem. You may operate on automatic pilot when it comes to your use of information. But when you are explicitly aware of the importance of information, you are much more careful in the conclusions you come to. You seek information when others would ignore the need to do so. You question the information you have, as well as the information others are using. You realize that your thinking can only be as good as the information you use to come to conclusions. You understand that your behavior is greatly impacted by the ways you see and use information.

Information, Assumptions, and Inferences in Relationship

But how do humans make use of information in reasoning? This is done through our interpretations of the information, which are guided by our assumptions. Assumptions are the beliefs we have formed which we now take for granted, and that we therefore do not feel the need to question. They lie primarily at the unconscious level, but we humans naturally and regularly make inferences based on these assumptions. We must do so to make sense of where we are, what we care about, and what is happening. Assumptions and inferences permeate our lives precisely because we cannot act without them. We make judgments, form interpretations, and come to conclusions based on the assumptions we have formed, the information we use in our reasoning, and how we perceive that information (see Figure 6.6).

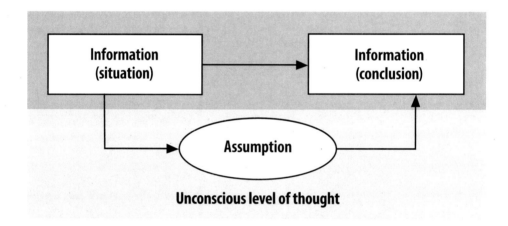

Figure 6.6: Humans routinely draw conclusions in situations. These conclusions are based on assumptions that usually operate at the unconscious level.

If you put humans in any situation, they start to give it some meaning or other. People automatically make inferences to gain a basis for understanding and action. So quickly and automatically do we make inferences that we do not, without training, notice them as such. You see dark clouds and infer rain. You hear the door slam and infer that someone has arrived. You see a frowning face and infer that the person is angry. If your friend is late, you might infer that she is being inconsiderate. You meet a tall man and infer that he is good at basketball, an Asian woman and infer that she will be good at math. You meet a well-dressed person and infer that he or she is successful. You think of the business you would like to start and infer it will be successful, because you desire what it will sell. You are told you are worthless and infer that this is true.

As you see, many of our inferences are justified and reasonable, but many are not. As always, an important part of critical thinking is the art of bringing what is unconscious in your thought to the level of conscious realization. This includes the skill of identifying and reconstructing the inferences you make, so the various ways in which you view your experiences through your inferences become more and more apparent to you. This skill enables you to identify and separate two elements of reasoning that contribute to your impression of your own experiences: information and inferences. In other words, you learn to distinguish the raw data of your experiences from your *interpretations* of those data—i.e., from the inferences you are making about them.

In turn, you need to realize that the inferences you form are heavily influenced by your point of view, and by the assumptions you make about people and situations. This realization allows you to broaden the scope of your outlook, to see situations from more than one point of view, and, hence, to become more openminded and mentally well.

It should be clear then that different people often draw different inferences because they bring to situations different points of view, leading them to see the data differently. And they have different assumptions about what they see. For example, if two people see a man lying in a gutter, one might infer, "There's a drunken bum." The other might infer, "There's a man in need of help." These inferences are based on different assumptions about the conditions under which people end up in gutters, and these assumptions are connected to the point of view about people that each has formed. The first person assumes, "Only drunks are to be found in gutters." The second person assumes, "People lying in the gutter need help."

The first person may have developed the point of view that people are fundamentally responsible for what happens to them, and that they should be able to take care of themselves. The second person may have developed the point of view that the problems people have are often caused by forces and events beyond their control. The reasoning of these two people, in terms of their inferences and assumptions, could be characterized in the following way:

Person One
- Situation: A man is lying in the gutter.
- Inference: That man's a bum.
- Assumption: Only bums lie in gutters.

Person Two
- Situation: A man is lying in the gutter.
- Inference: That man needs help.
- Assumption: Anyone lying in the gutter needs help.

As a person concerned with developing your thinking to improve your mental health, you want to begin noticing the inferences you are making, the assumptions you are basing those inferences on, and the point of view you are holding. To do this, you need lots of practice in noticing your inferences and then figuring out the assumptions that lead to them.

INTERNALIZE THE IDEA: DISTINGUISH BETWEEN INFORMATION, INFERENCES, AND ASSUMPTIONS

It is essential that you are able to distinguish among information, inferences, and assumptions. Whenever you are in a situation, you naturally make inferences. You come to conclusions about the situation or give it meaning through your interpretations. And these inferences result from the assumptions you have made or are making.

- If it were 12:00 noon, what might you infer? (It's time for lunch.)
- If there are black clouds in the sky? (It's probably going to rain.)
- If Jack comes to work with a black eye? (He was probably in a fight and hit by someone.)
- If there are webs in the corners of the ceiling? (Spiders made them.)
- If there is heavy traffic on the freeway? (I will probably be late for work).

For example:

- If it were 12:00 noon and you inferred that it was time for lunch, what did you assume? (That whenever it is 12:00 noon, it is time for lunch.)
- If there are black clouds in the sky and you infer that it's probably going to rain, what did you assume? (That it usually rains when there are black clouds in the sky.)
- If Jack comes to work with a black eye and you infer that he must have been hit by someone, what did you assume? (That people develop black eyes only when they have been hit by someone.)

INTERNALIZE THE IDEA: DISTINGUISH BETWEEN INFORMATION, INFERENCES, AND ASSUMPTIONS: CONTINUED

In the following activity, you will be provided with situations (information). Figure out what someone might infer (rightly or wrongly) in the situation. Usually there is a range of possible inferences different people might make, depending on their various beliefs.

Then, having stated what you think someone might infer, figure out the assumption that would lead someone to make that specific inference. As a suggestion, first figure out a likely inference (whether rational or irrational); then, and only then, try to figure out the assumption. The assumption will be a generalization that led the person to make the inference. Two examples have been provided to help you begin.

Information	Possible Inferences	Assumptions Underlying These Inferences
1. A police officer trails your car closely for several blocks.	The officer is going to pull me over.	When police officers trail people, they are planning to pull them over.
2. You do not get an increase in salary while others in your department do.	It is unfair that I did not get a raise.	Whenever others in my department get a raise, I should get one too, or it is unfair.
3. You see a child crying next to her mother in the grocery store.		
4. Your child yells at you when you tell him to clean his room.		
5. You notice a man in the bookstore reading a book by Karl Marx.		

DISTINGUISH BETWEEN INFORMATION, INFERENCES, AND ASSUMPTIONS: CONTINUED

Information	Possible Inferences	Assumptions Underlying These Inferences
6. While in a restaurant, your friend orders a steak cooked very rare.		
7. A colleague tells you she is pregnant and is going to have an abortion.		
8. Your teenage son comes home late from a late-night date.		
9. Your spouse is talking to an attractive member of the opposite sex at a late-night party.		
10. The telephone rings in the middle of the night.		
11. Your significant other does not call you when promised.		

Get Command of Your Inferences and Assumptions

Because all human thinking is inferential in nature, commanding your thinking depends on commanding the inferences embedded in it and the assumptions underlying it. In other words, becoming aware of the inferences you make and the assumptions that underlie your thinking enables you to gain more control over your thinking. Consider the way in which you plan and think your way through everyday events: you think of yourself as preparing for breakfast, eating your breakfast, getting ready for work, arriving on time, attending meetings, completing necessary tasks, making plans for lunch, paying bills, engaging in small talk, and so on. Another way to put this is that you are continually interpreting your actions, giving them meanings, and making inferences about what is going on in your life.

Throughout this process, you must choose among a variety of possible meanings. For example, am I "relaxing" or "wasting time"? Am I being "determined" or "stubborn"? Am I "joining" a conversation or "butting in"? Is someone "laughing with me" or "laughing at me"? Am I "helping a friend" or "being taken advantage of"? And every time you interpret your actions, every time you give them a meaning, you are making one or more inferences on the basis of one or more assumptions. Realize that whenever you make an inference, you may be wrong. Inferences are not facts. Inferences are your tentative conclusions in a given situation. Every time you make an inference, you might have made a different one. Practice saying, I infer X, but I may be wrong.

As humans, we continually make assumptions about ourselves, our jobs, our partners, our therapists, our parents, and the world in general. We take some things for granted simply because we can't question everything, but sometimes we take the wrong things for granted. For example, I run off to the store (assuming I have enough money with me) and arrive to find that I have left my money at home. I assume I have enough gas in the car, only to find that I have run out of gas. I assume that an item marked down in price is a good buy, only to find that it was marked up before it was marked down. I assume I mean well in my dealings with others; I assume my children will behave respectfully to others if we teach respect in our home.

We make hundreds of assumptions each day without knowing it—without thinking about it. Many of them are sound and justifiable. Many, however, are not. The question then becomes, "How can you begin to recognize the inferences you are making and the assumptions you are basing those inferences on?"

As you become skilled in identifying your inferences and assumptions, you are in a better position to question the extent to which any one of your assumptions is justified. For example, are you justified in assuming that you need validation from others to be mentally well? Are you justified in assuming that you need your spouse always to agree with you? Are you justified in assuming that someone is your friend when you have evidence that this person is talking ill of you behind your back? The point is that you need to be able to recognize and question the many assumptions you make in daily life. As you develop these critical intuitions, you should increasingly notice your inferences and those of others. You should increasingly notice what you and others are taking for granted. You should increasingly notice how your point of view shapes your experiences. You should become more skilled at making reasonable inferences, which should have a direct impact on how you see the world and, consequently, on your mental health.

INTERNALIZE THE IDEA: GETTING MORE PRACTICE IN DIFFERENTIATING INFERENCES FROM ASSUMPTIONS

Using the same format as we used in the previous activity, come up with ten "episodes" of thinking for yourself, which include a situation, a possible inference in the situation, and the assumption leading to the inference.

Information	Possible inference one might make	Assumption leading to the inference
1.		
2.		
3.		
4.		
5.		
6.		
7.		
8.		
9.		
10.		

When you explicitly identify inferences, and then figure out the assumptions leading to these inferences, you gain more control over your thinking and, therefore, your life. You begin to uncover the assumptions or beliefs you take for granted, that are guiding your actions. If, for instance, you assume that all supervisors are arbitrary, controlling people, this is what you will see in every supervisor you have. If you take for granted that the industrial pollution caused by your company doesn't cause health problems, you won't be motivated to check this assumption to see if it is justified, given the evidence. If you assume your spouse will always be there for you, no matter how badly you treat him or her, you might be in for an unwelcome surprise later on.

One additional point of clarification: People often say, "I assume X is true, or I assume X," when what they mean is "I infer X is true," or "I infer X." If they assumed it, they probably wouldn't state it; they would take it for granted and therefore, would not feel the need to state it. They would likely think that others shared their view as well (and therefore would not check their assumptions with those other people). Remember that assumptions usually lie at the unconscious level of thought and are thus not always easily accessible.

INTERNALIZE THE IDEA: BEGIN TO NOTICE YOUR INFERENCES IN EVERYDAY LIFE

Once you understand the differences among information, inferences, and assumptions, take time each day to notice the inferences you and others make. When faced with a new situation, ask yourself, "How am I making sense of this? What am I inferring right now? What assumption is leading to this inference? Is this a logical inference in this situation or context?"

UNDERSTAND HOW YOUR *CONCEPTS* DRIVE YOUR THINKING AND BEHAVIOR

Concepts are ideas we accumulate and use to guide our thinking and make sense of the world. Humans have both shared and individualized concepts; shared concepts come from common usage, while individualized concepts are the specific ideas you formulate and the specific ways in which you use them.

On shared concepts: it is safe to assume that many of your current ideas were uncritically assimilated into your thoughts. Much of this happened as you were growing, at a time when you (like other children) would have lacked developed critical capacities to see through problematic ideas and belief systems. However, some of this also happened in adulthood, as the uncritical adoption of ideas is a human tendency and not simply a childhood tendency. Like most people, you have likely never seriously examined many of these ideas, because you have taken them for granted from your past. These ideas, existing mainly at the unconscious level, are not easily accessed—yet they are the notions, beliefs, and ideologies through which you largely order and perceive what is happening in the world.

Shared concrete concepts are typically easy to understand and unambiguous. Because of the era you have been brought up in, you can easily envision the concept of a couch, chair, computer, world wide web, mobile phone, table, hand, face, kitchen, car, and so forth. However, grasping abstract concepts can be far more complex, regardless of the historical era in which one is living. Consider your concept of love, intimacy, family, career, happiness, or fulfillment. Being intangible, these concepts may be difficult to pin down. People vary in their ideas of each one. Yet to be a responsible thinker, you should understand the constraints embedded in each of these concepts. You should not use the term love, for instance, to manipulate someone into thinking you deeply care for her or him. Similarly, when others say they "love" you, you should not accept their usage of the term when they clearly do not understand you and when they show no concern for your growth, development and well-being.

Ideas are to us like the air we breathe. We take them in, often uncritically, then project them everywhere. Yet we rarely notice this. Most people have no notion of what a concept or idea even is, despite that we use ideas to create our very way of seeing things. What we experience, we experience through ideas, often funneled into the categories of "good" and "bad." We assume ourselves to be good. We assume our enemies to be evil. We use positive terms to cover up the indefensible things we do. We use negative terms to condemn even the good things our enemies do. We conceptualize things personally, by means of experience unique to ourselves (often distorting them to fit our world view). We conceptualize things socially, based on the ways in which we have been indoctrinated or socially conditioned, while often having little to no understanding of how we have been indoctrinated or conditioned.

You have already been introduced to a number of core concepts which, if taken seriously, can improve your life. Beginning with chapter two, you were introduced to the *elements of reasoning, intellectual standards*, and *intellectual virtues*, all of which are central ideas in critical thinking. Each of these primary ideas entails a number of concepts, which together formulate a constellation of concepts. The barriers of egocentric and sociocentric thinking also represent foundational concepts in a robust conception of critical thinking. One of our goals is for you to increasingly utilize these concepts, explicitly, as you transform yourself into the person you want to be.

In the section focused on purpose, we explored several key concepts which, when internalized, should give you additional leverage for improving your thinking and hence the quality of your life. These include *free agent, existential vacuum, group pathologies, economics, capitalism,* and *the will to achieve.*

Ideas, then, are our paths to either reality or self-delusion. Yet we don't typically recognize ourselves as engaged in idea-construction of any kind, whether illuminating or distorting. In our everyday lives, we don't consciously experience ourselves shaping what we see and constructing the world through our thoughts.

To the uncritical mind, it is as if people in the world came to us with our labels for them inherent in who they are. "He is a scoundrel." "She is a flirt." "They are savages." And it is as if we ourselves are permanently labeled in our own minds. Through a sense of inferiority, for instance, you may conceptualize yourself as follows: "I am worthless." "I could never achieve like her." "I just can't ever get things right." "I am not lucky." Or, through a sense of superiority or intellectual arrogance, you may conceptualize yourself in the following manner: "I am the smartest person here." "I should be the leader since I always know best." "I am inherently right." "Give me all the power; everyone else is to do what I say!" Both forms of irrationality—orientations of inferiority or superiority—are self-handicapping. It is easy to see that when you feel inferior and continually tell yourself you are incapable of accomplishing anything of value, you will have great difficulty achieving within your capacities. On the opposite end, when you continually tell yourself you are the best, smartest, and brightest of all, you are typically unable to see where your thinking needs improvement, and are likely to become self-righteous when challenged.

Underachievers can fall into both of the above categories. People frequently maintain within themselves an odd mixture of intellectual arrogance (as in, "I am right even though I am unwilling to consider—or have not even sought out—the evidence"), while in other situations, feeling a sense of inferiority (as in, "I'm too stupid to learn X"). Like those with overblown self-regard, such people typically become self-righteous when challenged.

To achieve mental well-being, you must come to recognize the ideas through which you see and experience the world. You must become the master of your own ideas. You must learn how, in good faith, to think within alternative ideas and alternative "world views." As general semanticists remind us: "The word is not the thing! The word is not the thing!" If you are trapped in one set of concepts (ideas, words), your thinking is then limited and limiting. The word and the thing become one and the same in your mind (such as in the earlier example of the term love being used as a manipulative tool). You are unable, then, to act as a truly free person, being trapped in your own narrow ideas while allowing people to manipulate you through their distorted use of language.

In this section, you will find some examples of how to improve the ways you think and live by targeting the concepts that guide your reasoning. Although we are now focusing on concepts, you will note that throughout this section—as in every section on the elements of reasoning—the other seven elements can and may be brought into view at any time.

Key Concepts in Rational Emotive Behavior Therapy

One rigorous therapeutic school that relies on some core critical thinking principles lies in the work of Albert Ellis, through his rich conception of *Rational Emotive Behavior Therapy* (REBT). Throughout his professional life, Ellis wrote and co-authored many books designed to help people become less self-defeating. To benefit from REBT, I recommend his culminating book, *A Guide to Rational Living* (Ellis & Harper, 1975) as a starting place. Ellis develops (and, in some cases, captures in clever whimsical terms) concepts that guide dysfunctional thinking. For instance, he admonishes people to avoid what he calls *musterbating*, or obsessing over and upsetting yourself about things outside your control. He warns people to avoid *self-downing*, or dumping on yourself and telling yourself you are no good (i.e., a *no-goodnik*). He continually advises people to avoid *awfulizing* and *horriblizing* situations and events, or exaggerating their importance and blowing them out of proportion.

In the diagram on the next page, you see a brief snapshot of Ellis' primary concepts (as I perceive them) through the lens of critical thinking. Note how the elements of reasoning can be used to open up any reasoning—including the reasoning of any mental-health theoretician or therapist.

"What disturbs men's minds is not events but their judgments on events." –Epictetus → **Theory of Albert Ellis REBT**

The purpose of life is happiness, but many/most people are too self-defeating to be happy; they don't see that they can become independent, happy people by taking command of their pathological tendencies.

Conceptual Understanding of Irrationality

All human behavior has clear-cut ideological antecedents; people continually re-indoctrinate themselves using irrational and unjustifiable ideologies; only if they continually re-evaluate the ways they have been indoctrinating themselves will irrational people get better. All behavior comes from thoughts; people create their own thoughts; so they create their own pathological thoughts. Therefore they can intervene with more logical or rational thoughts.

Key concepts and emotions of self-defeating people:

- low frustration tolerance
- musterbating
- irrational interpretations of information & experiences
- ignoring evidence
- disturbing themselves about people & things they can't change
- perfectionism
- re-indoctrinating oneself into pathological beliefs
- self-downing
- re-creating "bad memories"
- sexual frustration
- awfulizing & horriblizing
- self-fulfilling prophesies
- deep emotional disturbances that come from pathological thinking

Strategies for Actively Attacking Irrationality

People need to create and employ strategies for actively intervening in their irrational thoughts (the therapist uses direct questioning).

Use the scientific method "to attack" irrational ideas:
- Look at the real evidence   • Is your thinking clear?   • Are you being logical?

Design and follow through on homework that forces you to face and dispute your irrational fears, no matter how uncomfortable. People must persistently block irrational ideas that cause them to suffer.

Focus on the language you use to explain situations; get underneath the superficial explanation to the real explanation (sane sentence followed by unsane sentence). First sentence is the info, second sentence is the interpretation. Target the interpretation.

People who actively work on their irrationality use these concepts in their thinking:

- actively fight against self-defeating tendencies
- evidence as a guiding force
- unconditional other-acceptance
- daily strategic homework
- encourage appropriate emotions: disallow debilitating emotions
- vigorously attack irrational thoughts
- unconditional life-acceptance
- dispute irrational beliefs
- unconditional self-acceptance
- logical interpretations

©2025 Linda Elder

The Logic of Albert Ellis' Reasoning on Rational Emotive Behavior Therapy

Going beyond key concepts, we may capture the logic of Albert Ellis's reasoning by focusing on all the elements of his thought, as you can see below. Some of this logic may make sense to you only when you have read his book, *A Guide to Rational Living.* [10]

1. The *purpose* of Ellis' REBT:

To help people with self-defeating tendencies realize that if they actively work on their pathological thinking, they can significantly reduce the amount of suffering it causes them, thereby living a much happier life.

2. The key *questions* at the heart of Ellis' thinking:

What do we need to know about the mind if we are to intervene in our self-defeating tendencies and live more fulfilling lives? What causes people to be self-defeating? What strategies are the most effective for people to learn, internalize, and practice daily if they are to effectively reduce the power of their self-defeating tendencies? What role does language play in human thought, as well as in the development and perpetuation of self-defeating tendencies?

3. The primary *information* Ellis uses in developing his theory:

   a. *Information about what has worked for him personally* in getting command of his own neuroses. This includes information from his own personal narrative—specifically, strategies he developed and used as a child that helped him take command of his negative thinking, focus on what he could control, and take positive action to enjoy life even in difficult conditions.

   b. *Information on his clients' thinking and behavior,* which he gained through many years of engaging in psychotherapy with thousands of patients (i..e, experiences with clients).

   c. *Information he was taught as a PhD student, and as a young psychotherapist,* while studying in primarily the Freudian and Rogerian Schools of thought. After about ten years, much of this information was rejected by Ellis as useless in helping people gain command of their pathological tendencies of thought.

   d. *Information on the role of language in thinking,* specifically from the thinking and works of Ludwig Wittgenstein, Bertrand Russell, the analytic philosophers, and semanticists.

4. Ellis' primary *inferences*:

---

10 For the full reference, see Recommended Readings.

a. People should understand that they can take command of their minds so as to significantly reduce the amount of emotional pain they cause themselves.

b. People need to create definitive strategies for intervening in their own pathological thoughts, and they must aggressively follow through on these strategies.

c. People need to understand the role of language in human thought and human life, especially as it relates to human pathologies. If people want to become less self-defeating, they must take command of the language they use to explain their problems. They must look underneath the conscious level of thought by paying close attention—not to the first sentence they tell themselves about what is happening in their lives, but to the second, third, etc. (which reveal deeper thoughts or problems).

d. People need to apply the tools of the scientific method to think more logically, and to look at evidence more clearly.

e. Irrational people need to recognize that they continually "re-indoctrinate" themselves into, and become trapped within, false ideologies that cause them to suffer emotionally. Using these ideologies, irrational people create pathological ideas and interpretations; however, with active intervention, they can create healthier ideas for guiding their thoughts and actions. To do so, they must vigorously and consistently attack their irrational thoughts throughout life.

5. Ellis' primary *assumptions*:

a. Theory that doesn't help people become less pathological, though it may have this goal and be embraced by mental health professionals, should be tossed out as useless and replaced with theory that does help people live more rationally.

b. To understand the mind, one should study the best thinking that has been done on the mind and learn from it. But one should also look at what logically makes the most sense when applied to real-life situations and real-life people.

c. People should aim to be happy and fulfilled; this is the ultimate goal of life.

d. People can be happy and fulfilled even if traumatic events happen to them in their lives, which is almost inevitable.

e. It isn't what happens to people that ultimately determines the quality of their lives, but rather how they interpret situations and whether they take command of those interpretations.

     f. People should work to develop themselves; they should not live solely to please others.

     g. The scientific method, or logical thinking, should be a guiding force in human life.

     h. If people follow his approach conscientiously and consistently, they will be far happier, more fulfilled persons. This approach is far simpler than people think it is, if they are just willing to practice and take the theory seriously.

     i. If people internalize and act on a few powerful ideas from REBT, their lives will significantly improve.

     j. Feelings come from thinking, and thinking is influenced by feelings; the key is to target the thinking and ask whether it is logical.

6. Ellis' primary *concepts*:

     a. Irrationality as created and perpetuated by human thought.

     b. The role (misuse) of language in pathological thought.

     c. The malleability of our interpretations. This is based partly on the insights of Epictetus, who said, "What disturbs men's minds is not events but their judgments on events." Ellis was heavily influenced by this belief, and Epictetus was a guiding force in his work.

     d. Memories of past experiences as under your command, not set in stone; past experiences as deliberately recreated in the moment; past experiences as created or "recreated" in the mind over and over again through active choice, rather than existing as permanent "memory" to be automatically relived, regardless of one's will; memories as under the command of one's will.

     e. "The scientific method"—specifically, looking at the real evidence in a situation, asking whether you are being logical, and making sure your thinking is clear. Ellis uses a number of intellectual standards implicitly, such as relevance, significance, and justifiability, and would likely place this theory under the scientific method. (However, it appears he means critical thinking more broadly, rather than the scientific method per se.)

     f. Low frustration-tolerance; mustivating; horriblizing; disturbing yourself over things you cannot change, or that you have no control over.

     g. Self-downing; overgeneralizing negative situations and events; negative self-fulfilling prophesies

     h. Re-indoctrinating yourself into pathological beliefs

i. Ego-centered thought as problematic for one's development; the deeds of a person as primary; avoiding an egotistic orientation towards your accomplishments or failures; understanding human thought as flawed in many ways.

j. Humans as intrinsically fallible; being comfortable with making mistakes as a natural part of life; learning from mistakes; adopting a positive attitude towards mistakes.

k. Emotional states as decisions that are under your influence; seeing yourself as capable of "disallowing" dysfunctional emotional states and recognizing them as a waste of precious energy.

l. *Negative emotions* resulting from deeply-held beliefs, reinforced over and over again and, hence, deeply ingrained; *negative feelings* as temporary, normal human states that all people experience, but which do not overwhelm or paralyze them.

m. Happiness as a fundamental human purpose; finding happiness in small things every day; living intensely in the moment, however you can, whatever your circumstances; focusing on what you can change, not on what you have no control over.

n. Having maximum self-command—controlling all aspects of your life that you can, including the people you allow to influence you or that you allow in your life.

o. Emphasizing logical possibilities as a guiding force in your life

p. Sexual frustration as a primary cause of irrationality in people.

q. Strategic thinking and daily homework for dealing with one's neuroses.

r. Consistently attacking one's own irrational beliefs

s. Avoiding perfectionist tendencies that cause pain when you are unable to live up to your unreasonable expectations; humans as given to making mistakes, and as always being in some state of imperfection; being comfortable with being flawed.

7. Ellis' *point of view*:

Ellis is looking at human irrationality, seeing it as fundamentally created and repeatedly recreated—by the mind; seeing the command of language as essential to living rationally, and to experiencing happiness; seeing irrational tendencies as requiring active, deliberate, skilled processes of intervention that must be developed and practiced over time if one is to be fulfilled.

8.a. If self-defeating people take Ellis' reasoning seriously, some likely important **implications** are:

    i. They will be far less irrational.

    ii. They will have definitive tools for intervening in their own pathological thoughts and actions.

    iii. They will experience more fulfilling intimate relationships.

    iv. They will less likely expect the world to be, and people to behave, as they wish them to be and behave.

    v. They will have far greater command of their personal lives and their personal relationships.

    vi. They will spend less time on people and pursuits that are a waste of their time, or that cause them emotional pain.

    vii. They will think far more logically.

    viii. They will be less sexually frustrated.

    ix. They will be in greater command of their emotional lives and experience more positive emotions.

b. If self-defeating people fail to take Ellis' reasoning seriously, some likely important implications are:

    i. They will continue to be irrational and suffer the consequences, because they will lack tools for actively intervening in their own irrational thinking. For instance, they will likely engage in such self-defeating tendencies as "musterbating," "self-downing," 'horribilizing," "awfulizing," etc.

    ii. They will be far less likely to enjoy life and intimate relationships.

    iii. They will have far less control of their personal lives than they might have if they were to discipline their minds.

    iv. In terms of their personal lives, they will rarely think logically, allowing their egocentric thoughts and emotions to cause them all manner of problems, emotional pain, and internal suffering.

    v. They will likely be sexually frustrated with no insight into how to change this.

    vi. They will often feel trapped within their own pathological thoughts; they will not be intellectually, emotionally, or sexually free persons.

This logic of Albert Ellis' reasoning helps illuminate the power in using the elements of reasoning to deconstruct the logic of a given theoretician's philosophy. To fully make sense of and benefit from what has been detailed above would require that you study the work of Ellis, which dovetails directly with some of the critical thinking theory introduced in this book (though Ellis rarely uses explicit critical thinking terms).

INTERNALIZE THE IDEA: IDENTIFYING CORE CONCEPTS OF ALBERT ELLIS' WORK

After reading this brief section on the work of Albert Ellis, and presupposing my analysis to be sufficiently accurate, complete these statements:

1. Albert Ellis uses the following concepts that I believe would be valuable for me to seriously consider . . .

2. These concepts are important to me because . . .

3. If I were to use these concepts more frequently in my thinking, I would likely experience the following results . . .

4. Therefore, I intend to . . .

Understand and Command Your Concept of Intimate Relationships

An important dimension of your personal life is your interpersonal relationships. Therefore, it is essential to analyze the personal relationships which often function as the core of your personal life. Let us begin by focusing on intimate relationships.

Critical thinkers realize the importance of seeing intimate relationships precisely for what they are. When you are reasoning critically, you face the facts within your intimate relationship. You seek to fully understand your partner. You do not deceive yourself into thinking the relationship is more, or less, that it is. You understand your own purposes in the relationship, as well as the purposes of your partner. You also understand your shortcomings as well as the shortcomings of your partner. You think deeply about the meaning of love, both in general terms and in your intimate relationship.

Intimate Love and Sexual Intimacy

As I have mentioned, people frequently have a distorted view of love. They often get their idea of love from the media, which romanticizes love or demeans it in any number of ways. But intimate love means caring deeply for the welfare, happiness, and development of your partner. It means finding fulfillment in seeing the other person blossom and thrive. It means deep and long-term commitment as long as the love relationship is shared. Conversely, it does not mean holding onto the other person in a dysfunctional way or using him or her as a security blanket. It never involves exploitation, cruelty, or domination.

In *The Art of Loving* (1956), Erich Fromm says, "Love is the active concern for the life and the growth of that which we love" (p. 22). He goes on to say that respect plays a large role in love. To Fromm, respect is

> . . . the ability to see a person as he is, to be aware of his unique individuality. Respect means the concern that the other person should grow and unfold as he is. Respect, thus, implies the absence of exploitation. I want the loved person to grow and unfold for his own sake, and in his own ways, and not for the purpose of serving me. If I love the other person, I feel one with him or her, but with him as he is, not as I need him to be as an object for my use. It is clear that respect is possible only if I have achieved independence; if I can stand and walk without needing crutches, without having to dominate and exploit anyone else. Respect exists only on the basis of freedom: "l'amour est l'enfant de la liberté" as an old French song says; love is the child of freedom, never of domination. (pp. 23-24)

Fromm goes on to say, "To love somebody is not just a strong feeling—it is a decision, it is a judgment, it is a promise" (p. 47). He juxtaposes this concept of love with that of selfishness:

> The selfish person is interested only in himself, wants everything for himself, feels no pleasure in giving, but only in taking. The world outside is looked at only from the standpoint of what he can get out of it; he lacks interest in the needs of others, and respect for their dignity and integrity. He can see nothing but himself; he judges everyone and everything from its usefulness to him; he is basically unable to love. (pp. 50-51)

INTERNALIZE THE IDEA: THINKING ABOUT YOUR CONCEPT OF INTIMATE LOVE

As you begin to analyze an intimate relationship in your life, or to think seriously about the kind of intimate relationship you might eventually seek, you will need to examine your concept of intimate love. Complete these statements:

1. My concept of intimate love is . . .

2. In other words, when I think of being in an intimate relationship, I see myself behaving in the following ways . . . And I expect my partner to behave in the following ways . . .

3. In analyzing my concept of intimate love, I realize . . . about myself.

4. In my current intimate relationship or past intimate relationships, I [have/have not] behaved in accordance with a reasonable concept of intimate love. I have come to this conclusion because . . .

5. A more reasonable conception of love than the one I've used historically would be . . .

Intimate love seems to be a basic human need and is undoubtedly one of our primary aims. In its most sublime form, it entails an ongoing, rich sexual life. Of course, sexuality is one of the great mysteries of human existence, since it comes to us through primitive instinct and is played out through primitive behavior. Yet as humans, we always bring language into our activities, however instinctive or primitive; we cannot escape giving meaning to our sexual experiences through ideas. In other words, though our sexual experiences are thrust upon us through primitive desires, we conceptualize them largely through language. This means we also impose restrictions on our sexual experiences through our ideas, which get in the way of sexual knowledge and pleasure. Sexual intimacy is a blissful state in which primitive desires are shared, in which all partners are equally drawn to one another sensually and sexually, and who entirely trust one another within the sexual experience. Intimate love in its most elevated form can only be realized when both sexual intimacy and intimacy outside the sexual realm are achieved, and then maintained, throughout the loving relationship.

Sadly, and perhaps it goes without saying, intimate love is rarely realized in human relationships. Where have you witnessed it? Where do you see models of it in videos, movies, or TV programs? Where do you see healthy intimate love depicted in social media or anywhere else on the internet? Have you ever experienced anything like it? How would you go about finding and developing intimate love? Does society encourage or discourage intimate love? What rules or laws does society improperly impose on people's sexual lives? How has your view of sexuality been affected by parental or societal influences? How do you conceptualize intimate love?

Intimate love is so rare in human life that only with great difficulty can most people see examples of it in their own circles of friends, colleagues, and family members. You may never find this form of love, but when you commit to a life of reasonability—including in your intimate and sexual life—you will be prepared to participate in it, should you be so lucky as to find the right partner for you along life's path. But do always keep firmly in mind that your ability to give and receive intimate love does not depend on whether you are in a relationship now. If specific others do not love you, it doesn't follow that you are not lovable. Within yourself, by your habits and deeds and through your world view, you create a lovable person (or not). You do not need others to love you in order to know you are worthy of love; to think otherwise is unreasonable.

Again, though you may seek far and wide for the intimate companion to share your love, you may still never find the person you seek. This is true for many reasons, including the fact that we humans, though of the same species, are each of us unique, living within the language of our own minds, living within the logic and habits of our own thoughts, living within belief systems and ideologies we have absorbed over time. In short, the challenge is to find a partner who can connect with your way of seeing the world, while also being physically and sexually attracted to you to the same degree and on the same level as you are to your partner. To find such a person requires some luck and exertion on your part. And, if and when such a partner is found, it requires deep commitment to a rich concept of love between you. But you have to live with the realization that when it comes to intimate relationships, as with the duration of life itself, nothing is guaranteed.

Are You Trapped Within Rigid Thinking About Your Intimate Relationship?

If you are unhappy in a current romantic relationship or marriage, as you assess the impact of this relationship on your mental well-being, you will need to figure out whether and to what degree you may be trapping yourself within rigid thinking. For example, many people feel trapped in marriage. Social pressures still frequently guide people to "Stay together for the sake of the kids," or to believe "You made your bed, now lie in it." When things go wrong in a marriage, and one of the spouses is taken advantage of by the other, the retort is often, "Marriage is a series of compromises." No doubt, marriage does involve compromise, and any number of reasons might exist for a bad marriage. But when you are doing far more compromising than your partner, should you stay or get out? If you feel trapped in your marriage, it is often, if not usually, the case that you are free to leave. You may be telling yourself that you cannot possibly leave the marriage. You may be telling yourself that you cannot afford to leave; or that if you were to find someone else, he or she would probably be worse than your current partner; or that your life isn't really as bad as it seems (even when the facts don't support this conclusion). You may be telling yourself that you will leave eventually, like when the children are grown (never considering the possibility that you are wasting precious time in an unhappy marriage, or worse, that you may not even be alive when the children leave home.)

You may be telling yourself that your children need both parents in the same home, that they deserve to grow up in an "intact" family. You may be doing this even when you and your partner routinely bicker and fight with one another, conveying to your children that normal intimate adult relationships involve bickering and fighting on a regular basis. You may be staying in the marriage, even when you know that children who grow up in households with daily parental disharmony frequently end up in marriages with the same sort of discord.

Much of the time, these reasons you give yourself are simply excuses—in other words, rationalizations—that keep you trapped in believing you are doing the best thing under the circumstances. When your mind does this, you are a victim of your own self-deception. You may tell yourself again and again that you have no choice but to stay in the relationship, when in fact you do have a choice. Due to your insecurities, you may be unable to face a future with uncertainties. It may be that you would rather stay miserable than face the fact that you need to get out of the relationship, and that this requires standing on your own two feet.

But you need not see yourself as ensnared in circumstances you can *in fact* change. Critical thinkers are adept at knowing what they can and cannot change. They face the truth about the lives they are living. They do not limit their options unreasonably. They see life as a wonderful opportunity to grow and develop. They do not allow themselves to be dragged down by people (including spouses) who are negative and oppressive. They control the decisions they make. They realize that it is never too late to get out of an unhappy and unproductive marriage. They realize that life is short, and that they have a right not be hurt or taken advantage of by a partner. They realize they might never find a rational person to intimately share their future with, but that if they do not, they can find much satisfaction from being masters of their own lives and free from the unpleasantness of irrational romantic relationships. In other words, they do not need others to validate them as worthy persons. They find strength from within, and they realize that to the extent true security can be found, it must be found in themselves as reasonable, ethical persons.

Could You be the Problem in Your Relationship?

Of course, reasonable people also recognize when *they* are creating the fundamental problems in their respective marriages. They are willing to face the problems in their thinking that lead them to unfair actions in their intimate partnerships. When they see themselves taking advantage of a partner through domination or submission, they actively work to stop themselves from doing so. They do not deceive themselves into thinking a partner is chiefly responsible for discord when the evidence points to the contrary.

In developing as a critical thinker, then, you begin to see your intimate relationship or marriage for what it is. You may decide to stay in a relationship that is not ideal when the positives outweigh the negatives, but most importantly, you are able to *accurately perceive* the marriage with whatever shades of gray are present. And if you decide to stay in a relationship that is less than what you would hope for, you do so with the full realization of what you are doing, with willingness to accept the other person for who and what they are. Do not expect the other person to change in any fundamental way if he or she is not committed to changing. Do not subtly "punish" your partner for not being the rational person you would like him or her to be.

As you assess your relationship, consider these questions:

- How often and to what degree do you and/or your partner stoop to underhanded stratagems to get back at one another, or to manipulate one another?
- Do you bicker and argue? Can you imagine a relationship in which you do not argue? Do you want to live in an argumentative relationship?
- Can you reasonably continue living in this relationship?
- Do you communicate openly with one another, or do you hide things from each other? If you hide things, why do you?
- Do you have shared values and goals? Do you enjoy being with one another, or do you avoid each other?
- Do you talk behind your partner's back, saying things about him or her that you would not say to his or her face, or that you would not openly admit to?
- Are you acting in bad faith in the relationship?
- Are you lying to your partner?

Emotionally well people do not remain in argumentative relationships, because these relationships keep them from developing into their capacities and living a life of peaceful contentment. They recognize senseless arguing as a type of pollution to be avoided. This view runs counter to some theories that encourage people to fight and bicker to let off steam. But encouraging this type of negativity only keeps people locked in unhealthy relationships, and leads to greater destruction to the psyches of all people involved.

For those not in an intimate relationship, but who seek one, the principles underlying your thinking should follow the above analysis. You must first understand your purpose in the relationship. What are you hoping to get out of it? What can you reasonably expect of the other person? What are you willing to give? To what extent do you yourself have a reasonable conception of love? To what extent do you understand what it means to be in a deep and loving intimate relationship with another person? To what extent are you even able to place the quality of another person's life on the same plane as your own?

As you begin to analyze your intimate relationship, and your purposes within it, this may be a difficult or painful process. You may have to face parts of yourself or your partner that you are uncomfortable facing. You may ultimately conclude that you cannot fully develop as a rational person if you remain in your marriage or with your partner, or you may have to finally see yourself as fundamentally selfish in the relationship. However painful this process might be, once you think through this relationship, you should emerge with a better understanding of the realities you face. You should be better able to conceptualize the relationship in its most true light, and to act in accordance with that recognition. And if you have to face that you are the primary problem in the relationship, do not beat yourself up about it. Recognize and face the problems in your thinking and then move on to do whatever is in your power to improve the situation.

INTERNALIZE THE IDEA: ANALYZING THE LOGIC OF YOUR INTIMATE RELATIONSHIP

Focusing on either your current intimate relationship or one from your past, figure out the logic of the relationship based on the elements of reasoning. Complete the following statements:

1. *My purpose* in the relationship is/was . . .

2. The most significant *concepts* operating in my thinking in this relationship is/was . . .

3. The main *conclusions* I have come to about the relationship are . . .

4. I base these conclusions on the following *information* about the relationship . . .

5. Some of the significant *assumptions* I make/made in the relationship are/were . . .

6. Some of the important *implications* of my thinking and behavior in the relationship are/were . . .

7. The most fundamental *questions* operating in my thinking in this relationship are were . . .

8. The *point of view* from which I view(ed) the relationship is/was . . .

Now, using the critical thinking standards outlined in Chapter Six, assess the extent to which the thinking you just outlined is rational. In other words, to what extent is your purpose justified? To what extent are you using justifiable concepts in your thinking (concepts such as love, respect, caring, etc.)? To what extent are the assumptions you use in the relationship reasonable? . . . and so forth.

Understand and Command Your Concept of Parenting

Just as you need to command your concept of intimate relationships, so do you need to command your concept of parenting if you are a parent (or intend to be one). From the beginning of their lives, you interact with your children in ways that directly flow from your concept of parenting. These interaction patterns influence the quality of your life as a family, and often have a significant impact upon your children's development. Thus, there are at least three fundamental aspects from which you should look at your relationships with your children:

1. First, consider your ultimate purposes as a parent and whether your daily interaction patterns with your children, and the model you provide for them,

are in keeping with those purposes. By doing so, you begin to clarify your *concept* of parenting and whether you are living up to that concept.

2. Second, in connection with this, think about the ways in which your behavior (and your spouse's behavior) influence the quality of your children's lives, the ways in which family members affect the quality of one another's lives, and the ways in which any of these influences may affect your children in the long run. In doing so you will realize that your concept of parenting is connected with your concept of *family*, and you should see some of the many ways in which your influence on your children, though important, is limited—even within the family.

3. Third, realize that your children come to you with their own predispositions, over which you may have little or no influence. These predispositions may determine how your children interact with those around them (including you), what they are drawn to, the challenges they might face, how difficult learning may be for them, how others may influence them, the trouble they may get into, and the achievements they may realize.

Let us first consider your influence on your children. As a parent, you *may* have significant influence on the ultimate quality of your children's lives. From your daily interaction patterns to the long-term plans you make for them (purposes), from the behavior you require of them to the decisions you make for them, from the activities you allow them to be involved in to the friends you allow them to have, from the moment of birth (and the months preceding) to the end of childhood, again and again and again, your treatment of your children is but *one* influencing factor in the ways they see the world and behave within it.

This said, parenting decisions are typically an important factor in a child's development. As such, you should realize that the quality of your parenting can only be as good as the quality of your thinking as a parent, and the thinking you do *about* your parenting. Yet few parents spend adequate time *thinking* earnestly about what they ultimately want for their children, whether these goals for their children are reasonable, and how (or if) they can realistically achieve these goals. To do so means to think through, for example, what your purposes are or should be for your children. It requires thinking through the important implications of your parenting on the ultimate quality of your children's lives, as well as how this may impact the way your children's behavior will affect others' lives. It means continually reevaluating your behavior in light of these aims to determine whether your choices will likely support these purposes or deter from them.

If, for example, you want your children to learn to read well, to read often and read for pleasure, then you need to create structures that support their reading on a regular basis at home (including having a home library and being a reader yourself). You need to *think* about how you can achieve this goal and how you might remove the obstacles to achieving it. You cannot assume that your children will reach this objective through the influence of schooling. In fact, they may inadvertently be learning in school that reading is neither valuable nor pleasurable. At the same time, realize that many children now view reading for depth of understanding as somewhat old-fashioned, given the electronic world they have been thrust into from birth. Why should they read books when they can be entertained by the internet or video games? Why should they struggle through complexities in the real world when they can hide in digital space? Given the many obstacles to your goal, you may require your children to read regularly at home. You may give rewards when they do so, or you may make activities they find more enjoyable than reading available to them only when they have finished the reading you require of them. Of course, the reading process you engage your children in needs to be enjoyable if they are to realize its full benefits; you might therefore let them pick out many of the books they read. At the same time, you encourage them to broaden their reading base—for example, from mediocre fiction to classic fiction, from fiction to non-fiction, and from the light-hearted to the more serious. Still, notwithstanding your best intentions about reading, your children may never come to appreciate its importance to the liberally-educated mind. Such outcomes can result from many reasons outside your control, and dwelling negatively and unproductively on these uncontrollable factors does not help you or your children.

In short, your parenting can only be as good as the thinking you do about your parenting, the ways in which you conceptualize parenting, and your ultimate purposes in parenting—all understood in interrelationship with the unique internal resources and motives of your children. You must therefore bring disciplined thinking to bear upon the relationships you have with your children, while accepting them as their own persons. Critical thinkers do not allow their parenting to become whatever it will become naturally. They realize that they, like all people, are given to egocentric thinking. They understand that they themselves may be easily influenced by social groups that do not have a healthy concept of parenting.

INTERNALIZE THE IDEA: THINKING CRITICALLY ABOUT YOUR PARENTING

Take some time to analyze at least part of the logic of your parenting as it is. Be as honest with yourself as you can. Then think through at least part of the logic of your parenting as you would wish it to be. Complete the following statements:

1. At present, given my behavior, my *purpose* in parenting seems to be . . .

2. At present, given my behavior, the main *inferences* (or conclusions) I have made about parenting are . . .

3. The *information* I have used to come to these conclusions is . . .

4. At present, given my behavior, some *implications* (or consequences) of my parenting are . . .

5. Some of the *assumptions* I have made about parenting are . . .

6. To this point, my *concept* (or my idea) of parenting has been . . .

Now let's turn to the logic of your parenting as you would like it to be. Complete the following statements:

1. Given my values, my *purpose* in parenting should be . . .

2. To achieve this purpose, the *information* I should use in my thinking is . . .

3. Considering this information, the main *inferences* (or decisions) I should make about parenting are . . .

4. If I pursued my purpose with commitment and follow-through, some *implications* for my behavior (and the behavior of my children) might be . . .

5. Some of the *assumptions* I would make are . . .

6. My *concept* of parenting would be . . .

Many people are unclear as to the concepts that drive their thinking as parents. And because they are unclear about these concepts, they are often unable to teach these ideas to their children. You may have some vague sense that you want your children to grow up to be decent people, for example. But if you have not thought through what it means to be a "decent" person, you will likely fall short of your goal. By the term *decent*, do you mean ethical? If so, do you yourself understand the difference between what is ethical and what is merely socially acceptable? Can you tell when the two overlap and when they diverge?

To think seriously about the concept of parenting itself, you need to ask and answer questions like these:

- What does it mean to be a parent in a full, rich sense of the word?
- How do rational persons comport themselves as parents?
- What are some ways in which irrational parents approach parenting?
- To what extent should you get your definition of parenting from social norms and standards?
- To what extent should you give in to your children?
- To what extent should you be more demanding?
- To what extent should you give your children consequences for inappropriate behavior? To what extent should you try to reason with them instead?
- When should you make decisions for your children, and when should you let them make decisions for themselves? In any specific situation, what are some important benefits and drawbacks to each approach?
- How do you determine whether you should guide your children in making a given decision? What guidelines do you use? If you seem justified in guiding your children, do you have sufficient knowledge to do so, or do you first need to gather more data?
- How can you help your children pursue the development of their unique capacities while contributing to the family and common good?

If you want your children to behave in accordance with rational concepts in human life, it is important to explicitly define and explain these concepts and behave in accordance with them yourself. To do this, for example, you might develop a weekly evaluation form that you can use with your children (depending on their ages), wherein you explicitly state the meaning of the concepts you want them to use. You could then ask them to evaluate, on a weekly basis, the extent to which they behaved in accordance with those concepts. As a parent, you should also complete the evaluation forms yourself, honestly stating whether and to what extent you are using these concepts in your thinking. The more often you admit to mistakes in your thinking, the more you model intellectual humility, and the more your children come to see you as an honest person. This also shows them the value in admitting one's mistakes.

Our form might look something like the form on the next two pages (*note the key concepts*).

Weekly Evaluation Family Goals

Date:

1) Harmony

We have harmony when we are working together and helping each other.

I contributed to family harmony by_____

_____

I diminished family harmony when I_____

_____

2) Thoughtfulness

We have thoughtfulness when we try to think of ways to make others happy.

I tried to make others happy by_____

_____

I was not thoughtful when I _____

_____

3) Kindness

We have kindness when we do things to help others, and when we are sympathetic or generous to others.

I tried to be kind by _____

_____

I was unkind when I _____

_____

4) Understanding

We have understanding when we listen carefully to what others say and represent what they say accurately.

I tried to show understanding by_____

_____

I was not understanding when I _____

_____

5) Respect

We have respect when we show consideration for others, when we speak to each other quietly and courteously, without sarcasm or ridicule.

I tried to show respect by _____

_____

I showed disrespect when I _____

_____

6) Justice

We have justice when we show that we care about the rights, needs, and desires of others.

I tried to be just by _____

_____

I was unjust when I _____

_____

7) A Place to Learn and Develop

Our home is a place to learn and develop when we recognize that our happiness tomorrow depends on what we learn today.

I demonstrated my commitment to learning by _____

_____

I showed I was not committed to learning when I _____

_____

Whatever means you use to encourage your children to develop as rational persons, again, remember that it is essential to fully face the limits of your influence. Though parents may have enormous influence on the long-term intellectual and social growth of their children, remember the many other powerful variables competing with this influence that can greatly diminish it (video games, social media, and other internet influences; peers, teachers, and school bureaucracies; movies, drug culture, the dystopian effect; etc.).

The video programming your children watch, for instance, can significantly influence their interactions with people. Indeed, it can deeply affect the very way they see the world. If your daughter watches movies depicting young female characters as overly emotional, reacting to the stress of dealing with daily problems by attempting suicide, she may be at greater risk of thinking this behavior normal and therefore acceptable. She may then emulate this behavior in her own life. As parents, it is difficult to counter these types of powerful emotional messages, especially in a world where children accessing social media even in elementary schools is the norm.

As you think about your parenting, then, consider it in relationship with other influences in your children's lives. Which of these influences can you sway or control? Which can you not control? Which should you try to control? What irrational influences can you counter with rational ones? The more carefully you ponder important purposes and questions in parenting, and the more you understand the key concepts you are using to guide your reasoning, the better your parenting will be.

Still, however children have been parented, they are ultimately responsible for their thoughts and actions as they grow into adulthood and navigate their way through life. Your parenting skills may be excellent, and your parenting behavior may be entirely reasonable, while your children may nevertheless turn out to be irrational, destructive persons.

Help Your Children Become Rational Persons

If you want your children to fully develop as rational persons, they should learn the same concepts and ideas you are learning in this book. In other words, they need to learn how to command their own minds. They need to learn how their own egocentrism can be a powerful deterrent to their development as reasonable, capable persons. They need to learn how sociocentric thinking works in human life and what we can do to diminish its power in our own lives. They need to learn how to take their own thinking apart and evaluate it for flaws, as well as how to appropriately analyze and assess the thinking of others. They need to learn to take command of their learning in order to master it. In short, they should be introduced to critical thinking as a set of tools and principles for the mind, and they need practice in applying the concepts of critical thinking in their lives every day. When we foster critical thinking in our children, they become better equipped to deal with flaws in their own reasoning, and to reason through the problems and decisions they will inevitably face in their lives.

Help Your Children Develop a Reasonable Concept of Themselves and Their Responsibilities to Others

Just as you can significantly influence your children's lives, so can your children significantly influence the quality of yours. Just as a child can be destroyed by a parent, so can a child destroy a parent.

When our children are very young, we essentially give to them, as we should. Because we love them and care about their development as human beings, we nurture and protect them. When they cry, we try to figure out what they need, and we answer those needs if we can. When they fall, we help them up and check for injury. We do our best to provide for their basic needs and many of their wants. We do this without asking anything in return.

But as our children grow and emerge from early childhood, as they approach adolescence and beyond, the relationship between parents and children will increasingly need to be based on mutual caring, respect, compassion, and love. This is also true of relations among children in the home. Otherwise, the atmosphere will over time become toxic, even with just one person behaving irrationally on a regular basis. When one or more people in the family are destructive, mean, petty, bullying, manipulative or otherwise irrational, the entire family suffers.

This can be a difficult time for parents and children, in part because we often think of our children as being entitled to unconditional love. And this concept of unconditional love can be erroneously defined as love that demands nothing, that accepts any and every form of behavior, however damaging, vicious, or destructive. And these pathological forms of living tend to creep up on families who began with good intent.

Because our children, like all of us, are by nature egocentric, they will tend to operate in the world in terms of how it can serve them. This means they may well expect us, as their parents, to essentially cater to them. And they may use manipulation in elaborate forms to get us to do this: they may cry to get their way. They may sulk. They may give sophisticated reasons for why they should get what they want. Alternatively, they may use various forms of domination to get what they want: they may yell at us, swear at us, or even push or hit us.

When we allow our children to get away with using these egocentric strategies to get what they want, at least two important consequences follow. First, we teach them that it is altogether acceptable to be self-centered persons and to act in bad faith. Second, peace of mind cannot be maintained in the atmosphere of the family, and therefore the quality of life for everyone in the family is diminished.

The fact is that every one of us must eventually be held accountable for our conduct, our children included. All persons capable of thinking about how their behavior influences the lives of others are responsible to contribute to, rather than impoverish, the quality of life for those around them. As soon as is reasonably possible, you should therefore begin teaching your children that they are responsible for becoming giving members of the family, and eventually of society. Children should learn that all humans are responsible to help make the world a better place, according to their capacities. This responsibility begins at home. To the extent that we fail in this, our children may well become users, first of us and then of others. They may then get better and better at manipulating others to serve their selfish desires, at dominating others or submitting to them, in pursuing their irrational goals.

Assuming your children are capable of doing so, they should become independent persons as they reach adulthood, no longer relying upon you to prop them up or give them what they need to survive. They should be able to objectively analyze their relationships to you and other family members, seeing each person as separate from the others, each with their own unique needs and desires. They should recognize your humanity. To the extent that you have made mistakes in parenting them, they should be able to accurately interpret those mistakes and the reasons for them. They should see that, just as they will eventually make mistakes with their children (assuming they have any), so did you with them. Ideally, they will be able to avoid making the same mistakes with their children that you made with them.

At the same time, you should never allow your children to dump on you, to control you in any way, or to negatively influence the quality of your life through unreasonable demands and emotional outbursts. Put another way, you should expect them to behave as well as is reasonable for them to behave, given their age and circumstances.

Consider Your Concept of Friendship

Now let us move beyond familial relationships to the relationships you have with friends. For our purposes, the concept of *friends* refers to people with whom you choose to develop long-term relationships, whom you deeply care about, and whose company you value and enjoy. The concept of friends in this context does not mean common acquaintances (frequently referred to as "friends"), but rather people with whom you have important things in common and whose welfare you are concerned with. For our purposes, the *Oxford English Dictionary* (March 2023) defines a friend as, "A person with whom one has developed a close and informal relationship of mutual trust and intimacy."

Friends are people who may significantly influence you, and whom you may significantly influence. Based on our discussion thus far, it should be clear that the quality of the influence your friends have on you will only be as good as the thinking they engage in, both in general terms and in relationship to you. In the same way, the influence you have on your friends can only be as good as the thinking you do while influencing them.

Many people seek friendships with those people who will gratify, humor, and indulge them and who will constantly tell them how wonderful and marvelous they are. They telephone their friends to offload their frustrations, to complain about their situation and the people around them, often to be told how correct and right they are in everything they do. Using this skewed concept of friendship, they are naturally disappointed when their friends point out weaknesses in their reasoning. They think of friends not as people who help them reflect on their true selves and improve who they are, but instead as those who agree with them and support their choices unconditionally. In short, many people seek friendships for the sheer purpose of being validated, rather than as relationships of mutual learning, contribution, and growth.

While we all need connections with other humans, it is essential to seek those friendships which enhance your life and that of the other person. Your group of true friends will naturally be small in number, since you have limited time to give to the lives and development of others. But where you do have friends, you, and they, should actively participate in the well-being of one another.

Expand Your Concept of Mental Wellness to Include the Common Good and the Greater Good

One way to elevate your mental health is to throw your excess energy into projects and activities that contribute to the lives of others. This requires conceptualizing the quality of your life as dependent on your ability to contribute to the greater good. Of course, this presupposes that you are first taking care of your basic needs. You can hardly contribute to others' well-being while neglecting your own. However, part of your welfare depends on your willingness to reach out to something bigger than yourself, to help improve things for others, to contribute your unique skills to a higher cause. People who work to improve (for example) the habitats of animals, or the lives of children, or the health of the planet demonstrate the endless ways and means available for making the world less sad and more compassionate. These people conceptualize their own well-being as intertwined with those they can help, even in small ways. Yet they do not depend on these others for their own sense of self. They give unconditionally to those in need, and to the health of the planet. They do not give of themselves to be thanked, esteemed, or "repaid;" they understand that self-worth comes from living a life of ethical sensitivity, and from believing in their own abilities to do what makes the best sense in each situation.

HOW YOUR *POINT OF VIEW* AFFECTS YOUR MENTAL HEALTH

Point of view is one of the most challenging elements of reasoning to master. On the one hand, it is highly intuitive to most people that when we think, we think within a point of view. On the other hand, when people are asked to identify or explain their point of view when reasoning something through, they are likely to begin expressing anything and everything they are thinking about. Clearly, most people do not have a clear sense of how to identify someone's point of view, including their own.

Let us begin by recognizing that there are many potential sources for your point of view: time, culture, religion, gender, discipline, profession, peer group, economic interest, emotional state, social role, or age group, to name a few. For example, you can look at situations from the viewpoint of:

- A point in time (e.g., the 1st, 9th, 17th, 20th, or 21st century)
- A culture (e.g., Western, Eastern, South American, Japanese, Turkish, or French)
- A religion or theology (e.g., Buddhist, Christian, Muslim, Jewish, atheist or agnostic)
- A gender (e.g., male, female, or gender-neutral)
- Sexual orientation (e.g., homosexual, heterosexual, bisexual, or pansexual)
- A profession (e.g., a lawyer, manager, psychologist, or teacher)
- A discipline (e.g., biological, chemical, geological, astronomical, historical, sociological, philosophical, anthropological, literary, artistic, musical, dance, poetic, medical, nursing, or athletic)
- A social group
- An intimate partner
- A parent
- A professional group
- An economical interest
- An emotional state
- An age group
- A company philosophy

Your point of view reflects some combination of these dimensions and others. But are you aware of the extent to which these factors shape your point of view? Typically, people do not say, "I am seeing this situation from the point of view of . . ." Instead, people characteristically say something that implies, "This is the way things are." Our minds tend to absolutize our experience. People usually have no sense that they are looking at things in a partial, rather than objective, way.

Your point of view entails what you are looking at, how you are seeing it (from what vantage point). When you look at your children, how do you see them? When you look at your career, how do you see it? When you look at the quality of your life, how do you see it? When you look at your intimate partner, or your romantic life, how do you see it? If, for instance, you look at your children as extensions of yourself, you might then expect them to behave as you do, to have the insights you have, and to follow the career path you are on or want for them.

But if you see your children as unique persons with their own intellectual and ethical challenges, you recognize them as distinct from you, as individuals, and are therefore not surprised when they behave accordingly. If you look at your career as satisfying and fulfilling, your mental health should reflect these positive feelings. But if you view your career as disappointing, you may then view yourself as a disappointment, having failed to follow a career path that would have been more fulfilling. If you see yourself as trapped in a career that seems to go nowhere, your mental health will be diminished accordingly. If you view your intimate partner as contributing to your well-being, you will feel more satisfied in your relationship than if you see your partner as selfish and self-centered.

It is essential to see in any given situation or set of circumstances what is in fact happening (to the greatest extent that you can) rather than an avoidably skewed interpretation of the situation. For instance, you may be in an intimate relationship in which you see yourself as deeply in love with your partner, while sensing that he or she does not share the same level of love for you. This can lead to feelings of inadequacy on your part. In such a situation, it is essential to understand accurately both your point of view and that of your partner. With this understanding, you are in a better position to make decisions about the relationship.

As in the case of all the elements of thought, you take charge of your point of view by practicing bringing it out in the open and examining it. The more you recognize points of view at work in your thinking and the thinking of others, and the more points of view you learn to think within, the more effectively you will use points of view in your thinking, and the more in command of your own point of view you will be.

INTERNALIZE THE IDEA: PRACTICE MAKING EXPLICIT YOUR POINT OF VIEW

What follows is a list of possible objects of our thinking. Choose from this list seven possible ones to think about, then identify how you would look at each from your point of view. For example, you might decide, "When I look at people, I see a struggle to find happiness," or, "When I look at the future, I see myself as a lawyer taking cases that protect the environment," or, "When I look at the health care system, I see a system that does not provide adequately for the poor." Once you write your sentence, see if you can further characterize how it explains your point of view.

my life	computers	our health care system	drug use
my past	the news	New Age ideas	science
my parents	my economic future	human sexuality	human values
my spouse	my future	marriage	abortion
my career path	the problems we face as a nation	life in my country	the police
human conflict		religion	elections
learning	the problems we face as a species	income tax	vegetarians
the past		lifelong learning	liberals
politics	mass transportation	the future	conservatives
power	the environment	welfare	radicals
art	my mental health	welfare recipients	people without health insurance
television			

Complete the following, given the seven objects you have chosen to look at:

1. When I look at _____ from my point of view, I see . . .

2. When I look at _____ from my point of view, I see . . .

3. When I look at _____ from my point of view, I see . . .

4. When I look at _____ from my point of view, I see . . .

5. When I look at _____ from my point of view, I see . . .

6. When I look at _____ from my point of view, I see . . .

7. When I look at _____ from my point of view, I see . . .

The Point of View of the Critical Thinker

Critical thinkers share a common core of purposes in keeping with the values of critical thinking. They recognize explicit command of the thinking process as the key to commanding their behavior. They understand what practice is required for consistently reasoning at a high level of quality. They see critical reading, writing, speaking, and listening as modes of skilled thinking that self-actualized persons routinely engage in.

When critical thinkers read, they see the text as a verbal representation of the thinking of the author. They strive to enter the writer's points of view in order to expand their own views. They strive to accurately reconstruct the author's thinking in their own minds. When they write, they think explicitly about the points of view of their intended audience. They use their insight into the thinking of the likely audience to present their own thinking in the most accessible way. Their speaking reflects a parallel emphasis; they use dialogue to find out the specific points of view and concerns of those with whom they are talking. They do not try to force their ideas on others. They recognize that people must think their own way to ideas and beliefs. They therefore share experiences and information more than "final" conclusions (since conclusions put an end to inquiry and discussion, rather than further it). They listen attentively to the thinking of others. They ask more questions than they make assertions. They recognize critical reasoning as essential to mental health, since it is often our inadequate or flawed reasoning that leads to mental health problems.

Critical thinkers have a distinctive point of view concerning themselves. They see themselves as mentally well persons. They have a "can-do" vision of their own life. They do not see opposing points of view as a threat to their own beliefs. They see most beliefs as subject to change in the face of new evidence or better reasoning. They see themselves as lifelong learners.

THINK THROUGH *IMPLICATIONS* WHEN DEALING WITH SIGNIFICANT ISSUES AND DECISIONS

Among the most important critical thinking skills is the ability to distinguish between what a statement or situation actually implies and what people may merely (and wrongly) infer from it. An inference, again, is a step of the mind that results in a conclusion. For example, if the sun rises, we can infer that it is morning. Critical thinkers try to monitor their thinking so as to infer only what is implied in a situation—no more, no less. If you feel ill and go to the doctor for a diagnosis, you want the doctor to infer exactly what your symptoms imply. For example, you do not want her to infer that you simply have a cold requiring no medication when, in fact, you have a bacterial infection requiring antibiotics. Your symptoms imply that you have a certain illness, which in turn (along with other factors, such as allergies to certain medications) implies a certain course of treatment. You want the doctor to accurately infer what your illness is, then accurately infer the proper treatment for it.

It is often the case that, in thinking, people fail to think successfully through the implications of a situation. They fail to think through the implications of a problem or decision. As a result, negative consequences often follow.

In any situation, three kinds of implications may be involved: *possible* ones, *probable* ones, and *necessary* ones. For example, every time you drive your car, one *possible* implication is that you may have an accident. If you drink alcohol heavily and drive very fast on a crowded roadway in the rain, one *probable* implication is that you will have an accident. If you are driving fast on a major highway, all the brake fluid drains out of your brake cylinders, and another car immediately in front of you comes to a quick stop, one *necessary* implication is that you will have an accident.

We reserve the word "consequences" for what actually happens in a given case. In short, a consequence is what in fact occurs in some situation. If you are good at identifying (making sound inferences about) possible, probable, and necessary implications, you can take steps to maximize positive consequences in your life and minimize negative ones. On the one hand, you do not want possible or probable negative implications to become real consequences. On the other hand, you do want to realize potential positive implications. You want to understand and take advantage of the real possibilities in a situation. In short, it is essential to think through all the implications (possible, probable, and necessary) of an important decision before carrying it out.

In addition to implications that follow from concrete situations, there are those that follow from the words we use. These come from meanings inherent in natural languages; there are always implications of the words we use in communicating with people. If, for example, I tell my daughter that she cannot go to a friend's house because she failed to clean her room, I am implying that she knew she had a responsibility to clean her room if she wanted to go to a friend's house. My statement to my daughter, and my view that she should have consequences for failing to clean her room, are reasonable if:

1. She is capable of doing what I have asked her to do.

2. It is reasonable to ask a child to keep her room clean, and my standard for "cleanliness" is appropriate for the child and context.

3. I have previously communicated to her my desire that she keep her room clean.

4. I have adequately explained my reasoning and the consequences that will follow if she fails to comply with my request.

Imply Only What You Mean to Imply; Infer Only What Is Implied

As a thinker, then, you want to be aware of precisely what you are implying when you say things. You also want to take into account whether what you are implying is reasonable. When you do, you say what you mean and mean what you say—an important principle of integrity.

Just as there are implications of the language you use in communicating, there are implications of the way you say things. Much human communication occurs through vocal tone and body language; for example, the question "Why didn't you clean the kitchen?" asked calmly has different implications than when it is shouted aggressively. In the first instance, you perhaps are implying only that the other person should have cleaned the kitchen, or that you thought they were going to clean it. In the second, you are implying that the other person's failure to do so is a serious matter, warranting a severe reprimand.

What is more, just as you may fail to notice the important implications in a situation or of what you say, you also may fail to notice important implications of what others say to you. People often struggle (knowingly or not) to infer precisely what others are, and are not, implying in their use of language. People often read things into what is being said, thereby inferring more than what is being implied. If, for example, your spouse says he wishes you had consulted him before making a large purchase and means to imply nothing more, you do not want to infer that he thinks you are an unwise decision-maker. Nor does his statement imply that he doesn't want you to ever make important decisions on your own, or that he thinks he is better at making decisions than you are. What he is implying comes from the words he says and how he says them, as well as what he has done and said in similar circumstances in the past.

In sum, as a developing thinker, you want to realize the important role of implications in your life. When you are thinking through a problem, issue, or question, think through all the significant implications of the decisions you might make. When faced with a new situation or a nagging concern, infer only what is actually implied in the situation. Whenever you use language, be aware of what you are implying. When others are speaking to you, either verbally or in writing, figure out what they are logically implying. In every case, your goal should be to precisely interpret the logic of what is going on, and infer only what is truly implied—no more, no less.

INTERNALIZE THE IDEA: THINKING THROUGH THE IMPLICATIONS OF YOUR POTENTIAL DECISIONS

The ability to think through the implications of a decision you are faced with or a problem you are trying to solve is an important critical thinking skill. For this activity, think of a problem you need to find a solution to or a decision you need to make. Complete these statements:

1. The problem or decision I am facing is . . .

2. Some potential solutions to the problem, or some potential decisions I might make, are . . .

3. For each of these solutions or decisions, some implications that might logically follow if I act upon the solution or make the decision are . . .

Implications of Dystopian Thinking

In the past hundred years or more, the idea of a dystopian world has increasingly taken root. The term *dystopian* has somewhat different uses, with its core definition referring to the opposite of the ideal (*utopian*) society. As a developing concept, dystopian thinking generally refers to imagining a human future marked by great suffering, oppression, and injustice. Many people see global warming and failures to sustain the earth's resources as dystopian, which may lead to a sense of hopelessness. In addition, dystopian thinkers spotlight how in many societies today, information, as well as independence of thought and freedom of thought, are restricted or censored. People are perceived as being under constant surveillance, with little or no rights to privacy (in accord with George Orwell's predictions in his book 1984), and consequently, these people may develop a fear of the outside world. According to dystopian thinking, people are under government control, religious control, bureaucratic control, and technological control. The consequence is loss of the individual and the growing view of society as an antagonist against which people must fight or dissent.

There is dystopian fiction, dystopian conversation, and private dystopian thinking. You may be influenced by any or all of these.

It is true that humans are in many ways restricted by societal impositions, by authoritarian or sophistic governments, and by the influences and controls of religion, bureaucracy, and technology. It is true that we live in an era of government and corporate surveillance which appears to be growing worse, with its attendant loss of privacy and dignity. It is also true that neither freedom of thought, freedom of speech, nor the other basic human rights are widespread across human societies. Despite all these dark realities and their implications, in the end, as a thinker, you have two primary options. You can accept that humans are imperfect (and, in many ways, absurd), while yourself living at the highest levels of self-fulfillment possible within societal constraints, and doing what you can to contribute to a better world. Alternatively, you can assume a persona of hopelessness in which you recoil into a cloud of depression caused by feelings of impotence.

I do not at all mean to deny or ignore the dystopian features of human cultures and governments. But as critical thinkers, we can only work to remedy these problems to the extent that we are able, while also working around them to achieve what personal goals we can in our lifetimes, in keeping with conscientious values. Each of us has the right to find happiness in ways that do not harm others, despite the deficient world in which we live. This cannot be done if you emotionally collapse under dystopian thinking.

Consider: what important implications follow, for you, from harboring a sense of hopelessness? What important implications follow from nurturing a sense of impotence in yourself? What implications come from dwelling on existing dystopian realities and future dystopian possibilities? What can you personally do to change anything at all about human societies? How can you preserve your sense of self and develop your creative talents while living in this very imperfect human world?

If you fall prey to dystopian thinking, realize how this will likely affect your mental health. How can you be other than depressed if you constantly think about how sick, ridiculous, and bizarre are people, governments, their beliefs, and their actions? Answered frankly, you cannot. Realize that you are not responsible for making the world a sane place, as much as you may want to, and as clearly as you may see a path to more cultivated ways of living. You are only responsible to do what you can to positively affect any part of life or the earth itself. Beyond that, you have every right to pursue activities that bring you pleasure. You are not required to carry the weight of the world on your back; in any case, you cannot.

INTERNALIZE THE IDEA: AVOIDING DYSTOPIAN THINKING

If you fall prey to dystopian thinking, complete these statements:

1. Dystopian thinking affects me in the following ways . . .

2. I get my dystopian ideas from . . .

3. I realize I need to replace dystopian thinking with the following reasoning . . .

4. Therefore, I intend to make the following changes in my life . . .

What Is Implied for Your Future, Given Your Behavior Today?

The decisions you make today, the way you treat people, and your general attitudes toward life have implications for your future in many ways which you cannot possibly foresee. By making good decisions today, you have a chance to build on them moving forward. By making poor decisions today, you have nothing positive to build upon, and instead must continually attempt to make up for those poor decisions while frequently losing time, your reputation, relationships, career possibilities, and many other opportunities.

If you closely examine how you are now living, you can figure out many of the important implications for your future, should you continue to follow the same path.

INTERNALIZE THE IDEA: WHAT IS IMPLIED FOR YOUR FUTURE?

Think through some of the important implications of following the path you are on now. Complete the following statements for each major part of your life:

1. One thing I am doing now which may have negative implications for my future is . . .

2. Some of these negative implications include . . .

3. To change what I am now doing, I would need to . . .

4. Therefore, I intend to . . .

Implications of Developing a Voice of Reason for Your Mental Health

As you go through life, you create a voice within your mind which has important implications. What voice are you creating throughout the day, throughout your parenting, and throughout your work life from moment to moment? What voice are you giving your experiences at any given time? What concepts are you using to construct your interpretations in any situation? What are you telling yourself from minute to minute when you are alone, when you are with friends, when you are at work, or when you are in nature? What does your voice inside your head say to you about yourself, your situation, and the people around you? Does your internal voice constantly criticize you? Does your voice tell you how incompetent or unlucky you are? Does it tell you that you are not good enough and never will be? Does it tell you that no matter how hard you try, you are sure to fail? Do you tell yourself that you are always being persecuted by someone or through circumstances, and that in the end, life is always unfair to you? Do you tell yourself that there is nothing wrong with your thinking, and that everyone else is the problem? Do you say to yourself that you need validation from others to feel secure within yourself? Do you tell yourself you would not be able to survive without your therapist, spouse, reputation, or fame? Is the voice inside your head dark and dreary, or is does it turn towards hope and possibility?

The only way to sanity in the human world is by using the voice of reason actively developed through your own resources. This idea comes to us through history from such thinkers as Socrates and the Stoics. For instance, in speaking of developing the inner self, Seneca (circa 62 CE/2004) says,

> Such is more or less the way of the wise man: he retires to his inner self, is his own company . . . Natural promptings (not thoughts of any advantage to himself) compel him towards friendship. We are born with a sense of the pleasantness of friendship just as of other things. . . The wise man, nevertheless, unequaled though he is in his devotion to his friends, though regarding them as being no less important and frequently more important than his own self, will still consider what is valuable in life to be something wholly confined to his inner self. (p. 52)

> Life would be restricted indeed if there were any barrier to our imaginations. (p. 109)

> There can be absolute bedlam without so long as there is no commotion within . . . the only true serenity is the one which represents the free development of a sound mind. (pp. 110-111)

Men and birds together in full chorus will never break into our thinking when that thinking is good and has at last come to be of a sure and steady character. (p. 112)

In the following passage, Socrates (Plato, circa 409 BCE/2003) illuminates the importance of developing one's mental and ethical faculties, rather than chasing material advantage:

I have never lived an ordinary quiet life. I did not care for the things that most people care about: making money, having a comfortable home, high military or civil rank, and all the other activities— political appointments, secret societies, party organizations—which go on in our city; I thought that I was really too fair-minded to survive if I went in for this sort of thing. So instead of taking a course which would have done no good either to you or to me I set myself to do you individually in private what I hold to be the greatest possible service: I tried to persuade each of you not to think more of practical advantages than of his mental and moral well-being, or in general to think more of advantage than of well-being in the case of the state or anything else. (pp. 64-65)

As these passages show, in the end, you must rely on yourself to develop as a mentally well person. What critical thinking theory adds to these ancient thoughts is a wealth of explicit concepts that aid in developing your voice of reason.

Implications of Examining and Commanding the Rooms in the House of Your Mind

In developing your voice of reason and your ability to live as a reasonable person, consider this analogy: Each of us can be said to have, within our minds, rooms representing every major part of our lives. In other words, you may have an intimate relationship room, a parenting room, an extended family room, a professional room, a room of economics in which you think about money, a civics room in which you attempt civic responsibility (such as voting or volunteering), a reading room, a hobbies room, a physical fitness room, a relaxation room, an education room, a religion/metaphysics/spirituality room, a club room, a nature room, a history-of-your-life room. Indeed, you may have a room in your mind for every active domain of your life. These rooms are guided by the ways in which you think about the subject of the room.

INTERNALIZE THE IDEA: DEVELOPING YOUR INNER VOICE OF REASON

Begin to actively examine the inner voice, created by your mind, that speaks to you throughout your waking hours. Closely examine the moves your mind makes as you maneuver through each day. Answer the following questions:

1. What do you tell yourself as you go through each part of your day?

2. What do you tell yourself about your relationships, about your life conditions, and about your future?

3. How does your voice change from circumstance to circumstance?

4. Is your inner voice more reasonable when you are at work than when you are at home with family? Are there other contexts in which your inner voice is more or less reasonable?

5. How can you create a reasonable inner voice at all times?

6. How can you intervene in irrational thinking that drives you to do things you know you should not do?

One of your goals should be to fully command your thoughts and actions within each of these parts of your life. For instance, to what degree do you command your mind while interacting with your significant other or your children? Are you in charge of your professional life and professional future, or do you allow yourself to achieve less than that of which you are capable? Are you skilled at managing your money, or do you always feel overwhelmed by the economic realities of your situation? Have you critically analyzed your religious beliefs, or do you hold them uncritically? (After all, most people follow the religion of their youth, accepting uncritically the views of their parents while telling themselves they are entirely objective about their religious beliefs—i.e., they deceive themselves into believing that even if they had been raised with a different religion, they would still come to the beliefs they hold now.) Which rooms within your mind do you frequent to remind yourself of how unfair your life has been? Perhaps you harbor emotional trauma from the past. Perhaps you frequently go into your trauma rooms, reliving and recreating experiences from the past that you have perceived as unpleasant. What is the good of opening the door to this room and revisiting past trauma? How does this help you? How might this harm you? Are you using the data in this room to grow and move forward, or are you engaging in emotional self-harm with no productive result? Are you able to leave the door to this room closed and locked? Sure, you can explore the room to make certain you know what is there; but once you know, what is your purpose in frequenting this room? Critical thinkers can close the doors to any rooms in their minds that are not helpful or productive when entered. Critical thinkers do not obsess over their past since the past cannot be changed. When memories of the past are too painful to be reminded of, once they have been figured out, mentally well persons diligently keep the door to those memories locked.

Which rooms within your mind do you fear entering? Perhaps you are unwilling to examine your intimate relationship or your parenting; there may be something in these rooms you cannot face about yourself or the other persons. Perhaps you cannot face your religion room, because you cannot abide the possibility that the religious beliefs you have always held do not make sense. Perhaps you would prefer a different career, but you fear what may be involved in pursuing one. Fear of entering a given room in your mind is often a sign that you need to enter that room, and to work through what is bothering you within it. This requires *intellectual courage*, or in other words, the courage to examine and objectively assess your beliefs.

INTERNALIZE THE IDEA: COMMANDING THE ROOMS OF YOUR MIND

Make a list of all the important areas of your life, each of which represents a room in your mind by way of analogy. Complete these statements:

1. The important rooms in my mind are . . .

2. The rooms I need to avoid are . . . This is because . . .

3. One room I need to explore is . . .

4. Within this room, I find . . .

5. I see that I need to change my thinking about this area of my life in the following ways . . .

6. Therefore, I intend to . . .

7. Repeat numbers 3-6 for each room in your mind you need to explore.

CHAPTER NINE
EXPLORE EVERY DIMENSION OF YOUR LIFE THROUGH POWERFUL QUESTIONS

The problem of how to live one's life and how to make the most of one's life is a challenge facing every reasoning adult. Each of us must make many complex decisions, within numerous important areas of life, throughout our lives. And this must be done in a world handed to us with voluminous flaws and pitfalls. Now that you are beginning to internalize the foundations of critical thinking, you are in a better position to use its concepts and principles to improve your life moving forward.

In this chapter, we go further into one element of our reasoning—questions—for further tools to improve our reasoning. You now should know that whenever you reason, there are one or more questions guiding your reasoning. Therefore, the quality of your life is determined by the quality of the questions you ask—both globally about your life overall, and daily as you move through every part of your day. Questions drive us in one direction or another. But who determines the questions you are asking and where are your questions driving you? In this chapter we help you answer this broad question by focusing on significant domains of your life, to find strengths and weaknesses in your thinking within these domains. For each primary part of your life, you are invited to answer questions focused on that dimension, with the goal of assessing the quality of your thinking in that dimension.

In other words, in this chapter, you are encouraged to take a bird's eye view of your life, to look closely at all its important areas, so that you are taking a holistic approach to your well-being rather than narrowing in on a few parts (which may mean ignoring important dimensions). Your mental health is not determined by one part of your life, but by the totality of your experience. You may have problems in your marriage while being perfectly satisfied at work. You may love your spouse but not be able to live with her for any number of reasons. You may be overbearing with your work colleagues while a perfect angel with your friends. You may be a competent parent while also continually purchasing things that throw you and your family into debt, which may then cause you to feel inept and depressed. In short, to live as a reasonable person while being content and fulfilled, you need to live well within all the significant domains of your life—not one or a few.

To be mentally well requires that you successfully reason within, for instance, these and other essential areas of thought: how you think about your professional or work life; how you think about sexuality, love, parenting, education, learning, technology, creativity, economics, religion or spirituality, and death; how you think about yourself in relationship with the rest of the world; how you relate to yourself; and how you think about the history of your life. Some of these concepts were briefly discussed in the last chapter. Hopefully, you have by now already begun to rework and improve ideas you are using to guide your thinking and actions within these domains. Now it should be helpful to examine each major domain of your life by looking closely at your decisions and actions within them, actively seeking areas where you need to improve your thinking (and seek additional resources) to be more mentally well.

Here are the domains you will find in this chapter, briefly discussed, followed by questions that can help you think critically about that part of your life (note that many more may be added):

- Professional Life
- Intimate Relationships
- Sexuality
- Parenting
- Friendships
- Physical Health
- Self-Development, Enrichment and Relaxation
- Psychological Dimension
- Social Life
- Your History
- Ecology and Your Relationship with Nature
- How You Think About Science and the Natural World
- Your Finances

- Civic and Ethical Responsibility
- Religion/Metaphysics/ Mortality

- Your Technological Orientation
- How You Think About Power

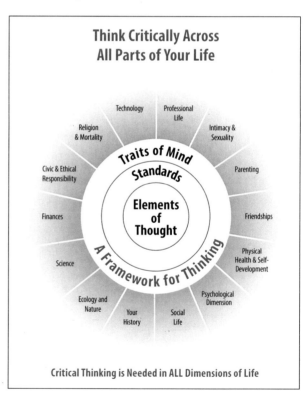

Think Critically Across All Parts of Your Life

Critical Thinking is Needed in ALL Dimensions of Life

For each section in this chapter, you should answer all the questions for each domain relevant to your life. Where you see deficiencies, you will need to dig deeper to figure out how to improve your thinking and actions within that domain. For instance, if you suspect you are not adequate as a parent, you should seek the best available advice on parenting *that addresses your precise parenting issues.* The basic tools of critical thinking reveal such questions as: "What exactly is the question that I need to answer about parenting to help me become a better parent? Where should I look for significant information relevant to the parenting issues I face? How do I know the information I have gathered is sufficient and relevant to my precise situation?" You should now be formulating questions such as these, based on your studies in previous chapters. The questions you will find in this chapter go beyond these types of general critical thinking questions and attempt to open up the domain of thinking being discussed in each section. Again, you may need to do further reading or research focused on any one of these domains, based on your unique situation and circumstances. See the *Recommended Readings* section for helpful resources within some of these dimensions.

PROFESSIONAL LIFE

Since you may spend a considerable amount of time at work, it is essential to examine whether and to what degree your work situation is helping or hindering your emotional well-being.

- Are you content with your professional path? If not, what do you need to do to be more satisfied with your professional path?
- Do you need to change careers entirely?
- Is your career path fine, but the conditions under which you work a problem?
- What type of career atmosphere would work better for you? How can you create the best atmosphere, professionally, by means within your control?
- How much control do you have over your work life? How much control might you have if you changed your career path or moved to another job?
- If you need to change your work situation, what real options do you have right now to make a change for the better?
- What work options have you ignored to feel "safe" in just having a job of any type?
- If you are unhappy working for others, might you create your own business or or nonprofit organization, using your capacities? If so, what further education or training do you need? How can you take steps right away to get this education or training? What other resources will you need to start your own organization? Can you access these resources?

- How can you create a long-term plan that would bring more of the satisfaction you need in your work life?

- Do you spend too much time at work while neglecting other parts of your life? If so, why? What do you gain and what do you lose by doing so?

- Are you trying to impress someone at work by putting in excessive hours? If so, why, and where is this getting you?

- Have you retired from work only to find yourself bored, and therefore in need of some productive work? What are your best options for developing a work (or perhaps volunteer) situation for yourself now?

INTIMATE RELATIONSHIPS

Most people desire an intimate relationship, but this may not be easy to achieve, given the complexities we humans bring to relationships. Sad to say, you may never find that ideal relationship. But if you do seek intimacy, you will need to figure out how to potentially meet someone who may be eligible as a partner, and who shares your most important values. This may mean joining certain types of groups with like-minded people working toward enlightening and fruitful goals. It may mean looking for someone through a dating website or app.

In the meantime, realize that while intimacy is highly desirable, this may not be a reality for you at present. Yet being in some loving relationships seems essential for human well-being. Most people simply cannot be loners and be well emotionally. Again, there are any number of ways you can give and receive love to meet at least part of your need for love and intimacy.

- If you are in a romantic relationship or have an intimate companion, to what degree are you satisfied in this relationship?

- When you objectively examine your behavior in your intimate relationship, what do you see? When you objectively examine your partner's behavior, what do you see?

- What precisely are the problems in the relationship? Why do these problems exist?

- To what degree do you behave reasonably in the relationship?

- To what degree does your partner behave reasonably in the relationship?

- How can you tell whether you and/or your partner are behaving reasonably? What criteria do you use?

- How do you handle conflict?

- Do you hold grudges against each other?

- Do you openly and honestly communicate, or do you hide things from each other?

- If you are hiding things from each other, what are you hiding, and why?
- Do you dominate your partner (or partners)? Are you subservient to your partner? Is your partner dominating or subservient towards you?
- What will you do to face the truth about your relationship and deal with these truths directly?
- Do you have irrational habits you bring to the relationship and cause your intimate partner to endure? If so, precisely what are these habits, and how can you stop acting in these ways?
- If you lack an intimate relationship, what are you doing to prepare yourself for the possibility that you may one day find a partner?
- What actions are you taking to involve yourself in such a relationship?
- Are you a reasonable partner? Why would someone want to live with you and become intimate with you?
- Are you avoiding an intimate relationship because you expect your behavior would be harmful toward or neglectful of a partner? If so, what patterns do you see in your thinking and behavior to create this concern, and how can you replace these with other thoughts and actions which are conducive to healthier relationships?
- Are you avoiding an intimate relationship because you know you are likely to allow yourself to be taken advantage of by the other person? Are you in such relationship now?
- Do you need to stop yourself from being with people who do not have your best interests at heart?
- How can you intervene in your destructive patterns of allowing others to run roughshod over you? Or are you running roughshod over others?
- How can you recognize your own worth in the relationship while respecting the needs and supporting the growth of the person you say you love?

SEXUALITY

Sexuality is largely misunderstood in humans. It is a natural human need, yet it can be very difficult to gratify. Other species do not seem to overlay complex communication and language ideologies onto sexuality. But humans do. And this can distort and confuse our understanding of how we should perceive healthy sex. The human need for sexuality tends to be interwoven with our need for intimacy. While sex in its raw form may be easy to achieve for some, it may be more like a massage than something deep and meaningful.

Sexuality is rarely discussed in a reasonable manner today, which largely results from the double bias of puritanism that has always prevailed in the U.S. (and in many other countries) coupled with views that stereotype men as toxic predators

328 | CHAPTER NINE

of women. Childhood sexuality has been all but crushed—given the popular, yet incorrect, view that it is unnatural for children to explore sexuality among themselves. Increasingly, children are treated as predators when they engage in sensual or sexual acts with other children. The literature on sexuality, expansive and exploratory in the 1970's, has diminished substantially; much of it has been removed from library shelves, replaced with sanitized mainstream views.

Distorted sexual views, many of which may have been thrust upon you at an early age, likely affect how you see sexuality and whether you can participate in healthy sexual relationships. Any sexual inhibitions you experience should be deeply explored to be fully understood and overcome.

Finding intimacy through a healthy sexual relationship (or relationships) is ideal, but again, you may never find this. Either way, you will need to deal with your instinctive sexual needs. Psychologist Albert Ellis has written on the importance of dealing with sexual needs through masturbation, a topic considered taboo for hundreds of years, but which is essential for most healthy people. Oddly enough, masturbation is still a forbidden topic in many circles, though it is considered by medical professionals to be healthy.

- Are you satisfied with your sexual life?
- Do you have regular orgasms?
- Are you able to effectively deal with your sexual needs, even though you may not have a partner or partners?
- If you are not having your sexual needs met, how do you channel these needs?
- Do you yell and scream at others or otherwise try to dominate them because you are sexually frustrated?
- If you are unsatisfied with your sexual life, what can you pragmatically do to become more satisfied? How can you deal with your sexual needs in healthy ways?

PARENTING

Parenting is an active decision requiring a lifetime of commitment (some would say angst, at least at times). Anyone who has grownup children will likely admit that the process of parenting was not as they had anticipated. Many things they wasted time worrying about as parents never happened; some things they did not worry about, did happen.

Children bring their own personalities and orientations to the family, which influence how they interact in the family and beyond. The family is a dynamic community that either advances reasonability, encouraging and supporting all family members equally, or there are problems. One or more bullying members can have a toxic effect on everyone else in the family.

As a parent, you have some power over family dynamics. You will want to use this power justifiably and compassionately, and you will need to help others in the family do the same. Depending on how dysfunctional the family is, this may not be possible. Whatever the case may be, you want to face it directly. Only in this way do you have any hope of addressing the problems.

Raising children means raising them into adults. In other words, we raise our children to become adults. Barring tragedy, most of the time spent in child-parent relationships will be between grown-up children and their parents. We have sons and daughters only for a short time as children. As our children move into adulthood, the rest of the time should entail adults forging healthy, mutually contributing, adult relationships.

- To what degree are you satisfied with your parenting efforts?
- How would your children rate your parenting abilities? Would they be correct?
- Are your children contributing members of the family?
- Have you allowed your children to behave irrationally to get what they want?
- How can you improve your parenting abilities and perspectives?
- How do you handle conflict within the family?
- Do you openly and honestly communicate with your children and invite them to do the same? Do you dominate your children? Do you easily lose your temper and shout at them?
- Do you allow your children to dominate you? In other words, are you subservient to your children? Do you allow them to abuse you?
- Do you expect to control and direct your children's lives into adulthood? Do you expect to control their careers?
- Do your children expect to lean on you into their adulthood, unwilling to pull their own weight?
- Is your home atmosphere pleasurable, or is it toxic? To the degree that it is toxic, what precisely are the pathologies causing this toxic environment, and what is causing these pathologies?
- Can you think of past examples where you behaved irrationally as a parent, but your ego prevented you from admitting this at the time? How can you use insights from these experiences to avoid irrational behavior in similar future cases?
- How can you face the truth about your parenting and family relationships, and how can you deal with these truths directly?

FRIENDSHIPS

Just as we all seek love, we all seek friendship. As mentioned in the previous chapter, the term "friendship" should be reserved for those people you trust, who you rely upon to help you make the best decisions when you need advice, who are there for you when you need emotional support, and for whom you do the same. Everyone needs one or a few such friends. One can of course be an intimate partner, and hopefully is. And it may be anyone you deeply care about and who deeply cares about you, as is evidenced in your behavior toward one another.

- Do you have any deep and lasting friendships?
- Are you too closed off from others to allow anyone into your life to become a friend you can trust and depend on?
- Do you have no time for friendships because you are busily engaged in other, less meaningful relationships and activities?
- Are you unable to trust another person you know to be trustworthy because you have been hurt in the past by others you considered to be friends?
- Do you have trouble finding true friends because you are gullible and therefore fall into the wrong types of relationships?
- Do you rely on your family to provide all your emotional support, rather than reaching out to someone you can relate to outside the family?
- Do you know how to seek healthy supportive relationships? Do you know where to look for them?

PHYSICAL HEALTH

Physical and mental health go together. As you nurture your physical body, you should experience a higher sense of overall well-being.[11] This means having a reasonable exercise program and eating regime. It means getting a reasonable amount of rest every day and doing everything else required for your physical health.

If you want to be mentally well but get no physical exercise, it may well be that physical exercise is the very thing needed for your sense of emotional well-being.

---

11 This is not necessarily true for every person, in that some people may be taking care of their physical body while still experiencing deeply negative, lasting emotional states. In these cases, since the physical dimension has been adequately addressed, there must (by logical implication) be other root causes of the emotions which will need to be determined and then addressed. This, however, does not negate the need for humans to be physically fit as a key component of mental health, since scientific studies increasingly reveal some of the connections between physical and emotional well-being. On the other side, many people experience emotional well-being who never give attention to their physical fitness. You will need to figure out the connection between the physical and emotional dimensions in your own life, using the data from your own experience, but do not assume there is no connection.

By ignoring this when it is required by your body, you can try many other things, but they may not get to the root of the problem. You cannot read or write or discuss your way out of depression when the cause of the problem is that you lack an effective exercise routine for your body and circumstances, or that you are failing to care for your physical body in any other number of other ways. This includes examining any and everything you take into your body such as alcohol, caffeine, various types of medicines (both legal and illegal), tobacco products, etc.

Humans are physical beings. We come from nature and are part of nature. In modern human societies, we have largely lost touch with our physical bodies as part of nature. We tend to live in contrived spaces, indoors, separate from nature. We still work in office spaces with unhealthy fluorescent lighting. We don't tend to think of ourselves as needing to physically move through nature as part of our everyday experience. In human societies, we create work, social, and political environments that impede people's abilities to meet their physical needs. Meeting human physical needs has never been central to industrialized societies or so-called advanced societies. Instead, we tend to be taught that our superficial appearance and what people think of us is more important than our physical health.

- Are you taking care of your physical well-being, or do you fail to prioritize this in the constant rush of life?
- Do you critically analyze and assess what you eat and your exercise patterns?
- Do you ignore the importance of getting sufficient sleep and rest every day?
- Do you know what a healthy diet consists of (for you), and do you adhere to such a diet?
- Do you spend a considerable amount of time every day on your superficial appearance while ignoring your need for physical fitness?
- Do you constantly give yourself excuses as to why you cannot exercise?
- Do you find that you simply do not have enough time in the day to exercise? If so, is this a reasonable way for you to be living, without setting aside enough time to even take care of your basic needs?
- If you see yourself as having too little time to exercise, can you see that the improved energy and focus from exercise will likely offset the time it requires?
- What can you do to create an exercise routine that works for you, and that you can maintain over many years or throughout your lifetime?
- Are you always taking care of other people's needs while ignoring your own?
- Are you in control of all the substances you take into your body that may affect your physical well-being? Do you try to minimize the significance of things like smoking, drinking alcohol, and taking non-essential medications

and supplements, any of which may have adverse consequences for your health?

SELF-DEVELOPMENT, ENRICHMENT AND RELAXATION

It is essential for you to recognize that your work life and family life may not provide enough sustenance for you to experience emotional well-being, however satisfying work and family life may be. Enriching your mind through creative endeavors such as art, gardening, music, writing, theatre, reading, and similar activities may be required for your sense of wellness. For many people, self-development in multiple directions is needed for them to be emotionally well and to experience fulfillment.

- Do you prioritize your own need for self-development through sufficient commitment to reading, writing, volunteering, sports, art, music, self reflection, relaxation, or other activities that help you feel content and satisfied in life?

- Have you neglected this essential part of yourself?

- Are you constantly doing things for others so that you no longer even know what you need to be happy?

- Do you tell yourself that your needs come second to those of others? While you can take care of others, or perform well at work while neglecting your basic needs, do you realize that this will take a toll on your mental health in the long run?

- How can you redesign your life to encompass the important aspects which are now missing? When you examine your life, do you find that you have become too entrenched in group expectations and therefore less centered in yourself?

- How can you more frequently and systematically engage yourself in things you truly enjoy, rather than constantly living according to work or family demands?

- Do you tell yourself you have no options for sharing responsibilities that overwhelm you, when really you do have alternatives that you have not pursued or explored?

- How can you get the help you need to offload some of your less enjoyable responsibilities and make way for enriching activities?

PSYCHOLOGICAL DIMENSION

The psychological dimension of life is not easily captured. Psychologists themselves are widely split on the fundamental logic of the subject, including its most basic assumptions. Many psychological traditions and perspectives compete against one another—Freudian, Adlerian, Jungian, Gestalt, humanist, cognitive behavioral, neuro-psychological, existentialist, constructionist, and so on—each seeking to persuade psychologists and therapists to join their camp. Mental health therapy, then, is to some extent a battleground between competing paradigms and conceptual frameworks, each emerging from divergent psychological orientations. The guiding principles of one psychologist are sometimes highly questionable to another. One and the same situation may be analyzed and evaluated in very different ways. Yet the field of psychology sees itself—and presents itself—as a science, misleadingly so. Psychology does entail scientific dimensions in certain contexts, but due to the human mind's inherent complexities and limitations, psychology can never reasonably be equated with science.

To understand and command your own psychology, we might approach psychology in its most literal form, deriving from the root words *psycho* and *logic*—which we can roughly capture as *the logic of the psyche*. Of course, the term "psyche" itself is ambiguous. Some refer to the psyche as entailing our deepest thoughts. At minimum, we can say that a significant part of the psyche lies within or is determined by the *unconscious* dimension of thought. This is where much of our thinking occurs, and this reality is crucial to understanding your own psychology as well as your psychologically dysfunctional patterns.

In short, if you want to be psychologically well or to reason well about your own psychology, you need to firmly understand and control the thinking that occurs at the unconscious level of your mind. This thinking may be pathological; in other cases, it may not be pathological, but it still must be understood and deliberately directed in order to maintain mental wellness. Your relationships with other people or groups, for example, are influenced by and frequently operate within the unconscious dimension of human thought—therefore affecting your psychology.

Your personality may also play a role in your psychology. If you are a sensitive, fragile, or fearful person, for instance, this may affect how you interact with others and how others affect you. On the other hand, if you are confident within yourself, this will affect how you interact with others and how others affect you. Ideally, your *character development* will (or has) become your primary guiding force. This means you are committed to being guided by intellectual virtues, rather than by your native egocentric and sociocentric psychological machinations, your personality (such as being introverted or extroverted), or your dysfunctional DNA propensities.

334 | CHAPTER NINE

We focus in the next chapter on primary psychological theories at the heart of counseling and therapy today. In the meantime, here are some initial questions you can ask to help you better understand the psychological dimension of your thought:

- To what degree are you aware that you have unconscious thoughts?
- What important dysfunctional unconscious thoughts might be driving the way you are living?
- Where do these unconscious thoughts come from?
- How can you better replace your irrational unconscious thoughts with more reasonable conscious thoughts?
- How has your personality affected your interactions with others?
- How has your personality affected your ability to better take charge of your mind?
- What mental characteristics do you think you may have been born with that have affected your development? How can you better control these characteristics for higher quality of life?

SOCIAL LIFE

All humans crave social contact with other humans. We may differ in how we need or can achieve appropriate and satisfactory social connection, but all of us need other humans. We are social animals. Of course, there is nothing wrong with this, and people should be encouraged to develop healthy social relationships.

Since groups are part of our (your) very nature, you largely live within groups that then influence you. You are affected by the groups of which you are a member, whether you have chosen these groups or not (such as your country, religious group, school groups). One key is to know precisely how you are affected by any groups in your life, including the sociocentric thinking occurring in these groups. It is also useful to understand how you have been influenced by groups you belonged to in the past, and how these influences shape your thinking and behavior today. And it is important to determine how you can intervene in your own inclination toward irrational groupthink of any kind and in any part of your life. In the chapter on the barriers to critical thinking, you were introduced to these ideas and to the insight that within every social group, there are tendencies toward sociocentric thinking. One of your goals should be to identify these tendencies and guard against their affecting you.

Questions you can ask yourself to better command your social dimension:

- To what extent has your behavior been controlled by society and culture throughout your life in its various dimensions?

- What cultural beliefs, customs, and taboos have come to dominate your life? Do you even know which of these beliefs influence your thinking and actions?
- What cultural beliefs, customs, and taboos are prevalent among your work colleagues, your family, and any other groups you belong to?
- To what extent do you tend to think for yourself in the face of established views?
- What are some important implications of, and possibilities for, your non-conforming behavior in any given setting or group you are in? What will happen if you do not conform to group ideas you have previously accepted?
- Focusing on the groups of which you are a member, what behaviors are required of everyone in the group, what behaviors are forbidden, and what range of free decision is allowed? Are some people privileged over others in the group?
- Are the groups in which you are a member healthy for you, or unhealthy? How can you remove yourself from unhealthy groups and move toward healthy groups?

YOUR HISTORY

Everyone thinks historically. In other words, everyone thinks about the past. But *few people think critically about how they have come to think about the past*. The stories we tell ourselves about the past are often riddled with distortions of our own making. Our view of the past is largely prejudiced by the ideologies of the cultures and groups that have influenced us, and by our own egocentric tendencies to see things according to what we want or wish were true. We see the past through the lenses we have created in our own minds. We want to see the past in certain ways, so we do. We have been taught to see the past in certain ways, so we see it in those ways. We rarely question the cultural norms, customs, beliefs, taboos, and values that influence how we see our own history.

In a broad sense, you are a historical thinker. You tell yourself stories about the past, as do all humans. You create memories of your past. You write or create these "memories" as they are happening, and you often rewrite or recreate them over time. Much of the story you create, or, in other words, much of your personal history, has been colored by wishful thinking and by the way you would like to see yourself and others. Much of your personal history is shaped by the people who have influenced you throughout your life—parents, teachers, siblings, spouses, friends, etc. The way you will think about your history in the future is being shaped by the people influencing you now. If you were to write an autobiography, it would not be an objective detailing of things that happened to you and things you have done; it would be a mixture of fact and distortion—of things that did happen and things that just seem (in your mind) to have happened.

You can be the master of your personal history. You can decide whether to write the story of your life in ways that mirror or distort reality. You can decide whether to write the story of your past in largely negative or positive terms. In writing your story, you can highlight the positives and give less attention to the negatives, or you can highlight the negatives and downplay the positives. You can write your story insightfully, or in a limited way. You can write your history according to social norms and taboos. You can think in a narrow, provincial way about your past, or you can look beneath the surface of events and happenings for deeper meanings.

You will, and do, tell the story of your life, in your mind, at every phase of your life. There is, in other words, an ongoing narrative you create which is, in your mind, the story of your life to that point. The following questions should help you better understand your personal history, and for you, there is perhaps no history more important.

- Are you trapped in the story you tell yourself about your past, or are you emancipated by it? In other words, do you define how you see your past?

- Are you actively shaping what you do today, rather than obsessing over memories?

- Does your interpretation of your past hold you back from future possibilities?

- How can you take command of the story you tell yourself about the past to let go of resentments towards those you perceive to have harmed you? What do you gain by holding onto these resentments?

- How much time do you spend ruminating on past events or your perceptions of past events?

- How can you take command of the story you tell yourself about the past so your experiences, or your perceptions of experiences, no longer haunt you?

- What were the dominant beliefs, concerns, values, and assumptions that influenced the way your parents or guardians raised you?

- Who were the people that influenced you the most? How did they influence you?

- When did you begin to have a sense of yourself as an individual with unique ways of seeing and doing things? How have others viewed your uniquenesses?

- What do you remember as the most significant events in your life, and why are they significant? How accurate is your interpretation of those events?

- What do others remember about you and the events that impacted you? How are the memories, perspectives, and conclusions of others about you different from your own? Which of these perceptions is most accurate? What can the memories, perspectives, and conclusions that others have about you teach you about your life?

- In what ways can your re-interpretation of your past help you become more mentally well?

ECOLOGY AND YOUR RELATIONSHIP WITH NATURE

Again, humans are part of nature. Our home is planet earth. It is an unavoidable fact that humans are intimately intertwined with ecological systems. Throughout our history, we have attempted to avoid or deny these truths; this has led to our vast destruction of animal and plant life, along with widespread destruction and elimination of natural habitat throughout the world. Due to our arrogance and selfishness, we have behaved as if we were above nature and hence could use nature for whatever purposes we chose. We have treated animals and plants as abominably as we wanted if doing so achieved our purposes. In short, we have acted as if the balance of nature and our treatment of nature were not important, as long as we humans could have what we wanted in the short term.

We are now experiencing increasingly severe consequences of this selfish reasoning, which has gone on for thousands of years. The destruction of the planet causes many people to experience a sense of hopelessness and depression, while others fail entirely to see the value of nature, so caught up in they are in the human world filled with endless artificial structures and materialistic products.

The past is gone, and nothing we do will—for example—bring back the old growth trees cut down by our ancestors and their ancestors. At the same time, nothing stops us from restoring and rewilding the earth where we can, in many directions, and working to maintain and restore as many species as we can. Your mental health may depend on it. Dystopian thinking about the earth will only bring you mental sorrow and sense of hopelessness; it will sap your energy, which is needed to aid the earth's health in any way you can.

There are many ways to expand your connection to nature. To name a few, you can start a vegetable garden, expand your vegetable garden, join or start a community garden, expand your garden of plants to encourage more insects and other creatures to thrive there, add a bird bath or fountain to your yard, add plants to your balcony, join bird watching groups, volunteer with wildlife rescue groups, initiate groups focused on wildlife support such as establishing free passages or corridors for animals across our countries, advocate for native gardens, help bring back the all-important beavers to help reestablish healthy waterways—the list goes on and on.

- What can you do reconnect with nature and immerse yourself in it?
- Have you lost your ability to appreciate nature, or did you ever have this appreciation?
- Do you fail to prioritize getting out in nature over other things that may not bring you the same satisfaction as immersing yourself in nature?

- Do you see how our disconnection from nature has led to horrific practices such as factory animal farming, which denies sentient creatures their basic rights?
- Do you see humans as superior to other creatures? If so, what gives you this idea?
- Do you take regular long walks in nature, as Henry David Thoreau would recommend?
- Do you have a garden?
- Do you find that you are more emotionally well when you work in the garden or get out in nature?

HOW YOU THINK ABOUT SCIENCE AND THE NATURAL WORLD

Humans are thrust into and are part of the scientific world. We ourselves are biological and chemical creatures; our physical nature cannot be denied. But do you think scientifically about your physical being, and do you think critically when it comes to scientific concepts? Many people take years of science courses in school and yet cannot think even in the most rudimentary ways about everyday scientific questions having to do with, for instance, the food they eat, the chemicals they take into their bodies, the effects of movement on their physical health, or the effects of air, water, light, and noise pollution on their well-being.

By asking and pursuing scientific questions, you can better understand the physical world and make better decisions about it. Some everyday scientific questions include:

- What aspects of life are important to think scientifically about?
- Do you think scientifically about your physical health, considering new relevant understandings that emerge over time?
- Do you even know how your body works and how it is affected by the many things you do to it, require of it, or put into it?
- How has scientific research been misused? How is it being misused now?
- How does scientific thinking contribute to your personal life? In what ways is it a threat?
- What are some limitations of science?
- Instead of using science where it is relevant, do you instead rely on superstition such as astrology and belief in unworldly phantoms? What is the basis for your superstitions? Are they logical? Are they conjured up by groups to make money or gain influence while manipulating you and making you feel good? Are they unreasonable explanations created through the poor reasoning of others, perhaps even with good intent, that you have accepted uncritically?

YOUR FINANCES

As I have mentioned, each of us lives in a complex economic set of realities. We were born into capitalistic systems which are themselves largely pathological, leading some few people to receive billions of dollars while innumerable other people live at or below the level of poverty. Capitalism, as we have come to conceptualize it, is based on the untenable assumption that more and more manufactured goods must always be cranked out onto the earth so people can constantly buy things, tire of them, and get rid of them, so that we can make more things to be bought.

Over the last few decades, the quality of our appliances has become increasingly inferior, lasting for briefer and briefer periods of time, so that we are required to continually purchase new ones. Our landfills get larger and larger with the junk we can no longer repair or are bored with. Unbridled capitalism has been a primary cause of the destruction of nature and its attendant loss of animal and plant life, since we need nature's resources to provide largely unneeded material goods for the billions of people living on earth, and to store the material items when they become trash.

And yet, like it or not, each of us must figure out how to fit ourselves into the world of capital. We need to think about how economics affects us and how to survive within existing capitalistic systems.

- How will you fit yourself into the capitalistic systems which run your country, and which largely control our world?
- Do you have any idea how you are affected by capitalistic messages that come to you through vast networks of sophisticated marketing—messages about your face, body, feet, hair, nails, about tattoos, relationships, medications, and indeed every aspect of your life?
- Do you worry about money and how you will make ends meet? Do you spend reasonably, or do you overspend? What problems does overspending cause you?
- How can you take command of your economic life, so that you are purchasing responsibly and living without monetary worries?
- How can you make enough money to live comfortably or meet your basic needs while taking minimal resources from the earth?
- What options have you not explored which would help you live more responsibly in terms of your finances, and in more fulfilling ways?

CIVIC AND ETHICAL RESPONSIBILITY

Everyone has civic and ethical responsibilities, since we humans live in groups where our behavior affects other people and non-human animals. We make numerous decisions in groups wherein some people have more power than others, and many have very little power. Those with little power, or who perceive themselves as having little power, are not likely to work toward more fair and equitable societies. Rational societies urge people to consider the public interest (which also encompasses their own individual interests) above the primitive desire for power (which can often undermine people's individual interests, often unbeknownst to them). These societies support efforts focused on the common good. Human emotional well-being depends upon living in accordance with what we ethically owe to others and what we owe to the greater good, as well as what we owe to ourselves.

A primary cause of depression and sense of hopelessness is when people spend an inordinate amount of time unproductively ruminating, going over again and again the same old thoughts that keep them in the same old rut. Your precious energy should be focused in ways that remove you from these ruminating loops, moving you toward activities and projects that help you achieve your capacities while contributing to more fairminded critical societies.

- Do you have any specific ways in which you contribute to the common good, or the public interest, or the protection of rights for all sentient creatures?

- Do you regularly pick up trash while walking along your favorite path?

- Do you volunteer for a nonprofit group?

- Consider how much energy you spend on contributing to a better world or enhancing someone else's life, versus the energy you spend on getting what you want for yourself, thinking about how bad things are, or thinking about how people seemingly don't appreciate you. How would you explain your answer to someone?

- Do you waste a lot of time on superficial pursuits and activities, or on worrying and fretting? What if you spent that time contributing to someone else's life, or on working toward the common good and the interests of sentient creatures?

RELIGION, METAPHYSICS, AND MORTALITY

Religious or spiritual thought is likely always to have been part of the human experience. This tendency may derive from perceived needs such as: control over our own destiny, protection of our loved ones, understanding our role in the universe, understanding the universe itself, and making sense of mortality. Humans appear to invent religious ideologies in attempting to control elements and circumstances that are beyond our control, as well as to give us comfort when we lose people we love or contemplate the problem of our own deaths. For some people, religious thinking provides a rationale for explaining the unexplainable (like losing a child to early death). The perceived security that comes from religious beliefs seems to be needed by some people to face life and its uncertainties.

Some people reject traditional religious beliefs and instead believe in astrology, which is based in ideas such as that star alignment determines your character, personality, and destiny. Others reject both of these orientations and instead see god as nature, with the central idea being that humans are connected with all of nature, with one another, and with the universe itself. Still others believe in any number of other spiritual beliefs, or rebuff the idea of religion or spirituality altogether.

Any religious belief system should be understood as mixed in quality, truth, and reasonability. None should be shielded from ethical concepts and principles; therefore, any religious practice that violates ethical principles must be rejected. If you were raised in an oppressive religious environment which still seems to persecute you, and you want to rid yourself of these harassing thoughts, you can begin by figuring out the religious beliefs you have uncritically accepted throughout your life. You will then need to assess these beliefs for accuracy, reasonability, and any other relevant intellectual standards. Many of your beliefs may need to be cast off entirely, though the ethical concepts embedded in them should remain as part of your thinking (such as *do unto others as you would have them do unto you*).

It is perhaps not problematic to participate in religious life, as long as your religion gives you comfort, you are not being indoctrinated into unsound beliefs, and you do not impose your arbitrary religious beliefs on others. But you should be skeptical about any religious group promoting the idea of a supreme being or beings with power over your destiny. Even if such beings ever did or do exist, there is no logical way they could control all the variables they would need to control for predestination to be realized even in a single case, much less for all eight billion people on planet earth. So, when an athlete thanks "God" for winning a game, you might ask why "God" did not do the same for the equally religious (or more religious) athlete who lost. And how would it be possible for a god to manipulate every single variable required for a given individual to win out over others who are as skilled as the winner? And then to do this across the world for all the religious people under said god's domain? To take a far more serious example, when innocent children are born into vicious families with no concern for the newborn's well-being, this cannot possibly be an act of God—for what did the infant do to deserve it? If God is all powerful, how could s/he allow such horrific and terrifying things to happen to innocent children? Cruelty toward children is caused by human ignorance, selfishness, and lack of compassion, and not while an ethical and all-powerful god stands by.

Many people have mental health problems due to religious ideologies being thrust upon them as children. Religious groups may provide a sense of security, and a feeling of being involved in community, which may help your mental health. But they should only be participated in if you see through all of their unreasonable ideologies, and if you do not fall prey to their irrationalities (this holds true for any group of which you are a member, religious or not).

In addition to the religious or spiritual dimension, some people obsess over death or get caught up in the metaphysical domain. Death is something that none of us understand and that many people fear. Most of us dread the idea of dying. It bothers us that we have no experience with it firsthand in order to prepare ourselves for its inevitability. We can't imagine the world going on without us. And yet we will die and the world will go on after we are gone. Fearing and fretting over the inevitable will only make you mentally unwell.

Similarly, many people get caught up in metaphysical questions which, by their very nature, cannot be answered. These include questions like, What is consciousness? How did we get here? Does god exist? What is the meaning of life? To live a satisfying life, it is likely best not to attempt to answer questions that cannot be answered, given all the questions facing us that can be answered and that are worth spending our time on. Some philosophers enjoy debating and discussing metaphysical questions. This is well and good for them, but it is likely not well and good for you if you become depressed or anxious while pursuing these questions.

Consider these questions:

- To what degree are you a religious person?
- What precisely are your religious beliefs?
- If you are a religious person, why have you chosen your specific religion? Were these religious beliefs internalized by you as a child? If so, how do you know they entail sound beliefs?
- To what degree do you uncritically accept the religious doctrines of this group?
- What emotional advantages do you believe you receive from this group?
- What beliefs within your religion are reasonable?
- What beliefs within your religion are unreasonable?
- To what extent can you remain within this religious group while continuing to develop as a fairminded critical thinker?
- Do you believe in phantoms or other superstitions? If so, upon what evidence do you base your superstitious beliefs?
- Do you believe in astrology? If so, upon what evidence do you base your astrological beliefs? Do you know the history of astrology?
- If you give up your religious beliefs, what will you replace them with?

- If you give up your religious groups, how will you get your emotional needs met that were met through these groups?
- Do you worry about death? If so, how can you best deal with your fears of death so that you are able to enjoy the life you have been given?
- Do you worry about other metaphysical questions that you can never answer and can do nothing about?

YOUR TECHNOLOGICAL ORIENTATION

All of us live in a world of technology. We cannot possibly avoid technology in industrialized countries. Many people seem to assume that any new technological idea is necessarily a good idea. Yet certain technological advancements may not be desirable and may even end our very existence.

You should actively determine and control to what degree you participate in technology. Many people today seem to be almost completely enthralled by their mobile phones. Who knows what technological obsessions may emerge in the future? But today many people rarely allow their phones to leave their hands and seem to be largely dominated by what comes to them through these phones. They constantly receive beeps and vibrations and other noises from their phones which alert them to presumably important things. They spend tremendous amounts of time on "social" media to feel some connection with other humans and get attention from them. They participate in video games and live online games. They visit websites that simulate casinos, sports, music, art, sex, and so forth, frequently forgetting that every minute spent in virtual reality is a minute that cannot be spent engaging in the real world.

The internet has its uses. Technology has its bright spots. A key is to know the strengths and weaknesses of all technologies. For your mental well-being, you need to have control over what technology you willingly engage with, how you engage with that technology, and how often you engage with it. You need to be keenly aware of what you are giving up when you spend time on the internet, looking at your phone, or watching television.

- How can you develop your critical capacities and unique talents while spending precious time on trivial websites, apps, and other technologies?
- Do you really need to be on alert through notifications coming to your phone, text messages, and beeps that constantly interrupt you? How important are these notifications in reality? In most cases, if you ignored them, what consequences would actually occur? Are these consequences as serious as you have assumed they are?
- During how much of your day do you actually need to be holding your mobile phone in your hand?

- To what extent are you engaged with technology (such as your phone) rather than with the people you have actual relationships with?
- How can you wean yourself from technologies that are not helping you develop your mind and general well being?
- How can you use technology to help you live more reasonably?
- Are there some forms of social interaction you have through the internet that improve your mental health? Do you connect with some important people through the internet that help you emotionally?

HOW YOU THINK ABOUT POWER

All people want and need power. All of us need to feel potent and effective within at least some parts of our lives. Some people want all the power—in the family, at the office, in a meeting, in government, etc. Some people do not use their power, but instead allow others to take their power from them. Some people pine for power they can never have, sometimes to the point of self-destruction. Some people are driven by the desire for raw power without realizing the consequences that may follow—for them and others in their power path. Recall that, in terms of the dominating ego and submissive ego discussed previously in the book, dominators most assuredly misuse power while submitters may misuse power through subtle, obsequious, manipulative behavior.

- Do you feel potent as an individual, with enough power to achieve what you would like to achieve without harming others?
- Do you tend to dominate others to feel powerful? If so, how precisely do you dominate them or try to dominate them? Can you let go of your irrational power needs and allow others more power appropriate to the context?
- Do you find that your competitive nature gets you into trouble or leads you in the wrong direction? When is it appropriate to be competitive, and when is it a problem in your life?
- Do you go through life feeling you have no real power? Do you feel that people dump on you or take advantage of you?
- Would you like to have more power, but without a sense of why or how to acquire it rationally?
- How can you best channel your need for power? What positive ways can you use your power in your life?
- If the ways you have pursued power in your life to this point are problematic based on your answers to the questions above, what steps can you immediately take to improve how you think about power and how you try to achieve it in your life? How can you be more fair to yourself and/or others as you pursue power?

INTERNALIZE THE IDEA: FORMULATE QUESTIONS WITHIN IMPORTANT DIMENSIONS OF YOUR LIFE

This chapter has focused on primary dimensions of human life and has offered some questions for your contemplation. Now create your own list of primary dimensions in your life, prioritizing them with the most important at the top of your list. Then for each primary dimension of life you list, make a list of questions you need to ask within those domains. Bring in any questions from the lists of questions found in this chapter. You may add dimensions to your list not covered in this chapter. Once you have a beginning list of questions for each dimension, spend time each day contemplating your answers to these questions, moving around within the domains on different days. Add to your list as needed, of both domains and questions.

CHAPTER 10
ASSESSING EXISTING MENTAL HEALTH THERAPIES AND THERAPISTS

If you have studied the explicit critical thinking concepts detailed in this book, and if you have practiced internalizing them by working through the activities provided, you should now have a sense of the power of your reasoning and your ability to command it. All your decisions ultimately come from, or are affected by, your reasoning, including the decision to continue studying critical thinking to improve your life. Hopefully you now see the importance of developing the skills, abilities, and characteristics of the fairminded critical thinker. And hopefully you now see them as essential to your mental health and to self-actualization.

Critical Thinking Therapy begins with the assumption that mental health requires reasonable thinking. Being mentally healthy implies living a reasonable life. And there are any number of ways to live a reasonable life. This has been the ultimate message in this book. To achieve at the highest levels within your capacity you must continue actively developing your mind, with readings and practice every day.

If you do desire or think you need a mental health therapist, you should have some awareness of the theories your therapist uses. This chapter offers suggestions for choosing a therapist as well as for choosing alternatives to traditional therapy. It also outlines the role of the *Critical Thinking Therapist*, and it briefly explains core concepts within primary classic therapeutic approaches, including critique of some of these primary therapies.

As you are learning, critical thinking is needed to help you appropriately assess your own reasoning, and it is needed to help you assess the reasoning of others; this includes assessing the reasoning embedded in any other approach to therapy or mental health you might become involved in. In other words, you need critical thinking tools to determine how to best assess the ideas thrust at you, that you run across, or that you seek—ideas that promise to offer hope for your mental well-being.

As you consider choosing a book that might help you, or a video you might watch to improve your outlook, keep in mind that the human mind is unimaginably complex. *Your* human mind is unimaginably complex. Anyone who suggests otherwise will be wrong. Many of the ideas presented to you through the various forms of media about how to improve your mental health will be oversimplified. Many will be problematic in other ways. Sadly, superficial, half-baked, and unsound ideas pervade the world of therapy, with various theoreticians and authors asserting inadequate, or even harmful, methods for mental health. Similarly, many ideas labeled "critical thinking" have emerged in the last half-century which are either incomplete, incorrect, or otherwise misleading.

Given the above, if you are considering possible therapeutic options beyond those in this book, you will want to know their strengths and weaknesses. Again, there are an unlimited number of activities, programs, and undertakings you can engage in to improve your mental outlook. A key is to identify those that will do the most for your mental and emotional well-being, given your uniquenesses and within your circumstances; then, immediately begin immersing yourself in these activities. Another key, if you now feel isolated, is to connect with people through these undertakings who you can relate with in shared community; this will help meet your social needs in healthy ways.

Many people go to therapy because they need someone to talk with in an open, inviting, calm, setting about what concerns them. They want to feel they are not being judged or criticized. Very often they want to be told that they are correct. Often, they seek therapy to deal with a specific problem. For most people with these common human needs, therapy can be avoided by cultivating a deep and loyal friendship with someone you can count on to support you and help you see when your thinking may be unreasonable. Where possible, this relationship should be fully reciprocal, so that you serve the same role for your friend(s). Of course, this may not be easy to achieve, but you can always take steps toward this type of relationship. And you will still need to continue studying and internalizing the tools of critical thinking.

ALTERNATIVE AND ORGANIC MENTAL HEALTH THERAPIES

You may not necessarily need someone to talk through your problems with. Or you may need something in addition to someone to talk to. You may need to expand your horizons to expand your mind. Consider the following mental health therapies people use to achieve happiness and self-fulfillment, whether or not they call them therapies. You will of course need to figure out exactly what undertakings will most gratify you and bring the highest levels of satisfaction to your life. Many more therapies, as well as examples within each category, can be added to this list.

- **Therapy through nature**—by gardening at home, walking, sitting in nature, joining or starting a community food and/or native garden.
- **Therapy through animals**—through horseback riding programs, volunteering at an animal shelter, bird watching, starting or volunteering at a wildlife rehab center, adopting a companion pet, or taking your pet to a care facility to visit the residents.
- **Therapy through art and creative processes**—by attending art classes and programs, starting art projects at home, or attending cooking classes.
- **Therapy through giving**—through volunteering to work with groups who share your values and are contributing to a more just world. There are many ways you can contribute through the various groups who are working to make the world a better place.
- **Music therapy**—by playing or listening to music, attending music classes or programs, or joining music groups.
- **Therapy through sports**—by joining a sports team or finding a partner for a sport such as tennis.
- **Therapy through exercise**—by developing a regular exercise program that you can commit to, or finding a partner to exercise with (such as a walking partner).
- **Therapy through meditation and relaxation**—including making sure you have time every day for relaxation in whatever form works for you. This may involve reading, sitting quietly by yourself and relaxing, joining a group that comes together regularly for relaxation, going camping with friends or family, etc.
- **Therapy through reading.** Reading can be used for relaxation as well as development of the mind. Identify reading material that will cultivate your mind and is found in printed books—not necessarily on the Internet.
- **Therapy through writing.** Regularly write out your thoughts in a journal, or develop written projects as an outlet for your creativity—such as writing a play, poem, novel, essay, letter to the editor, etc.
- **Therapy through work.** Many people spend too much time working at the expense of developing in other directions; yet, other people find great satisfaction in their work. If your work develops your creativity and mental well-being, use this as a source for your mental health (but keep your life balanced).
- **Therapy through dance.** There are many forms of dance, some of them individual and some of them in pairs or larger groups. Dance can be a wonderful way to meet people and find human connection. It can also be an excellent form of exercise coupled with social connection.

- **Therapy through intellectual development.** This entails studying and deepening your ideas to develop and expand your mind. See Appendix B to find recommendations for developing your intellect through classic literature readings.

- **Therapy through discussion groups.** All of us need to continue growing and developing through life. If you are interested in ideas, you may start a study group with like-minded people. This group can focus on, for instance, studying this book to learn the foundations of critical thinking. It can also focus on any other topics of interest to the group, such as current events and personal discoveries that anyone in the group may want to share. Additional readings can also be brought into the group. See the Recommended Readings section and Appendix B for books you may want to focus on in your study group.

- **Therapy through travel.** Some people find great benefit in traveling beyond their home base. If you are one of these people, plan regular trips within your budget that will enhance your emotional well-being.

- **Therapy through communal living.** Many people are drawn to community living situations to avoid living in isolation. There may be many advantages to communal living, so long as those within the community are striving to live rational, ethical lives. However, be aware that it is all too common for both egocentric and sociocentric thinking to pervade such communities. Choose wisely when living in community with others and be aware of indoctrinating or otherwise irrational tendencies with the group.

- **Sexual Therapies.** Some people are drawn to sexually explorative groups as a form of therapy. As with communal living situations, make sure you know the implications of getting involved in any such group before committing yourself.

- **Play Therapy.** Humans, like other animals, need play in their lives. This might include playing games such as board games, ping pong, sports, or outdoor games such as croquet and pickleball. Human play can come in many forms. Seek those forms that best fit your needs. But don't forget the importance of play in your life.

- **Therapy through almost anything that makes you happy as long as you are not harming anyone else**. As you see from the list above, there are an unlimited number of avenues for improving your mental well-being, in addition to gaining command of your reasoning overall. A key, again, is to choose one, two, three, or any number of these and begin putting your energy into them. Don't just look at the list and say, "Yes, this would be nice and that would be fun, but I don't have the energy for it," or, "I will get to that later. Right now I will just continue to stay home and hope for a better day tomorrow." Mentally well people actively create an environment that supports their mental wellness. For you, this means choosing activities that expand and cultivate your individual mind—the only mind with the power to command your well-being

INTERNALIZE THE IDEA: PLANNING FOR A MENTALLY HEALTHY LIFESTYLE

Read again the list of alternative therapies above, then complete the following statements.

1. Some activities that I believe would benefit my mental health if I were to commit to them are . . .

2. Some barriers that stop me from engaging in these activities are . . .

3. I can deal with these barriers in the following ways . . .

4. I therefore intend to engage in the following activities . . .

ON CHOOSING AND ASSESSING A THERAPIST

Perhaps after reading this book and fully engaging in all its activities relevant to your well-being, you still feel the need for a therapist, or for additional theory to address your issues. Remember that mental health professionals tend to lack explicit understanding of the vast toolbox of critical thinking and its vital importance to effective mental health therapies; therefore, you cannot necessarily count on therapists or other support persons to lead you on the right path toward your own best destiny. Making the most reasonable decisions about therapy or a given therapist, as with all parts of your life, will require your best critical thinking all along the way.

For more than a hundred years, therapies for mental health have been developing. These therapies go in many directions and frequently contradict one another. After more than a century of psychological, sociological, and philosophical research and theorizing, we still lack an agreed-upon set of coherent, efficacious tools for mental health. In part, perhaps this is because the logic of the dysfunctional human mind is itself elusive. It will not be easily pinned down by a given way of conceptualizing the mind, or in other words, by one theoretical school of thought.

New therapeutic approaches to mental health are continually popping up. Some are based in sound reasoning yet are not integrated into a cohesive conceptual framework for making sense of the many pathologies of the human mind. Others are plain nonsense. Many are a mixture of sound reasoning, plain nonsense, and something in between. For this reason, it is essential, again, for you to be grounded in critical thinking skills, abilities, and dispositions. With this grounding, you should be able to distinguish better from worse reasoning embedded in any therapeutic approach to mental health. Using critical thinking concepts and principles, it is possible to identify mental health therapies or activities for your individual development.

First and foremost, approaches to mental health should be understood in terms of *what is needed by you personally, as a unique individual.* An irrational person will need a therapeutic process that deals effectively with irrationality. A person who lacks meaning in life will need a therapeutic process that leads to the development of important purposes. A psychotic person will likely need a secure, safe place to overcome a psychotic episode and, over time, learn to successfully navigate what is perceived as a frightening and overwhelming world. People trying to overcome bullying, manipulative, or dishonest behavior in themselves will need to practice intervening in their irrational, destructive thoughts and actions that cause others harm. People needing to escape other people who are bullying or manipulative will need to practice intervening in their own irrational thoughts that enable others to harm them.

Therefore, therapies for mental health should be fundamentally self-determined. In short, as everyone is unique, everyone must find her or his best path to mental well-being. *Self-development and self-guidance* are required in all cases. No one can develop your mind for you. No one can make you mentally well. Only you can open, examine, and understand your mind, because only you can know (with time and effort guided by critical thinking) what is going on there. Others can help you. Books can be read by you. You may consider advice given to you. But ultimately, you will need to determine which ideas to accept and which to reject. This determination should be driven by intellectual humility and confidence in reason. The more actively you take command of your mind, using critical thinking, the more mentally well you are likely to be.

Any given psychological theory should be used as a tool appropriate within certain situations and under certain circumstances. In other words, as mentioned, if you are an anxious person, you may need one type of therapy. If you are a depressed person, you may need another type of therapy. If you are a highly fragile person, this may affect how you relate to a given therapeutic approach. Again and again, and again, we come back to the fact that reasonably making these and all decisions requires you to think critically.

It isn't, of course, that mental health professionals never use critical thinking. The best therapeutic approaches to mental health utilize critical thinking to some extent. Yet, clinicians do not always choose the best mental health therapies. This is true because they don't always know *how* to choose among the theories and therapies within the various schools of thought relevant to cultivating mental health. In other words, they are frequently unclear as to the standards they should use in deciding on the best therapeutic strategies. Nor can therapists necessarily effectively apply the best theories when they do choose them, for this also requires critical thinking. And even the best approaches to mental health have limitations or weaknesses. Again, critical thinking is required to figure out these limitations.

Therapists typically neither use nor impart a comprehensive, explicit conception of critical thinking in their work with clients because they are rarely, if ever, taught such a conception. They may themselves *think critically*, even to a large degree, on any number of topics. But if they are limited by their overall lack of overt *knowledge of critical thinking* when attempting to advance critical thinking in the therapeutic setting (assuming they are even making such an attempt), their efforts may fail or be only marginally helpful. Clinicians frequently employ *some* explicit critical thinking concepts and principles when working with clients, but this is often without awareness of the broader range of critical thinking concepts and principles from which they could be choosing. This conceivably limits their ability to foster the critical reasoning skills and characteristics you need as a client to gain full command of your thoughts, feelings, and desires.

In short, critical reasoning as an object of study has not been a primary focus for psychologists, psychiatrists, social workers, and counselors throughout the histories of these professions. Predictably then, critical reasoning has never been at the heart of most mental health programs. There are some notable exceptions, but these exceptions are frequently overlooked or watered down by mainstream mental health professionals. Instead of relying on the cultivation of critical, creative, ethical reasoning for mental health, some counselors still encourage people to re-create "bad memories" from their past, and then re-live these "memories" repeatedly (traditional analytic psychology, typically using Freudian theory). They may assume that their clients' irrational behavior (such as habitually or even frequently yelling at their children) results from childhood conditioning or abuse (again a Freudian perspective), when this may not be the case. Or they may want their clients simply to *feel good*, rather than focusing them on taking responsibility for their selfish, dominating behavior (for instance) and for living a sensible life.

Many psychiatrists, entrenched in the "medical model," typically give medications to treat mental health problems. They sometimes prescribe these in enormous quantities that include many different pharmaceuticals, frequently with limited or untested long-term effectiveness, while often actually harming clients. Many mental health clinicians still use such archaic assessment tools as the *Rorschach inkblot test*, which has no scientific evidence to support its use; in the process, these clinicians make inferences that cannot be logically deduced from the evidence of the person's responses. Therapists frequently ignore the essential role of ethical reasoning in the healthy person; they themselves are frequently unclear as to the distinction between ethics and social ideologies.

How then do counselors decide on the therapies they use? *More specifically, what standards do they use to determine which therapies to accept and which to reject? How can you trust your therapist to be using the best therapies for your situation?* These questions are difficult to answer, because even when therapists presumably subscribe to specific schools of therapeutic thought, they often stray from these schools and instead use an intuitive approach.[12, 13] Still, the rest of the chapter will give you some sense of the primary orientations of mental health therapists today, beginning with the fact that there is not an organized, agreed-upon, system of understandings in mental health.

BRIEF OVERVIEW OF PRIMARY MENTAL HEALTH THERAPIES

Research shows two things to be particularly helpful in mental health therapy: a warm therapeutic approach that feels welcoming to the client, and an approach that includes a strong cognitive dimension with strategies clients can use to intervene in their irrational thinking, thereby improving their lives. While a supportive therapeutic setting can help you, a kind, caring person to talk to will not change the overall structure and quality of your reasoning, which is likely at the root of your problems; this kind of change requires the *tools* of critical reasoning. Cognitive behavioral therapy (CBT) methods tend to be successful when they help you discover the thinking underneath your irrational behaviors and detect irrational thinking and actions in others. Cognitive behavioral therapies derive from, but now frequently and may vastly differ from, their origins which are based in the work of Albert Ellis's Rational Emotive Behavior Therapy, to be further discussed presently.

---

12 For instance, one study found "considerable diversity in the way therapists work even when they subscribe to the same psychotherapeutic approach and work with the same type of clients." See: Roubal J, Hytych R, Čevelíček M, Řiháček T. *Personal therapeutic approach in Gestalt therapists working with clients suffering from medically unexplained psychosomatic symptoms*. Res Psychother. 2021 Dec 20;24(3):535. doi: 10.4081/ripppo.2021.535. PMID: 35047424; PMCID: PMC8715264. Found at https://www.ncbi.nlm.nih.gov/pmc/articles/PMC8715264/

13 One clinical psychologist I spoke with about this book put it this way: "Every therapist has his own unique cosmology." This implies a spiritual, religious or metaphysical dimension as part of therapy. Or does it? Given the established uses of the term cosmology, I wonder how many therapists would agree with this clinical psychologist, or whether he himself is clear on his meaning.

When we canvas the research on therapy, we find that most techniques used in counseling fall under the rough category of *talk therapy* centered on the client, or in other words, *therapist as questioner and advisor, and client as talker*. In talk therapy, clients are expected to discuss their problems with the therapist. Person-centered therapy is the primary form of talk therapy today, and talk therapies are typically referred to as psychotherapy. Many therapists will require you to return week after week to their offices to talk—operating under the assumption that talking things out in a warm, non-judgmental environment will lead you to a higher level of mental health. Some therapists refrain from giving advice, but instead question you, the client, to help you explore your thoughts, and then reflect or mirror back to you what they think you are saying or possibly implying.

In addition to focusing on questioning and responding, many therapists today use an eclectic, miscellaneous approach with clients, pulling in and mixing ideas primarily from person-centered therapies, Freudian theory, and/or cognitive behavioral therapies. The person-centered, feel-good approach primarily emphasizes making clients feel welcomed in a warm, undemanding atmosphere. Freudian or other psychoanalytic theory frequently points clients back in time, especially to their childhoods, to search for damaging experiences that supposedly explain current unhealthy behaviors and thoughts (such as neuroses). Cognitive behavioral therapies, now used by a growing number of therapists, encourage clients to uncover their irrational thoughts, but these approaches vary widely in terms of quality and effectiveness. Few are guided by the broad range of explicit critical thinking tools.

Question-centered and talk therapies (again, typically referred to as psychotherapy) include titles such as person-centered therapy, psychoanalysis, psychodynamic therapy, dialectical behavior therapy, narrative therapy, and interpersonal therapy. Then you have hypnotherapy, mindfulness therapy, pharmaceutical therapy, and electric shock treatment, as well as fringe therapies such as Eye Movement Desensitization and Reprocessing (EMDR), Thought Field Therapy (TFT), and Visual-Kinesthetic Dissociation (VKD).

There are perhaps as many approaches to mental health therapy as there are therapists. And it may well be the case that a therapist lacks clarity about the theories or methodologies she or he is employing. However, we can roughly summarize the primary theoretical schools guiding mental health programs and individual therapists. You need this background knowledge to understand what theories a therapist is using, or might be using, in your therapy sessions. Therefore, the rest of this chapter focuses on helping you become aware of these principal theoretical orientations, and begins to explore some major concerns about some of them from the point of view of critical thinking. In a few cases, readings are suggested. These are strictly introductory comments and represent only brief summaries (and in some cases beginning critique) of each school of thought.[14] You can dig deeper into any one of these therapeutic schools of thought.

Here are the therapies to be briefly discussed in the rest of the chapter:

- Critical Thinking Therapy
- Psychotherapy
  - *Humanism, Existentialism, Person-Centered, and Gestalt Therapies*
  - *Psychoanalysis*
- Rational Emotive Behavior Therapy
- Cognitive Behavioral Therapy
- Mindfulness
- Hypnosis
- Drug Treatment and Electroshock Therapy in Psychiatry

Finally, realize that, as in any field of health, there can be risks to the client. Because some forms of therapy, whether talk-centered or not, may harm you, rather than being neutral or helping you, it is vital that you, as a client pursuing better mental health, equip yourself with accurate information and assess what treatment is best for your needs.

CRITICAL THINKING THERAPY: A NEW FORM OF THERAPY

In addition to fostering and encouraging explicit use of critical thinking tools, critical thinking therapists aim, through their own developed critical thinking skills, to effectively pull together and employ the best therapeutic approaches that have come to us through such fields as psychology, philosophy, sociology, and anthropology. In developing or using the tools of critical thinking, these therapists do not ignore the best ideas on mental health that have already been worked through by important thinkers from the past, but instead appropriate and build on these best ideas. In other words, they do not rely on any individual

---

14 As you read the following summaries of primary approaches to therapy, remember that I am canvassing them from the point of view of critical thinking, using my best thinking given the state of therapy today. I am not a therapist; therefore, I am not approaching these theories from within the field of counseling. I am not approaching them as a therapist with preconceived notions about therapy. I am assessing these therapies from an outside, independent position, and in terms of critique of the field. In short, the tools of critical thinking are being used in this section to understand and critique primary forms of therapy in common use today, just as these tools might be used to understand and critique any other domain, subject, or profession.

school of psychological or social thought, but instead pull together the best ideas from *any field of thought* relevant to the mental health of their clients (for instance, suggesting art or music therapy for specific clients, or astronomy activities for others).

Critical thinking therapists do not accept the erroneous assumption that the most recent theories or practices in the field of mental health are necessarily best. They reach back anywhere through history to find the best ideas developed about the human mind that are relevant to mental health. They read widely through the literature to locate these best ideas, and they work to interconnect and deepen their ideas in a web of understandings that then guide their practices with clients. For instance, they begin with the assumption that all humans are intrinsically sociocentric (which we can learn to chiefly modify or control); this they accept as a reasonable generalization. They also realize that sociocentric thinking leads to many mental health problems, and they therefore read in sociological literature to understand some of these connections. They read widely in psychological theory, philosophical theory, educational theory, critical theory, and sociological theory.

Critical Thinking Therapy relies, then, not only on its own foundational tools for reasoning, as outlined in this book, but also on the best thinking that has been done about mental health historically by theoreticians in the diverse relevant fields of study. For example, Critical Thinking Therapists advocate for *Rational Emotive Behavior Therapy* because it offers sound therapeutic techniques for taking command of one's self-defeating attitudes by way of certain essential critical thinking concepts. They highlight parts of *existentialism* as linked to the vital importance of finding and pursuing one's higher purposes in life. They rely on some classic works from antiquity for early critical thinking theory, including Socratic thought and Stoic philosophy.

Critical Thinking Therapists recognize the value of intellectual, cultural, and creative development to mental health. They focus on the importance of helping clients live according to the meanings and purposes they themselves design for their own well-being, as well as the human responsibility to live an ethical life. They help clients internalize the tools of critical thinking through an ongoing educational process. In other words, they see themselves fundamentally as teachers of critical thinking concepts and principles, and as coaches helping clients apply critical thinking throughout their lives.

Critical Thinking Therapists see the importance of perceiving humans as living in nature, as being part of nature, rather than disconnected from it, as a requirement for mental health. This deep connection is also required if humans are to appreciate, enrich, and preserve nature, which is an ethical responsibility.

Critical Thinking Therapists are themselves committed to embodying intellectual virtues. They do not try to teach others something they themselves do not understand. Only those therapists committed to understanding and enhancing their own minds through critical thinking, as tools in their own lives, can foster these understandings in clients. Critical Thinking Therapists are interested in ideas and how ideas affect behavior. They are coaches assisting clients in internalizing ideas that make sense because they are based in sound reasoning. They are facilitators of self-empowerment through the tools of reasonability.

In therapy involving adults and adolescents, the therapists' emphasis on reasoning should be primary, and should focus specifically on clients taking full command of their reasoning using the tools of critical thinking. In the case of child and teen therapy, the emphasis should still be on the reasoning of the clients themselves—in this case, the children or teens—if they are mature enough to reason at a rudimentary level at minimum. But it must also focus on the reasoning of the adults caring for the children, and that of everyone else in the household who can or is influencing the child. This is because the problem often lies with the parents' reasoning or the reasoning of both parents and children (or teens), as well as others in the family with influence or power over the child. A primary goal in working with the entire family is to foster fairminded critical thinking among all its members across daily life; this is so that reasonable questions are encouraged as a rule, and children are educated to develop in their own right (within their capacities and in context of their needs and desires) while also learning to contribute to the greater good. In short, the ideal we reach for in therapy is the development of intellectual and ethical character across the family, with everyone committed to learning the explicit critical thinking tools in this book.

A primary or exacerbating problem for many children and teens may be the school setting they are embedded within. The vast majority of students are extremely ill-served by their schools in the US and in all countries where education is not the motivating factor, and where instead indoctrination, politics, and economics largely determine the school culture. Schools have traditionally been set up to serve the status quo, and this means keeping students in their seats, quiet, and accepting of mainstream views. This approach stifles learning at all levels for all students. For many learners, the situation is untenable and intellectually debilitating. They simply cannot fit themselves into the school structure without harm to their emotional well-being. Therefore, the influence of the school on the child must be considered. This includes whether the school has encouraged inappropriate use of psychotropic medications for a child or teen, which is likely to have detrimental physical and cognitive effects. This is now a widespread problem, leading many children and teens to become addicted to prescription medications and then carry this addiction into adulthood. We have known for some time that the developing brain of the child and teen should not be subjected to psychotropic drugs except *possibly* under extreme conditions. Yet psychiatrists continue to prescribe these medications inappropriately, and school personnel continue to push them onto children to keep them docile while at school. These concerns, along with the glaring problems implicit in social media use, especially for teens' mental health, should be carefully examined in therapy.

In Critical Thinking Therapy, all clients have their own printed versions of this book where at all possible (including those children and teens in therapy who can read and understand it). Critical Thinking Therapists do not attempt to teach critical thinking or use Critical Thinking Therapy without clients owning their own printed versions of this book, with some rare exceptions, nor do they rely on their own vague or partial conceptions of critical thinking. Wherever feasible, they foster deep understandings and uses of explicit critical thinking language, principles, and theory in helping clients become more mentally well. In other words, the therapist fosters fairminded critical thinking where possible as the core focus of therapy, since high-level, ethical, reasoning tends to be at the heart of genuine mental health.

When a client does not appear able to benefit from learning *any* tools of critical thinking immediately, or ever, the Critical Thinking Therapist relies on other forms of therapy (as briefly discussed presently), critiquing any therapy according to its relevance and potential effectiveness for a specific client. In this process, such therapists use critical thinking to identify the best therapies for their clients.

To be mentally healthy in our multifaceted world requires that you be an intellectually independent (in other words, intellectually autonomous) thinker. Therapists who make their clients depend upon them are not doing the most for their clients and are frequently harming them. Critical Thinking Therapy is designed to, as soon as possible and as much as possible, move the client away from dependence on the therapist and toward self-control and self-development using the tools of critical thinking. This is done through encouragement of regular critical thinking practice—for example, by asking clients to complete the activities and read the chapters in this book, discussing homework in therapy, then encouraging clients to revisit the chapters and activities again and again, over time, until ongoing mental health is more fully achieved. The process of development through critical thinking will take many years; therefore, the therapy time frame may require several years, and should continue until the client has developed built-in mechanisms for commanding and ensuring his or her ongoing mental well-being.

As you move away from meeting with a therapist (or decide against having a therapist at all), it will be essential to continue actively reading, writing, and applying critical thinking tools and concepts; this can be done through a long-term study group focused on critical thinking fundamentals and exemplars of critical thinking found in literature. The idea is that you need an ongoing system for continuing your development after ceasing therapy or after reducing how often you meet with your therapist.

Critical Thinking Therapists are both students and teachers of critical thinking. They work to internalize the critical thinking concepts and principles found throughout this book and are committed to living in accordance with these critical thinking foundations. They recognize the development of critical thinking abilities and virtues as a personal journey required for the highest level of mental and emotional well-being, as well as for self-actualization. While teaching clients critical thinking, they themselves continue to learn it with the understanding that one is never finished developing his or her critical thinking skills and dispositions. Instead, critical thinking requires lifelong commitment and continual work.

In short, through deep understanding and illumination of critical thinking concepts and principles, therapists can help clients intervene in pathological or otherwise irrational thinking. Clients themselves are encouraged to internalize and use the tools of critical thinking as a central part of becoming mentally well. Further, through a robust conception of critical thinking, therapists and clients alike can learn to effectively assess all existing therapeutic techniques which purport to improve mental health.

One final note on Critical Thinking Therapy. At this moment in history, and contrary to what has been implied in this section, there are no critical thinking therapists, per se. To our knowledge, no one is using all the tools as laid out in this book in the therapeutic process with clients. Therefore we can offer no exemplars for critical thinking therapy within the clinical setting. This does not mean such exemplars do not exist. It simply means that to our knowledge, no such exemplars exist. This also does not mean that there are not exceptional clinicians, because clearly there are. It means that the vast toolbox of explicit critical thinking concepts, principles, skills, and virtues do not tend to be at the heart of mental health therapies. Therefore there are no persons yet certified as critical thinking therapists. There are no schools of critical thinking therapy yet. There are no degrees specializing in critical thinking therapy. Therefore, there are no critical thinking therapists we can recommend to you. We hope this changes with this book.

PSYCHOTHERAPY

Now let us consider existing therapies by beginning with the broad category of psychotherapy, which generally refers to talk therapy and may entail any number of techniques on the part of the therapist. Most mental health therapists fall under this category, but the theories they use can vary wildly. Still, psychotherapies tend to fall under the rough category of *Therapist as Questioner and Advisor, and Client as Talker.*

Again, question and talk therapies include titles such as person-centered therapy, psychotherapy, psychoanalysis, psychodynamic therapy, dialectical behavior therapy, and interpersonal therapy. Psychodynamic therapy borrows from psychoanalysis, and dialectical behavior therapy is a form of cognitive behavior therapy, so they are not discussed in this chapter. You can find books on all these forms of therapy. I am concerned here primarily with focusing on classic theories from which latter theories have been derived.

Humanism, Existentialism, Person-Centered, and Gestalt Therapies

Humanistic psychotherapies tend to focus on the free will of the client, along with the importance of self-discovery and cultivating their own potential. These therapies include Existentialism, Person-Centered, and Gestalt Therapies, among others.

A primary form of psychotherapy today, *Person-Centered Therapy*, is based in the assumption that therapy should not be intimidating in any way, but instead should focus on just what the client wants to discuss—nothing else. The therapist's role is simply to bring out the thinking the client wants to explore by asking open-ended questions that help the person articulate their own thoughts. Carl Rogers initiated this school of thought, and you can read his books to better understand his philosophy.

On the one hand, it seems clear that all therapies for mental health should focus on the person seeking help through therapy; in other words, such therapies should be client-centered. Clients in psychotherapy should feel that they can openly communicate their thoughts in an unthreatening environment, so that they can begin to examine these thoughts within the therapeutic setting. But in most cases, for therapy to have a long-term impact will require more than making clients feel good: it will require that clients rework their faulty thinking. This necessitates critical thinking.

For people who are searching for meaning in life, the literature focused on logotherapy may be helpful. Logotherapy was developed by psychiatrist Viktor Frankl who believed the primary motivator for people is to find their own meaning in life. Rather than focusing on experiencing pleasure or aspiring to power, Frankl believed in existentialist thought—most specifically that people must find their own meaning in life and actively, fully direct their energy toward that self-determined meaning. His moving book, *Man's Search for Meaning*, briefly outlines *Logotherapy* and details to some degree his experiences in Nazi concentrations camps (in which he continually applied his concepts to survive and remain in command of his mind). Also recommended is Frankl's book *The Will to Meaning*.

Erich Fromm was an important humanistic, existential philosopher and social psychologist who focused on underlying problems in human life that frequently lead to psychological problems. Reading Fromm is a must for those who require a deep critique of human customs and human trappings that lead to psychological troubles. Though some of his ideas are dated, the bulk are relevant and very helpful for seeing through social ideologies and understanding their potential influences on us as individuals. For instance, Fromm points out how unbridled capitalism deters people from what is important and essentially good in living a human life. In his works he deals with pathologies that run through human life where capitalism is the primary determinant of life's purposes (he was a student of Marx, though pathological forms of capitalism can be critiqued through non-Marxist lenses as well). He also developed a rich conception of love in his book *The Art of Loving*. In addition to this book, I recommend the following books by Fromm: *Escape from Freedom*, *The Sane Society*, *To Have or to Be*, and *The Art of Being*.

Gestalt Therapists focus on helping people become aware of themselves, grasp their freedom as individuals, and direct themselves more fully in life. They emphasize the development of the whole person, rather than simply critiquing the person's individual behaviors, and they encourage living in the moment and integrating the many parts of one's personality in any given situation. You might read the works of Fritz Perls, who developed Gestalt Therapy to better understand this therapeutic approach.

Psychoanalysis

Psychoanalysis, as practiced today, focuses primarily on digging up unconscious memories the therapist believes may be affecting the client's ability to function satisfactorily in the world. Psychoanalysts tend to assume that their clients harbor repressed memories due to the unpleasant or traumatic nature of original experiences leading to these memories, which are thought to negatively impact the client's life.

Psychoanalysis originates from Sigmund Freud, who believed that unconscious repressed memories need to be brought to the surface to release the client from the torment, sadness, and dysfunctional behaviors resulting from these hidden memories. There are many facets and much depth to Freud's thinking, some of which can be useful in commanding your mind, some of which are routinely misunderstood or misused, and several of which have seeped into collective human conversations beyond therapy. Free association, wish fulfillment, reality principle, defense mechanisms, Freudian slips, anal-retentive personality, obsessive compulsive behavior, narcissism, libido, the pleasure principle, and the death wish are some examples.

Freud believed that in our early childhood, we are largely molded and receive our script for adulthood. Traditional psychoanalysts encourage clients to uncover repressed memories during the therapy process. One obvious potential problem with this is that the client may have no significant repressed memories, yet may be encouraged to ferret these out as sources of their irrational behavior. Another problem is that the client may have already worked through issues from the past and therefore may not need to, nor want to, revisit them. A third problem is that negative experiences or memories from one's past may not be the fundamental cause of poor mental health.

Freud has had tremendous influence over how western traditions view the influence of conditioning as against genetic predispositions, with Freud emphasizing the role of conditioning over genetics. In the end, we know that both conditioning and genetics play powerful roles in molding individual human thought and action. How given persons perceive the world, how self-absorbed or potent they are, what and how they achieve their goals, all depend on many variables, within any history period.

Freud's distinctions of the id, ego, and superego may be brought into the therapy process. In Freud's view, the id represents the impulsive primitive urges of the mind. The superego represents the influences of society on the person, the socially acceptable and ethical dimensions, as well as the parenting voice which frequently results in harsh and therefore inappropriate self-criticism. The ego, in Freud's representation, refers to the part of the mind that balances the id's impulses and the superego's critical nature. The ego moderates the desires of the id by finding socially acceptable ways to satisfy its primitive desires. (Note that this use of the term "ego" differs from the use of the term "egocentric" throughout this book).

Though Freud's theory of mind changed over time, we can roughly say that he distinguished between the conscious mind, the subconscious mind, and the unconscious mind. The conscious mind includes all the thoughts, desires, and feelings readily available to the person. The subconscious mind represents the thoughts one can easily bring to the level of consciousness when needed, but that are not always conscious. The person feels no conflict in accessing these subconscious thoughts. The unconscious mind represents all the thoughts, feelings, and desires that are difficult to access because the person is motivated not to do so, primarily due to fear of re-experiencing trauma from past negative situations or to hide something from oneself. The unconscious mind also includes primitive and instinctual desires.

The unconscious mind is able to maintain its irrational views via self-deception and through defense mechanisms such as projection, stereotyping, sublimation, distortion, and repression (developed by Anna Freud). Through these contrivances, the mind deceives itself into believing that what is false is actually true. Accordingly, thoughts left at the unconscious level cannot be examined by rational forces of the mind. Hence, a primary goal in psychoanalysis is to bring these unconscious thoughts to the conscious level. Symbolism through language and dream interpretation are significant to Freud as in his view they provide clues to the unconscious mind.

Freud was highly concerned with the sexual dimension of life and considered humans to be naturally sexual, both toward their gender-opposite parents in childhood and more generally as they move through life. He referred to a male's sexual attraction to his mother as the Oedipus Complex, and a female's sexual attraction to her father as the Electra Complex. He believed that sexual dysfunction frequently results from our inability to deal in healthy ways with our hidden sexual thoughts and desires. And he believed that sexual repression affects our behavior in other parts of our lives. Many people have been critical of Freud's views on sexuality; but it behooves us all to understand how our sexual functioning has been affected by our natural sexual inclinations, our sexual conditioning during childhood, and the influences of society's rules, norms, and taboos on our sexual views. To understand the roots of psychoanalysis, it is best to read the works of Freud, such as his *Introduction to Psychoanalysis*. The vast amount of literature in psychoalysis continues to branch out and specialize. For a broader understanding of Freud's philosophy, I suggest *Civilization and Its Discontents*, and *The Future of an Illusion*; to develop a healthy attitude toward sexuality, however, you might read *Sex Without Guilt* by Albert Ellis. For a revisionist or neo-Freudian view of psychoanalysis, you might read the works of Karen Horney, including *Neurosis and Human Growth: The Struggle Towards Self-Realization* and *Our Inner Conflicts: A Constructive Theory of Neurosis*.

When we consider the expanse of Freud's work, we find that most of his theory, so popular throughout the 20th century, is little in use today. This is especially true since psychiatry has turned almost wholly to psychotropic medicines as the primary treatment form. But Freud's theory that is in use still plays a powerful role in much mental health therapy, namely the ideas that childhood experiences can greatly influence mental health (and that these need to be revisited to be dealt with) and that unconscious thoughts frequently control our actions, resulting in all manner of irrational decision-making.

It seems clear that each of us should be keenly aware of the unconscious thoughts within us that give rise to illogical, narrowminded, unjustifiable behavior, including those we bring forward from our past. But the sooner we can properly analyze and move on from these the better. Further, we all should be aware of our sexual nature so we can adequately and properly guide it (within the confines of what is ethically justifiable and socially allowed). And we need to be keenly aware of how our unconscious thoughts affect our actions. But it is critical thinking that enables us to reveal what needs to be examined in our unconscious minds and that should determine both the thoughts we allow into our minds and the weight we give those thoughts. It is critical thinking that should determine whether we should "remember" something or refuse to allow it into our minds. It is critical thinking that illuminates and routinely scans and searches the mind for unconscious egocentric and sociocentric thoughts that attempt to stay hidden while impeding our development as rational persons.

RATIONAL EMOTIVE BEHAVIOR THERAPY[15]

For most people needing mental health support, the most effective primary mental health therapies entail a strong cognitive component in which client thinking is targeted as the chief instrument for improvement. These therapies now fall under the broad category of cognitive behavioral therapy (CBT). But there are better and worse approaches to CBT. The most rigorous approach was originated and developed by Albert Ellis, named Rational Emotive Behavior Therapy (REBT), and has since been largely watered down and subsumed under the CBT heading (though REBT predated and powerfully influenced the beginnings of CBT). Because CBT is a mishmash of approaches, I separate it from REBT, which is a rigorous approach to irrationality and other common mental health concerns.

This section elaborates on my introduction to REBT in Chapter Eight and discusses this therapy in relationship to CBT more generally. Further, since there are many connections between REBT and Critical Thinking Therapy, some of these connections are discussed here.

Rational Emotive Behavior Therapy (REBT), developed beginning in the 1940s by Albert Ellis, was the first break-through mental health therapy that marked a definitive, lucid path away from psychoanalysis, and which emphasized the importance of rational thinking as the key to dealing with personal neuroses. REBT utilizes several core critical thinking concepts, including the importance of following out logical implications on a routine basis, understanding interrelationships between one's thoughts, emotions, and behavior, and accepting reality as it exists.

Unlike traditional psychoanalysis, which presupposes that ideas and experiences from our past naturally reappear from the unconscious mind to plague us, REBT is based in the premise that ideas are actively generated by the thinker in the present. Classic psychoanalytic philosophy posits that people are molded in the first six years of life through conditioning and are then, if their childhood was deficient, continually victimized throughout life by psychological pain caused by past events over which they have no control; conversely, REBT teaches that people can command their minds to a large degree, notwithstanding their past experiences. This is also a natural tenet of critical thinking.

Though over time REBT was to importantly influence the field of mental health, again, the powerful concepts developed by Ellis have unfortunately been to some

15 Also see pp. 282-289 (Key Concepts in REBT)

degree (and in some cases a large degree) diluted or entirely misinterpreted, most significantly by cognitive behavioral therapists who have come after Ellis or used his ideas during his lifetime. Therefore, if you need further help gaining command of your self-defeating behavior, I suggest beginning with the work of Ellis and his colleagues.

Some of Ellis' powerful concepts include *musterbating*—obsessing over the idea that people and the world must behave according to your wishes; *awfulizing and horriblizing*—exaggerating a situation perceived as negative; *self-downing*—telling yourself you are worthless and a *no-goodnick* when you make mistakes or are unable to achieve what you would hope; and *disturbing yourself* over any number of things that are not within your power to change.

Ellis believed that people can find at least some happiness, even in difficult and trying situations, by intervening in negative thought processes. This, and most all of Ellis's approach to the mind, directly correlate with a rich conception of critical thinking.

Like Rational Emotive Behavior Therapy, critical thinking typically targets problems in thinking that lead to problems in behavior. But critical thinking goes further.

Critical thinking does not simply focus on individual characteristics or behaviors, as is commonly done in traditional cognitive behavioral therapies. Instead, all of your needs and essential desires, as well your capacities, are understood in relationship with one another using a holistic orientation. The ultimate goal in critical thinking is to cultivate fairminded critical societies in which rational ways of thinking and communicating are the norm, rather than the exception as they are today. To achieve this goal, it will not do to simply target your individual irrationalities. Instead, you must learn to apply the explicit tools of critical thinking across all important domains of your life (as you learned in the last chapter).

Ellis wrote many articles and books in his lifetime on a number of topics which can easily be obtained in print or digital format. For those who have difficulty finding happiness and self-fulfillment due to intrusive unhelpful thoughts, I recommend his books *A Guide to Rational Living and Reason and Emotion in Psychotherapy*.[16] Debbie Jolle-Ellis continues his work and coauthored with Ellis the book *Rational Emotive Behavior Therapy*, which I also recommend. As a therapist, Ellis was considered to some degree controversial for what may have been perceived as a confrontational style. However, irrational thoughts that lead

---

16 Also see videos of Ellis on YouTube or otherwise online—for instance this 1965 exploratory first meeting with a client named Gloria: https://www.youtube.com/watch?v=Jg5o0479uUQ. Compare Ellis's approach with that of Carl Rogers (Person Centered Therapy): https://www.youtube.com/watch?v=nc5v3HNZhjw&ab_channel=Person-CenteredApproachVideos or that of Fritz Perls (Gestalt Therapy), all with the same client in a first session: https://www.youtube.com/watch?v=cpUVR43jZHk&ab_channel=Person-CenteredApproachVideos

to irrational ways of living must eventually be confronted and dealt with. We can dance around the truths about ourselves that we would rather not face, but we will then be the losers in quality of life. It is far better, as Ellis would agree, to directly target and actively address problems in your thinking that cause problems in your emotions and behavior. This will be uncomfortable until you break through to higher understandings about yourself and begin to appreciate the process of self-cultivation.

The growing field of cognitive behavioral therapy derives its primary concepts from the work of Ellis, though as mentioned, much of Ellis' more significant work and deeper philosophical perspective have been largely ignored in traditional cognitive behavioral approaches. In an article entitled *Rational-Emotive Therapy and Cognitive Behavior Therapy: Similarities and Differences* (1980), Albert Ellis provides a well-developed analysis of why REBT (initially termed RET) is to be preferred over CBT, while acknowledging strengths in CBT. For instance, Ellis points out that RET is based in deep philosophical foundations, not on simple techniques. Ellis says:

> RET tries to help people comprehend and accept several ideas that are still revolutionary in our culture: (1) They largely (though not exclusively) create their own emotional disturbances by strongly believing in absolutistic, irrational beliefs. (2) Having a distinct measure of self-determination or "free will," they can actively choose to disturb or undisturb themselves. (3) To change, they had better actively work at modifying their thoughts, feelings, and behaviors. (4) If they decide to profoundly change one major philosophy, this may help modify many of their own emotional and behavioral reactions. (5) They will usually find a philosophy of long-range hedonism more healthful and productive of happiness than one of short-range hedonism. (6) A scientific rather than an unscientific, devoutly religious, or mystical outlook is likely to bring them greater emotional health and satisfaction (pp. 326-327).
>
> While RET, like CBT, is often interested in, or at least will settle for, symptom removal, it primarily strives for deep-seated emotional and behavioral change. It works for—but, of course, does not always achieve—a remarkably new psychological set on the part of its clients that will enable them not only to feel better and be relieved of their presenting symptoms but also to bring a radically revised outlook to all new, present and future, situations that will semiautomatically help them to stop disturbing themselves, in the first place, or to quickly undisturb themselves, in the second place. (p. 327)

COGNITIVE BEHAVIORAL THERAPY

Cognitive behavioral therapy (CBT) has gradually begun to take root in mental health therapy over the past several decades because, from a research perspective, it is one of the few primary forms of therapy that systematically results in positive outcomes for the client. But what are these outcomes? If the primary goal is a higher degree of perceived emotional well-being, which is usually the case, this may or may not be appropriate in context (e.g. in cases where clients are systematically harassing or otherwise abusing another person or sentient creature, or where they are engaging in dangerous wishful thinking). In any case, to the extent that CBT holds to the tenets of Albert Ellis' philosophy and the principles of critical thinking, it is to be expected that the therapeutic process would improve their mental health. Why? Because as you now know, it is the thinking underlying your behavior and emotions that you must command if you are to be mentally well. You *can* pick and choose methodologies for doing this, and some are better than others. But at minimum, you will need to understand that thinking is the key to feelings, desires, and behaviors; you will need to command your thinking through the tools of reasonability. And you will need a rigorous approach to the mind.

Sadly, since the original work of Ellis, the field of CBT has gradually been watered down until the deep essence of Ellis' ideas have been largely removed from much of CBT as it is now practiced. In some cases, authors have implied that their work is superior to Ellis' work because it has been made more *accessible* or *simpler*. But when we look closely at how these new works are crafted, we see that in fact authors are frequently misleading clients by oversimplifying human thought and experience, and by distorting what is required to command thoughts, feelings, and desires. Once you have studied the concepts and principles of critical thinking and applied them to your mental health, and when you have read the recommended readings on REBT (Ellis) and internalized his ideas, you should then be in a good position to critique *other* works in CBT (should you be interested in doing so).

Critical Thinking Therapy does not belong within cognitive behavioral therapy, because if it is subsumed within it, it will be diluted and distorted by it just as REBT has. Critical Thinking Therapy naturally entails a cognitive behavioral component in that it focuses on thinking underlying behavior, but it is far more than this. It is a way of living in which one is continually reaching towards self-actualization while also contributing to the lives of others, and to a better world. And remember that critical thinking tools are required to critique all other forms of therapy.

Aaron T. Beck, a leading theoretician in cognitive therapy, first began emphasizing the importance of the thinking underlying emotions and motivations based on Ellis' influence. Beck was a contemporary of Ellis, and seems to have taken powerful ideas from him, but in many cases he simplified them in the interest of research based in "scientific evidence." However, understanding the human mind can never be reduced to, or confined to, scientific analysis. Humans are far too complex, and many neurological underpinnings of cognition are not even accessible for thorough study by contemporary instruments.

In an interview on CBT, Judith Beck (Beck & Frances 2020)—Aaron Beck's daughter, who continued his work after his death—states on the one hand that CBT must be based in scientific research, and on the other hand that clinicians should not "follow the manual" to CBT. In advising therapists, she emphatically states, "never use manuals," though manuals are precisely what she and others in CBT largely produce. How can a therapy be based in scientific evidence alone, while at the same time be treated as if you should in some instances throw out the manual which presumably details the science you are to follow? The short answer is that it cannot. The longer answer is that though we can use scientific analysis to some degree in understanding the mind, we also need to understand fundamental concepts about the mind that are not proven through science (such as the fact that whenever we reason, we reason for a purpose; or that whenever we reason, we use information; or that the best reasoning adheres to universal intellectual standards such as clarity, accuracy, relevance, significance, logicalness, and so forth; or that all people are at times egocentric or sociocentric. None of these need be proven scientifically, since they are conceptual constructs that, when understood, help you reason better).

In recent years, Judith Beck's interest has been in creating positive emotions in therapy, and this conception seems to be catching on in CBT. On the face of it, this seems reasonable. But what if people in therapy routinely engage in behaviors that are harmful, manipulative, or are in any number of other ways unethical to others? Should they be made to feel positive emotions during therapy, or should they be made to face what they are doing, and have done, to cause pain and suffering to others? Moreover, what if patients in therapy engage in behaviors which all but guarantee severe negative emotions in their future life, however happy they may feel in the meantime?

Clearly, the positive-emotions-oriented therapy should be used in certain situations with clients experiencing specific types of problems, such as those having extremely low self-esteem. Again, therapists would need to determine when and where to advance the idea of encouraging positive emotions in therapy. But a key to self-fulfillment is to take command of the thinking that gives rise to your low self-esteem. Unless and until irrational thoughts are directly changed at the root level of your thinking (by altering your assumptions, concepts, point of view, etc.), any gain in self-esteem is likely to be passing rather than permanent.

Further, many questions asked in CBT could be replaced with much more powerful critical thinking questions. In therapy, Judith Beck frequently begins with what she terms a "mood" check—as in "How do you feel?" At best, this may help some clients clarify their feeling states—by revealing the thinking that gives rise to their feelings; at worse, it is a traditional psychoanalytic move that may be off-putting or unhelpful to others. Instead of a mood check, therapists might begin with any of these questions:

- How have you benefited from your homework between this session and last session?
- What have you learned about yourself this week?
- What have you learned about others who are important to you, such as how you affect them?
- What have you learned about how you need to change your thinking or behavior for the better?
- What steps have you taken to deal with your egocentric nature?
- What steps have you taken to become less dependent on the views of others?
- What are you doing to stop dumping on yourself?
- What are you doing to see yourself in a more realistic light?
- What activities have you done, or strategies have you used, to improve your thinking and your ability to control your emotional life?
- How has the homework helped you this week? Can you be more specific?

As you know, directly addressing your own irrationality is a key to improving your mental health. But this is often side-stepped in CBT. For instance, in a book on CBT entitled *Retrain Your Brain: Cognitive Behavior Therapy in 7 Weeks*, author Seth Gillihan (2016) details a therapy session in which a mother, Alex, tells him that sometimes her young daughter does not get ready to go in time for Alex to get to her office meeting—"because Bunny, her favorite stuffed animal, was sleeping in her room and she didn't want to wake her up." Alex becomes exasperated and eventually says to her daughter, "Put your dress on now or Bunny goes in the trash." The therapist asks the mother to describe "what she would say to someone she loved if he or she told her they'd done something similar." The account continues:

> She smiled and said, "It's funny; that actually came up over the weekend. I was running with Laura, and I told her how upset I was at myself for losing patience and threatening to get rid of Bunny. 'That's nothing,' she told me. 'You'd be shocked to hear some of the things that come out of my mouth when the kids are really aggravating me.' She told me some of them and to be honest—I was kind of shocked. I mean, it wasn't anything abusive, but I would feel terrible if I said those things."
>
> "So that must have really changed your feelings about Laura, huh?"
> (p. 116)

Gillihan goes on in this tone, apparently trying to coax Alex into believing she is being too hard on herself (in an attempt to make her feel good about herself). This has apparently been confirmed by her friend, whose behavior inappropriately reassures Alex that she actually must be a pretty good parent when the friend details her own, even worse examples of irrational behavior toward her children.

No matter how rushed, tired, or exhausted a parent is, allowing excuses for your own irrationality (such as threatening to throw away a child's cherished toy)—and telling yourself that though you may have been unreasonable, at least you are not as unreasonable as others—is not a defensible position. Of course, beating yourself up for being irrational is also never helpful, but implicitly encouraging clients to ignore their irrational behaviors which hurt others (in this example, her own small child) is not a justifiable form of therapy. This is just one of many superficial approaches to cognitive therapy you might come across in any of the CBT books that have become popular in recent years. What is needed in the example above, in part, is for the client to come to terms with her overall lifestyle. If work is overwhelming her, how does parenting fit into her life? Can she move to a part-time work position while her children are young? When we have children, we are responsible to care for them first and foremost. Therefore, the realities of child-rearing should be considered before people have children. We have created a world in which parents want to pursue a powerful career while also raising children, but we have not necessarily figured out how this can be successfully accomplished, or if in many contexts it is even possible. The work-home balance is something all people who work should seriously think through before having children. I am not suggesting that any of this is simple; I am suggesting that the notion that young children must be made to fit into our fast-paced, sometimes insane lifestyles is neither realistic nor fair to the children we bring into this world.

To the extent that CBT deals with the workings of the mind in a superficial way, only superficial changes are to be expected. On the other hand, to the extent that CBT—or any other therapy—focuses on revealing, dissecting, and fully understanding the irrational thinking underlying irrational behaviors and negative emotions, and then improving on that thinking, such therapy will in many cases lead people to develop as rational persons (assuming those persons are motivated to change).

The broad range of critical thinking concepts and principles should underlie all cognitive therapies, since cognition is improved through better reasoning for which critical thinking provides the tools. If you plan to rely on CBT therapists or literature, you will first need to make sure you have internalized the critical thinking concepts in this book. You will then have the background necessary to properly critique and benefit from the CBT methods being used. Be sure to ask yourself whether the ethical dimension is included in any given approach, since developing as an ethical reasoner is essential to authentic mental health.

MINDFULNESS THERAPY

The concept and practice of mindfulness have recently gained in use in mental health therapies and are often coupled with other therapies including cognitive behavioral therapies. Though the concept of mindfulness may be somewhat ambiguous in everyday life, therapists seem to primarily perceive mindfulness as being fully present in the moment, appreciating what is happening in one's present circumstances (as against worrying over the past or future), noticing one's breathing patterns, and engaging in breathing exercises to reduce stress, anxiety or other negative emotional states. Research indicates that these specific practices may significantly help some clients who experience ongoing negative feelings, as well as those who experience addiction issues or chronic health conditions. For more on *mindfulness*, see the glossary.

HYPNOSIS

Hypnosis is a form of therapy designed to help the client relax and enter a state of calm and tranquility in an unthreatening therapeutic setting. Results in terms of effectiveness for mental health have been mixed. Hypnosis can be likened to meditation or mindfulness, and has been linked with reductions in pain and anxiety for some people. More research is needed to determine the effectiveness and best uses of hypnosis.

DRUG TREATMENT, ELECTROSHOCK THERAPY, AND PSYCHIATRY

The treatment of mental health issues through physiological treatments such as medications (psychopharmacology) is still the primary line of defense for psychiatrists, who are first trained medical doctors and then specialize in psychiatry. Psychiatrists typically prescribe medications and some few may still engage in talk therapy. They base their medical prescriptions on the notion that mental health issues are characteristically caused by diseases of the brain.

However, the medical model of mental health is fraught with conceptual and practical problems. Though there are clear connections between brain and mind, we are in the infancy stages in terms of understanding these connections in ways useful to mental health. And though drugs are typically given to people with all types of emotional issues, the long-term efficacy of these drugs and their safety must frequently be called into question. This may apply to the new emphasis on and research into using psychedelic drugs for certain conditions such as depression and PTSD (since positive effects resulting from the controlled use of psychedelic drugs, where they are found, are at present known only to last a few months and because repeated use may be harmful to the brain).

As medical doctors, psychiatrists have an interest in advancing the medical model of the mind. This viewpoint seems to take precedence over the scientific studies that show serious adverse consequences for people taking psychiatric drugs long-term.

Here are a few primary questions you can ask of your psychiatrist:

1. Do you use a medical model for understanding the mind? In other words, do you see pharmaceuticals and medical procedures as primary methods for helping clients?

2. What studies can you point me to that show this medication you are prescribing is safe to use and under what conditions it is safe? How do I know it is safe to use all these medications together?

3. Do you also offer therapy sessions? If so, what theories do you use in therapy to help clients?

The rest of this section highlights some critical analyses of psychiatry by professionals who have researched and/or worked in the field. Much of this critique goes against mainstream views.

Thomas Szasz (1974; 2010), a long-term critic of traditional psychiatry, points out that psychiatrists tend to perceive and present psychiatry as scientific in nature, with their reliance on pharmaceuticals and other medical treatments, while also routinely engaging clients in any form of talk therapy (which is certainly not scientific). Szasz sees this mixture as a clear contradiction:

> … there is no such thing as "mental illness." … Alchemist and astrologers … spoke of mysterious substances and concealed their methods from public scrutiny. Psychiatrists have similarly persisted in speaking of mysterious mental maladies and have continued to refrain from disclosing fully and frankly what they do. Indeed, whether as theorists or therapists, they may do virtually anything and still claim to be, and be accepted as, psychiatrists (p. 1).

> There is… a serious discrepancy between what psychotherapists and psychoanalysts do and what they say they do. What they do, quite simply, is to communicate with other persons (often called "patients") by means of language, nonverbal signs, and rules; they analyze—that is, discuss, and explain, and speculate about—the communicative interactions which they observe and in which they themselves engage; and they often recommend engaging in some types of conduct and avoiding others… But what do these experts tell themselves and others concerning their work? They talk as if they were physicians, physiologists, biologists, or

even physicists. We hear about "sick patients" and "treatments," "diagnoses" and "hospitals," "instincts" and "endocrine functions" and of course "libido" and "psychic energies," both "free" and "bound." All this is fakery and pretense whose purpose is to medicalize certain aspects of the study and control of human behavior (pp. 3-4).

Many diagnoses commonly propagated by psychiatry are questionable. In the book *Rethinking Madness: Towards a Paradigm Shift In Our Understanding and Treatment Of Psychosis*, Paris Williams (2012) contends that there is no medical support, for instance, for the diagnosis of schizophrenia:

> … in fact, the diagnosis of schizophrenia is highly controversial. Despite over a century off intensive research, no biological markers or physiological tests that can be used to diagnose schizophrenia have been found, its etiology continues to be uncertain, and we don't even have clear evidence that the concept of schizophrenia is a valid construct. However, diagnosis and treatment based upon the diagnosis continues unhindered by these serious problems. (p. 16)

In his book *Smoke and Mirrors: How You Are Being Fooled About Mental Illness, An Insider's Warning To Consumers*, Chuck Ruby (2020), clinical psychologist and Executive Director of the International Society for Ethical Psychology and Psychiatry, eschews the medical model and argues for rethinking how we label those considered mentally ill:

> Using different terms when talking about human suffering would make things clearer and more honest. We would be better served with terms that don't give the impression of illness, disease, and medicine but more accurately described the very real and distressing problems people endure. It would be especially helpful if we could find good substitutes for the very terms "mental illness" and "mental health," as they falsely imply medical problems and defective people (p. 7).
>
> This medical language is probably the single most deceptive, yet subtle, influence in perpetuating the myth [of mental illness]. You are being fooled about it by the very language used in talking and thinking about it (p. 8).
>
> …the problems that get called "mental illness" are not caused by something malfunctioning in the person. They are meaningful but problematic personal reactions to difficult life situations. They are not illnesses… Instead, something in the person's life is not working right. Who would want industry professionals labeling us ill for being upset about difficult life challenges or dictating the best way to react to those challenges? I don't think many of us would want them determining what it is healthy living, except when that kind of living interferes with the

mechanical and chemical ways our bodies function to sustain life. And we certainly wouldn't want them to have the authority to force us into living in prescribed ways or believing in prescribed things (p.5).

Focusing on the problem of prescribing antipsychotic drugs over the long-term, Williams references the views of an ex-director at the National Institute of Mental Health (NIMH).

Hyman, neuroscientist, provost of Harvard University… summarized over 40 years of research on the mechanism underlying the effects of antipsychotic drugs. One of the main conclusions he arrived at was that the use of antipsychotics actually creates, rather than corrects, a biochemical imbalance within the brain. Prior to treatment, those diagnosed with schizophrenia have no known biochemical imbalances within the functioning of their neurons, but once they are placed on antipsychotics, the brain goes through a dramatic modification that results in abnormal neurotransmission (pp. 23-24).

In their book, *Psychiatry Under the Influence: Institutional Corruption, Social Injury, And Prescriptions For Reform*, Robert Whitaker and Lisa Cosgrove (2015) attack the chemical imbalance theory with considerable evidence and point out the need for psychiatrists to keep the medical model myth alive to serve their vested interests. They contend that:

… the field [of psychiatry] has an evident economic need to maintain societal belief in the integrity of its research, the validity of its diagnoses, and the merits of psychiatric drugs… In the United States, psychiatry is in competition for patients with psychologists, social workers, counselors, and other therapists to provide psychological services to people struggling with psychiatric issues. If psychiatric drugs are not seen as helpful, the field cannot hope to thrive in this competition (p. 180)… in 2009…it was reported that 90% of the panel members responsible for developing the APA clinical practice guidelines for schizophrenia, bipolar, and major depressive disorder had financial ties to pharmaceutical companies (p. 185)… although the APA 1999 textbook acknowledged that a chemical imbalance theory of mental disorders had never panned out, it wasn't until 2011 that representatives of mainstream psychiatry, in various forms, began admitting that fact to the public… If that was so, why had the public been led to believe otherwise? Why had the public been led to believe that psychiatric drugs fixed chemical imbalances in the brain? (p. 186)… Psychiatrists told the chemical imbalance story to patients to give them confidence that their psychiatrists knew what they were doing (p. 187)… Psychiatry has no special expertise in psychological or social matters… There are many in American society who are turning to nutrition, exercise, meditation, and other pursuits to get well and stay well. Meanwhile, from a scientific standpoint, psychiatry is clearly facing a legitimacy crisis (p. 206).

In his critique of psychiatry, Jeffrey Masson (1990) discusses the training he received as a student. He says:

> The major treatment was mind altering drugs. No doubt these drugs masked the symptoms of illness, but they also completely ravaged the personalities of the people who took them. There was no black market or street trade in any psychiatric drugs—every patient avoided them like the poison they were (p. 52).

Medical journalist Robert Whitaker (2001), in his book *Mad in America: Bad Science, Bad Medicine, and The Enduring Treatment of The Mentally Ill*, illuminates the fact that schizophrenics in America fare worse than patients in the world's poorest countries and possibly more than asylum patients in the early 19th century. In summary, he says:

> … if we wanted to be candid today in our talk about schizophrenia, we would admit to this: Little is known about what causes schizophrenia. Antipsychotic drugs do not fix any known brain abnormality, nor do they put brain chemistry back into balance. What they do is alter brain function in a manner that diminishes certain characteristic symptoms. We also know that they cause an increase in dopamine receptors, which is a change associated both with tardive dyskinesia and an increased biological vulnerability to psychosis, and that long-term outcomes are much better in countries where such medications are less frequently used. Although such candor might be humbling to our sense of medical prowess, it might also lead us to rethink what we, as a society, should do to help those who struggle with "madness."

> But none of this, I'm afraid, is going to happen… there will be no rethinking of the merits of a form of care that is bringing profits to so many. Indeed, it is hard to be optimistic that the future will bring any break with the past. There is no evidence of any budding humility in American psychiatry that might stir the introspection that would be a necessary first step toward reform. At least in the public arena, all we usually hear about are advancements in knowledge and treatment, as if the march of progress is certain… Hubris is everywhere, and in mad medicine, that has always been a prescription for disaster. In fact, if the past is any guide to the future, today we can be certain of only one thing: the day will come when people will look back at our current medicines for schizophrenia and the stories we tell to patients about

their abnormal brain chemistry, and they will shake their heads in utter disbelief (p. 291).

Beyond pharmaceuticals, electroconvulsive therapy (ECT) is still frequently used today to treat certain so-called mental illnesses. During his training, when expressing concern that a given patient did not need ECT, Masson recalls this conversation he had with a supervising psychiatrist:

> Who gets electroshock and who doesn't is not a medical decision, it is a political decision, and it depends on who has the power. One thing you can be sure, the power will never lie with the patient, or with anybody who wants to help him… if you think your complaint is going to alter the system, you are naïve (pp. 53-54).

About his discussion later with the director of the hospital regarding his concern over the use of ECT in a given patient, Masson says:

> The director was not cynical, he was absolutely persuaded, he told me, that nothing could be better for my friend's mental health than to have a dose of ECT, no matter who prescribed it. Better it should come from a physician, but the nurses have been here so long that they have learned the danger signs and know when a particular patient requires the soothing surges of 120 volts to the brain. He had nothing to be frightened of; why, it was totally harmless, and whatever pain was felt was forgotten afterward, because the shock to the brain was so great that many brain cells involved in memory were destroyed, and nobody remembered the actual pain (p. 54).

It should now be clear that if you are taking medications or undergoing other physical treatments through psychiatry, you want to know exactly the consequences, both short and long-term, of these treatments. Be wary of any psychiatrist (or any other therapist) who tries to avoid answering your questions or who treats you in a condescending manner.

Beyond medical treatments, if the psychiatrist is using a form of talk therapy, the sections above focused on client-centered therapy and other forms of therapy will be useful. In other words, psychiatrists will employ the same sorts of theories in therapy as psychologists, social workers, or others who call themselves a mental health therapist.

For those struggling with psychosis, rather than the heavy administration of psychotropic medications, Williams (2012) points to successful residential facilities designed to support the client through the crisis:

> …in such facilities, an environment of maximal freedom contained within a structure of maximal safety is maintained in several ways: the residents are allowed the freedom to follow their experiences and

maintain full choice regarding the use of psychiatric drugs while firm limitations are placed on activities that may cause harm to themselves, others, or property; they receive … support in the form of having their basic needs met – healthy food, water, shelter, clothing, and relative comfort; and they receive continuous nourishment in the form of 24-hour care by staff who are trained to hold them within an atmosphere of empathy, unconditional positive regard, and authenticity (p. 282)… By not subscribing to the brain disease model and instead expecting that these individuals will recover and eventually move onto rich and meaningful lives, the factors of *hope, meaning, and the development of a hopeful understanding of their psychosis* are supported. By not losing sight of the humanity of these individuals and maximizing their freedom and sense of agency, they are supported in *connecting with their aliveness.* In being surrounded by an empathetic, supportive community, they are supported in *cultivating healthy relationships and distancing from and/or healing unhealthy relationships* (p. 283).

For more on the problem of the medical model and to learn more about approaches to effectively addressing psychosis without medication, I suggest you read the books referenced in this section as well as those on the Recommended Reading list.

FOREWARNING: ETHICAL REASONING TENDS TO BE IGNORED IN THERAPY

As a reminder, most therapies give little attention to, or entirely ignore, the ethical dimension in human thought. Yet developing ethical reasoning abilities is as important to your mental health as developing critical thinking abilities. This is true because you live in community with others. You affect other people, and they affect you. There are ethical implications for almost everything we do where other viewpoints are relevant.

The proper role of ethical reasoning is to highlight acts of two kinds: those which enhance the well-being of others—that warrant our praise—and those that harm or diminish the well-being of others and thus warrant our criticism. Developing one's ethical reasoning abilities is crucial because there is in human nature a strong tendency toward egotism, prejudice, self-justification, and self-deception. These tendencies are exacerbated by powerful sociocentric cultural influences that shape our lives. These tendencies can be actively combated only through the systematic cultivation of fairmindedness, honesty, integrity, self-knowledge, and deep concern for the welfare of others.

The ultimate basis for ethics is clear: human behavior has consequences for the welfare of others. We are capable of acting toward others in such a way as to increase or decrease the quality of their lives. We are capable of helping or harming. What is more, we are theoretically capable of understanding when we are doing the one and when the other. This is so because we have the capacity to put ourselves imaginatively in the place of others and recognize how we would be affected if someone were to act toward us as we are acting toward others.

Thus nearly everyone gives at least lip service to a common core of general ethical principles—for example, that it is morally wrong to cheat, deceive, exploit, abuse, harm, or steal from others, that everyone has an ethical responsibility to respect the rights of others, including their freedom and well-being, to help those most in need of help, to seek the common good and not merely their own self-interest and egocentric pleasures, to strive in some ways to make the world more just and humane.

Unfortunately, mere verbal agreement on ethical principles alone will not accomplish important ethical ends nor change the world (or you) for the better. Ethical principles mean something only when manifested in behavior. They have force only when embodied in action. Yet to put them into action requires intellectual skills as well as ethical insights.

Through example and encouragement, we can cultivate important intellectual traits. We can learn to respect the rights of others and not simply focus on fulfilling our desires. The main problem is not so much distinguishing between helping and harming, but our natural propensity to be focused almost exclusively on ourselves and those closely connected with us.

It is up to each of us to determine the extent to which we are actively developing our ethical capacities. Of course we can only contribute to others' well being to the degree that we ourselves are physically, emotionally and mentally well ourselves. For more on ethical reasoning, see pp. 92-93 and pp. 266-268.

CONCLUSION

Critical thinking is implicit, or even explicit, in some mental health therapies. However, where we do find it in the mental health literature, critical thinking tends to be used in limited ways, employing only some of its transformative concepts, and frequently mixing them in with less sound, or even harmful, therapies. This smorgasbord approach may work to improve the mental health of some people (just as some people work out their problems without therapists). But for others, more overt and a broader range of critical thinking tools are needed. Further, the ethical dimension of human life is frequently ignored in therapy while making the client feel good is frequently the primary goal. This may be true even when the client has engaged in highly unethical acts.

Mentally healthy people who rely on explicit tools of criticality consistently and accurately assess their own reasoning as well the reasoning of relevant others in their lives. Remember that to assess reasoning, critical thinkers routinely use critical thinking standards—standards such as *clarity, accuracy, relevance, significance, logicalness, depth, breadth, sufficiency, justifiability,* and *fairness.* The best mental health therapies employ critical thinking because their primary goal is to help you, the person in distress or crisis, or in need of further development, *improve your reasoning* so you can take better command of your life. And Critical Thinking Therapy may entail using any of the best ideas developed by mental health experts as discussed in this chapter or elsewhere, including examining your past for issues that still get in the way of your development. In short, Critical Thinking Therapy includes knowledge of all therapies that may help a client, as well as the explicit toolbox of critical thinking detailed throughout this book.

APPENDIX A

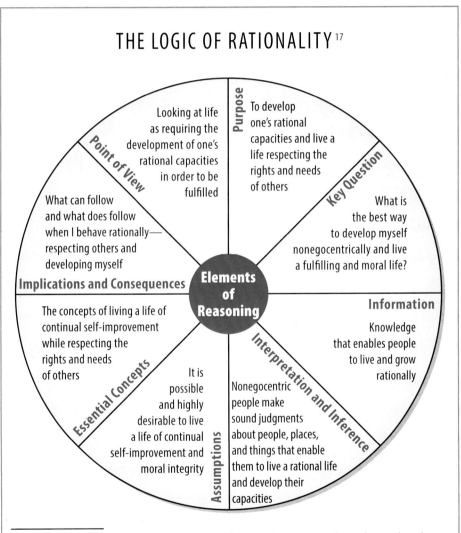

THE LOGIC OF RATIONALITY [17]

Purpose
To develop one's rational capacities and live a life respecting the rights and needs of others

Point of View
Looking at life as requiring the development of one's rational capacities in order to be fulfilled

Key Question
What is the best way to develop myself nonegocentrically and live a fulfilling and moral life?

Implications and Consequences
What can follow and what does follow when I behave rationally—respecting others and developing myself

Elements of Reasoning

Information
Knowledge that enables people to live and grow rationally

Essential Concepts
The concepts of living a life of continual self-improvement while respecting the rights and needs of others

Assumptions
It is possible and highly desirable to live a life of continual self-improvement and moral integrity

Interpretation and Inference
Nonegocentric people make sound judgments about people, places, and things that enable them to live a rational life and develop their capacities

17 An overview of the elements of reasoning, which provide a structure for understanding this logic and the others in this appendix, can be found in Chapters Seven and Eight.

THE LOGIC OF EGOCENTRISM

Egocentrism has a self-contained logic. To itself, it appears logical. By focusing on its logic we can figure out how it functions. We can figure out its purpose, assumptions, point of view, etc.

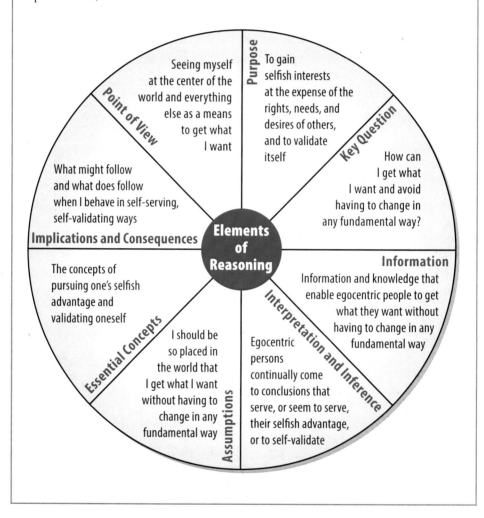

THE LOGIC OF EGOCENTRIC DOMINATION

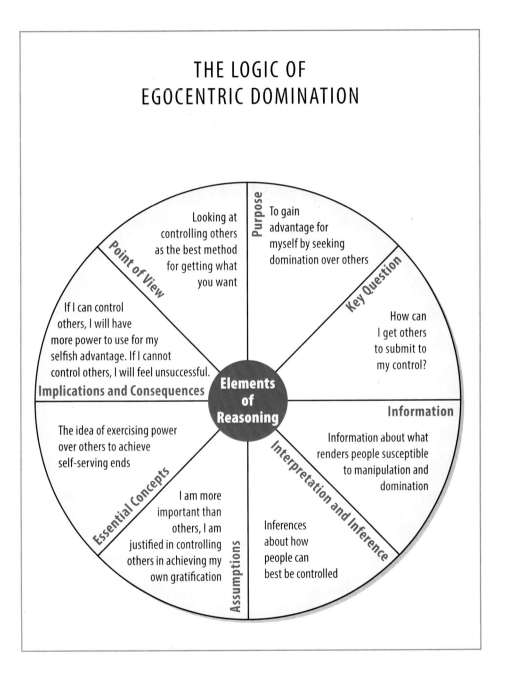

Purpose
To gain advantage for myself by seeking domination over others

Point of View
Looking at controlling others as the best method for getting what you want

Key Question
How can I get others to submit to my control?

Implications and Consequences
If I can control others, I will have more power to use for my selfish advantage. If I cannot control others, I will feel unsuccessful.

Information
Information about what renders people susceptible to manipulation and domination

Elements of Reasoning

Essential Concepts
The idea of exercising power over others to achieve self-serving ends

Assumptions
I am more important than others, I am justified in controlling others in achieving my own gratification

Interpretation and Inference
Inferences about how people can best be controlled

THE LOGIC OF EGOCENTRIC SUBMISSION

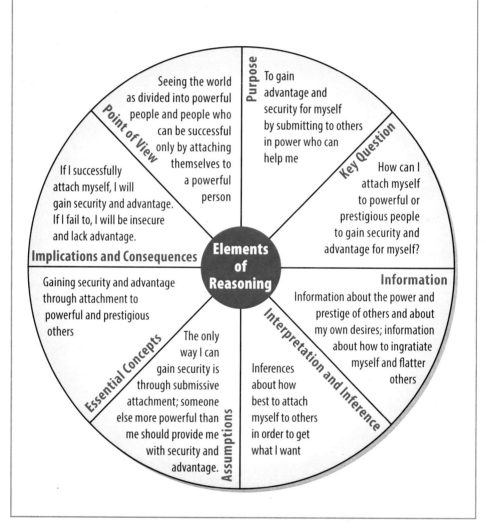

Purpose
To gain advantage and security for myself by submitting to others in power who can help me

Key Question
How can I attach myself to powerful or prestigious people to gain security and advantage for myself?

Information
Information about the power and prestige of others and about my own desires; information about how to ingratiate myself and flatter others

Interpretation and Inference
Inferences about how best to attach myself to others in order to get what I want

Assumptions
The only way I can gain security is through submissive attachment; someone else more powerful than me should provide me with security and advantage.

Essential Concepts
Gaining security and advantage through attachment to powerful and prestigious others

Implications and Consequences
If I successfully attach myself, I will gain security and advantage. If I fail to, I will be insecure and lack advantage.

Point of View
Seeing the world as divided into powerful people and people who can be successful only by attaching themselves to a powerful person

Elements of Reasoning

SOCIOCENTRICITY:
THE LOGIC OF GROUPISHNESS

Point of View
Seeing our group as the center of the world and everything and everyone else as a means to getting what we want.

Purpose
To pursue group interests at the expense of the rights, needs, and desires of those outside the group.

Key Questions
How can we as a group achieve our group purposes (without having to examine our beliefs or change in any fundamental way)?

Implications and Consequences
By deliberately pursuing group agendas and ignoring the effects of our actions on others, we are most likely to get what we want.

Elements of Reasoning

Assumptions
Our group should be so placed in the world as to get what we want without having to change in any fundamental way, or to consider the rights and needs of others.

Information
Information that enables the group to achieve its purposes and get what it wants.

Essential Concepts
The concepts of group superiority and group privilege.

Inferences
The group continually comes to conclusions that serve, or seem to serve, its agenda.

©2025 Linda Elder

SOCIOCENTRICITY:
THE LOGIC OF GROUP VALIDATION

Point of View
Seeing our beliefs as correct and good and true, without regard to objective reality.

Purpose
To maintain the beliefs and ideologies of the group in which one is a member.

Implications and Consequences
By constantly validating group beliefs, we can believe what we want and are justified in judging everyone outside the group according to whether they agree with us.

Key Questions
How can we assimilate all information so as to maintain our group's beliefs? How can we best rationalize our position so we don't have to consider other viewpoints?

Elements of Reasoning

Assumptions
Our group should never have to consider views it doesn't want to consider; we are entirely justified in maintaining our beliefs.

Information
Information selectively chosen that enables us to maintain our views; ignoring information that goes against our views.

Essential Concepts
The concept of telling one another within our group that our views are the best.

Inferences
Interpreting information so as to maintain the views already held by the group, or the views that appeal to the group.

©2025 Linda Elder

SOCIOCENTRICITY: THE LOGIC OF GROUP CONTROL

Point of View
Seeing group control as necessary for survival, and group acceptance of rules as a necessity.

Purpose
To maintain order and control within groups.

Key Questions
How can we ensure that people in the group conform to the group's beliefs, rules, customs, and taboos? How will we deal with group members who violate group rules?

Implications and Consequences
If people abide by the rules, taboos and conventions of the group, the group will survive and prosper. If they don't, the group will suffer.

Assumptions
For the group to prosper, order must be maintained. Group members must follow the rules of the group. Group members who dissent are a threat to our groups.

Elements of Reasoning

Information
Information that enables us to maintain control over the group — includes information about group members, human nature, rules to be followed, punishment methods, etc.

Essential Concepts
Humans as group animals in need of control by those who know how to maintain law and order.

Inferences
Judgments about (1) which behaviors will be rewarded in the group, which will be punished, which will be allowed; (2) how to deal with those who "violate" the rules; (3) who gets power and who doesn't.

©2025 Linda Elder

SOCIOCENTRICITY: THE LOGIC OF CONFORMITY

Elements of Reasoning

Point of View
Seeing conformity as necessary for survival; seeing groups as hierarchical in nature, requiring conformity to rules and conventions.

Purpose
To survive and be accepted within groups; to be validated by those in control.

Key Questions
How can I survive and be accepted within this group? What rules must I follow? What beliefs must I accept? If I disagree with the rules, how far can I bend them before getting into trouble?

Implications and Consequences
As long as I follow the rules of the group, I can survive in the group. If I go against group beliefs and rules I will be punished.

Assumptions
To survive, I must learn to fit into groups; I will get into trouble if I question certain rules, taboos or customs of the group.

Essential Concepts
Conformity as necessary for survival and acceptance; humans as existing in hierarchies with beliefs and rules to which group members are expected to adhere.

Inferences
Judgments about group beliefs, rules, conventions and taboos that help me understand the group so as to be accepted in it and not get into trouble.

Information
Information and knowledge about how the group functions, about its rules, taboos and customs which will enable me to survive and be accepted in the group.

APPENDIX B
IMPROVE YOUR MENTAL HEALTH BY READING CLASSIC LITERATURE

For many people, mental malaise comes at least in part from the fact that their intellects have not been properly developed. This often begins in childhood when people are not given proper education from parental guidance and/or in school systems. Many people have a great need to learn and explore ideas. But most societies, schools, colleges, and universities are not set up to address these needs. Beginning at a young age, many people become disconnected from the world because their intellectual needs are not met, and they therefore do not perceive themselves as able to achieve at high levels within their capacities. These people are frequently labeled troublemakers in school. Many are given medications by psychiatrists to dull their emotions (often referred by teachers and school administrators). Consequently, these people are predictably left feeling inadequate as thinkers. They lack a sense of self-efficacy. They lack power over their own minds, because they have never been taught how to develop their thoughts and explore ideas.

Of course, not everyone needs to study and explore ideas for mental well-being. But those who do have this need likely cannot satisfy it in any way other than by learning how to pursue and examine concepts on their own, using their best thinking through the tools of critical reasoning described earlier in this book. Everyday mundane conversation and experience, however pleasant, yet leaves them unfulfilled.

To develop the intellect is to internalize and potentially build upon powerful ideas that have come to us from distinguished thinkers throughout history. In fact, most, if not nearly all, powerful ideas about the mind can be traced through history to classic literature. Yet these thoughts, as they come to us through modern writers, are frequently diluted, partial or distorted because they are not deeply understood and/or are exploited for economic reasons. We see these ideas in much of the so-called self-help literature, typically written by people with superficial notions and the goal of making money, along with the aid of agents and marketing experts. Yet, it is always best to seek out for yourself the thinkers who have offered the deepest perspectives on the most significant, universal topics that have faced, and do face, humans.

Of course, classic literature is not all equal, either in soundness or value. It is therefore left up to you to work your way through the literature, seeking gems of wisdom that can bring you to higher levels of self-understanding and self-realization, while passing by or discarding unsound ideas.

This appendix highlights a few of the ideas that come to us through classic literature that might be considered essential reading for any discerning person. My goal here is merely to introduce a few enduring thoughts that come to us through classic literature—to give you an idea of the importance of studying substantive, illuminating and enlightening ideas that have stood the test of time. By way of example only, then, I include some of the reasoning of Socrates (as was recorded by his student Plato), and of these Stoic thinkers: Epictetus, Seneca, and Marcus Aurelius. This is followed by a list of recommended readings in classic literature as a starting place for further reading.

It is important to note that many distinguished thinkers through history have been mixed in their reasoning abilities, sometimes offering reasonable, powerful ideas, while at other times being off the mark entirely. Therefore, when reading the classics, or indeed any literature, it is up to you to distinguish among the wisdom, the lukewarm ideas, and the utter nonsense.

In this appendix, I do not give much historical background to the ideas written by a given author, though clearly this historical background is important in and of itself. Instead, I intend primarily to quote from the actual writings, or thoughts, of a few important sages, and to offer some little commentary of my own where I think it may be helpful. If your intellect has been malnourished, any one of these ideas, taken seriously, could greatly influence your mental attitude. Life-long reading in classic literature, when well-chosen, can profoundly improve your life.

THE IMPORTANCE OF SOCRATES

Let us begin with Socrates (469-399 BCE), the first documented substantial theoretician of critical reasoning. Approximately 2,400 years ago, Socrates was indicted and convicted of two things: first, believing in gods other than those sanctioned by the state, and second, of corrupting the minds of the youth. Regarding the first claim, it seems clear that Socrates held spiritual views consistent with those of the times, though he apparently did question what seemed contradictory in the views of sanctioned gods that had been passed down through antiquity. As to the second accusation, Socrates apparently made it his life's mission to foster critical thinking in both himself and the populace of Athens, Greece. He did this through disciplined questioning of anyone who would listen:

students sincerely interested in his teachings, politicians with whom he came into contact, arrogant teachers who spread false claims and unreasonable ideas, naysayers trying to avoid his open inquiring mind, and friends who appreciated his intellectual prowess. Socrates consistently and repeatedly emphasized the importance of honesty and consideration in living the examined life; he placed at the front and center of his dialogue the essential need to live according to ethical principles. He was often reaching for, and exploring, these ethical principles in his dialogues with others. It is his emphasis on critical, disciplined reasoning, coupled with the importance he placed on living an ethical life, that secures his place in history as a distinguished thinker. It also led to his execution, since he was in fact a danger to those in power who hankered after money, prestige, and power instead of seeking out truth, much like those in power today.

Because Socrates left nothing of his own writings, we must turn to his students (namely Plato and Xenophon) for a written picture of his rare critical thinking abilities. One of the most well-known texts in history comes to us from Plato, titled the *Apology of Socrates* (often published or described as *Apology* or "Plato's *Apology*"). This work begins with Socrates' opening statement to the court, in his own defense, after the prosecution warns the jury that Socrates will try to mislead them. In paradigmatic style, Socrates says:

> What effect my accusers have had upon you, gentlemen, I do not know, but for my own part I was almost carried away by them; their arguments were so convincing. On the other hand, scarcely a word of what they said was true. I was especially astonished at one of their many misrepresentations: the point where they told you that you must be careful not to let me deceive you, implying that I am a skillful speaker. I thought that it was peculiarly brazen of them to have the nerve to tell you this, only just before events must prove them wrong, when it becomes obvious that I have not the slightest skill as a speaker – unless, of course, by a skillful speaker they mean one who speaks the truth. If that is what they mean, I would agree that I am an orator, and quite out of their class. (p. 39)

Revealed in this passage, among other things, is the fact that Socrates was highly critical of sophistic thinkers—people skillful at using language in deceitful, manipulative, unethical ways. This included the very politicians who indicted and ultimately convicted him, who had themselves been his students.

Socrates was deemed the wisest man of the day by the Oracle of Delphi, a claim he himself denied at first, but which his own investigation later evidenced. He says:

> . . . when I heard about the Oracle's answer, I said to myself, "what is the god saying, and what is his hidden meaning? I'm only too conscious that I have no claim to wisdom, great or small; so what can he mean by asserting that I am the wisest man in the world? . . . After puzzling about it for some

time I set myself at last with considerable reluctance to check the truth of it in the following way. I went to interview a man with a high reputation for wisdom, because I felt that here if anywhere I should succeed in disproving the Oracle and pointing out to my divine authority, "you said that I was the wisest of men, but here is a man who is wiser than I am." . . . Well, I gave a thorough examination to this person . . . and in conversation with him I formed the impression that although in many people's opinion, and especially in his own, he appeared to be wise, in fact he was not. Then when I began to try to show him that he only thought he was wise and was not really so, my efforts were resented both by him and by many of the other people present. However, I reflected as I walked away: "well, I am certainly wiser than this man. It is only too likely that neither of us has any knowledge to boast of; but he thinks that he knows something which he does not know, whereas I am quite conscious of my ignorance. At any rate it seems that I'm wiser than he is to this small extent, that I do not think that I know what I do not know." (pp. 44-45)

From that time on I interviewed one person after another. I realized with distress and alarm that I was making myself unpopular, but I felt compelled to put the gods' business first; since I was trying to find out the meaning of the Oracle, I was bound to interview everyone who had a reputation for knowledge . . . it seemed to me as I pursued my investigations . . . that the people with the greatest reputations were almost entirely deficient, while others who were supposed to be their inferiors were much more noteworthy for their general good sense. (p. 45)

After I had finished with the politicians I turned to the poets, dramatic, lyric, and all the rest, in the belief that here I should expose myself as a comparative ignoramus . . . it is hardly an exaggeration to say that any of the bystanders could have explained those poems better than their actual authors . . . I also observed that the very fact that they were poets made them think that they had a perfect understanding of all other subjects, of which they were totally ignorant . . . last of all I turned to the skilled craftsmen . . . these professional experts seemed to share the same failing which I had noticed in the poets; I mean that on the strength of their technical proficiency they claimed a perfect understanding of every other subject. (p. 45)

Importantly, not only did Socrates embody intellectual humility as we see in the above passages, he also consistently and unfailingly advanced the importance of living an ethical life:

I have incurred a great deal of bitter hostility; and this is what will bring about my destruction, if anything does . . . the slander and jealousy of a very large section of the people. They have been fatal to a great many other innocent men and I suppose will continue to be so; there is no likelihood that they will stop at me. But perhaps someone will say, "do you feel no compunction, Socrates, in having pursued an activity which puts you in danger of the death penalty?" I might fairly reply to him, "you are mistaken, my friend, if you think that a man who is worth anything ought to spend his time weighing up the prospects of life and death. He has only one thing to consider in performing any action; that is, whether he is acting justly or unjustly, like a good man or a bad one. (p. 54)

. . . and so long as I draw breath and have my faculties, I shall never stop practicing philosophy and exhorting you and indicating the truth for everyone that I meet. I shall go on saying, in my usual way, "my very good friend, you are an Athenian and belong to the city which is the greatest and most famous in the world for its wisdom and strength. Are you not ashamed that you give your attention to acquiring as much money as possible, and similarly with reputation and honor, and to give no attention or thought to truth and understanding and the perfection of your soul?" And if any of you disputes this and professes to care about these things, I shall not at once let him go or leave him; no, I shall question him and examine him and put him to the test; and if it appears that in spite of his profession he has made no real progress towards goodness, I shall reprove him for neglecting what is of supreme importance, and giving his attention to trivialities. I shall do this to everyone that I meet . . . wealth does not bring goodness, but goodness brings wealth and every other blessing . . . and whether you acquit me or not; you know that I am not going to alter my conduct, not even if I have to die a hundred deaths. (pp. 55-56)

You will find that throughout my life I have been consistent in any public duties that I have performed, and the same also in my personal dealings: I have never countenanced any action that was incompatible with justice on the part of any person . . . (p. 60)

I have never lived an ordinary quiet life. I did not care for the things that most people care about: making money, having a comfortable home, high military or civil rank, and all the other activities – political appointments, secret societies, party organizations – which go on in our city; I thought that I was really too fair-minded to survive if I went in for this sort of thing. So instead of taking a course which would have done no good either to you or to me I set myself to do you individually in private what I hold to be the greatest possible service: I tried to persuade each of you not to think more of practical advantages than of his mental and moral well-being, or in general to think more of advantage than of well-being in the case of the state or anything else. (pp. 64-65)

. . . I tell you that to let no day pass without discussing goodness and all the other subjects about which you hear me talking and examining both myself and others is really the very best thing that a man can do, and that life without this sort of examination is not worth living. (p. 66)

. . . I suggest, gentlemen, that the difficulty is not so much to escape death; the real difficulty is to escape wickedness . . . when I leave this court I shall go away and condemned by you to death, but [my accusers] will go away convicted by truth herself of depravity and injustice. (p. 68)

I tell you my executioners that as soon as I am dead, vengeance shall fall upon you with a punishment far more painful than your killing of me. You have brought about my death in the belief that through it you will be delivered from submitting the conduct of your lives to criticism; but I say the result will be just the opposite. (p. 68)

When my sons grow up, gentleman, if you think that they are putting money or anything else before goodness, take your revenge by plaguing them as I plagued you; and if they fancy themselves for no reason, you must scold them just as I scolded you, for neglecting the important things and thinking that they are good for something when they are good for nothing. If you do this, I shall have had justice at your hands – I and my children. (p. 70)

Socrates comments on the pervasive problem of corruption in politics, still widespread today, and how involvement in politics by the just and reasonable can be life-threatening:

. . . because you may be quite sure, gentlemen, that if I had tried long ago to engage in politics, I should long ago have lost my life . . . no man on earth who conscientiously opposes either you or any other organized democracy, and flatly prevents a great many wrongs and illegalities from taking place in the state to which he belongs, can possibly escape with his life. The true champion of justice, if he intends to survive even for a short time, must necessarily confine himself to private life and leave politics alone. (pp. 58-59)

For further readings on Socrates, I suggest the full version of the *Apology of Socrates* by Plato, as well as these early Platonic dialogues: Euthyphro, Crito, and Phaedo. (Be aware that other Platonian works divert significantly from Socratic philosophy.) For a slightly different but also intriguing view of Socrates, read Xenophon's *Conversations of Socrates*.

STOIC PHILOSOPHY

Socrates' place in history was established during his lifetime, and at least some of his views were carried forward through other philosophers such as Plato and later the Cynics, the Epicureans, and most notably the Stoic philosophers. Stoic thinking, in particular, built upon intellectual foundations laid by Socrates, especially in terms of living an examined life through rationality and contributing to the common good (though it would not be until the 20th century that more explicit methodologies for ethical critical thinking would emerge). Stoic philosophy began with Zeno of Citium (c. 335-263 BCE), considered its founder, and continued through the writings of Marcus Aurelius (121-180 CE). After reading this chapter, in addition to continuing reading within Stoic philosophy, you may want to read in the available Cynics and Epicureans (see Recommended Readings at the end of this appendix).

Stoic philosophers view the world as a single community in which all people are interconnected. They believe everyone to be responsible for living in accord with nature's laws, and resigning themselves completely and utterly to those things beyond their control, without complaint and without obsessing or fixating over what they themselves cannot control. They believe people should not rely for their well-being on anything that may be taken away from them. Only then can people "discover that true, unshakable peace and contentment to which ambition, luxury and above all avarice are among the greatest obstacles" (Campbell 2004). Stoics highly value reasoning and living the rational life, believing, generally speaking, that people have the inborn capacity to develop as skilled reasoners if only they will recognize this capacity and constantly cultivate it. By taking command of their reasoning capacities, they can accept and more easily deal with pain, grief, and injustice, as well as the fear of death. The importance of intellectual discipline is explicit in Stoic philosophy, which entails the need to command one's will to effectively manage forces within one's control, such as desires for pleasure and passion that may lead in a wrong direction. Though in ancient times Stoicism was widely accepted among intellectuals, it failed to take hold among the populace, perhaps because people found it too difficult to live up to Stoic principles.

Most ancient Stoic writings have been lost. However, surviving texts do give us a good sense of Stoic views and how these views can help us live a rational life—of course, only if we take them seriously on a daily basis.

Again, this section offers a glimpse of the extant writings and thoughts of the two primary Stoic philosophers available to us, Lucius Annaeus Seneca the Younger (c. 1-65 CE) and Epictetus (c. 50-130 CE), and one emperor who employed Stoicism, Marcus Aurelius (121-180 CE).

As you read the following excerpts, you should be able to easily discern why these principles still find little favor in human societies today. And you will see interconnections between Stoic and critical thinking philosophies.

SENECA

Lucius Annaeus Seneca the Younger (c. 4 BCE - 65) apparently wrote extensively during his lifetime, but little remains of his writings. The best-known works that have made it to us through history are his 124 letters to Lucilius Junior, which are early essays on how to live according to Stoic principles. The following excerpts are drawn from these letters. Seneca opens his second letter by focusing on the importance of reading and rereading works by distinguished authors in seeking wisdom rather than reading superficial works. He then elaborates on the link between happiness and cultivating wisdom through daily reflections on important ideas (c. 64 CE; 2004):

> You should be extending your stay among writers whose genius is unquestionable, deriving constant nourishment from them if you wish to gain anything from your reading that will find a lasting place in your mind . . . so always read well-tried authors, and if at any moment you find yourself wanting a change from a particular author, go back to the ones you have read before. (pp. 33-34)

> We need to set our affections on some good man and keep him constantly before our eyes, so that we may live as if he were watching us and do everything as if he saw what we were doing . . . misdeeds are greatly diminished if a witness is always standing near intending doers. The personality should be provided with someone it can revere, someone whose influence can make even its private, inner life more pure. Happy the man who improves other people not merely when he is in their presence but even when he is in their thoughts! . . . Choose someone whose way of life as well as words . . . have won your approval . . . there is a need, in my view, for someone as a standard against which our characters can measure themselves. (p. 56)

> . . . no one can lead a happy life, or even one that is bearable, without the pursuit of wisdom . . . the perfection of wisdom is what makes the happy life, although even the beginnings of wisdom make life bearable. Yet this conviction, clear as it is, needs to be strengthened and given deeper roots through daily reflections; making noble resolutions is not as important as keeping the resolutions you have made already. You have to persevere and fortify your pertinacity until the will to good becomes a disposition to good. (p. 63)

Seneca encourages people to think philosophically, and by this he means living the examined life and developing one's character in the way Socrates advised:

> . . . you've no grounds for forming a ready, hasty belief in yourself. Carry out a searching analysis and close scrutiny of yourself in all sorts of different lights. Consider above all else whether you've advanced in philosophy or just

in actual years . . . Philosophy is not an occupation of a popular nature . . . it moulds and builds the personality, orders one's life, regulates one's conduct, shows one what one should do and what one should leave undone, sits at the helm and keeps one on the correct course as one is tossed about in perilous seas. Without it no one can lead a life free of fear or worry. (pp. 63-64)

A good character is the only guarantee of everlasting, carefree happiness. (p. 64)

Seneca stresses the importance of carefully choosing who one associates with, pointing out how other people can lead you to wrong thinking and wrong living. Note how he illuminates the pervasive problem of sociocentricity via the need for approval:

You asked me to say what you should consider it particularly important to avoid. My answer is this: a mass crowd. It is something to which you cannot entrust yourself yet without risk. I at any rate am ready to confess my own frailty in this respect. I never come back home with quite the same moral character I went out with; something or other becomes unsettled where I had achieved internal peace . . . Associating with people in large numbers is actually harmful: there is not one of them that will not make some vice or other attractive to us, or leave us carrying the imprint of it . . . and inevitably enough, the larger the size of the crowd we mingle with, the greater the danger . . . what do you take me to mean? That I go home more selfish, more self-seeking, and more self indulgent? Yes, and what is more, a person crueler and less humane through having been in contact with human beings . . . [Even] A Socrates . . . might have been shaken in his principles by a multitude of people different from himself: such is the measure of the inability of any of us, even as we perfect our personality's adjustment, to withstand the onset of devices when they come with such a mighty following . . . you should neither become like the bad because they are many, nor be an enemy of the many because they are unlike you. Retire into yourself as much as you can. Associate with people who are likely to improve you. Welcome those who are capable of improving . . . The many speak highly of you, but have you really any grounds for satisfaction with yourself if you are the kind of person the many understand? (pp. 41-44)

Away with the world's opinion of you—it's always unsettled and divided. (p. 71)

Seneca speaks of developing the inner self:

Such is more or less the way of the wise man: he retires to his inner self, is his own company . . . Natural promptings (not thoughts of any advantage to himself) compel him towards friendship. We are born with a sense of the pleasantness of friendship just as of other things . . . The wise man,

402 | APPENDIX B

nevertheless, unequalled though he is in his devotion to his friends, though regarding them as being no less important and frequently more important than his own self, will still consider what is valuable in life to be something wholly confined to his inner self. (p. 52)

Life would be restricted indeed if there were any barrier to our imaginations. (p. 109)

There can be absolute bedlam without so long as there is no commotion within . . . the only true serenity is the one which represents the free development of a sound mind. (pp. 110-111)

Men and birds together in full chorus will never break into our thinking when that thinking is good and has at last come to be of a sure and steady character. (p. 112)

Seneca points out the problem of seeking unnecessary wealth and he argues for simple, frugal living as a key to happiness.[18] He says:

Set aside now and then a number of days during which you will be content with the plainest of food, and very little of it . . . endure this for three or four days at a time, sometimes more, so that it is a genuine trial and not an amusement . . . There is no reason, mind you, why you should suppose yourself to be performing a considerable feet in doing this—you will only be doing something done by thousands upon thousands of slaves and paupers . . . [Regarding possessions] I am not, mind you, against your possessing them, but I want to ensure that you possess them without tremors; and this you will only achieve in one way, by convincing yourself that you can live a happy life even without them, and by always regarding them as being on the point of vanishing. (pp. 67-69)

On learning, Seneca argues:

But something that can never be learnt too thoroughly can never be said too often. With some people you only need to point to a remedy; others need to have it rammed into them. (p. 75)

---

18 Seneca has been criticized for being a wealthy person, and having extravagant properties, which seems to contradict his stoic injunctions. He did contend, and may have defended himself on the grounds, that it is acceptable to enjoy one's wealth within reasonable boundaries, as long as one does not attach undue importance to wealth or what it brings, and as long as one can give up unneeded wealth without whining, complaining, or feeling that anything important has been lost. Some unconvinced persons might then respond, "Physician, heal thyself." Indeed it is not uncommon for theoreticians to argue in one way and live in another. The important thing for you, in the process of cultivating your mind and transforming the way you live, is to take the gems of wisdom you can gain from any distinguished thinker and incorporate them into your own thinking. The important question is whether the theory is sound and potentially powerful, and, if sound, whether you yourself are using it—not whether a given theoretician lives, or has lived, in accordance with his or her stated principles.

Seneca admonishes against simply quoting and memorizing from others, instead arguing for the importance of intellectual autonomy. He says:

> It is disgraceful that a man who is old or in site of old age should have a wisdom deriving solely from his notebook. 'Zeno said this.' And what have you said? 'Cleanthes said that.' What have you said? How much longer are you going to serve under others' orders? Assume authority yourself and utter something that may be handed down to posterity. Produce something from your own resources . . . it is one thing . . . to remember, another to know . . . the men who pioneered the old routes are leaders, not our masters. (pp. 80-81)

To the subject of death, Seneca returns many times.

> Well, we should cherish old age and enjoy it. It is full of pleasure if you know how to use it. Fruit tastes most delicious just when its season is ending . . . 'It is not very pleasant, though,' you might say, 'to have death right before one's eyes.' To this I would say, firstly, that death ought to be right there before the eyes of a young man just as much as an old one – the order in which we each reach our summons is not determined by our precedence in the register – and secondly, that no one is so very old that it would be quite unnatural for him to hope for one more day. (p. 58)

> 'Rehearse death'. To say this is to tell a person to rehearse his freedom. A person who has learned how to die has unlearned how to be a slave . . . There is but one chain holding us in fetters, and that is our love of life. There is no need to cast this love out altogether, but it does need to be lessened somewhat so that, in the event of circumstances ever demanding this, nothing may stand in the way of our being prepared to do at once what we must do at some time or other. (p. 72)

> The man . . . whom you should admire and imitate is the one who finds it a joy to live and in spite of that is not reluctant to die. (p. 105)

> Let us never feel a shudder at the thought of being wounded or being made a prisoner, or of poverty or persecution. What is death? Either a transition or an end. I am not afraid of coming to an end, this being the same as never having begun, nor of transition, for I shall never be in confinement quite so cramped anywhere else as I am here. (p. 124)

> . . . but life is never incomplete if it is an honorable one. At whatever point you leave life, if you leave it in the right way, it is a whole. (p. 125)

> Someone, though, will say, 'But I want to live because of all the worthy activities I'm engaged in. I'm performing life's duties conscientiously and energetically and I'm reluctant to leave them undone.' Now, surely you know that dying is also one of life's duties? You're leaving no duty undone, for

there's no fixed number of duties laid down which you're supposed to complete. Every life without exception is a short one. (p. 130)

... There's nothing so very great about living ... what is, however, a great thing is to die in a manner which is honorable, enlightened and courageous. (p. 126)

You want to live – but do you know how to live? You're scared of dying – and, tell me, is the kind of life you lead really any different from being dead? (p. 129)

On grieving when others close to us die, Seneca says:

... we can be pardoned for having given way to tears so long as they have not run down in excessive quantities and we have checked them for ourselves. When one has lost a friend one's eyes should be neither dry nor streaming. Tears, there should be, but not lamentation ... your face will cease to be its present picture of sadness as soon as you take your eyes off yourself. At the moment you're keeping a watch on your grief—but even as you do it is fading away ... let us see to it that the recollection of those we have lost becomes a pleasure to us. (p. 114)

On the fact that people generally do not appreciate critical thinking, Seneca says:

A sound mind can neither be bought nor borrowed. And if it were for sale, I doubt whether it would find a buyer. And yet unsound ones are being purchased every day.

On attempting to run away from one's problems, Seneca quotes Socrates:

Here is what Socrates said ... 'how can you wonder your travels do you no good, when you carry yourself around with you? You are saddled with the very thing that drove you away ... are you really surprised, as if it were something unprecedented, that so long a tour and such diversity of scene have not enabled you to throw off this melancholy and this feeling a depression? ... You are running away in your own company. You have to lay aside the load on your spirit. Until you do that, nowhere will satisfy you. Once you have rid yourself of the affliction there, though, every change of scene will become a pleasure. You may be banished to the ends of the earth, and yet in whatever outlandish corner of the world you may find yourself stationed, you will find that place, whatever it may be like, a hospitable home. Where you arrive does not matter so much as what sort of person you are when you arrive there ... the thing you are looking for, the good life, is available everywhere. (pp. 75-77)

On bringing about improvement in oneself, Seneca says:

'A consciousness of wrongdoing is the first step to salvation.' This remark of Epicurus' is to me a very good one. For a person who is not aware that he is doing anything wrong has no desire to be put right. You have to catch yourself doing it before you can reform . . . So – to the best of your ability – demonstrate your own guilt, conduct inquiries of your own into all the evidence against yourself. Play the part first of prosecutor, then of judge and finally of pleader in mitigation. Be harsh with yourself at times. (pp. 77-78)

There are my terrors to be quieted, incitements to be quelled, illusions to be dispelled, extravagance to be checked, greed to be reprimanded: which of these can be done in a hurry? (p. 84)

. . . man is a rational animal. Man's ideal state is realized when he has fulfilled the purpose for which he was born. And what is it that reason demands of him? Something very easy – that he lives in accordance with his own nature. Yet this is turned into something difficult by the madness that is universal among men; we push one another into vices (pp. 88-89) . . .

[Yet] each man has a character of his own choosing. One is a slave to sex, another to money, another to ambitions; all are slaves to hope or fear . . . only an absolute fool values a man according to his clothes, or according to his social position, which after all is only something that we wear like clothing. . . and there's no state of slavery more disgraceful than one which is self-imposed. (pp. 94-95)

On the impoverished ways in which philosophers typically approach reasoning (still a serious problem today), Seneca says:

. . . in the midst of all this what you people do for me is pull words about and cut up syllables. One is led to believe that unless one has constructed syllogisms of the craftiest kind, and reduced fallacies to a compact form in which a false conclusion is derived from a true premise, one will not be in a position to distinguish what one should aim at and what one should avoid. It makes one ashamed – that men of our advanced years should turn a thing as serious as this into a game . . . 'mouse is a syllable, and a mouse nibbles cheese; therefore, a syllable nibbles cheese.' . . . what childish fatuities these are! Is this what we philosophers acquire wrinkles in our brows for? . . . Is this the way to our supreme ideal? Do we get there by means of all that 'if X, Y, or if not Y, Z' one finds in philosophy? . . . Keep clear, then . . . as far as you can, of the sort of quibbles and qualifications I've been mentioning in philosophers. Straightforwardness and simplicity are in keeping with goodness . . . isn't it the height of folly to learn inessential things when time is so desperately short! (pp. 97-100)

On the importance of keeping one's body physically fit, Seneca says:

I've just this moment returned from a ride in my sedan-chair, feeling as tired as if I'd walked the whole distance instead of being seated all the way. Even to be carried for any length of time is hard work, and all the more so, I dare say,

406 | APPENDIX B

because it is unnatural, nature having given us legs with which to do our own walking just as she gave us eyes with which to do our own seeing. Soft living imposes on us the penalty of debility. (p. 106)

On dealing with physical suffering, which Seneca had considerable experience with throughout his lifetime, he says:

> What in fact makes people who are morally unenlightened upset by the experience of physical distress is their failure to acquire the habit of contentment . . . they have instead been preoccupied by the body. That is why a man of noble and enlightened character separates body from spirit and has just as much to do with the former, the frail and complaining part of our nature, as is necessary and no more, and a lot to do with the better, the divine element . . . so do not go out of your way to make your troubles any more tiresome than they are and burden yourself with fretting... If . . . you start giving yourself encouragement, saying to yourself, 'it's nothing – or nothing much anyway – let's stick it out, it'll be over presently,' then in thinking it a trivial matter you will be ensuring that it actually is. Everything hangs on one's thinking . . . A man is as unhappy as he has convinced himself he is. And complaining away about one's sufferings after they are over . . . is something I think should be banned . . . (you know the kind of language: 'No one had ever been in such a bad state. The torments and hardships I endured! No one thought I would recover. The number of times I was giving up for lost by the family! The number of times I was despaired of by the doctors! A man on the rack isn't torn with pain the way I was'). Even if all this is true, it is past history. What's the good of dragging up sufferings which are over, of being unhappy now just because you were then? What is more, doesn't everyone add a good deal to his tale of hardships and deceive himself as well in the matter? . . . When some trouble or other comes to an end the natural thing is to be glad. (pp. 133-135)

EPICTETUS

Born a slave, Epictetus (c. 50-135) was considered one of the most influential Stoic philosophers of his time. He inspired, for instance, the writings of Marcus Aurelius. Epictetus was likely owned for a time by the powerful freedman Epaphroditus, and he studied with the Stoic teacher Musonius Rufus. Epictetus taught philosophy in Rome and, when banished from Rome in the year 89 along with other philosophers, he established a school on the Adriatic coast of Greece. His student Arrian, an important historian and writer, recorded and published informal lectures by and conversations with Epictetus (c. 108). What remains of these writings fall under the headings, "Discourses," "Fragments," and "Handbook." The following quotes come from these writings found in *The Discourses of Epictetus*, as translated by Robin Hard (c. 108; 2014).

On reason as the key to understanding and assessing all modes of thought, and the importance of developing one's reasoning capacities, Epictetus says:

> Among all the arts and faculties, you'll find none that can take itself as an object of study, and consequently none that can pass judgment of approval or disapproval upon itself . . . what will tell you, then? The faculty that takes both itself and everything else as an object of study. And what is that? The faculty of reason. For that alone of all the faculties that we've been granted is capable of understanding both itself – what it is, what it is capable of, and what value it contributes – and all the other faculties too . . . What else can judge music, grammar, and the other arts and faculties, and assess the use that we make of them, and indicate the proper occasions for their use? None other than this. (p. 4)

One of the primary ideas Epictetus uses repeatedly is the idea that though there are many things we as humans cannot control, the important thing is to be able to distinguish between what we can and cannot control by making proper use of what he terms "impressions." He says people have been given

> . . . this faculty of motivation to act and not to act, of desire and aversion, and, in a word, the power to make proper use of impressions; if you pay good heed to this, and entrust all that you have to its keeping, you'll never be hindered, never obstructed, and you'll never groan, never find fault, and never flatter anyone at all. (p. 5)

> So what was it that Agrippinus used to say? 'I won't become an obstacle to myself.' The news was brought to him that 'your case is being tried in the Senate.' – 'May everything go well! But the fifth hour has arrived' – this was the hour in which he was in the habit of taking his exercise and then having a cold bath – 'so let's go off and take some exercise.' When he had completed his exercise someone came and told him, 'You've been convicted' – 'To exile,' he asked, 'or to death?' – 'What about my property?' – 'It hasn't been confiscated.' – 'Then let's go away to Aricia and eat our meal there.' This is what it means to train oneself in the matters in which one ought to train oneself, to have rendered one's desires incapable of being frustrated, and one's aversions incapable of falling into what they want to avoid. (p. 6)

On accepting the inevitability of death, Epictetus says:

> I'm bound to die. If at once, I'll go to my death; if somewhat later I'll eat my meal since the hour has arrived for me to do so, and then die afterwards. And how? As suits someone who's getting back that which is not his own. (p. 6)

On living up to one's responsibilities, not overreaching one's capacities, and, again, not fearing death, he says:

> When Vespasian sent word to [Helvidius Priscus] to tell him not to attend a meeting of the Senate, he replied, 'it lies in your power not to allow me to be a Senator, but as long as I remain one, I have to attend meetings.' – 'Well, if you attend, hold your tongue.' – 'If you don't ask for my opinion, I'll hold my tongue.' – 'But I'm bound to ask you.' – 'And I for my part must reply as I think fit.' – 'But if you do, I'll have you executed. – 'Well, where have I ever claimed to you that I'm immortal? You fulfill your role, and I'll fulfill mine. It is yours to have me killed, and mine to die without a tremor; it is yours to send me into exile, and mine to depart without a qualm.' (p. 8)

MARCUS AURELIUS

Marcus Aurelius (121-180) intensely studied the thinking of Epictetus and attempted to bring Stoic philosophy to his everyday life experience as Emperor (from 161-180 CE) in a deteriorating Rome. His writings, found in *Meditations*, should be read as notes to himself, as they were written. Since his writings seem to primarily derive from the thoughts of Epictetus' thinking, only a few quotes from Aurelius are included here. Aurelius (c. 170-180; 1940) begins with dedications to those who have most strongly and positively influenced him.

> From Maximus I learned self-government, and not to be led aside by anything; and cheerfulness in all circumstances, as well as in illness; and a just admixture in the moral character of sweetness and dignity, and to do what was set before me without complaining. I observed that everybody believed that he thought as he spoke, and in all that he did he never had any bad intentions; and he… was never in a hurry, and never put off doing a thing, nor was perplexed nor dejected, nor did he ever laugh to disguise his vexation …He was accustomed to do acts of beneficence, and was ready to forgive, and was free from all falsehoods; and he presented the appearance of a man who could not be diverted from right rather than of the man who had been improved … He had also the art of being humorous in an agreeable way. (p. 493)

> Begin the morning by saying to thyself, I shall meet with the busy body, the ungrateful, arrogant, deceitful, envious, unsocial. All these things happen to them by reason of their ignorance of what is good and evil. (p. 497)

> … those who do not observe the movements of their own minds must of necessity be unhappy. (p. 498)

> If thou workest at that which is before thee, following right reason seriously, vigorously, calmly, without allowing anyone else to distract thee… if they'll holdest to this, expecting nothing, fearing nothing, but satisfied

with thy present activity according to nature and with heroic truth in every word and sound which thou utterest, thou wilt live happy. (p. 506)

In the morning when thou risest unwillingly, let this thought be present – I am rising to the work of a human being. Why then am I dissatisfied if I am going to do the things for which I exist and for which I was brought into the world? Or have I been made for this, to lie in the bed-clothes and keep myself warm? – But this is more pleasant. – Dost thou exist then to take thy pleasure, not at all for action or exertion? Dost thou not see the little plants, the little birds, the ants, the spiders, the bees working together to put in order their several parts of the universe? And art thou unwilling to do the work of the human being, and dost thou not make haste to do that which is according to thy nature? – But it is necessary to take rest also. – It is necessary: however nature has fixed bounds to this too: she has fixed bounds both to eating and drinking, and yet thou goest beyond these bounds, beyond what is sufficient... So thou lovest not thyself, for if thou didst, thou wouldst love thy nature and her will ...(p. 517)

WHERE DO YOU GO FROM HERE?

If the ideas in this appendix have piqued your interest, I suggest you go further with classic readings. As you see, these ideas are only a beginning place. Below are some beginning recommendations for further reading aimed at developing your intellect by expanding your constellation of ideas.

NONFICTION:

The Apology of Socrates, Euthyphro, Crito, and Phaedo... Plato

Conversations of Socrates... Xenophon

The Cynic Philosophers: From Diogenes to Julian

Epicurus – Principal Doctrines, Fragments, The Life of Epicurus

Letters from a Stoic... Seneca

Discourses of Epictetus... Epictetus

Meditations... Marcus Aurelius

Autobiography... Benjamin Franklin

Narrative of the Life of Frederick Douglass: An American Slave... Frederick Douglass

Autobiography... John Stuart Mill

The Spirit of the Age... John Stuart Mill

On Liberty... John Stuart Mill

The Subjection of Women... John Stuart Mill

On the Duty of Civil Disobedience... Henry David Thoreau

Walden... Henry David Thoreau

Slavery in Massachusetts... Henry David Thoreau

On Walking... Henry David Thoreau

The Story of My Life... Helen Keller

Among the Nudists... Merrill and Merrill

The Tyranny of Words... Stuart Chase

Thinking with Concepts... John Wilson

The Scope and Nature of University Education... John Henry Newman

Unpopular Essays... Bertrand Russell

Why I am Not a Christian... Bertrand Russell

A History of Western Philosophy... Bertrand Russell

The Art of Being... Erich Fromm

To Have or to Be?... Erich Fromm

The Art of Loving... Erich Fromm

Man's Search for Meaning... Viktor E. Frankl

The Autobiography of Malcolm X... Malcolm X

The Souls of Black Folk... W.E.B. Du Bois

50 Years of Freedom of Thought... George E. Macdonald

Long Walk to Freedom... Nelson Mandela

Man the Manipulator... Everett L. Shostrom

The Soul of Man Under Socialism... Oscar Wilde

The True Believer... Eric Hoffer

The Presentation of Self in Everyday Life... Erving Goffman

Medical Nemesis... Ivan Illich

The Collected Poems of Langston Hughes... Langston Hughes

The Ralph Nader Reader... Ralph Nader

The Reign of Error: Psychiatry, Authority and the Law... Lee Coleman

Obedience to Authority... Stanley Milgram

A Theory of Global Capitalism... William Robinson

Animal Liberation Now... Peter Singer

Famine, Affluence, and Morality... Peter Singer

Requiem for the American Dream... Noam Chomsky

Secrets: A Memoir of Vietnam and the Pentagon Papers... Daniel Ellsberg

The Doomsday Machine: Confessions of a Nuclear War Planner… Daniel Ellsberg

Freethinkers: A History of American Secularism… Susan Jacoby

The Myth of Monogamy: Fidelity and Infidelity in Animals and People… Barish and Lipton

In the Shadow of Man… Jane Goodall

Seeds of Hope: Wisdom and Wonder from the World of Plants… Jane Goodall

The Practicing Stoic… Ward Farnsworth

NOVELS:

Frankenstein… Mary Shelley

The Death of Ivan Ilyich… Leo Tolstoy

War and Peace… Leo Tolstoy

The Novels of Anton Chekhov

Jane Austen's finished novels

Charles Dickens' novels

The Bronte sisters' novels

Silas Marner… George Eliott

Les Miserables… Victor Hugo

Barchester Towers… Anthony Trollope

Tom Brown at Oxford… Thomas Hughes

Doctor Pascal… Émile Zola

Wives and Daughters… Elizabeth Gaskell

North and South… Elizabeth Gaskell

Tess of the d'Urbervilles… Thomas Hardy

The Scarlet Letter… Nathaniel Hawthorne

Uncle Tom's Cabin… Harriet Beecher Stowe

The Good Earth… Pearl S. Buck

A Room with a View… E.M. Forster

Howard's End… E.M. Forster

Maurice… E.M. Forster

Rebecca… Daphne du Maurier

Lady Chatterley's Lover… D.H. Lawrence

The Grapes of Wrath… John Steinbeck

Of Mice and Men… John Steinbeck

The Rise of Silas Lapham… William Dean Howells
1984… George Orwell
Animal Farm… George Orwell
Brave New World… Aldous Huxley
Go Tell It on the Mountain… James Baldwin
Invisible Man… Ralph Ellison
The Color Purple… Alice Walker
Of Human Bondage… Somerset Maugham
The Picture of Dorian Grey… Oscar Wilde
Lolita… Vladimir Nabokov
To Kill a Mockingbird… Harper Lee
Mrs. Dalloway… Virginia Wolfe

PLAYS:

Shakespeare's Plays
Tartuffe… Molière
Cyrano de Bergerac… Edmond Rostand
The Importance of Being Earnest… Oscar Wilde
The Three Sisters… Anton Chekhov
The Cherry Orchard… Anton Chekhov
Uncle Vanya… Anton Chekhov
The Glass Menagerie… Tennessee Williams
A Streetcar Named Desire… Tennessee Williams
Raisin in the Sun… Lorraine Hansberry
Death of a Salesman… Arthur Miller
Pygmalion… George Bernard Shaw
A Doll's House… Henrik Ibsen
Frost/Nixon… Peter Morgan

BOOKS ON CRITICAL THINKING, READING, AND WRITING, FOR FURTHER INTELLECTUAL AND ETHICAL DEVELOPMENT:

How to Read a Book… Mortimer Adler

The Art of How to Read a Paragraph: The Art of Close Reading… Richard Paul & Linda Elder

The Art of How to Write a Paragraph: The Art of Substantive Writing… Richard Paul & Linda Elder

The Thinker's Guide to Ethical Reasoning… Richard Paul & Linda Elder

The Thinker's Guide to Socratic Questioning… Linda Elder & Richard Paul

The Art of Asking Essential Questions… Richard Paul & Linda Elder

Fact Over Fake: A Critical Thinker's Guide to Media Bias and Political Propaganda… Richard Paul & Linda Elder

The Thinker's Guide to Ethical Reasoning… Richard Paul & Linda Elder

Critical Thinking: Tools for Taking Charge of Your Professional and Personal Life… Richard Paul & Linda Elder

Liberating The Mind: Overcoming Sociocentric and Egocentric Thinking… Linda Elder

NOTE TO THE THERAPIST

A primary reason for this book is to provide the therapist with a holistic approach to therapy using the broad range of critical thinking tools. This will most likely appeal to therapists already using a cognitive behavioral therapy approach, since the main emphasis is on uncovering faulty thinking that leads to problematic expectations or behavior. But remember that there are better and worse approaches to cognitive behavioral therapy, as discussed in Chapter Ten. And critical thinking is required to critique all other forms of therapy, including cognitive behavioral therapies. Therefore, critical thinking therapy should not be subsumed under the label cognitive behavioral therapy.

An ultimate goal in critical thinking is the development of ethical character as we reach toward self-actualization. It is not a vague approach that simply looks for thinking underlying behavior. Rather, it is a way of living in which we reach for the highest levels of thought and action across all parts of our lives, and in which we believe in the power of our own minds.

Therapists need available to them all the concepts and principles in critical thinking if they are to effectively assist clients in finding a reasonable path to contentment and happiness in a complex world. To this point in time, explicit critical thinking, with emphasis on both the barriers to criticality and a holistic framework for improving thinking, has been chiefly missing from the therapeutic setting. My hope is that you, the therapist, will find in this book tools for therapy which will help you better reach your clients and that you will become a Critical Thinking Therapist. The deeper you understand critical thinking concepts and principles, the more tools you have for reaching the uniquenesses of each client. Since critical thinking therapy is new to the field of counseling, I invite you to contact me with your feedback on how you are using the ideas in this book and how these ideas are working out in therapy with your clients (contact me at: lindaelder@criticalthinking.org).

Skilled therapists use a complex set of understandings to address the range of issues facing their clients. This includes the fundamentals of critical thinking as well as knowledge of best practices in therapy, which itself requires critical thinking. You are well aware that every client is unique and therefore brings an array of her or his own issues and problems to the therapeutic setting. My recommendation is that you provide this book to the client, and that you guide the client through the parts of the book most useful to that particular client. Some will be interested in the entire book, and therefore you can work through the book with them, over time. Some may only benefit from the activities, and for these clients you can simply assign one or two activities to write out per week in a journal, as homework.

The therapeutic setting is best conceptualized as a place of learning and retraining the mind to take command of itself. Therefore, the emphasis is on helping clients internalize the understandings implicit in critical thinking and use these understandings in explicit ways throughout each day as they interact with family members, colleagues, and everyone else, and as they plan their futures. The best way for you, the therapist, to learn the theory of critical thinking offered through our framework is to work through it with your clients, learning as you go. Do not place pressure on yourself to learn all the theory in this book before using it in therapy with clients. Critical thinking is learned over years, through deep commitment and routine application to one's own thinking and to the reasoning of others. The more you apply these ideas to your own reasoning and throughout your life, the better you should be able to help clients grasp and use them.

In addition to all the ideas already developed and discussed in this book, including the section in Chapter Ten on Critical Thinking Therapy, you might benefit from the following list of critical thinking questions. Use these questions in therapy as you deem appropriate with a given client.[19]

QUESTIONS OF CLARIFICATION

- What do you mean by _____?
- What is your main point?
- How does _____ relate to _____?
- Could you put that another way?
- What do you think is the main issue here?
- Is your basic point _____ or _____?
- Could you give me an example?
- Would this be an example: _____?
- Could you explain that further?
- Would you say more about that?

---

19 These questions were adapted from those found on pp. 22-25 of *The Thinker's Guide to Socratic Questioning* by Richard Paul and Linda Elder, NY: Rowman and Littlefield, 2019.

- Why do you say that?
- Let me see if I understand you; do you mean _____ or _____?
- How does this relate to our discussion/problem/issue?
- What do you think John meant by his remark? What did you take John to mean?
- Jane, would you summarize in your own words what Richard has said? Richard, is that what you meant?

QUESTIONS THAT PROBE PURPOSE

- What is the purpose of _____?
- What was your purpose when you said _____?
- What was your purpose when you acted as you did?
- How do the purposes of these two family members vary?
- Was your purpose justifiable in the situation?
- What is the purpose of addressing this question at this time?

QUESTIONS THAT PROBE ASSUMPTIONS

- What are you assuming?
- What is this person assuming?
- What could we assume instead?
- You seem to be assuming _____. Do I understand you correctly?
- All of your reasoning depends on the idea that _____. Why have you based your reasoning on _____ rather than _____?
- You seem to be assuming _____. How would you justify taking this for granted?
- Why do you think your assumption holds here?

QUESTIONS THAT PROBE INFORMATION, REASONS, EVIDENCE, AND CAUSES

- What would be an example of your point?
- How do you know?
- What are your reasons for saying that?
- Why did you say that?
- What other information do we need to know before we can address this question?
- Why do you think that is true?

- Could you explain your reasons to us?
- What led you to that belief?
- Is this good evidence for believing that?
- Do you have any evidence to support your assertion?
- Are those reasons adequate?
- How does that information apply to this case?
- Is there reason to doubt that evidence?
- What difference does that make?
- Who is in a position to know if that is the case?
- What would convince you otherwise?
- What would you say to someone who said _____?
- What accounts for _____?
- What do you think is the cause?
- How did this come about?
- By what reasoning did you come to that conclusion?
- How could we go about finding out whether that is true?

QUESTIONS ABOUT VIEWPOINTS OR PERSPECTIVES

- You seem to be approaching this issue from _____ perspective. Why have you chosen this rather than that perspective?
- How would other types of people respond? Why? What would influence them?
- How could you answer the objection that _____ would make?
- Can/did anyone see this another way?
- What would someone who disagrees say?
- What is an alternative?
- How are your and your spouse's ideas alike? Different?

QUESTIONS THAT PROBE IMPLICATIONS AND CONSEQUENCES

- What are you implying by that?
- When you say _____, are you implying _____?
- But if that happened, what else would also happen as a result? Why?
- What effect would that have?
- Would that necessarily happen or only probably happen?

- What is an alternative?
- If this and this are the case, then what else must be true?
- Have you followed out the important implications of continuing to behave in these ways?

QUESTIONS ABOUT THE QUESTION

- How can you find out?
- Is this the same issue as _____?
- How can you settle this question?
- Can you break this question down at all?
- Is the question clear? Do you understand it?
- How would _____ put the issue?
- Is this question easy or difficult to answer? Why?
- What does this question assume?
- Would _____ put the question differently?
- Why is this question important?
- Do you need more facts to answer this question?
- Do you both agree that this is the question?
- To answer this question, what other questions would you have to answer first?
- I'm not sure I understand how you are interpreting the main question.

QUESTIONS THAT PROBE CONCEPTS

- What is the main idea you are dealing with?
- Why/how is this idea important to the quality of your life?
- Do these two ideas conflict? If so, how?
- What was the main idea guiding the thinking of your supervisor, that upset you?
- Is this idea that you have about (marriage) causing problems?
- What main theories do you need to consider in figuring out _____?
- Are you using this term "_____" in keeping with educated usage?
- What main distinctions should you draw in reasoning through this problem?
- What idea is your child using in her or his thinking? Is there a problem with it?

QUESTIONS THAT PROBE INFERENCES AND INTERPRETATIONS

- What conclusions are you coming to about _____?
- On what information are you basing this conclusion?
- Is there a more logical inference you might make in this situation?
- How are you interpreting her behavior? Is there another possible interpretation?
- What do you think of _____?
- How did you reach that conclusion?
- Given all the facts, what is the best possible conclusion?
- How shall you interpret these data?

RECOMMENDED READINGS

RATIONAL EMOTIVE BEHAVIOR THERAPY

Ellis, A. (1961; 1997) *A guide to rational living.* Chatsworth, CA: Melvin Powers Wilshire Book Company.

Ellis, A. (2001). *Overcoming destructive beliefs, feelings, and behaviors.* Amherst, N.Y.: Prometheus Books.

Ellis, A. (2002). *Overcoming resistance.* New York, NY.: Springer Publishing.

Ellis, A. (2003). *How to keep people from pushing your buttons.* New York, NY: Citadel.

Ellis, A. (2004a). *Rational emotive behavior therapy—It works for me, it can work for you.* Amherst, N.Y.: Prometheus Books.

Ellis, A. (2004b). *The road to tolerance.* Amherst, N.Y.: Prometheus Books.

Ellis, A. (2016). *How to control your anxiety before it controls you.* New York, NY: Kensington Publishing Group.

Ellis, A. (2016). *How to stubbornly refuse to make yourself miserable about anything—yes, anything!* New York, NY: Citadel.

Ellis, A. (1994). *Reason and emotion in psychotherapy: A comprehensive method of treating human disturbances.* New York, NY: Carol Publishing Group.

Ellis, A. & Ellis, D.J. (Collaborator). (2010). *All out! An autobiography.* New York, NY: Prometheus Books.

Ellis, A. & Ellis, D.J. (2019). *Rational Emotive Behavior Therapy: Second edition.* Washington DC: American Psychological Association.

ON THE RELATIONSHIP BETWEEN RATIONAL EMOTIVE BEHAVIOR THERAPY AND COGNITIVE BEHAVIORAL THERAPY

Ellis, A. (12003). Similarities and differences between rational emotive behavior therapy and cognitive therapy. *Journal of Cognitive Psychotherapy: An International Quarterly*, 17(3), 225-240. DOI:10.1891/jcop.17.3.225.52535

Ellis, A. (2005). Discussion of Christine A. Padesky and Aaron T. Beck, "Science and Philosophy: Comparison of Cognitive Therapy and Rational Emotive Behavior Therapy". *Journal of Cognitive Psychotherapy*, 19(2), 181–185. DOI:10.1891/jcop.19.2.181.66789

Ellis, D.J. (2017). Rational emotive behavior therapy and individual psychology. *Journal of Individual Psychology*, 73(4), 272-282. DOI: 10.1353/jip.2017.0023

Padesky, C. & Beck, A.T. (2003). Science and philosophy: Comparison of cognitive therapy and rational emotive behavior therapy. *Journal of Cognitive Psychotherapy: An International Quarterly*, 17(3), 211224. DOI:10.1891/jcop.19.2.181.66789

PSYCHOSIS, SCHIZOPHRENIA, AND THE CONCEPT OF MADNESS

Brown, K.W. (2021). *Easy crafts for the insane.* New York, NY: Putnam.

Jamison, K.R. (1996). *An unquiet mind.* New York, NY: Vintage Books.

Laing, R.D. (1969). *The divided self.* New York, NY: Pantheon Books.

Laing, R.D. & Esterson, A. (2017). *Sanity, madness, and the family.* New York, NY: Routledge.

May, R. (1953). *Man's search for himself.* New York, NY: W. W. Norton & Company.

Szasz, T. S. (2010). *The myth of mental illness: Foundations of a theory of personal conduct.* New York, NY: Harper Perennial.

Wang, E. W. (2019). *The collected schizophrenias: Essays.* United Kingdom: Penguin Books.

Whitaker, R. (2002). *Mad in America: Bad science, bad medicine, and the enduring mistreatment of the mentally ill.* Cambridge, MA: Perseus Publishing.

Williams, P. (2012). *Rethinking madness: Towards a paradigm shift in our understanding and treatment of psychosis.* San Rafael, CA: Sky's Edge Publishing.

THE PROBLEM OF USING THE MEDICAL MODEL FOR MENTAL HEALTH

Gotzsche, P.C., Young, A.H., & Crace, J. (2015). Does long term use of psychiatric drugs cause more harm than good? *The BMJ, 350.* https://doi.org/10.1136/bmj.h2435

Moncrieff, J., Cohen, D., & Porter, S. (2013). The psychoactive effects of psychiatric medication: The elephant in the room. *Journal of Psychoactive Drugs, 45*(5), 409-415. https://doi.org/10.1080%2F02791072.2013.845328

Moncrieff, J. (2008). *The myth of the chemical cure: A critique of psychiatric drug treatment.* New York, NY: Palgrave Macmillan.

Ruby, C. (2020). *Smoke and mirrors: How you are being fooled about mental illness.* Welcome, MD: Clear Publishing.

Whitaker, R. (2015). *Anatomy of an epidemic: Magic bullets, psychiatric drugs, and the astounding rise of mental illness in America.* New York, NY: Broadway Books.

Whitaker, R. and Cosgrove, L. (2015). *Psychiatry under the influence: Institutional corruption, social injury, and prescriptions for reform.* New York, NY: Palgrave Macmillan.

DEPRESSION

Yapko, M. D. (2009). *Depression is contagious: How the most common mood disorder is spreading around the world and how to stop it.* New York, NY: Free Press.

Yapko, M. D. (2016). *Keys to unlocking depression: An internationally known depression expert tells you what you need to know to overcome depression.* Fallbrook, CA: Yapko Publications.

ON DEPRESSION AND THE SUN: UNRAVELING THE SUN'S ROLE IN DEPRESSION

WebMD. (2023, September 14). *Understanding depression – the basics.* https://www.webmd.com.depression/understanding-depression-basics

Kent, S.T., McClure, L.A., Crosson, W.L., Arnett, D.K., Wadley, V.G., & Sathiakumar, N. (2009). Effect of sunlight exposure on cognitive function among depressed and non-depressed participants: a REGARDS cross-sectional study. *Environmental Health, 8.* https://doi.org/10.1186/1476-069X-8-34

Tri-City Medical Center. *5 ways the sun impacts your mental and physical health.* https://www.tricitymed.org/2018/08/5-ways-the-sun-impacts-your-mental--and-physical-health/

Hidaka, B.H. (2012) Depression as a disease of modernity: Explanations for increasing prevalence. *Journal of Affective Disorders,* 140(3), 205-214. https://doi.org/10.1016/j.jad.2011.12.036

CLASSICS ON MENTAL HEALTH

Berne, E. (1975). *What do you say after you say hello?: The psychology of human destiny.* New York, NY: Bantam Books.

Frankl, V. (1959; 2006). *Man's search for meaning.* Boston, MA: Beacon Press.

Fromm, E. (1989; 1992). *The art of being.* New York, NY: The Continuum Publishing Company.

Fromm, E. (1956; 2019). *The art of loving.* New York, NY: HarperCollins Publishers.

Fromm, E. (1969). *Escape from freedom.* New York, NY: Avon Books.

Fromm, E. (1955). *The sane society.* New York, NY: Holt Paperbacks.

Horney, K. (1972). *Our inner conflicts: A constructive theory of neurosis.* New York, NY: W. W. Norton & Company.

Maslow, A. (1962; 1968). *Toward a psychology of being.* New York, NY: Van Nostrand Reinhold Co.

Rogers, R. R. & Stevens, B. (1967). *Person to person: A new trend in psychology.* New York, NY: Real People Press.

Rosen, R. D. (1977). *Psychobabble: Fast talk and quick cure in the era of feeling.* New York, NY: Atheneum.

Tavris, C. (2011). *Psychobabble and biobunk: Using psychological science to think critically about popular psychology.* Upper Saddle River, NJ: Prentice Hall.

CRITICAL THINKING, ETHICAL REASONING AND SOCIAL CONVENTIONS

Elder, L. (2019). *Liberating the mind: Overcoming sociocentric thought and egocentric tendencies.* Lanham, Maryland: Rowman & Littlefield.

Paul, R. & Elder, L. (2013). *The thinker's guide to ethical reasoning.* Dillon Beach, CA: Foundation for Critical Thinking.

Sumner, W. (1906; 2012). *Folkways: A study of the sociological importance of usages, manners, customs, mores, and morals.* New York, NY: Library of Alexandria.

ON INTELLECTUAL DEVELOPMENT

See recommended readings at the end of Appendix B.

MINDFULNESS

Creswell, J.D. (2017). Mindfulness interventions. *Annual Review of Psychology, 68,* 491-516. https://doi.org/10.1146/annurev-psych-042716-051139

REFERENCES

About mental health. (2023). Retrieved from https://www.cdc.gov/mentalhealth/learn/index.htm

Beck Institute for Cognitive Behavior Therapy (2020, October 6). *What's new in the third edition of cognitive behavior therapy: basics and beyond? [Video.] YouTube.* https://www.youtube.com/watch?v=PrVRGFpC7mc

Campbell, R. (2004). Introduction. In L.A. Seneca - *Letters from a Stoic.* New York, NY: Penguin Books.

Ellis, A. (1980). *Rational-emotive therapy and cognitive behavior therapy: similarities and differences. Cognitive Therapy and Research, 4,* pp. 325-340.

Epictetus. (2014). *Discourses, fragments, handbook.* (R. Hard, Trans.). Oxford, UK: Oxford University Press. (Original work published c. 108.)

Frankl, V.E. (2006). *Man's search for meaning.* (I. Lasch, Trans.) Boston, MA: Beacon Press. (Original work published 1946.)

Fromm, E. (1988) *To have or to be.* New York, NY: The Continuum Publishing Company.

Gillihan, S.J. (2016) *Retrain your brain: cognitive behavior therapy in 7 seven weeks.* Berkeley, CA: Althea Press.

Masson, J.M. (1990). *Final analysis: The making and unmaking of a psychoanalyst.* New York, NY: Pocket Books.

Oates, W.J. (Ed.). (1940). *The Stoic and Epicurean philosophers: The complete extant writings of Epicurus, Epictetus, Lucretius and Marcus Aurelius.* New York, NY: Random House.

Oxford University Press. (n.d.). Friend. In *Oxford English dictionary.* Retrieved June 21, 2023 from https://www.oed.com/dictionary/friend_n

Peters. R. S. (1973). *Reason and Compassion.* London: Routledge & Kegan Paul.

Plato. (2003). *The last days of Socrates: Euthyphro; apology; crito; phaedo.* (H. Tarrant, Ed.). (H. Tarrant & H. Tredennick, Trans.). New York, NY: Penguin Books. (Original work published c. 409 BCE.)

Ruby, C. (2020). *Smoke and mirrors: How you are being fooled about mental illness.* Welcome, MD: Clear Publishing.

Seneca (2004). *Letters from a Stoic.* New York, NY: Penguin Books. (Original work published c. 62.)

Szasz, T. (2010). *The myth of mental illness.* New York, NY: Harper Perineal.

Sumner, W. (1906;1940). *Folkways: A Study of the Sociological Importance of Usages, Manners, Customs, Mores, and Morals.* New York: Ginn and Co.

Whitaker, R. and Cosgrove, L. (2015). *Psychiatry under the influence: Institutional corruption, social injury, and prescriptions for reform.* New York, NY: Palgrave McMillan.

Williams, P. (2012). *Rethinking madness: Towards a paradigm shift in our understanding and treatment of psychosis.* San Rafael, CA: Sky's Edge Publishing.

GLOSSARY[20]

ANALYZE:

To decompose into constituent parts; to examine in detail so as to determine the nature of, to look more deeply into an issue or situation; to find the essence or structure of; to take apart and examine the structures of something.

Analyzing thought is a fundamental goal of critical thinking. It represents one of the three sets of essential understandings in critical thinking (the other two being the assessment of thought and the pursuit of intellectual virtues). Since reasoning is a fundamental "activity" of the human animal, becoming skilled at taking reasoning apart and examining its parts for quality is essential to consistently reasoning at a high level of skill. You should routinely analyze your ideas, claims, experiences, interpretations, judgments, and theories. Do the same with those you hear and read.

COGNITIVE PROCESSES:

Generally understood as operations of the intellect that are innate or naturally occurring in the human mind.

It is important to understand cognitive processes in human thought – processes such as classifying, inferring, assuming, planning, analyzing, comparing, contrasting, synthesizing. However, we should not assume that engaging in these processes automatically ensures skilled and disciplined reasoning. For example, whenever we plan, we do not necessarily plan well. Sometimes we plan poorly. The mere fact of planning does not automatically carry with it high quality cognition. To ensure excellent thought, we need to consistently meet intellectual standards when engaging in (natural) cognitive processes.

---

20 Most of the concepts in this glossary are included in A *Glossary of Critical Thinking Terms & Concepts* by RIchard Paul and Linda Elder, and were included in Richard Paul's earlier works. Terms related to mental health have been added here.

CONTRADICT/CONTRADICTION:

To assert the opposite of; to be contrary to, go against; a statement in opposition to another; a condition in which things tend to be contrary to each other; inconsistency; discrepancy; a person or thing containing or composed of contradictory elements.

Contradictions are common in human life, since humans often act in ways that are not in keeping with what they profess to believe. This is a natural byproduct of human egocentric and sociocentric thought, and stands in the way of intellectual integrity.

CRITICAL SOCIETY:

A society which systematically cultivates critical thinking and hence systematically rewards reflective questioning, intellectual independence, and reasoned dissent.

To begin to conceptualize a critical society, one must imagine a society in which independent critical thought is embodied in the concrete day-to-day lives of individuals. William Graham Sumner, a distinguished anthropologist, explicitly formulated the ideal:

> The critical habit of thought, if usual in a society, will pervade all its mores, because it is a way of taking up the problems of life. Men educated in it cannot be stampeded by stump orators and are never deceived by dithyrambic oratory. They are slow to believe. They can hold things as possible or probable in all degrees, without certainty and without pain. They can wait for evidence and weigh evidence, uninfluenced by the emphasis or confidence with which assertions are made on one side or the other. They can resist appeals to their dearest prejudices and all kinds of cajolery. Education in the critical faculty is the only education of which it can be truly said that it makes good citizens. (Folkways, 1906)

Until critical habits of thought pervade our society (if this ever occurs in the future), there will be a tendency for schools as social institutions to transmit the prevailing world view more or less uncritically, to transmit it as reality, not as a picture of reality. Education for critical thinking, requires that schools and classrooms become microcosms of a critical society. There are at present no existing critical societies on a broad scale. Critical societies will develop only to the extent that:

- critical thinking is viewed as essential to living a reasonable and fairminded life.
- critical thinking is routinely taught; consistently fostered.
- the problematics of thinking are an abiding concern.
- closed-mindedness is systemically discouraged; open-mindedness systematically encouraged.

- intellectual integrity, intellectual humility, intellectual empathy, confidence in reason, and intellectual courage are everyday social values.
- egocentric and sociocentric thinking are recognized as a bane in social life.
- children are routinely taught that the rights and needs of others are equal to their own.
- a multi-cultural world view is fostered.
- people are encouraged to think for themselves and discouraged from uncritically accepting the thinking or behavior of others.
- people routinely study and diminish irrational thought.
- people internalize universal intellectual standards.

CRITICAL THINKER:

Critical thinkers are persons who consistently attempt to live rationally, fairmindedly and self-reflectively.

Critical thinkers are keenly aware of the potentially flawed nature of human thinking (when left unchecked). They strive to diminish the power of their egocentric and sociocentric tendencies. They use the intellectual tools that critical thinking offers to analyze, assess, and improve thinking. They work diligently to develop intellectual virtues: intellectual integrity, intellectual humility, intellectual civility, intellectual empathy, intellectual sense of justice and confidence in reason. They realize that no matter how skilled they are as thinkers, they can always improve their reasoning abilities. They recognize that they will at times fall prey to mistakes in reasoning, human irrationality, prejudices, biases, distortions, uncritically accepted social rules and taboos, selfish and vested interests. They strive to contribute to a more rational, civilized society in whatever ways they can. They strive to consider the rights and needs of relevant others. The extent to which anyone can be properly described as a "critical thinker" depends upon the skills, abilities, and traits of critical thinking the person exhibits on a daily basis. There is no "critical thinker" in the sense of "perfect" or "ideal" thinker, nor will there ever be.

CULTURAL ASSOCIATIONS:

Cultural associations are ideas linked in the mind, often inappropriately, due to societal influences.

Many, if not most, of our important ideas are connected with, or guided by, cultural associations. Media advertising juxtaposes and joins logically unrelated things to influence our buying habits (e.g. if you drink this particular brand of beverage, you will be "sexy"; if you drive this type of car, you will be "attractive" and "powerful"). Raised in a particular country or within a particular group within it, we form any number of mental links which, if they remain unexamined, unduly influence our thinking and behavior.

Of course, not all cultural associations are problematic. Only through disciplined examination can we distinguish between those that are and those that are not.

CULTURAL ASSUMPTION:

Unassessed (often implicit) belief adopted by virtue of upbringing in a society and taken for granted.

Raised in a culture, we unconsciously adopt its point of view, values, beliefs, and practices. At the root of each of these are many assumptions. Not knowing that we perceive, conceive, think, and experience within assumptions we have formulated uncritically, we take ourselves to be perceiving "things as they are," not "things as they appear from a cultural perspective." Becoming aware of our cultural assumptions so that we might critically examine them is a crucial dimension of critical thinking. It is, however, a dimension largely missing from the educational process. Indeed, schools, and even colleges and universities, often implicitly and unknowingly foster blind acceptance to group ideologies.

DEFENSE MECHANISMS:

Self-deceptive process used by the human mind to avoid dealing with socially unacceptable or painful ideas, beliefs or situations.

The human mind routinely engages in unconscious processes that are egocentrically motivated, and that strongly influence our behavior. When functioning egocentrically, we seek to get what we want. We see the world from a narrow self-serving perspective. Yet, we also see ourselves as driven by purely rational motives. We therefore disguise our egocentric motives. This disguise necessitates self-deception. Self-deception is achieved by means of defense mechanisms. Defense mechanisms, generally speaking, represent one constellation of irrational processes that utilize egocentric and/or sociocentric thinking while defending itself against realities or information it does not want to accept. All egocentric and sociocentric thoughts require self-deception. Therefore, on the whole, defense mechanisms will entail self-deception. Exceptions to this include sublimation, since it can often be dealt with rationally. Through the use of defense mechanisms the mind can avoid conscious recognition of negative feelings such as guilt, pain, anxiety, etc. The term 'defense mechanisms' is used in Freudian psychoanalytic theory generally to mean psychological strategies used by the unconscious mind to cope with reality and to maintain a positive self-image. The theory of defense mechanisms is complex, with some theoreticians suggesting that the range of defense mechanisms may at times be healthy (particularly in childhood). However, when these mechanisms are allowed to freely operate in the mind of the normal adult, they pose significant barriers to rationality and the creation of critical societies. All humans engage in self-deception; however, critical thinkers consistently strive to act in good faith, to minimize their self-deceptive tendencies, to understand these tendencies and work toward diminishing their frequency and power.

Some of the most common defense mechanisms (and those included in this glossary) are: denial, identification, projection, repression, rationalization, stereotyping, scapegoating, sublimation, and wishful thinking.

DENIAL:

When a person refuses to believe indisputable evidence or facts in order to maintain a favorable self-image or favored set of beliefs.

Denial is one of the most commonly used defense mechanisms. All humans sometimes deny what they cannot face, for example, some unpleasant truth about themselves or others. A basketball player, for example, may deny that there are any real flaws in his game in order to maintain an image of himself as highly skilled at basketball. A "patriot" may deny—in the face of clear-cut evidence— that his country ever violates human rights or acts unjustly.

DIAGNOSTIC AND STATISTICAL MANUAL OF MENTAL DISORDERS (DSM):

A classification system of mental disorders as defined and conceptualized by the American Psychiatric Association (APA).

The DSM, now in its 5th edition and therefore referred to as the DSM-5, is considered the authoritative guide for diagnosing mental disorders in the U.S. (the DSM-1 was published in 1952). However, though this publication is widely used and almost universally accepted in the U.S., it is considered problematic by some clinicians. Gerald Young (May 16, 2016), in his book *DSM-5: Basics and Critics*, points out that "The critique of the DSM-5 has focused on deficits in its utility, reliability, and validity. In addition, often it sets a bar too low, and exposes both vulnerable people and normal ones to the risks of overdiagnosis and of pathologizing normal conditions." Young suggests instead adopting a biopsychosocial approach in psychiatry and revising the DSM-5 accordingly. See his chapter on critique of DSM-5 at this link: https://doi.org/10.1007/978-3-319-24094-7_22

Social worker Arnold Cantu (2023) has recently suggested replacing the DSM with a problem-based coding system. In his article "Toward a Descriptive Problem-Based Taxonomy for Mental Health: A Nonmedicalized Way Out of the Biomedical Model" (*Journal of Humanistic Psychology*, 0[0]), Cantu writes on how U.S. regulations require inappropriate use of the biomedical model in mental wellness contexts:

Psychiatric disorders tend to be subsumed under the biomedical model of mental health and have been critiqued for contributing to iatrogenic harm and stigma in addition to fundamental concerns about their validity and reliability. However, current practice of requiring psychiatric diagnoses within health care systems occurs due to federal regulations and does not allow for the formal use of alternative taxonomies, forcing clinicians and clients into the biomedical model.

Cantu introduces "an organizing framework, borrowing from the field of social work accompanied by an example of how the field can move away from the biomedical model given the regulations at play." He proposes "the interdisciplinary development of an alternative nonmedicalized, psychosocial, and codified descriptive problem-based taxonomy that can decouple psychiatric diagnosis from the eligibility for and provision of mental health services."

The idea of labeling humans according to categories of mental illness is fraught with problems. The articles above point out some of these problems. It may be best to have no labels whatsoever for so-called mental illnesses, given the problems implicit in any such classification system. This may be an issue for the insurance reimbursement process for clinicians, but insurance should not drive the way people are labeled, which affects how they see themselves and their sense of self-efficacy. If we are to maintain a system of reimbursement to clinicians for clients with mental health concerns, the process might simply entail general statements such as "the person needs mental health assistance," rather than definitive labels.

EGOCENTRICITY:

A tendency to view everything in relationship to oneself, to confuse immediate perception (how things seem) with reality, to be self-centered, or to consider only oneself and one's own interests; selfishness; to distort "reality" in order to maintain a particular viewpoint or perception.

One's desires, values, and beliefs (seeming to be self-evidently correct or superior to those of others) are often uncritically used as the unconscious norm for much judgment and "experience." Egocentricity is one of the fundamental impediments to critical thinking. As one learns to think critically in a strong sense, one learns to become more rational, and less egocentric.

EGOCENTRIC DOMINATION:

The egocentric tendency to seek what one wants through the unreasonable use of direct power over, or intimidation of, people (or other sentient creatures).

Egocentric domination of others may be overt or covert. On the one hand, dominating egocentrism can involve harsh, dictatorial, tyrannical, or bullying behavior (e.g., a physically abusive spouse). On the other hand, it might involve subtle messages and behavior that imply the use of control or force if "necessary" (e.g., a supervisor reminding a subordinate, by quiet innuendo, that his or her employment is contingent upon unquestioning obedience). Human irrational behavior is often some combination of dominating and submissive acts. In the "ideal" Fascist society, for example, everyone (except the dictator) is submissive to everyone above him and dominating to everyone below him.

EGOCENTRIC IMMEDIACY:

The irrational tendency (noted by Piaget) wherein a person over-generalizes from a set of positive or negative events to either an "Isn't life wonderful?" or "Isn't life awful?" state of mind.

Egocentric immediacy is a common pattern of human thought which operates as a barrier to critical thinking. Instead of accurately interpreting situations, egocentric immediacy causes the mind to over-generalize, to see the world either in sweeping negative or positive terms.

EGOCENTRIC SUBMISSION:

The irrational tendency to psychologically join and serve "powerful" people to get what one wants.

Humans are naturally concerned with their interests and motivated to satisfy their desires. In a world of psychological power and influence, people generally learn to "succeed" in two ways: to psychologically conquer or intimidate (subtly or openly) those who stand in their way (through egocentric domination), or, alternatively, to psychologically join and serve more powerful others, who then: (1) give them a sense of personal importance, (2) protect them, and (3) share with them some of the benefits of their success. Irrational people use both techniques, though not to the same extent.

When people submit to more powerful others, they are engaging in what can be termed 'egocentric submission.' Those who use overt force and control are engaging in what can be termed 'egocentric domination.' Both of these forms of behavior can be seen publicly, for example, in the relationship of rock stars or sport stars to their admiring followers. Most social groups have an internal "pecking order," with some playing the role of leader and most playing the role of follower. A fairminded rational person seeks neither to dominate nor to blindly serve someone else who dominates. Opposite is egocentric domination.

ELEMENTS OF REASONING—THE PARTS OF:

Elements of reasoning: the parts of thinking embedded or pre-supposed in all reasoning—purpose, question, information, inferences, assumptions, concepts, implications, point of view; also termed 'parts of thinking,' 'elements of thought,' 'structures of thought.'

All reasoning contains a universal set of elements, each of which can be monitored for possible problems. In other words, whenever we think, we think for a purpose within a point of view based on assumptions leading to implications and consequences. We use concepts, ideas, and theories to interpret data, facts, and experiences (information) in order to answer questions, solve problems, and resolve issues. Critical thinkers develop skills of identifying and assessing these elements in their thinking and in the thinking of others. Analyzing reasoning into its elements or structures represents one of the three sets of essential understandings in critical thinking; the other two focus on the assessment of thought (intellectual standards) and the development of intellectual virtues. See analysis, purpose, question, information, inference, concepts, assumption, implication, point of view.

EMOTION:

A feeling aroused to the point of awareness; often a strong feeling or state of excitement.

Our emotions are integrally related to our thoughts and desires. These three mental structures—thoughts, feelings, and desires—are continually influencing one another in reciprocal ways. We experience negative *feelings*, for example, when we *think* things are not going well for us. Moreover, at any given moment, our thoughts, feelings, and desires are under the influence of either our rational faculties or our native irrational tendencies. When our *thinking* is irrational, or egocentric, irrational *feeling* states are actuated. When this happens, we are excited by (what is perhaps) infantile anger, fear, and jealousy, which can cause our objectivity and fairmindedness to decrease.

Thus, emotions serve to signal whether things are working "for us or against us." There is a range of emotional states regularly experienced by humans, from the "highs" to the "lows—from excitement, joy, pleasure, satisfaction, to anger, defensiveness, depression, and so on. The same, or very similar, feeling state may be experienced in connection with rational or irrational thoughts and behavior. We may feel "satisfied," for example, when successfully dominating someone (see egocentric domination), or when successfully teaching a child to read. We may feel "angry" when someone refuses to follow our irrational orders, or when we perceive some injustice in the world. Therefore, the feeling of satisfaction or anger itself may tell us little or nothing about the quality of thought leading to the feeling.

In any case, emotions or feelings are intimately connected with thoughts. For example, strong emotions can keep us from thinking rationally, may cause paralysis of thought and action. And because there is always a cognitive dimension to our emotions, having the ability to analyze the thinking that causes emotions is critical to living a rational life.

Critical thinkers, for example, strive to recognize when dysfunctional thinking is leading to inappropriate or unproductive feeling states. They use their rational passions (for example, the passion to be fair) to reason themselves into feelings appropriate to the situation as it really is, rather than egocentrically reacting to distorted views of reality. Thus, emotions and feelings are not in themselves irrational; they are irrational only when they arise from and feed egocentric thoughts. Strong-sense critical thinkers are committed to living a life in which rational emotions predominate and egocentric feelings are minimized

EMOTIONAL INTELLIGENCE:

Bringing intelligence to bear upon emotions; using skilled reasoning to take command of one's emotional life.

The basic premise behind this idea is that high quality reasoning in a given situation will lead to more satisfactory emotional states than low quality reasoning. Taking command of one's emotional life is a key purpose of critical thinking.

In recent years, the term 'emotional intelligence' has been largely connected with a growing body of "brain" research in which attempts are made to connect brain chemistry to mental functioning, to connect, in other words, neurological processes that occur in the brain to cognitive/emotional processes in the mind. One must be careful not to overstep what can reasonably be inferred from this research. For example, some researchers have suggested that the amygdale (a so-called "primitive" part of the brain) can cause an emotional response to situations before the mind has had a chance to "think." This process has been blamed for things like murder (e.g. "he emotionally reacted and killed someone before his higher order mental functions could stop him from doing it"). Yet, *every emotional response is connected with some thinking* of some kind, however primitive. If I jump in fear at a loud sound, I do so because I think something is potentially dangerous. Again the thinking may be primitive; it may be split second; *but it is thinking nevertheless.*

For the "average" person, taking command of one's emotional life does not require technical knowledge of brain chemistry and neurology. By studying the mind and its functions (thinking, feeling, wanting), we have an abundance of knowledge we can use to develop emotional intelligence. For example, if we begin with the basic premise that emotions are always connected to some thinking, we can analyze the thinking that leads to our emotions, and the ways in which our emotions keep us from thinking rationally or reasonably in given situations. We can analyze the circumstances that tend to lead to irrational thoughts, and accompanying irrational emotions.

ETHICAL REASONING:

Thinking through problems or issues that entail implications for harming or helping sentient creatures.

Despite popular beliefs to the contrary, ethical reasoning is to be analyzed and assessed in the same way as any other domain of reasoning. Ethical reasoning entails the same elements as does all reasoning, and is to be assessed by the same standards of clarity, accuracy, precision, relevance, depth, breadth, logic, significance, etc. Understanding ethical principles is as important to sound ethical reasoning as understanding principles of math and biology are to mathematical and biological reasoning. Ethical thinking, when reasonable, is ultimately driven by ethical concepts (for example, *fairness*) and principles (for example, "*Like cases must be treated in a like manner*"), as well as sound principles of critical thought.

Ethical principles are guides for human conduct and imply what contributes to good or harm and what one is either obligated to do or obligated not to do. They also enable us to determine the ethical value of a behavior even when that behavior is not, strictly speaking, an obligation. Ethical questions, like questions in any domain of thought, can either imply a clear-cut answer or competing reasonable answers (matters requiring our best judgment). However, they are not matters of personal preference. It makes no sense to say, "Oh, you prefer to be fair. Well, I prefer to be unfair!"

Ethics is often confused with other modes of thinking, such as social conventions, religion, and the law. When this happens, we allow ethics to be defined by cultural rules and taboos, religious ideologies, or legal statutes. For instance, if a religious group advocates killing the first born male, or sacrificing teen girls to the gods, and *religion is equated with ethics*, then these practices would be seen as the right way to behave, or, in other words ethically correct. Clearly this collapsing of ethics with any other system of thought has significant implications for the way we live, how we define right and wrong, what behaviors we punish and what behaviors we advocate or "allow."

ETHNOCENTRICITY:

A tendency to view one's own race or culture as superior to all others, and therefore judging other cultures according to one's own cultural standards.

Ethnocentrism can be understood as a form of egocentrism extended from self to one's group. Much uncritical or selfish critical thinking is either egocentric or ethnocentric in nature. (Ethnocentrism and sociocentrism are often used synonymously though sociocentricity is broader, relating to any group, including, for example, sociocentric identification with one's profession.) The "cure" for ethnocentrism or sociocentrism is routine empathic thought within the perspective of opposing groups and cultures. Such empathic thought is rarely cultivated in the societies and schools of today. Instead, many people develop an empty rhetoric of tolerance without seriously considering the value in the beliefs and practices of other groups, the meaning of these beliefs to those others, and their reasons for maintaining them.

FAIRMINDEDNESS:

A cultivated disposition of mind that enables the thinker to treat all perspectives relevant to an issue in an objective manner, without privileging one's own views, or the views of one's group.

Fairmindedness implies being conscious of the need to treat all relevant viewpoints alike without reference to one's own feelings or selfish interests, or the feelings or selfish interests of one's friends, community, nation, or species. It implies adherence to intellectual standards without reference to one's own advantage or the advantage of one's group. There are three primary reasons why people lack this disposition: 1) native egocentric thought, 2) native sociocentric thought, 3) lack of intellectual skills necessary for reasoning through complex ethical issues.

HUMAN MIND:

That which thinks, perceives, feels, wills; the seat of conscious as well as unconscious thought.

The mind is an organized set of capacities by which sentient creatures think, feel, and want. These capacities continually interact. Thus, the human mind entails a cognitive dimension (that of thought), as well as an affective dimension (that of feelings and desires).

In recent years, many studies have been conducted to understand the relationships between the cognitive and affective dimensions of the human mind. Yet much is known about the human mind that cannot yet be connected to precise neurological processes in the brain. For example, one natural mechanism of the human mind is its tendencies toward selfishness. This fact can be documented in hundreds of thousands of ways through simple observation. In short, we know much about the mind and comparatively little about the brain/mind interconnection.

HUMAN NATURE:

The common qualities, instincts, inherent tendencies, and capacities of human beings.

People have both a primary and secondary nature. Our primary nature is spontaneous, egocentric, and subject to irrational belief formation. It is the basis for our instinctual thought. People need no training to believe what they want to believe: what serves their immediate interests, what preserves their sense of personal comfort and righteousness, what minimizes their sense of inconsistency, and what presupposes their own correctness. People need no special training to believe what those around them believe: what their parents and friends believe, what is taught to them by religious and school authorities, what is repeated often by the media, and what is commonly believed in their nation and culture. People need no training to think that those who disagree with them are wrong and probably prejudiced. People need no training to assume that their own most fundamental beliefs are self-evidently true or easily justified by evidence. People naturally and spontaneously identify with their own beliefs. They often experience disagreement as personal attack. The resulting defensiveness interferes with their capacity to empathize with, or enter into, other points of view.

On the other hand, people need extensive and systematic practice to develop their secondary nature, their implicit capacity to function as rational persons. They need extensive and systematic practice to recognize the tendencies they have to form irrational beliefs. They need extensive practice to develop a dislike of inconsistencies in their thought, a love of clarity, a passion to seek reasons and evidence and to be fair to points of view other than their own. People need extensive practice to recognize that they live inferentially, that they do not have a direct pipeline to reality, and that it is perfectly possible to have an overwhelming inner sense of the correctness of one's views and still be wrong.

IDENTIFICATION:

A person's (often unconscious) association with or assumption of the qualities, characteristics, or views of another person or group; developing an emotional attachment such that the thing associated with is seen as a part of the person.

Identification is a common defense mechanism in which one's self image is connected with the self-image of others. This sociocentric phenomenon, innate in human thought, leads people to unconsciously take on the views of those around them without critically analyzing and assessing those views. By assuming the views of one's group, one's own self image and sense of self-worth are elevated. Examples: a football fan experiencing an inner sense of triumph when his team wins, a parent experiencing a triumph in the success of his children, a citizen feeling elevated by the triumph of his nation's armed forces.

INTELLECTUAL STANDARDS:

The standards or criteria necessary for reasoning at a high level of skill and for making sound judgments. Intellectual standards are necessary for forming knowledge (as against unsound beliefs), for understanding, and for thinking rationally and logically.

Intellectual standards are fundamental to critical thinking. Some essential intellectual standards are *clarity, accuracy, relevance, precision, breadth, depth, logicalness, significance, consistency, fairness, completeness,* and *reasonability.*

Intellectual standards are presupposed in every domain of human thought, in every discipline and subject.

To develop one's mind and discipline one's thinking using these standards requires regular practice and long-term cultivation. Of course, achieving these standards is a relative matter and varies to some degree among domains of thought. Being precise while doing mathematics is not the same as being precise while writing a poem, describing an experience, or explaining a historical event. We may roughly classify intellectual standards into two categories: "micro intellectual standards" and "macro intellectual standards." Micro intellectual standards are those intellectual standards that pinpoint specific aspects of intellectual assessment. For example: Is the thinking *clear*? Is the information *relevant*? Are the purposes *consistent*? Though essential to skilled reasoning, meeting one or more micro standards does not necessarily fulfill the intellectual task at hand. This is true because thinking can be clear but not relevant; it can be relevant but not precise; it can be accurate but not sufficient, and so forth. When the reasoning we need to engage in is monological, (that is, focused on a question with an established settlement procedure), micro intellectual standards may suffice. But to reason well through multilogical issues, (that is, problems or issues that require that we reason within conflicting points of view), we need not only micro, but 'macro intellectual standards' as well. Macro intellectual standards are broader in scope; they integrate our use of micro standards; they expand our intellectual understandings. For example, when reasoning through a complex issue, we need our thinking to be reasonable or sound (satisfying, in other words, broad intellectual standards). For thinking to be *reasonable* or *sound*, it needs, at minimum, to be *clear*, *accurate*, and *relevant*. Moreover, when more than one viewpoint is *relevant* to an issue, we need to be able to compare, contrast, and integrate insights from relevant viewpoints before taking a position on the issue ourselves. Thus the use of macro intellectual standards (such as *reasonability* and *soundness*) help guide the reasoning toward depth, comprehensiveness, and integration of thought.

INTELLECTUAL TRAITS / DISPOSITIONS / VIRTUES:

The traits of mind and character necessary for right action and thinking; the dispositions of mind and character essential for fairminded rationality; the virtues that distinguish the narrowminded, self-serving critical thinker from the openminded, truth-seeking critical thinker.

Intellectual traits include, but are not limited to: *intellectual sense of justice, intellectual perseverance, intellectual integrity, intellectual humility, intellectual empathy, intellectual courage, intellectual curiosity, intellectual discipline, (intellectual) confidence in reason*, and *intellectual autonomy*.

The hallmark of the strong-sense critical thinker is the embodiment of and deep commitment to these intellectual virtues. Yet, the extent to which anyone

©2025 Linda Elder

lives in accordance with them on a daily basis is a matter of degree, no actual person achieving that of the hypothetical ideal thinker.

Intellectual traits are interdependent. Each is fully developed only in conjunction with the development of the others. They develop only through years of commitment and practice. They cannot be imposed from without; they must be cultivated by encouragement and example.

IRRATIONAL / IRRATIONALITY:

Lacking the power to reason; contrary to reason or logic; senseless, unreasonable, absurd.

Humans are both rational and irrational. We have innate egocentric and sociocentric tendencies that often lead us to do things that are illogical (though they seem to us at the time to be perfectly logical). We don't *automatically* sense what is reasonable in any given situation. Rather, the extent to which we think and act rationally depends upon how well our rational capacities have been developed. It depends upon the extent to which we have learned to go beyond our natural prejudices and biases, beyond our narrow, self-serving viewpoint, to see what makes most sense to do and believe in a given situation. Critical thinkers are alert to their irrational tendencies. They strive to become rational, fairminded persons.

IRRATIONAL EMOTIONS:

Feelings based on unreasonable beliefs.

Emotions are a natural part of human life. Irrational emotions reflect irrational beliefs or irrational responses to situations. They occur when our natural egocentricity leads us to behave in unproductive or unreasonable ways or when we are unsuccessful in getting our way (irrationally). Critical thinkers consistently work to diminish the power of irrational emotions in their life.

IRRATIONAL LEARNING:

Learning that results in unreasonable beliefs.

Rational learning presupposes rational assent. Yet, much that we learn in everyday life is distinctively irrational. It is quite possible, in other words, to believe for irrational reasons; because those around us believe, because we are rewarded for believing, because we are afraid to disbelieve, because our vested interest is served by belief, because we are more comfortable with belief, or because we have an egocentric need to maintain belief. In all of these cases, our beliefs are without rational grounding, without good reason and evidence, without the foundation a rational person demands. We become rational, on the other hand, to the extent that our beliefs and actions are grounded in good reasons and evidence; to the extent that we recognize and critique our own irrationality; to the extent that we are not moved by unsound reasons and a multiplicity of irrational motives, fears, and desires; to the extent that we have cultivated a passion for clarity, accuracy, and fairmindedness. These global skills, passions, and dispositions, integrated into behavior and thought, characterize the rational, the educated, the critical person.

MENTAL HEALTH / MENTAL ILLNESS:

Mental health is generally referred to as one's overall sense of well-being as perceived through one's thoughts, feelings, and desires. This includes one's sense of self-efficacy, or critical and creative potency. When people are said to be *mentally well*, or to enjoy *mental* or *emotional well-being*, they are perceived as characteristically effective in working through life's problems, as having adequate control over the direction of their lives, as handling everyday stress with equanimity, and as maintaining an inner sense of well-being (barring tragedy). They work their way through the issues they face, while dodging the many societal pathologies and irrational people they must frequently avoid. They communicate effectively with others and maintain social connections appropriate to and healthy for themselves as individuals. They are contributing people—giving of themselves to others to help improve things. But they do not allow others to control their thoughts, actions or feelings. They take care of their emotional well-being as a top priority. These principles that form mental and emotional wellness are essential to self-actualizing.

The term *mental illness* implies problems in any of these areas. Whether and to what degree one can be said to be mentally ill or emotionally unwell may be influenced by the circumstances of one's life, and may change over time and given new circumstances, but in any case, will be largely determined by one's overall ability to cope with life's problems and concerns while maintaining emotions appropriate to the context.

One's overall mental health will occur on a continuum from the highest to the lowest. Those experiencing the highest degrees of mental health are those who are self-actualizing, since they spend their energy developing themselves, creating fruitful products of their reasoning, and contributing to the lives of others.

Though we can begin with basic conceptualizations as detailed above, the concepts of *mental health* and *mental illness* are unfortunately burdened with problems in terms of their use and misuse. These problems result primarily from the fact that these terms have historically been seen through a biomedical lens and are often taken literally rather than analogically. In other words, the use of the terms *health* and *illness* in connection with *mental* has led to the notion that there is something biological underlying mental issues, though this may not at all be the case. For this reason, some have argued that the terms *mental health* and *mental illness* should *not* be used in speaking of the mind and its interrelated functions: thoughts, feelings, desires, and actions. The Centers for

Disease Control and Prevention website states that "Mental health includes our emotional, psychological, and social well-being. It affects how we think, feel, and act. It also helps determine how we handle stress, relate to others, and make healthy choices." ("About Mental Health," 2023.) Nothing in this definition implies a medical or biological problem.

Again, many variables affect how a person may function mentally and emotionally, and these variables frequently change over time. How a society deals with what are considered "mental illnesses" largely determines the outcomes of those so-called illnesses. By medicalizing mental health, answers to mental health problems often inappropriately involve pharmaceuticals or other physical interventions. But we might ask: how much of what we term *mental illness* is either caused by society, or is poorly handled by society and by clinicians who proport to be experts in dealing with such conditions? How much of what we label *mental illness* does not rise to the level of illness at all?

Some critics argue that the terms *mental health* and *mental illness* should be eliminated, because they tend to be medicalized rather than being seen as psychological processes. But to do this, we would first need viable replacements, which we do not at present appear to have. It may be that what we need, instead, is to remember that the terms *mental health*, *mental illness*, and other related medical-referenced terms are merely analogies for speaking about the cognitive and affective dimensions of the mind.

In any case, the most fruitful and hopeful concept of mental health (whatever we might call it) entails directly controlling the workings of one's own mind, leading to the most positive or appropriate emotions in the circumstances of one's life, and to the most reasonable actions accordingly. This has been the message throughout this book.

One further point: early in the book, I distinguish between two types of mental health. *Genuine mental health* refers to being in rational command of one's thoughts, feelings, desires, and actions, thereby experiencing mostly appropriate and/or positive emotional states that come from honesty within oneself and honest presentation of self to others. *Sham mental health*, on the other hand, entails living a lie, deceiving others and/or oneself, and yet perceiving oneself to be emotionally well. Sham mental health entails significantly hiding from oneself (in other words, suppressing the truth within oneself) and presenting a false front to others, resulting in a lack of authenticity. Inauthentic persons may feel positive emotions and project them toward others while suppressing the negative emotions that would emerge if they were honest, straightforward and authentic.

MINDFULNESS:

The practice of intentionally focusing on the present moment for the purpose of better dealing with stress, anxiety, or some other negative emotion, or for dealing with addiction, illness, or other negative habitual processes or life conditions. Mindfulness training may involve meditation and/or focusing on one's breathing, bodily sensations, mental state, or attempting to achieve a state of non-thinking and/or non-judgment of oneself.

The concept of mindfulness, like others in the mental health profession, is fraught with problems. It may seem obvious that a proper amount of relaxing the mind and deliberately living in the moment are essential to living a life of satisfaction and enlightenment. And, though mindfulness *may* be clearly conceived, operationalized, and researched[21] its use in daily life tends to be nebulous, imprecise or hazy. For instance, many people connect mindfulness with the spiritual dimension of Buddhism, whence it originates. Spiritualism is itself an ambiguous term, rejected by many who on the other hand would readily open their minds to intentional focus on and appreciation of the moment. Further, because there does not appear to be an agreed-upon conception of mindfulness, operationalizing it for research will be less than optimal, and comparing studies may also be problematic.

These things considered, we might ask: To what extent is mindfulness now a cohesive conception across therapists and theoreticians of mindfulness, so that it can be properly studied and assessed? What is a robust, reasonable, agreed-upon conception of mindfulness that can be supported by theoreticians and researchers across human societies? Does mindfulness rise to the level of a third wave of therapy (coming after cognitive behavioral therapies) as some have suggested? How do mindfulness practices interconnect with or enhance other therapy methods? What precise methods are used in mindfulness and what standards should be applied to it?

Components of mindfulness typically include:
- Intention: Choosing to cultivate your awareness
- Attention: Paying attention to the present moment as well as current sensations and thoughts
- Attitude: Being kind, curious, and non-judgmental

Some common recommendations for practicing mindfulness include:
- Noticing one's breathing patterns
- Breathing in and out slowly and deliberately
- Meditating

---

21 For a helpful article that surveys the research on mindfulness, see "Mindfulness Interventions" by J.D. Creswell in *Annual Review of Psychology* (2017).

- Use of guided imagery
- Relaxation of mind and body
- Focusing on one thing at a time while attending to and appreciating the moment
- Slowing down
- Eating slowly and deliberately while appreciating the process
- Limiting phone and computer time
- Movement
- Spending time in nature

NAÏVE THINKERS:

People having or showing a lack of experience, judgment, or information; lacking understanding and reasoning abilities; showing or characterized by a lack of sophistication and critical judgment.

Naïve thinkers are contrasted with critical thinkers (either fairminded or sophistic critical thinkers). Lacking in critical reasoning abilities, they are easily manipulated. Naïve thinkers generally do not see the importance of developing their reasoning abilities. They often depend on others to think for them. They are easily influenced by media bias and propaganda. They generally conform to the "rules" of society, rarely questioning those rules (and when they do, they are usually going along with someone else who is questioning them). They too easily follow authority figures. They often acquiesce to things that are not in their best interests. If we take a close look at history, we may well find that the masses in all human cultures tend to be largely naïve thinkers.

NEUROTIC / NEUROSIS:

Maintaining a debilitating negative emotional state that typically involves excess sensitivity and vulnerability to stress coupled with a reactive emotional temperament. The neurotic person is one who, unlike the psychotic person, is typically able to function within society and is in touch with reality, though depressed, anxious, or maintaining some other negative pervasive emotional state. Neurosis commonly entails perceiving ordinary situations as threatening, hence results in an ongoing feeling of anxiety or depression. Neurotic persons often perceive minor frustrations as hopelessly difficult to work through. They may be pessimistic and will characteristically lack a sense of potency, self-efficacy, or in other words, control over their lives. This leads to habitual self-defeating patterns of thought and action. Though neurotic persons may have the capacity to take command of their thoughts and actions, and thereby to strongly influence their own futures, they typically do not see this capacity within themselves.

In understanding your own frame of mind, which may tend toward the neurotic as conceptualized above, it may be useful to ask such questions as: What if the society within which you are attempting to cope or survive is in many ways pervasively and highly dysfunctional? Isn't it true that human cultures are themselves frequently unreasonable, commonly tending toward the farcical, the preposterous and the bizarre? Doesn't it follow, then, that societal conditions and power structures wield the power to radically warp the individual trying to survive within them? We humans face almost constant pressure from outside sources, frequently without support from likeminded people with whom we relate on a deep level. Further, there are any number of unjust conditions caused by humans one-to-one, group-to-group, and toward other sentient creatures. It only stands to reason that even the strongest and most rational person may at times be exasperated, infuriated or outraged. And it should be no surprise that many people, especially those who are more sensitive, will not be able to modify themselves enough to both fit into our warped society and retain a healthy sense of self without extensive work on their own thinking (such as you have been doing in this book).

Compassionate, reasonable people try to mitigate unjust conditions where possible using critical thinking. But most of what happens in the world we have no personal control over, especially those situations we view from afar. Rational persons focus their efforts safely within their circle of power, using their energy as wisely as possible while protecting themselves as best they can. These people manage not to succumb to self-defeating ways of living. When personally caught up in unjust conditions, they realize they have no choice but to do their best reasoning to get through them.

Neurotic people, on the other hand, frequently try to step out of their circle of influence to control things they cannot control—specifically other people and much within the situations they face. They may obsess over what they can do nothing about. They may care about other people, the earth and other creatures but perceive themselves as having no power. Therefore, instead of doing what little they can to help, they instead suffer thoughts of impotency, helplessness and hopelessness. This leads to feelings like distress, sadness and anguish, and may even amount to self-torture. Being disappointed with one's life achievements can make neurotic persons more dysfunctional and increase their chances of falling into long-term depression. Neurotic individuals tend to experience life as entailing primarily negative events, and they tend to have worse psychological well-being overall than those who are not neurotic. Neurotic thinking and behavior, despite being in touch with reality, can manifest in any number of ways and occurs on a continuum from the lowest to highest levels of self-defeating thoughts and behavior. Here are some of the ways that neurosis may be manifest, all of which result in emotional suffering at some level and are ultimately self-defeating:

• anxiety
• depression

- bipolar tendencies
- phobias
- feelings of impotence
- resentment
- addictive orientation
- high sensitivity to stress
- obsessive behaviors
- exacting behaviors
- avoidance of others
- avoidance of reality
- worrying
- obsessing

The terms *neurosis* and *neurotic* have fallen from clinical use as the medicalization of the mind has become increasingly dominant. Many clinicians have abandoned the terms for more narrow concerns, specifically anxiety disorder or depressive disorder. But an argument can be made to retain their use as psychological concepts as described above.

PATHOLOGICAL:

As a psychological term, *pathology* or *pathological* refers to any number of dysfunctional ways in which humans live, interact with one another, see themselves or relate in the world.

The terms *pathological* or *pathology* may be used in a scientific or medical sense. They may also be used in a psychological sense, which is the case throughout this book.

There are many ways in which human societies are dysfunctional and which cause stress to individuals living in those societies. Humans create rules, taboos, customs, mores, and traditions that are then imposed on the individual. These rules and taboos may be irrational or illogical in any number of ways, and hence may be termed pathological. Humans may also engage in any number of irrational, dysfunctional or illogical behaviors, which may also loosely be termed pathological.

PSYCHOTIC / PSYCHOSIS:

A state of mind in which the person is not in touch with reality and cannot reason logically. It may entail emotional and mental suffering.

There are many reasons why people may become disconnected from human reality, given the stressors humans place on themselves along with possible genetic predispositions. Some psychotic conditions include schizophrenia, bipolar disorder or severe depression. Psychosis may include hallucinations and delusions and may be connected with medical conditions such as Alzheimer's disease, stroke, Addison's disease, and multiple sclerosis. It may also result from misuse of alcohol or other recreational drugs, or from head injuries.

Barring a medical condition, psychotic episodes frequently dissolve on their own when the person experiencing the episode is given proper support. However, due to the medicalization of the human mind, non-medical psychosis is still primarily treated with psychotropic drugs in the U.S. and other countries. Taken over the long term, these medications may lead to medically-induced permanent psychosis. Psychotropic drugs for treating psychosis may also lead to any number of other problems such as bizarre behaviors, dangerous behaviors, threatening or deadly behaviors, sexual dysfunction, postural hypotension, cardiac complications, metabolic dysfunction, neurological damage such as in tardive dyskinesia, organ failure, and brain damage. These drugs may also lead to death, including by suicide. It may be that use of these medications is justified under certain narrow, limited conditions, and typically only for the short term; but extreme caution should be exercised before beginning psychotropic drug use, due to the many potential adverse effects of these medications.[22] Cognitive behavioral therapy has been proven useful in alleviating symptoms of psychosis, as has a supportive, caring program or atmosphere.

PERSONAL CONTRADICTION:

When people say one thing and do another, or use a double standard, judging themselves and those with whom they identify by an easier standard than that used for others; a form of hypocrisy typically "justified" through self-deception.

Everyone engages in personal contradictions in one form or another at times. As with most egocentricity, personal contradictions generally function at the unconscious level. People too often ignore the difficulty of becoming intellectually and ethically consistent themselves, instead tending to focus on the personal contradictions of others. Personal contradictions are more likely to be discovered, analyzed, and reduced when people are encouraged to openly discuss their own contradictions and where people work together to diminish the frequency and power of this egocentric tendency. As it now stands, in most human societies people are penalized, rather than rewarded, for admitting their personal contradictions. For example, admitting contradictions in one's thinking in the workplace is generally viewed as a weakness, rather than a strength.

---

22 For more on the problems associated with using psychotropic medications for psychosis, read "The Psychoactive Effects of Psychiatric Medication: The Elephant in the Room" by J. Moncrieff, D. Cohne, and S. Porter in *Journal of Psychoactive Drugs* (2013). Also read "Does Long Term Use of Psychiatric Drugs Cause More Harm than Good?" by P.C. Gotzsche, A.H. Young, and J. Crace in *The BMJ* (2015).

PROJECTION:

When a person attributes to another person what he or she feels or thinks, usually in order to avoid unacceptable thoughts and feelings such as guilt.

Projection is one defense mechanism used by the human ego to avoid some part of reality which is unpleasant (like taking responsibility for one's actions). A wife who doesn't love her husband may accuse him of not loving her (when he really does) in order to unconsciously deal with her dishonesty in the relationship.

It is important to avoid projecting onto others motives or behaviors of which we ourselves are guilty. An essential dimension of critical thinking is identifying and overcoming ways in which we engage in any form of self-deception.

RATIONAL / RATIONALITY:

Being guided by the intellect (rather than emotions), or having to do with reason; being consistent with or based on logic; that which conforms to principles of good reasoning, is sensible, shows good judgment, is consistent, logical, relevant and sound.

In everyday discourse, there are at least three different common uses of the term 'rational' or 'rationality.' One refers to a person's general ability to think well. A second refers to a person's ability to use his intellect to achieve his purposes (irrespective of whether or not these purposes are ethically justified). A third refers to one's commitment to think and act only in ways that are intellectually and ethically justified. Behind these three uses lie these distinctions: skilled thinker, sophistic thinker, Socratic thinker. In the first use, we mark the skills only of the thinker. In the second we mark the skills used "selfishly" (as the Sophists of old). In the third we mark the skills used fairmindedly (as Socrates did).

Critical thinkers, in the strong sense, are concerned with developing their capacities to reason with skill while also respecting the rights and needs of others. They are fairminded in the use of their intellectual skills.

RATIONAL EMOTIONS:

The affective dimension of skilled reason and critical thought.

Emotions are an integral part of human life. Whenever we reason, there is always some emotion linked with our thoughts. Rational emotions are those connected with reasonable thought and action.

R. S. Peters (1973) explained the significance of "rational passions" as follows:
There is, for instance, the hatred of contradictions and inconsistencies, together with the love of clarity and hatred of confusion without which words could not be held to relatively constant meanings and testable rules and generalizations stated. A reasonable man cannot, without some special explanation, slap his sides with delight or express indifference if he is

told that what he says is confused, incoherent, and perhaps riddled with contradictions.

Reason is the antithesis of arbitrariness. In its operation it is supported by the appropriate passions which are mainly negative in character—the hatred of irrelevance, special pleading, and arbitrary fiat. The more developed emotion of indignation is aroused when some excess of arbitrariness is perpetuated in a situation where people's interests and claims are at stake. The positive side of this is the passion for fairness and impartial consideration of claims. . .

A man who is prepared to reason must feel strongly that he must follow the arguments and decide things in terms of where they lead. Insofar as thoughts about persons enter his head, they should be tinged with the respect which is due to another who, like himself, may have a point of view which is worth considering, who may have a glimmering of the truth which has so far eluded himself. A person who proceeds in this way, who is influenced by such passions, is what we call a reasonable man.

RATIONAL SELF:

Human character and nature to the extent that we seek to base our beliefs and actions on good reasoning and evidence; the capacity of humans to think and behave in a reasonable manner (in contrast to thinking and behaving egocentrically).

Each of us has both a "rational" and "irrational" self, a reasonable side and an unreasonable side. While the irrational or egocentric side functions naturally, without cultivation, critical thinking is essential to the development of one's "rational self." Put another way, our rational capacities do not develop themselves. They aren't automatic in the mind, but must be developed by us. Present societies do not tend to cultivate rational persons, but rather (perhaps inadvertently) tend to encourage egocentric and sociocentric thought.

REPRESSION:

When thoughts, feelings or memories unacceptable to the individual are prevented from reaching consciousness.

Repression is a defense mechanism which often occurs when memories are considered too painful to remember. It can also be a form of "forgetting" because the person doesn't want to remember something unpleasant (such as a dental appointment). Repression may serve a useful purpose—for example, when suppressing painful memories that may be best handled by simply not rehashing them. However, some repression may be dysfunctional—for example, when suppressing the fact that one has behaved in unethical ways (such as irresponsibly hurting someone). Critical thinkers work to increase awareness of instances of repression in their thinking and emotions. They seek to understand why they are engaging in repression. They actively work to diminish the extent to which they repress ideas which cause them to behave in dysfunctional ways. It should be noted, however, that deeply repressed ideas are highly resistant to rational critique.

SCAPEGOATING:

When a person attempts to avoid criticism of himself by blaming another person, group or thing for his own mistakes or faults.

One common form of egocentric thought is to avoid facing one's own weaknesses and faults. Scapegoating is a frequently used defense mechanism which enables us to hide from problems in our thought and behavior by blaming others. Critical thinkers try to squarely face and deal with their own mistakes or faults, rather than blaming others for them.

SELF-DECEPTION:

The natural human (egocentric) tendency to deceive oneself about one's true motivations, character, or identity.

This phenomenon is so common to humans that the human species might well be defined "the self-deceiving animal." All of the defense mechanisms are facilitated by this egocentric tendency. Through self-deception, humans are able to ignore unpleasant realities and problems in their thinking and behavior. Self-deception reinforces self-righteousness and intellectual arrogance. It enables us to pursue selfish interests while disguising our motives as altruistic or reasonable. Through self-deception, humans "justify" flagrantly unethical acts, policies, and practices.

All humans engage in self-deception—but not to the same degree. Overcoming self-deception through critical thinking is a fundamental goal of strong-sense critical thinkers.

SOCIAL CONTRADICTION:

An inconsistency between what a society "preaches," or professes to believe, and what it practices.

Every society has some degree of inconsistency between its image of itself and its actual character. When a group, for example, professes to be spreading peace throughout the world, while at the same time systematically engaging in unjust wars, it is demonstrating a social contradiction. Social contradiction is typically connected with sociocentric thought and correlated with human self-deception on the part of the group.

SOCIALIZATION:

A continuing process of learning to conform to the values, norms, traditions, manners, customs, taboos, and ideologies of one's society; assuming social skills appropriate to one's "social position."

For the most part, humans live together in groups. Accordingly, they must learn to live together reasonably in those groups, to get along, to respect the rights and needs of others with whom they interrelate and interact. But the process of socialization often goes beyond a defensible conception of living together reasonably. It often leads to oppression and the violation of individual rights. Because humans create complex ideas and ideologies through which they see the world, these ideas are a necessary part of the "socialization process." At a very young age children within every culture begin to think within these ideas, seeing them, not as one possible way to think, but as the right way to think (e.g. no elbows on the table, napkin in your lap, no nudity allowed). Part of the ideology of any culture, then, is the laying down of rules, the creation of customs, the forbidding of certain behaviors. Accordingly, people living within every culture are expected to uncritically accept the largely arbitrary rules, customs, and taboos of their culture. Every day, very young children in the U.S., for example, are expected to stand up and "pledge allegiance to the flag of the United States of America." In doing so, they have no real sense of what they are pledging, of what it would mean to take their pledge seriously, of what it would mean to critically analyze it, of how to skillfully argue for and/or against it. This is just one example of many forms of indoctrination that often come hand in hand with socialization.

One important part of the socialization process has to do with social stratification. People in modern societies are layered according to a political/economic "pecking order," to put it somewhat crudely. Those at the top have most of the power and advantages. Those in the middle have a low to modest amount of power, and significant advantages. Those at the bottom have very few advantages and very little power. Part of the socialization process of every culture is to pass on the "correct behavior" for one's "social status," according to the system of social stratification within the culture. It is essential to critically analyze the social rules, customs, taboos, and power structure of one's culture so as not to be intellectually imprisoned by them.

SOCIOCENTRICITY:

The belief in the inherent superiority of one's own group or culture; a tendency to judge alien people, groups or cultures from the perspective of one's own group.

As social animals, humans cluster together. Indeed, the very survival of the human species depends upon a lengthy rearing process so that all humans survive, in the first instance, because they are cared for within a group. Accordingly, children learn from an early age to think within the logic of the group. This is required for their "acceptance" in the group. As part of this socialization process, they (largely uncritically) absorb group ideologies. Sociocentricity is based on the assumption that one's own social group is inherently and self-evidently superior to all others. When a group or society sees itself as superior, and so considers its views as correct or as the only reasonable or justifiable views and when a group perceives all of its actions as justified, it has a tendency to think closed-mindedly. Dissent and doubt are considered disloyal and are rejected. Few people recognize the sociocentric nature of much of their thought. Sociocentric thought is connected with the term 'ethnocentricity,' though ethnocentricity is often used more narrowly to refer to sociocentric thought within an ethnic group.

SOPHISTIC CRITICAL THINKERS:

Skilled thinkers who use the tools of critical thinking to manipulate others, usually to serve their selfish or group interests. The term 'sophistic' commonly refers to those who use subtle, tricky, superficially plausible, but often fallacious methods of reasoning to win an argument or convince someone that something is true (when it may be only partially true or not true at all).

For example, they may use deliberately invalid arguments in a persuasive way (displaying ingenuity in reasoning). The term "sophist" is traceable to the Greek words 'sophos' or 'sophia,' originally used to mean "wise" or "wisdom." Use of the term evolved over time, especially in the second half of the 5th century BCE, most notably at Athens, where 'sophist' came to denote a class of itinerant intellectuals who taught courses in "excellence" or "virtue," generally focusing on how to persuade or convince others to accept a position as true. Sophists claimed that they could find the answers to all questions. Over time, the term 'sophist' came to be used in reference to argumentation sometimes designed to make "the weaker argument appear the stronger," (for a deeper understanding, read the works of Plato and Aristotle on sophistry).

STEREOTYPING:

When a person lumps people together based on some common characteristic, forming a rigid, biased perception of the group and the individuals in the group.

One primary form of stereotyping comes from cultural bias wherein people assume that practices and beliefs in their culture are superior to those in other cultures simply by virtue of being part of their culture. They take this group to be the measure of all groups and people.

STRONG-SENSE CRITICAL THINKERS:

Fairminded critical thinkers; skilled thinkers characterized predominantly by the following traits: (1) the ability and tendency to question deeply one's own views; (2) the ability and tendency to reconstruct sympathetically and imaginatively the strongest versions of viewpoints and perspectives opposed to one's own; and (3) the ability and tendency to reason dialectically (multilogically) in such a way as to determine when one's own point of view is at its weakest and when an opposing point of view is at its strongest; (4) the ability and propensity to change one's thinking when the evidence would require it, without regard to one's own selfish or vested interests.

Strong-sense critical thinkers are fundamentally concerned with reasoning at the highest level of skill, considering all the important available evidence, and respecting all relevant viewpoints. Their thought and behavior is characterized primarily by intellectual virtues or habits of mind. They avoid being blinded by their own viewpoints. They recognize the framework of assumptions and ideas upon which their own viewpoints are based. They realize the necessity of putting their assumptions and ideas to the test of the strongest objections that can be leveled against them. Most importantly, *they can be moved by reason*; in other words, they are willing to abandon their own ideas when other ideas prove more reasonable or valid.

SUBCONSCIOUS THOUGHT:

Thoughts or beliefs operating in the mind beneath the level of conscious awareness, but which the thinker would have no problem acknowledging.

Most of what we believe is not conscious to us at any given moment. Our beliefs come into conscious perception in context, when they seem to be relevant to thinking through an issue, problem, etc. Subconscious thoughts may be recalled simply by directing attention to them. They are contrasted with unconscious thoughts, which the thinker is, for some reason, motivated to avoid.

UNCONSCIOUS THOUGHT:

Thinking that occurs without awareness; ideas, experiences, assumptions, etc. beneath the level of awareness but that have a pronounced influence on behavior (and on conscious thoughts); thoughts lying below the level of perception and not easily raised into consciousness; thoughts we are unaware of, and which we would rather avoid explicitly perceiving.

There are at two distinctly different uses of this term for our purposes here. The first use is equated with the term 'subconscious thought.' It simply refers to thoughts in our minds that we are not explicitly aware of at any given moment, but from which we have no "need" to hide.

The second use refers to suppressed thoughts—thoughts in our minds we are unaware of that influence our conscious thoughts and behavior, and which we are for some reason motivated to avoid recognizing. These may be painful or unpleasant "experiences," or they may be dysfunctional patterns of thought—such as rationalization or other forms of self-deception. Much human thinking is unconscious. It is quite common for people to be guided by ideas, assumptions, perspectives that exist in their minds, but of which they have little or no awareness. All egocentric and sociocentric thoughts have some unconscious dimension to them because these thoughts can't stand the light of day. In other words, if we were to face the fact that these thoughts were operating in our thinking, we would be "forced" to deal with them. This may require us to give up something we hold dear. Any thoughts that we cannot openly "own" have an unconscious dimension.

To the extent that thoughts are unconscious in the mind, we have little chance of analyzing and assessing them. We have little chance of exploring how they are influencing our thoughts and behavior. Critical thinkers are aware of this, and therefore routinely work to bring unconscious thoughts to the level of consciousness in order to examine them for quality.

WEAK-SENSE CRITICAL THINKER:

Those who use the skills, abilities, and to some extent, the traits of critical thinking to serve their selfish interests; unfair or unethical critical thinkers.

Weak-sense, or unethical critical thinkers, have the following pronounced tendencies:

(1) They do not hold themselves or those with whom they ego-identify to the same intellectual standards to which they hold opponents.

(2) They do not reason empathically within points of view or frames of reference with which they disagree;

(3) They tend to think monologically (within one narrow perspective).

(4) They do not genuinely accept, though they may verbally espouse, the values of fairminded critical thinking.

(5) They use intellectual skills selectively and self-deceptively to foster and serve their selfish interests at the expense of truth.

6) They use critical thinking skills to identify flaws in the reasoning of others and sophisticated arguments to refute others' arguments before giving those arguments due consideration.

(7) They routinely justify their irrational thinking through highly sophisticated rationalizations.

(8) They are highly skilled at manipulation.

WISHFUL THINKING:

When a person unconsciously misinterprets facts in order to maintain a belief. Wishful thinking leads to false expectations and usually involves seeing things more positively than is reasonable in the situation.

The woman who interprets a man's behavior as intending to attract her for romantic reasons, when in fact he is merely being friendly, is an example of wishful thinking. The teacher who believes she is deeply engaging the intellects of her students through lecture, followed by massive memorization for testing, is engaging in wishful thinking. Critical thinkers avoid engaging in wishful thinking, instead seeking the truth, however painful that truth might be.

INDEX

professional life xxxi, 109, 257, 282, 318,
324-325
projection 136, 156, 179, 363, 437, 454
psychiatry xxxiv, 353, 356, 358, 361, 364,
372-378, 393, 437-438, 453
psychoanalysis 355-356, 361-365
psychological dimension of life 333
psychosis 242, 374, 376-378, 452-453
psychotherapy 284, 355-356, 360-361, 366
purposes xxxv, 46, 60, 87-88, 101, 128,
138, 182, 218-219, 237-255, 257,
289, 295-298, 303, 310, 337, 352,
357, 362, 387, 417, 445, 454

R

rational capacities xxx, 96, 99, 119, 124,
126, 446, 455
rational emotions 454-455
Rational Emotive Behavior Therapy
(REBT) 282-289, 365-368
rationality xxx-xxxi, 112, 116, 122-123,
138-139, 167, 185, 383, 399, 436,
445, 454
rationalization 99, 136, 150, 157, 183,
293, 437, 460
rational self 455
rational thinking 113-114, 126, 141, 143,
365
rational thought 95, 122, 128, 144-145
reasonable xxiii, xxxiv-xxxv, 49-51, 53-55,
60-63, 65, 68, 70-71, 75, 78-79, 84,
90-92, 107-108, 111-112, 114-115,
119, 121, 123, 137-138, 141-142,
145, 147, 149-150, 157, 159, 170,
173, 178-179, 183, 185, 187, 195,
200, 209, 227-228, 230, 234-235,
241, 244, 247, 252-255, 261, 264,
267, 273, 278, 291, 293-297, 303,
305, 311-312, 317-318, 323, 327,
330-331, 334, 342, 347, 351, 357-
369, 394, 398, 402, 415, 434, 442,
445-446, 448-449, 451, 454-456,
458-459, 461
reasoning 78, 88, 217-218, 234, 237, 284,

378, 387-390, 413
relevance xxiv, 84, 87-88, 91-92, 167, 196-
199, 221, 237, 262, 286, 359, 369,
380, 442, 444
religion 120, 122, 174, 267, 307, 309, 313,
317-319, 324, 341, 342, 442
religious beliefs 341
religious thinking 340-343, 266-268
repression 136, 244, 364, 455-456
resentment 48-49, 69
Ruby, Chuck 374
Russell, Bertrand 284

S

scapegoating 137, 456
schizophrenia 242, 374, 375-376, 452
science 324, 338, 376
scientific concepts 338
self-actualization xxiv, xxix, 76, 79, 100,
163, 189, 193, 347, 360, 368, 415
self-centered 96, 124, 146, 165, 304, 308,
438
self-deception 76, 78-79, 97, 126-127, 135,
138, 143-144, 150, 167, 293, 363,
378, 436-437, 453-454, 456, 460
self-development 59, 76, 119, 123, 332, 359
self-downing 282, 286, 288, 366
selfish critical thinker, 85, 162, 164
selfishness xxix, xxx, 120, 149, 151, 183-
184, 211-212, 269, 290, 337, 341, 438,
443
self-justifying thoughts 78
self-realization xxix, xxiii, 75, 364, 394
Seneca 316, 394, 399-406
sexual intimacy 290-291, 295
sexuality 121, 158, 267, 290-292, 309, 324,
327-328, 364
sham mental health xxxv, 75, 180, 448
significance xxiv, 49, 87-88, 91-92, 167,
196-198, 211, 239, 286, 369, 380,
442, 444
sleep xxxii-xxxiii
social contradiction 456
social dimension 334

The Foundation for Critical Thinking seeks to promote essential change in education and society through the cultivation of fairminded critical thinking—thinking committed to intellectual empathy, intellectual humility, intellectual perseverance, intellectual integrity, and intellectual responsibility. A rich intellectual environment is possible only with critical thinking at the foundation of education. Why? Because only when we learn to think through the content we are learning in a deep and substantive way can we apply what they are learning in our lives. Moreover, in a world of accelerating change, intensifying complexity, and increasing interdependence, critical thinking is now a requirement for economic and social survival.

Join our subscription community at www.criticalthinkingcommunity.org, which houses the world's largest critical thinking digital library, along with self-paced activities designed to help you further advance your critical thinking abilities. Our *Center for Critical Thinking Community Online* also hosts webinars and study groups and offers a host of other resources.

Contact us online at criticalthinking.org to learn about our publications, videos, workshops, conferences, and professional development programs.

For More Information

Phone	707-878-9100
Toll Free	1-800-833-3645
Fax	707-878-9111
E-mail	cct@criticalthinking.org
Web site	www.criticalthinking.org
Mail	Foundation for Critical Thinking PO Box 31080 Santa Barbara, CA 93130